ROBERT *the* BRUCE
A LIFE CHRONICLED

D0931816

NOT FOR RESALE
This is a Free Book
Bookthing.org

ROBERT *the* BRUCE
A LIFE CHRONICLED

CHRIS BROWN

TEMPUS

For Pat
Bbofts pobn

First published 2004

Tempus Publishing Limited
The Mill, Brimscombe Port,
Stroud, Gloucestershire, GL5 2QG
www.tempus-publishing.com

© Chris Brown, 2004

The right of Chris Brown to be identified as the Author
of this work has been asserted in accordance with the
Copyrights, Designs and Patents Act 1988.

All rights reserved. No part of this book may be reprinted
or reproduced or utilised in any form or by any electronic,
mechanical or other means, now known or hereafter invented,
including photocopying and recording, or in any information
storage or retrieval system, without the permission in writing
from the Publishers.

British Library Cataloguing in Publication Data.
A catalogue record for this book is available from the British Library.

ISBN 0 7524 2575 7

Typesetting and origination by Tempus Publishing Limited
Printed in Great Britain by Midway Colour Print, Wiltshire.

Contents

Acknowledgements   6

Introduction – King Robert and the written record   9

1   Excerpts from the *Scalacronica*
of Sir Thomas Grey of Heton (1296–1329)   15

2   Excerpts from the *Chronicle of John Fordoun* (1296–1329)   33

3   Excerpts from the *Lanercost Chronicle* (1296–1329)   53

4   The Acts of King Robert (1306–1329)   83

5   Extracts from the Chamberlain's Rolls for 1328   91

6   The Bruce family in English State records   95

7   Why was there a battle at Stirling in 1314?   149

8   The more we know, the more we know we don't know   157

9   The people of King Robert   173

10 Storys that suthfast wer... have doubill
plesance in heryng   185

11 *The Bruce* – John Barbour (1306–1329)   201

12 King Robert in romance   397

Glossary   400

Notes   401

Bibliography   406

List of illustrations   408

Index   409

Acknowledgements

The first debt of gratitude is, of course, to King Robert himself, without whom, as they say, 'none of this would have been possible'. There are several other people, however, whose contributions, direct and indirect, have indeed made this possible. I am indebted to my son Robert, whose computing skills prevented several disasters and rescued several more; to Jonathan Reeve at Tempus Publishing, whose confidence in me is a continuing source of amazement, not only to myself but also to everyone I know; to Dr William Knox, who persuaded the University of St Andrews to admit me to the Scottish History Department to read for a PhD; to Dr Michael Brown, my supervisor, whose patience I have undoubtedly tried and of whose expansive knowledge, not only of medieval Scotland but also of medieval Europe as a whole, I have continually taken unreasonable advantage; to Dr Hamish Scott, Head of Post-Graduate Admissions at St Andrews, for gambling on a rank outsider; to Dr Colin Martin, formerly of the Archaeology Department, for his course 'Archaeology and the Historian' which has saved me from making an even larger fool of myself; to the late W. Douglas Simpson, whom I met as a small boy and who impressed me immeasurably; to Dr Grant Simpson and Dr Geoffrey Barrow, both of whom were kind enough to advise me twenty years ago, when I was not a student and when (I'm sure) they had better things to do with their time; to Major George Athey, RAEC

– a positively inspirational history teacher; to Bob Lawson at Scotland in Focus; to the staff of Penicuik Public Library, who have relentlessly pursued inter-library loans on my behalf and who could show many far more august institutions a thing or two; to my parents, Peter and Margaret Brown, for not throttling me at birth (tempting as that must have been) and to my children, Robert, Charis, Christopher and Colin, and my son-in-law, Alex, for listening to me drone on about medieval Scotland. It is a sad reflection on my lack of imagination that I *still* have found no viable means of making other people responsible for my intellectual shortcomings and I can therefore categorically assure the reader that all mistakes in this book are mine and mine alone.

Craigard, Penicuik, 2004

INTRODUCTION

King Robert and the written record

That Robert I is the greatest of Scotland's heroes is not a remark likely to provoke widespread disagreement. To most people he is an almost legendary figure; *almost* legendary in the sense that his existence is not in dispute and quite legendary in the sense that what most people 'know' about him are in fact legends – spiders in caves and mysterious Knights Templar conspiracies. This is hardly surprising, it is part of the nature of heroic figures, but it is not altogether appropriate. There is a good deal of fourteenth-century written evidence relating to King Robert's life; this volume is only a selected sample from some of the more important groups.

Robert Bruce's earliest extant dated act as king is a 'credence' – a form of 'power of attorney' enabling an emissary to speak on behalf of a principal – given on 28 March 1306 to the abbot of Inchaffray so that he could approach the earl of Strathearn in the hope of gaining the earl's support for Robert's kingship.

His last known 'act' was issued at his manor house in Cardross on 31 May 1329. In the period of more than twenty years that separates the two, Robert Bruce was party to hundreds, probably thousands, of documents and was the subject of, or mentioned in, a great many more. Obviously some quantity – and probably a large quantity – have failed to survive and with luck there may be a number, though sadly it must surely be a very small number, that have survived and are yet to be discovered. This is an attempt to make some of the material that has survived more readily available. The comments added to the text excerpts are not a substitute for reading analytical histories of the period and the texts themselves are not a substitute for an in-depth biography of Robert I; Professor Barrow's *Robert the Bruce and the Community of the Realm of Scotland* is certainly the definitive work on the subject to date (2003).

Although several features of fourteenth-century life in Scotland are touched upon in this volume it is not in any sense a general picture of the 'community' of King Robert's realm; there are several volumes that address the political, legal, economic and diplomatic conditions which surrounded his kingship and the reader is recommended to search the reading list at the end of this book to further his or her knowledge of those topics.

MATERIAL FROM ENGLISH CROWN RECORDS

Most of the material relating to Robert's life before his seizure of the Crown in 1306 comes from English state documents. The Bruce family held extensive lands in England and were therefore subjects of English kings, owing them the same sort of military, financial and administrative service for their properties in England as they owed to Scottish kings for Scottish properties. As English barons we find them paying their dues − or not − running up debts with the king or serving as sheriffs and constables. As Scottish barons we find them doing much the same thing but a far greater proportion of English record survives. Consequently the bulk of official (state) evidence for the career of Robert before 1306 is to be found in English, rather than Scottish, records. Conveniently for Scottish historians most of the relevant material was compiled in the later nineteenth century by Joseph Bain in his four-volume *Calendar of Documents Relating to Scotland* or is included in the 'Supplementary' fifth volume edited by Dr Grant Simpson and Dr J. Galbraith and published in the 1980s. The original volumes are not easily available, nor are they likely to be reprinted in the foreseeable future; what appears here is a compilation of the items relating to the Bruces.

Before the period of wars triggered by Edward I in the 1290s the Bruces − and other lords, both Scottish and English − had seldom been obliged to compromise the service owed to one king on the strength of responsibilities to the other, simply because there had been very little conflict between Scotland and England for the better part of a century. The Bruces might be closely involved in the political communities of two different countries, but as long as there was peace there was no reason why they should not continue those involvements; and even when war came they would endeavour to protect their family interests in both countries, until Robert made his bid for kingship.

Obviously Robert continued to appear in English documents after 1306, but the record is supplemented thereafter by the surviving grants and instructions issued by his own administration. There are nearly 600 of these, and they show King Robert in all the roles of medieval kingship. We see him as soldier, judge, legislator and diplomat through the instruments of his government, but we also see a man who liked his sport – chiefly hunting, it would seem, given his interest in 'parks' (areas reclaimed for the chase) and 'messing about in boats', shown by the maintenance of his 'great ship'; but in general his collected acts tell us rather more about what people wanted from their king than they do about what he expected of them. They petition the king for office, they have their transactions confirmed, they ask for respite of taxes or other dues, but the documents seldom give much detail of what is expected in return, and thus give us little insight to the requirements of the king.

MATERIAL FROM SCOTTISH CROWN RECORDS

The most significant sources for Scottish state records of this period are the 'acta' of King Robert and exchequer rolls of his government and household. The former can be studied in their entirety in volume five of 'Regesta Regum Scottorum' compiled and edited by Professor A.A.M. Duncan, and the latter in *The Exchequer Rolls of Scotland*, compiled and edited by J. Stewart (*et al.*) in the late nineteenth and early twentieth centuries. The paucity of Scottish records of this period is, perhaps, a little over-stated; they are slender, but not non-existent. Although virtually all of the Chamberlains' accounts date from 1328–29 we can be reasonably confident that what survives (with the exception of the 'Contribution for Peace' (part of the 'final peace' of 1328), is not 'abnormal' but represents a random sample of the rather ordinary transactions; the day to day running of the king's household for example, which comprised the vast majority of Crown record in Scotland just as it did in any other medieval nation. The 'Declaration of Arbroath' has not been included here; it is readily available elsewhere and readers are particularly recommended to avail themselves of Dr Duncan's study.

CHRONICLES

Chronicle accounts are burdened with a weight of suspicion not generally deserved. The mistaken names or dates which inevitably crop up from time to time are more than outweighed by the social and political information in which they abound. The *Lanercost Chronicle* and the *Chronicle of John of Fordoun* were both written within a lifespan of the events they describe, they are invaluable for what we might call a civil perspective of the period to complement Sir Thomas Grey's *Scalacronica*, the interpretation of a military professional who made a career out of fighting the Scots.

King Robert features in several other chronicles, but these are the ones closest to the events they portray, geographically as well as temporally, and therefore have been given priority over Walter Bower, the Scottish abbot and historian, writing 100 years later.

The extracts presented here do not, of course, constitute all the chronicle references to Robert I by a very wide margin indeed. Brut, Guisborough, Le Bel and many others contain relevant material, but they are also — relatively — accessible in printed form and are understandably rather less focused on Scottish affairs.

A NOTE ON CURRENCY IN THE FOURTEENTH CENTURY

The only coins minted in Scotland in the thirteenth and early fourteenth century were silver pennies of a similar weight and fineness to those produced in the Low Countries and England. Large sums obviously needed to be expressed in a more convenient way than simply so many hundreds or thousands of pennies. The major units of money were pounds, shillings and merks. The pound (£ or I or L) comprised twenty shillings of 12 pence each: a score of dozens. The merk (or mark in England) was equivalent to two thirds of a pound, though this was not the rationale behind its value. The merk was an expression of eight-score pennies, that is eight times twenty, or 160 pence or thirteen shillings and four pence. Small sums of money were often expressed in pennies, i.e. 12d or 24d instead of 1s or 2s. There are several good volumes on medieval coinage, and an excellent guide to the financial realities of medieval Scotland in Mayhew and Gemmill's *Changing Value of Money*.

THE BRUCE

No account of King Robert's life can ignore Barbour's epic (in both the traditional and modern colloquial senses of the word) poem *The Bruce*. To include the text in its entirety does smack of self-indulgence; it would be tempting to excise the tracts devoted to Edward Bruce's adventures in Ireland, but his operations are an integral part of King Robert's strategy. To ignore the war in Ireland is to compromise our understanding of the Scottish campaigns in England and to ignore a serious drain on the resources of Edward II. The text presented here is not 'absolutely and perfectly intact' as Barbour wrote it; indeed there is a real possibility that each of the various surviving texts that have come down to us has been modified by at least one other hand. For reasons of personal taste and no more I have chosen not to include all of the variations that have survived and in that sense this is a synthetic edition; however since only a mere handful of lines have been excluded out of many thousands one hopes that little damage has been done to Barbour's classic epic. For a serious study of *The Bruce* one must look to Professor Duncan's edition (Canongate, 1997) not only for his erudite translation of the text itself but for his copious explanatory notes. This applies particularly to university undergraduates, who will require an edition with line numbers. I have adopted almost without exception Professor Duncan's spelling and literary conventions, and his interpretation of manuscript 'E', for the simple reason that I do not think they can be bettered.

A page from the Scalachronica of Sir Thomas Grey of Heton. Constable of Norham Castle in 1355, when it was captured by the Scots, Sir Thomas Grey was imprisoned in Edinburgh Castle for two years, and there he wrote this chronicle. On this page is his account of the removal of the Stone of Destiny from Scone; 'the stone whereon the kings of Scotland were wont to be seated at the beginning of a reign, and caused it to be taken to London at Westminster, and made it the seat of a priest at the high altar'.

I

Excerpts from the *Scalacronica* of Sir Thomas Grey of Heton (1296-1329)

*U*nsurprisingly, the majority of chronicle narratives were compiled by ecclesiastics in monastic institutions. Scalacronica is the work not only of a layman but also of a professional soldier. Head of a minor Northumberland landowning family, Sir Thomas, like his father before him, made a career of military service. Both father and son served extensively against the Scots and both had the misfortune to become prisoners of war and be held for ransom, an occupational hazard for medieval military professionals. Thomas senior was captured on the first day of Bannockburn (see below). A generation later Thomas junior whiled away his own captivity by writing Scalacronica.

As a soldier his observations of the military practices and operations of the Scots are particularly valuable – we must assume that since he was in the way of risking his neck against the Scots on a regular basis he had a vested interest in understanding them. Interestingly he sees no general distinction between the Scots and the English, militarily or socially. In his view the key to almost every engagement is in the behaviour of the men-at-arms. He sees no difference between Scottish men-at-arms and English ones; it was not apparent to him, or his contemporaries, that the Scots could not support the required quality of horseflesh to mount armoured men. This is interesting given that that very deficiency is more or less universally acknowledged by historians!

Additions to the text in square brackets are by the translator; this writer is responsible for the additions and comments in italics.

At this same time, Robert de Brus, Earl of Carrick, who retained a strong following through kinsmanship and alliance, always hoping for the establishment of his claim of succession to the realm of Scotland, on the 4th of the kalends of February in the year of grace 1306 sent his two brothers, Thomas and Neil from Lochmaben to Dalswinton to John Comyn, begging that he would meet him [Robert] at Dumfries at the [church of the] Minorite Friars, so that they might have a conversation. Now he had plotted with his two brothers aforesaid that they should kill the said John Comyn on the way. But they were received in such a friendly manner by the said John Comyn that they could not bring themselves to do him any harm, but agreed between themselves that their brother himself might do his best. The said John Comyn, suspecting no ill, set out with the two brothers of the said Robert de Brus in order to speak with him [Robert] at Dumfries, went to the Friars [Church] where he found the said Robert, who came to meet him and led him to the high altar. The two brothers of the said Robert told him secretly – 'Sir,' they said, 'he gave us such a fair reception, and with such generous gifts, and won upon us so much by his frankness, that we could by no means do him an injury.' – 'See!' quoth he, 'you are right lazy: let me settle with him.' He took the said John Comyn, and they approached the altar.

'Sir,' then spoke the said Robert de Brus to the said John Comyn, 'this land of Scotland is entirely laid in bondage to the English, through the indolence of that chieftain who suffered his right and the franchise of the realm to be lost. Choose one of two ways, either take my estates and help me to be the king, or give me yours and I will help you to be the same, because you are of his blood who lost it, for I have the hope of succession through my ancestors who claimed the right and were supplanted by yours; for now is the old age of this English King.'
'Certes,' then quoth the said John Comyn, 'I shall never be false to my English seigneur, forasmuch as I am bound to him by oath and homage, in a matter which might be charged against me as treason.'
'No?' exclaimed the said Robert de Brus; 'I had different hopes of you, by the promise of yourself and your friends. You have betrayed me to the King in your letters, wherefore living thou canst not escape my will – thou shalt have thy guerdon!*'

* *reward*

So saying, he struck him with his dagger, and the others cut him down in the middle of the church before the altar. A knight, his [Comyn's] uncle, who was present, struck the said Robert de Brus with a sword in the breast, but he [Bruce] being in armour, was not wounded, which uncle was slain straightway.

The said Robert caused himself to be crowned as King of Scotland at Scone on the feast of the Annunciation of Our Lady by the Countess of Buchan, because of the absence of her son, who at that time was living at his manor of Whitwick near Leicester, to whom the duty of crowning the Kings of Scotland belonged by inheritance, in the absence of the Earl of Fife, who at that time was in ward of the King of England. The said Countess this same year was captured by the English and taken to Berwick, and by command of King Edward of England was placed in a little wooden chamber in a tower of the castle of Berwick with sparred sides, that all might look in from curiosity.

King Edward of England, perceiving the revolt that Robert de Brus and his adherents was making in Scotland, sent thither Aymer de Valence, Earl of Pembroke, with other barons of England and several Scottish ones, descended from the blood of John Comyn, who all set themselves against the said Robert de Brus. The said Earl of Pembroke went to the town of Saint John★ and remained there for a while. Robert de Brus had gathered all the force of Scotland which was on his side, and some fierce young fellows easily roused against the English, and came before the town of Saint John in two great columns, offering battle to the said earl and to the English. He remained before the said town from morning until after high noon. The said Earl of Pembroke kept quite quiet until their departure, when, by advice from the Scottish lords who were with him in the town, friends of John Comyn and adherents of the English – the lords de Moubray, de Abernethy, de Brechin and de Gordon, with several others – he [Pembroke] marched out in two columns. Their Scottish enemy had decamped, sending their quartermasters to prepare a camp at Methven; they formed up as best they could and all on horseback attacked the said sortie; but the Scots were defeated. John de Haliburton caught the reins of the said Robert de Brus, and let him escape directly that he saw who it was, for he [Brus] had no coat armour, only a white shirt.

★ *Perth*

Thomas Randolf, nephew of the said Robert de Brus, he who was afterwards Earl of Moray, was taken at this same battle of Methven, and was released at the instance of Adam de Gordon, and remained English until at another time he was retaken by the Scots.

Robert de Brus, most of his following being slain or captured at this battle of Methven, was pursued into Cantyre★ by the English, who invested the castle of the said country, thinking that the said Robert was within it, but upon taking the said castle they found him not, but found there his wife, a daughter of the Earl of Ulster, and Neil his brother, and soon after the Earl of Athol was taken, who had fled from the said castle. The said Neil, brother to the said Robert de Brus, with Alan Durward and several others, was hanged and drawn by sentence at Berwick, and the wife of the said Robert was sent to ward in England. The Earl of Athol, forasmuch as he was cousin of the King of England, [being] the son of Maud of Dover his [Edward's] aunt, was sent to London, and, because he was of the blood royal, was hanged on a gallows thirty feet higher than the others.

In the same year the King made his son Edward, Prince of Wales, a knight at Westminster, with a great number of other noble young men of his realm, and sent him with a great force to Scotland with all these new knights. Thomas Earl of Lancaster and Humfrey de Bohun Earl of Hereford, passing through the mountains of Scotland, invested the castle of Kildrummie and gained it, in which castle were found Christopher de Seton with his wife, the sister of Robert de Brus, who, as an English renegade, was sent to Dumfries and there hanged, drawn and decapitated, where he had before this caused to be slain a knight, appointed sheriff of a district for the King of England. The Bishops of Glasgow and St Andrews and the Abbot of Scone were taken in the same season and sent to ward in England.

Piers de Gaveston was accused before the King of divers crimes and vices, which rendered him with unfit company for the King's son, wherefore he was exiled and outlawed.

In the year of Grace 1306 King Edward having come to Dunfermline, his son Edward Prince of Wales returned from beyond the mountains, and lay with a great army at the town of Perth. Meanwhile, Robert de Brus having landed from the Isles and collected round him a

★ Kintyre

18

mob in the defiles of Athol, sent a messenger having a safe conduct to come and treat, to arrange for a treaty of peace with the said son of the king. He came to the bridge of the town of Perth, and began negotiation in order to ascertain whether he could find grace, which parley was reported to the King at Dunfermline on the morrow.

He was almost mad when he heard of the negotiation and demanded: 'Who had been so bold as to attempt treating with our traitors without our knowledge?' and would not hear speak of it.

The King and his son moved to the Marches of England. Aymer de Valence remained the King's lieutenant in Scotland. Robert de Brus resumed [his] great conspiracy; he sent his two brothers Thomas and Alexander into Nithsdale and the vale of Annan to draw [to him] the hearts of the people, where they were surprised by the English and captured, and taken by command of the King to Carlisle, and there hanged, drawn and decapitated. Robert de Brus had assembled his adherents in Carrick. Hearing of this, Aymer de Valence marched against him, when the said Robert de Brus encountered the said Aymer de Valence at Loudoun, and defeated him, and pursued him to the castle at Ayr; and on the third day [after] the said Robert de Brus defeated Rafe de Monthermer, who was called Earl of Gloucester because Joan the King's daughter and Countess of Gloucester had taken him for a husband out of love [for him]. Him also he [Brus] pursued to the castle of Ayr, and there besieged him until the English army came to his rescue, which [army] reduced the said Robert de Brus to such distress that he went afoot through the mountains, and from isle to isle, and at the same time in such plight as that occasionally he had nobody with him. For, as the chronicles of his actions testify, he came at this time to a passage between two islands all alone, and when he was in the boat with the two seamen they asked him for news — whether he had heard nothing about what had become of Robert de Brus. 'Nothing whatever,' quoth he. 'Sure,' said they, 'would that we had hold of him at this moment, so that he might die by our hands!' 'And why?' enquired he. 'Because he murdered our lord John Comyn,' [said they]. They put him ashore where they had agreed to do, when he said to them, 'Good sirs, you were wishing that you had hold of Robert de Brus — behold me here if that pleases you; and were it not that you had done me the courtesy to set me across this narrow passage, you should have had your wish.' So he went on his way, exposed to perils such as these.

Although a prisoner of war, Sir Thomas evidently had documentary material available for his studies. This story of the two boatmen also surfaces in Barbour's poem.

The aforesaid King Edward of England had remained at this same time exceedingly ill at Lanercost, whence he moved for change of air to await his army, which he had summoned to re-enter Scotland. Thus he arrived at Burgh-on-sands, and upon the death of his uncle Charles, so that another collateral, the son of the uncle of the aforesaid Charles, was crowned King by means of his supporters, especially of Robert of Artois (to whom he was afterwards the greatest enemy), because no other challenged the right at the proper time, nor until a considerable time after, as will be recorded hereafter; which [thing] is correct, and ought to be a notable thing and remembered everywhere.

At this time Thomas de Gray was warden of the castle of Cupar and Fife, and as he was traveling out of England from the King's coronation to the said castle, Walter de Bickerton, a knight of Scotland, who was an adherent of Robert de Brus, having espied the return of the said Thomas, placed himself in ambush with more than four hundred men by the way the said Thomas intended to pass, whereof the said Thomas was warned when scarcely half a league from the ambush. He had not more than six-and-twenty men-at-arms with him, and perceived that he could not avoid an encounter. So, with the approval of his people, he took the road straight towards the ambush, having given his grooms a standard and ordered them to follow behind at not too short interval.

The enemy mounted their horses and formed for action, thinking that they [the English] could not escape from them. The said Thomas, with his people, who were very well mounted, struck spurs to his horse, and charged the enemy right in the centre of their column, bearing many to the ground in his course by the shock of his horse and lance. Then, turning rein, came back in the same manner and charged again, and once again returned through the thick of the troop, which so encouraged his people that they all followed him in like manner, whereby they overthrew many of the enemy, whose horses stampeded along the road. When they [the enemy] rose from the ground, they perceived the grooms of the said Thomas coming up in good order, and began to fly to a dry peat moss which was near, wherefore almost all [the others] began to fly to the moss, leaving their horses for their few assailants. The said Thomas and his men could not get near them on horseback, wherefore he caused their horses to be driven before them along the road to the said castle, where at night they had a booty of nine score saddled horses. (*One wonders if 'covered' or 'barded' – meaning armoured – might have been a more appropriate translation.*)

Another time, on a market day, the town being full of people from the neighbourhood, Alexander Frisel, who was an adherent of Robert de Brus, was ambushed with a hundred men-at-arms about half a league from the said castle, having sent others of his people to rifle a hamlet on the other side of the castle. The said Thomas, hearing the uproar, mounted a fine charger before his people could get ready, and went to see what was ado. The enemy spurred out from their ambush before the gates of the said castle, so doing because they well knew that he *(Sir Thomas)* had gone forth. The said Thomas, perceiving this, returned at a foot's pace through the town of Cupar, at the end whereof stood the castle, where he had to enter on horseback, [and] where they had occupied the whole street. When he came near them he struck spurs to his horse; of those who advanced against him, he struck down some with his spear, others with the shock of his horse, and, passing through them all, dismounted at the gate, drove his horse in, and slipped inside the barrier, where he found his people assembled.

This King Edward the Second after the conquest bestowed great affection during his father's life upon Piers de Gaveston, a young man of good Gascon family; whereat his father became so much concerned lest he [Piers] should lead his son astray, that he caused him [Piers] to be exiled from the realm, and even made his son and nephew, Thomas of Lancaster, and other magnates swear that the exile of the said Piers should be for ever irrevocable. But soon after the death of his father, the son caused the said Piers to be recalled suddenly, and made him take to wife his sister's daughter, one of Gloucester's daughters, and made him Earl of Cornwall. Piers became very magnificent, liberal, and well-bred in manner, but haughty and supercilious in debate, whereat some of the great men of the realm took deep offence. They planned his destruction while he was serving the King in the Scottish war. He had caused the town of Dundee to be fortified, and had behaved himself more rudely there than was agreeable to the gentlemen of the country, so that he had to return to the King because of the opposition of the barons. On his way back they surprised and took him at Scarborough, but he was delivered to Aymer de

Valence upon condition that he was to be taken before the King, from whose [Aymer's] people he was retaken near Oxford, and brought before the Earl of Lancaster, who had him beheaded close to Warwick, whereat arose the King's mortal hate, which endured for ever between them.

Adam Banaster, a knight bachelor of the county of Lancaster, led a revolt against the said earl by instigation of the King: but he could not sustain it, and was taken and beheaded by order of the said earl, who had made long marches in following his [Banaster's] people.

During the dispute between the King and the said earl, Robert de Brus, who had already risen during the life of the King's father, renewed his strength in Scotland, claiming authority over the realm of Scotland, and subdued many of the lands in Scotland which were before subdued by and in submission to the King of England; and [this was] chiefly the result of bad government by the King's officials, who administered them [the lands] too harshly in their private interests.

The castles of Roxburgh and Edinburgh were captured and dismantled, which castles were in the custody of foreigners Roxburgh [being] in charge of Guillemyng (*William*) Fenygges, a knight of Burgundy, from whom James de Douglas captured the said castle upon the night of Shrove Tuesday, the said William being slain by an arrow as he was defending the great tower. Peres (*Peter*) Lebaud, a Gascon knight, was Sheriff of Edinburgh, from whom the people of Thomas Randolph, Earl of Moray, who had besieged the said castle, took it at the highest part of the rock, where he suspected no danger. The said Peter became Scots in the service of Robert de Brus, who afterwards accused him of treason, and caused him to be hanged and drawn. It was said that he suspected him [Peter] because he was too outspoken, believing him nevertheless to be English at heart, doing his best not to give him [Bruce] offence.

The said King Edward planned an expedition to these parts, where, in [attempting] the relief of the castle of Stirling, he was defeated, and a great number of his people were slain, [including] the Earl of Gloucester and other right noble persons; and the Earl of Hereford was taken at Bothwell, whither he had beaten retreat, where he was betrayed by the governor. He was released [in exchange] for the wife of Robert de Brus and the Bishop of St Andrews.

As to the manner in which this discomfiture befell, the chronicles explain that after the Earl of Atholl had captured the town of St John for the use of Robert de Brus from William Oliphant, captain [thereof] for the King of England, being at that time an adherent of his [Edward's], although shortly after he deserted him, the said Robert marched in force before the castle of Stirling, where Philip de Moubray, knight, having command of the said castle for the King of England, made terms with the said Robert de Brus to surrender the said castle, which he had besieged, unless he [de Moubray] should be relieved; that is, unless the English army came within three leagues of the said castle within eight days of Saint John's day in the summer next to come, he would surrender the said castle. The said King of England came thither for that reason, where the said constable Philip met him at three leagues from the castle, on Sunday the vigil of Saint John, and told him that there was no occasion for him to approach any nearer, for he considered himself as relieved. Then he told him how the enemy had blocked the narrow roads in the forest.

[But] the young troops would by no means stop, but held their way. The advanced guard, whereof the Earl of Gloucester had command, entered the road within the Park, where they were immediately received roughly by the Scots who had occupied the passage. Here Peris de Mountforth, knight, was slain with an axe by the hand of Robert de Brus, as was reported.

Here Sir Thomas is, for once, misinformed; it was of course Sir Henry de Bohun who fell to King Robert's axe.

While the said advanced guard were following this road, Robert Lord de Clifford and Henry de Beaumont, with three hundred men-at-arms, made a circuit upon the other side of the wood towards the castle, keeping the open ground. Thomas Randolph, Earl of Moray, Robert de Brus's nephew, who was leader of the Scottish advanced guard, hearing that his uncle had repulsed the advanced guard of the English on the other side of the wood, thought that he must have his share, and issuing from the wood with his division marched across the open ground towards the two afore-named lords.

Sir Henry de Beaumont called to his men: 'Let us wait a little; let them come on; give them room!'

'Sir,' said Sir Thomas Gray (*the author's father*), 'I doubt that whatever you give them now, they will have all too soon.'

'Very well!' exclaimed the said Henry, 'if you are afraid be off!'

'Sir,' answered the said Thomas, 'it is not from fear that I shall fly this day.' So saying he spurred in between him [Beaumont] and Sir William Deyncourt, and charged into the thick of the enemy. William was killed, Thomas was taken prisoner, his horse being killed on the pikes, and he himself carried off with them [the Scots] on foot when they marched off, having utterly routed the squadron of the said two lords. Some of whom [the English] fled to the castle, others to the king's army, which having already left the road through the wood had debouched upon a plain near the water of Forth beyond Bannockburn, an evil, deep, wet marsh, where the said English army unharnessed and remained all night, having sadly lost confidence and being too much disaffected by the events of the day.

The Scots in the wood thought they had done well enough for the day, and were on the point of decamping in order to march during the night into the Lennox, a stronger country, when Sir Alexander de Seton, who was in the service of England and has come thither with the King, secretly left the English army, went to Robert de Brus in the wood, and said to him 'Sir, this is the time if ever you intend to undertake to reconquer Scotland. The English have lost heart and are discouraged, and expect nothing but a sudden, open attack.'

Then he described their condition, and pledged his head, on pain of being hanged and drawn, that if he [Bruce] would attack them on the morrow he would defeat them easily without [much] loss. At whose [Seton's] instigation they [the Scots] resolved to fight, and at sunrise on the morrow marched out of the wood in three divisions of infantry. They directed their course boldly upon the English army, which had been under arms all night, with their horses bitted. They [the English] mounted in great alarm, for they were not accustomed to dismount to fight on foot; whereas the Scots had taken a lesson from the Flemings, who before that had at Courtrai defeated on foot the power of France. The aforesaid Scots came in line of 'scholtroms', and attacked the English columns, which were jammed together and could not operate against them [the Scots], so direfully were their horses impaled on the pikes. The troops in the English rear fell back upon the ditch of Bannockburn, tumbling one over the other.

The English squadrons being thrown into confusion by the thrust of pike upon the horses, began to fly. Those who were appointed to [attend upon] the King's rein, perceiving the disaster, led the King by the rein off the field towards the castle, and off he went, though much against the grain. As the Scottish knights, who were on foot, laid hold of the housing of the King's charger in order to stop him, he struck out so vigourously behind him with a mace that there was none whom he touched that he did not fell to the ground.

As those who had the King's rein were thus drawing him always forward, one of them, Giles de Argentin, a famous knight who had lately come over sea from the wars of the Emperor Henry of Luxemburg, said to the king:

'Sire, your rein was committed to me; you are now in safety; there is your castle where your person may be safe. I am not accustomed to fly, nor am I going to begin now. I commend you to God!'

Then, setting spurs to his horse, he returned into the mellay, where he was slain.

The King's charger, having been piked, could go no further; so he mounted afresh on a courser and was taken round the Torwood, and [so] through the plains of Lothian. Those who went with him were saved; all the rest came to grief. The King escaped with great difficulty, traveling thence to Dunbar, where Patrick, Earl of March, received him honourably, and put his castle at his disposal, and even evacuated the place, removing all his people, so that there might be neither doubt nor suspicion that he would do nothing short of his devoir to his lord, for at that time he [Dunbar] was his liegeman. Thence the King went by sea to Berwick and afterwards to the south. Edward de Brus, brother to Robert, King of Scotland, desiring to be a king [also], passed out of Scotland into Ireland with a great army in hopes of conquering it. He remained there two years and a half, performing there feats of arms, inflicting great destruction both upon provender and in other ways, and conquering much territory, which would form a splendid romance were it all recounted. He proclaimed himself King of the kings of Ireland; [but] he was defeated and slain at Dundalk by the English of that country [because] through over confidence he would not wait for reinforcements, which had arrived lately, and were not more than six leagues distant.

At the same time the King of England sent the Earl of Arundel as commander on the March of Scotland, who was repulsed at Lintalee in the forest of Jedwort, by James de Douglas, and Thomas de Richmond was slain. The said earl then retreated to the south without doing any more.

On another occasion the said James defeated the garrison of Berwick at Scaithmoor, where a number of Gasçons were slain. Another time there happened a disaster on the marches at Berwick, by treachers of the false traitors of the marches, where was slain Robert de Neville; which Robert shortly before had slain Richard fitz Marmaduke, cousin of Robert de Brus, on the old bridge of Durham, because of a quarrel between them [arising] out of jealousy which should be reckoned the greater lord. Therefore, in order to obtain the King's grace and pardon for this offence, Neville began to serve in the King's war, wherein he died.

At the same period the said James de Douglas, with the assistance of Patrick, Earl of March, captured Berwick from the English, by means of the treason of one in the town, Peter de Spalding. The castle held out for eleven weeks after, and at last capitulated to the Scots in default of relief, because it was not provisioned. The constable, Roger de Horsley, lost there an eye by an arrow. Aymer de Valence, Earl of Pembroke, traveling to the court of Rome, was captured by a Burgundian, John de la Moiller, taken into the empire and ransomed for 20,000 silver livres, because the said John declared that he had done the King of England service, and that the King was owing him his pay.

This James de Douglas was now very busy in Northumberland. Robert de Brus called all the castles of Scotland, except Dunbarton, to be dismantled. This Robert de Brus caused William de Soulis to be arrested, and caused him to be confined in the castle of Dunbarton for punishment in prison, accusing him of having conspired with other great men of Scotland for his [Robert's] undoing, to whom [de Soulis] they were attorned subjects, which the said William confessed by his acknowledgement. David de Brechin, John Logie, and Gilbert Malherbe were hanged and drawn in the town of St John, and the corpse of Roger de Mowbray was brought on a litter before the judges in the Parliament of Scone, and condemned. This conspiracy was discovered by Murdach of Menteith, who himself became earl afterwards. He had lived long in England in loyalty to the King, and, returned home in order to discover this conspiracy. He became Earl of Menteith by consent of his niece, daughter of his elder brother, who, after his death at another time, became countess.

The King of England undertook scarcely anything against Scotland, and thus lost as much by indolence as his father had conquered; and also a number of fortresses within his marches of England, as well as a great part of Northumberland which revolted against him.

Gilbert de Middleton in the bishopric of Durham, plundered two Cardinals who came to consecrate the Bishop, and seized Louis de

Beaumont, Bishop of Durham, and his brother Henry de Beaumont, because the King had caused his [Gilbert's] cousin Adam de Swinburne to be arrested, because he had spoken too frankly to him about the condition of the Marches.

This Gilbert, with adherence of others upon the Marches, rode upon a foray into Cleveland, and committed other great destruction, having the assistance of nearly all Northumberland, except the castles of Bamborough, Alnwick, and Norham, of which the two first named were treating with the enemy, the one by means of hostages, the other by collusion, when the said Gilbert was taken through treachery of his own people in the castle of Mitford by William de Felton, Thomas de Heton, and Robert de Horncliff, and was hanged and drawn in London.

On account of all this, the Scots had become so bold that they subdued the Marches of England and cast down the castles of Wark and Harbottle, so that hardly was there an Englishman who dared to withstand them. They had subdued all Northumberland by means of the treachers of the false people of the country. So that scarcely could they [the Scots] find anything to do upon these Marches, except at Norham, where a [certain] knight, Thomas de Gray, was in garrison with his kinsfolk. It would be too lengthy a matter to relate [all] the combats and deeds of arms and evils for default of provender, and sieges which happened to him during the eleven years that he remained [there] during such an evil and disastrous period for the English. It would be wearisome to tell the story of less [important] of his combats in the said castle. Indeed it was so that, after the town of Berwick was taken out of the hands of the English, the Scots had got so completely the upper hand and were so insolent that they held the English to be of almost no account, who [the English] concerned themselves no more with the war, but allowed it to cease.

At which time, at a great feast of lords and ladies in the county of Lincoln, a young page brought a war helmet, with a gilt crest on the same, to William Marmion, knight, with a letter from his lady-love commanding him to go to the most dangerous place in Great Britain and [there] cause this helmet to be famous. Thereupon it was decided by the knight [present] that he should go to Norham, as the most dangerous [and] adventurous place in the country. The said William betook himself to Norham, where, within four days of his arrival, Sir Alexander de Mowbray, brother of Sir Philip de Mowbray, at that time governor of Berwick, came before the castle of Norham with the most spirited chivalry of the Marches of Scotland, and drew up before the castle at the hour of noon with more than either score men-at-arms. The alarm was given in the castle as they were sitting down to dinner. Thomas de Gray, the constable, went with his garrison to his barriers, saw the enemy near drawn up in order of battle, looked behind him, and beheld the said knight, William Marmion, approaching on foot, all glittering with gold and silver, marvellous finely attired, with the helmet on his head. The said Thomas, having been well informed of the reason for his coming [to Norham], cried aloud to him: 'Sir knight, you have come as knight errant to make that helmet famous, and it is more meet that deeds of chivalry be done on horseback than afoot, when that can be managed conveniently. Mount your horse: there are your enemies: set spurs and charge into their midst. May I deny my God if I do not rescue your person, alive or dead, or perish in the attempt!'

The knight mounted a beautiful charger, spurred forward, [and] charged into the midst of the enemy, who struck him down, wounded him in the face, [and] dragged him out of the saddle to the ground.

At this moment, up came the said Thomas with all his garrison, with levelled lances, [which] they drove into the bowels of the horses so that they threw their riders. They repulsed the mounted enemy, raised the fallen knight, re-mounting him upon his own horse, put the enemy to flight, [of whom] some were let dead in the first encounter, [and] captured fifty valuable horses. The women of the castle [then] brought out horses to their men, who mounted and gave chase, slaying those whom they could overtake. Thomas de Gray caused to be killed in the Yair Ford, a Fleming [named] Cryn, a sea captain, a pirate, who was a great partisan of Robert de Brus. The others who escaped were pursued to the nunnery of Berwick.

Another time, Adam de Gordon, a baron of Scotland, having mustered more than eight score men-at-arms, came before the said castle of Norham, thinking to raid the cattle which were grazing outside the said castle. The young fellows of the garrison rashly hastened to the furthest end of the town, which at that time was in ruins, and began to skirmish. The Scottish enemy surrounded them. The said men of the sortie defended themselves briskly, keeping themselves within the old walls. At that moment Thomas de Gray, the said constable, came out of the castle with his garrison [and], perceiving his people in such danger from the enemy, said to his vice-constable: 'I'll hand over to you this castle, albeit

I have it in charge to hold in the King's cause, unless I actually drink of the same cup that my people over there have to drink.'

Then he set forward at great speed, having of common people and others, scarcely more than sixty all told. The enemy, perceiving him coming in good order, left the skirmishers among the old walls and drew out into the open fields. The men who had been surrounded in the ditches, perceiving their chieftain coming in this manner, dashed across the ditches and ran to the fields against the said enemy, who were obliged to face about, and then charged back upon them [the skirmishers]. Upon which came up the said Thomas with his men, when you might see the horses floundering and the people on foot slaying them as they lay on the ground. [Then they] rallied to the said Thomas, charged the enemy, [and] drove them out of the fields across the water of Tweed. They captured and killed many; many horses lay dead, so that had they [the English) been on horseback, scarcely one would have escaped. The said Thomas de Gray was twice besieged in the said castle – once for nearly a year, the other for seven months. The enemy erected fortifications before him, one at Upsettlington, another at the church of Norham. He was twice provisioned by the Lords de Percy and de Nevill, [who came] in force to relieve the said castle; and these [nobles] became wise, noble and rich, and were of great service on the Marches.

Once on the vigil of St Katherine during his [Gray's] time, the fore-court of the said castle was betrayed by one of his men, who slew the porter [and] admitted the enemy [who were] in ambush in a house before the gate. The inner bailey and the keep held out. The enemy did not remain there more than three days, because they feared the attack of the said Thomas, who was then returning from the south, where he had been at that time. They evacuated it [the forecourt] and burnt it, after failing to mine it.

Andrew de Harcla had behaved gallantly many time against the Scots, sometimes with good result and sometimes with loss, [performing] many fine feats of arms; until he was captured by them and ransomed at a high price.

In the summer following the death of the Earl of Lancaster the King marched with a very great army towards Scotland, having, besides his knights and esquires, an armed foot-soldier from every town in England. These common people fought at Newcastle with the commons of the town, where, on the bridge of the said town, they killed the knight, John de Penrith, and some esquires who were in the service of the Constable, and the Marshal, because they tried to arrest the ruffians so as to quell the disturbance; so insolent were the common folk in their conduct.

The said King marched upon Edinburgh, where at Leith there came such sickness and famine upon the common soldiers of that great army, that they were forced to beat a retreat for want of food; at which time the King's light horsemen, foraging at Melrose were defeated by James de Douglas. None [dared] leave the main body to seek food by foray. So greatly were the English harassed and worn with fighting that before they arrived at Newcastle there was such a murrain in the army for want of food, that they were obliged of necessity to disband.

The King retired upon York with the great men of his realm; when Robert de Brus having caused to assemble the whole power of Scotland, the Isles and the rest of the Highlands, pressed ever after the King, who, perceiving his approach, marched into Blackhow Moor, with all the force that he could muster on a sudden. They [the Scots] took a strength on a hill near Biland, where the King's people were defeated, and the Earl of Richmond, the Lord of Sully, a baron of France, and many others; so that the King himself scarcely escaped from Rivaulx, where he was [quartered]. But the Scots were so fierce and their chiefs so daring, and the English so badly cowed, that it was no otherwise between them than as a hare before greyhounds.

The Scots rode beyond the Wold and [appeared] before York, and committed destruction at their pleasure without resistance from any, until it seemed good to them to retire.

From this time forward the King made a truce with the Scots for thirteen years. He kept himself quite quiet.

When Robert de Brus, then King of Scotland, had laid siege to the castle of Norham, whereof Robert de Manners was the constable, he [Manners] made a sortie one day with his garrison and defeated the watch of the Scottish enemy before the castle gate, where a banneret of Scotland, William Mouhaud, was slain. The commander of the watch would not allow them to be rescued because of the flood, so that none of those in the town could get near them.

Presumably Grey means that the main body of the Scots held the town and were separated from the area in front of the castle gate by a water course which prevented effective reinforcement.

The Earl of Moray, with James de Douglas, had then besieged the Lord Percy in Alnwick, where there were great jousts of war by formal agreement; but these lords did not maintain the siege, but marched to Robert their King at the siege of Norham. At which time the Lord Percy with the men of the Marches made a raid upon the side of Teviotdale, remaining scarcely ten leagues distant. No sooner was James de Douglas informed of this, than he suddenly threw himself from Norham with his troops between the Lord Percy and his castle of Alnwick; which forced him [Percy] to make a night march toward Newcastle, so demoralised were the English in time of war.

The aforesaid council of the King of England sent a man of law, William de Denoun, to the said Robert de Brus at Norham [to negotiate] peace, and arranged a marriage between David, son of the said Robert, and Joan, sister of the King of England, which afterwards took place at Berwick.

By the time Sir Thomas was writing his chronicle the whole question of Scottish independence had been reopened; Edward III had denied the validity of the 'final peace' of 1328 and was supporting Edward Balliol, son of the deposed John I, as king of Scotland against his own brother-in-law, David II.

Edward I. His aggressive interventions in Scotland destroyed the generally positive relationship between Scotland and England for a century. Despite his posthumous nickname 'Malleus Scottorum' (Hammer of the Scots) Edward failed miserably in his attempt to annex Scotland.

2

Excerpts from the *Chronicle of John Fordoun* (1296–1329)

Chronica Gentis Scotorum, edited by W.F. Skene, 1872

A s we might expect from a Scottish chronicle, Fordoun makes the most of heroic figures generally and King Robert in particular. A churchman, he was at pains to stress the importance of the will of God in the affairs of Scotland and for that matter the affairs of all nations and individuals – King Robert leads the Scots to battle, but it is God who gives victory. Like the Lanercost Chronicle, *Fordoun's work has a distinctly patriotic tone; not simply 'anti' English, but positively 'pro' Scottish. The idea of a national consciousness was perhaps still in its infancy in the early fourteenth century, but personal consciousness of nationality was a factor in people's lives. Notes in square brackets are by the translator, those in italics by me.*

CXII
Rise of Robert of Bruce, King of Scotland

After the withdrawal of the king of England, the English nation lorded it in all parts of the kingdom of Scotland, ruthlessly harrying the Scots in sundry and manifold ways, by insults, stripes, and slaughter, under the awful yoke of slavery. But God, in His mercy, as is the wont of His fatherly goodness, had compassion on the woes, the ceaseless crying and sorrow, of the Scots; so He raised up a saviour and champion unto them – one of their own fellows, to wit, named Robert of Bruce. This man, seeing them stretched in the slough of woe, and reft of all hope of salvation and help, was inwardly touched with sorrow of heart; and, putting forth his hand unto force, underwent the countless and unbearable toils of the heat of day, of cold and hunger, by land and sea, gladly welcoming weariness, fasting, dangers, and the snares not only of foes, but also of false friends, for the sake of freeing his brethren.

CXIII
League of King Robert with John Comyn

So, in order that he might actually give effect to what he had gladly set his heart upon, for the good of the commonwealth, he humbly approached a certain noble, named John Comyn (who was then the most powerful man in the country), and faithfully laid before him the unworthy thraldom of the country, the cruel and endless tormenting of the people, and his own kind-hearted plan for giving them relief. Though, by right, and according to the laws and customs of the country, the honour of the kingly office and the succession to the governance of the kingdom were known to belong to him before any one else, yet, setting the public advantage before his own, Robert, in all purity and sincerity of purpose, gave John the choice of one of two courses: either that the latter should reign, and wholly take unto himself the kingdom, with its pertinents and royal honours, forever, granting to the former all his own lands and possessions; or that all Robert's lands and possessions should come into the possession of John and his forever, while the kingdom and the kingly honour were left to Robert. Thus, by their mutual advice as well as help, was to be brought to maturity the deliverance of the Scottish nation from the house of bondage and unworthy thraldom; and an indissoluble treaty of friendship and peace was to last between them. John was perfectly satisfied with the latter of the aforesaid courses; and thereupon a covenant was made between them, and guaranteed by means of sworn pledges, and by their indentures with their seals attached thereto. But John broke his word; and, heedless of the sacredness of his oath, kept accusing Robert before the king of England, through his ambassadors and private letters, and wickedly revealing Robert's secrets. Although, however, Robert was more than once sounded thereupon by the aforesaid king, who ever showed him the letters of his adversary who accused him, yet, inspired by God, he always returned an answer such that he over and over again softened the king's rage by his pleasant sayings and skilful words. The king, however, both because he was himself very wily and shrewd, and knew full well how to feign a sham friendship, and also because Robert was the true heir of the kingdom of Scotland, looked upon the latter with mistrust – the more so because of John's accusations. So, because of his aforesaid grounds for mistrust, Edward bade Robert stay always at court; and he delayed putting him to death – or, at least, in prison – only until he could get the rest of this Robert's brothers together, and punish them and him at once, in one day, with sentence of death.

The demands of patriotism, in a time when the king of England had long been, and continued to be, identified (not unreasonably) as an aggressive and acquisitive neighbour, meant there was no room for dissent among the Scots. The murder of John Comyn required justification if a killing in front of the very altar were to be considered anything other than the most dreadful sacrilege. 'Explaining' the actions of King Robert was absolutely essential if Fordoun were to be able to show Robert as a paragon of knightly values and Christian sentiment. Fordoun's relation of an offer by Robert to forego his claim to the throne bears little weight; any Comyn claim to the kingship would be extremely tenuous to say the least.

CXIV
King Robert accused before
the King of England, by John Comyn

As the said John's accusations were repeated, at length, one night, while wine glittered in the bowl, and that king was hastening to sit down with his secretaries, he talked over Robert's death in earnest – and shortly determined that he would deprive him of his life on the morrow. But when the Earl of Gloucester, who was Robert's true and tried friend in his utmost need, heard of this, he hastily, that same night, sent the aforesaid Robert, by his keeper of the wardrobe, twelve pence and a pair of spurs. So the keeper of the wardrobe, who guessed his lord's wishes, presented these things to Robert, from his lord, and added these words: 'My lord sends these to you, in return for what he, on his side, got from you yesterday.' Robert understood, from the tokens offered him, that he was threatened by the danger of death; so he discreetly gave the pence to the keeper of the wardrobe, and forthwith sent him back to the Earl with greeting in answer, and with thanks. Then, when twilight came on, that night, after having ostentatiously ordered his servants to meet him at Carlisle, with his trappings, on the evening of the following day, he straightaway hastened towards Scotland, without delay, and never stopped travelling, day or night, until he was safe from the aforesaid king's spite. For he was under the guidance of One of whom it is written: 'There is no wisdom, no fore-sight, no understanding against the Lord, who knoweth how to snatch the good from trial, and mercifully to deliver from danger those that trust in Him.'

The earl of Gloucester mentioned here held the title through his wife (ius uxoris) who died in 1307. He was not therefore the same man as the earl of Gloucester killed in action at Stirling in 1314, but his father.

CXV
Death of John Comyn's messenger

Now, when Robert was nearing the borders of the marches, there met him a messenger whom, when he sighted him afar off, he suspected, both from the fellow's gait and from his dress, to be a Scot. So, when he got nearer, he asked him whence he came and whither he was making his way. The messenger began to pour forth excuses for his sins; but Robert ordered his vassals to search him. Letters, sealed with Robert's seal about the covenant entered into between him and John Comyn, were found addressed to the king of England through this messenger, and were forthwith pulled out. The messenger's head was thereupon struck off, and God very much be praised for His guidance in this pros-perous journey.

It would be interesting to know what exactly Fordoun means when he tells us the Robert knew that an approaching man was a Scot by his 'dress and gait'. We have no evidence to suggest that Lowland Scots dressed any differently to people elsewhere.

CXVI
Death of William Wallace

In the year 1305, William Wallace was craftily and treacherously taken by John of Menteith, who handed him over to the king of England; and he was, in London, torn limb from limb, and, as a reproach to the Scots, his limbs were hung on towers in sundry places throughout England and Scotland.

CXVII
John Comyn's death

The same year, after the aforesaid Robert had left the king of England and returned home, no less miraculously than by God's grace, a day is appointed for him and the aforesaid John to meet together at Dumfries; and both sides repair to the above-named place. John Comyn is twitted with his treachery and belied troth. The lie is at once given. The evil-speaker is stabbed, and wounded unto death, in the church of the Friars; and the wounded man is, by the friars, laid behind the altar. On being asked by those around whether he could live, straightaway his answer is : 'I can.' His foes, hearing this, give him another wound; and thus was he taken away from his world on the 10th of February.

The earliest surviving description of this event is from the chronicler Walter of Guisborough, an English writer. Unsurprisingly the two accounts are diametrically opposed to one another in ascribing honourable or wicked intentions. To Walter, Bruce is a murderous rebel attempting to undermine the decent and worthy rule of a great man – Edward I, whereas John of Fordoun excuses the sacrilegious deed of his hero by stressing the treachery of John Comyn and the desperate plight of the nation.

CXVIII
Coronation of King Robert Bruce

Now, when a few days had rolled on, after the said John's death, this Robert of Bruce, taking with him as many men as he could get, hastened to Scone; and, being set on the royal throne, was there crowned, on the 27th March 1306, in the manner wherein the kings of Scotland were wont to be invested; and great was the task he then undertook, and unbearable were the burdens he took upon his shoulders. For, not only did he lift his hand against the king of England, and all partakers with him, but he also launched out into a struggle with all and sundry of the kingdom of Scotland, except a very few wellwishers of his, who, if one looked at the hosts of those pitted against them, were as one drop of water compared with the waves of the sea, or a single grain of any seed with the multitudinous sand. His mishaps, flights, and dangers; hardships; and weariness; hunger, and thirst; watchings, and fastings; nakedness, and cold; snares, and banishment; the seizing, imprisoning, slaughter, and downfall of his near ones, and — even more — dear ones (for all this had he to undergo, when overcome and routed in the beginning of his war) — noone, now living, I think, recollects, or is equal to rehearsing, all this. Indeed, he is reported to have said to his knights, one day, when worn out by such numberless and ceaseless hardships and dangers: 'Were I not stirred by Scotland's olden bliss/Not for earth's empire would I bear all this.'

Moreover, with all the ill-luck and numberless straits he went through with a glad and dauntless heart, were anyone able to rehearse his own struggle, and triumphs single-handed — the victories and battles wherein, by the Lord's help, by his own strength, and by his human manhood, he fearlessly cut his way into the columns of the enemy, now mightily bearing these down, and now mightily warding off and escaping the pains of death — he would, I deem, prove that, in the art of fighting, and in vigour of body, Robert had not his match in his time, in any clime. I will, therefore, forbear to describe his own individual deeds, both because they would take up many leaves, and because, though they are undoubtedly true, the time and place wherein they happened, and were wrought, are known to few in these days. But his well-known battles and public exploits will be found set down below, in the years wherein they took place.

Fordoun wants his readers to see King Robert's concern for his country as proof of the righteousness of his cause. Whether or not a sense of national identity was a major factor in the wars of independence has been an issue among historians for generations, but it would seem that Fordoun and Barbour were convinced of the importance of patriotic motivation. This does not mean, of course, that Robert's career was governed by medieval nationalism, but we should not be in too much of a hurry to discount national identity as a factor in the popularity of the Bruce cause. It is clear that people were well aware of their nationality; how widely that consciousness of identity drew support to the Bruce family is a more thorny question.

CXIX
Battle of Methven

The same year, on the 19th day of June, King Robert was overcome and put to flight, at Methven, by Odomar *(Aymer)* of Valence, who was then warden of Scotland on behalf of the king of England, and was staying at the then well-walled town of Perth, with a great force of both English and Scots★ who owed fealty and submission to the king of England. Now, though the aforesaid king did not lose many of his men in this struggle, yet, because of the bad beginning, which is often crowned by an unhappy ending, his men began to be disheartened, and the victorious side to be much emboldened by their victory. Then, all the wives of those who had followed the king were ordered to be outlawed by the voice of a herald, so that they might follow their husbands; by reason whereof, many women, both single and married, lurked with their people in the woods, and cleaved to the king, abiding with him, under shelter.

CXX
Conflict at Dalry, in the borders of Argyll

The same year, while this king was fleeing from his foes, and lurking with his men, in the borders of Athol and Argyll, he was again beaten and put to flight, on the 11th of August, at a place called Dalry. But there, also, he did not lose many of his men. Nevertheless, they were all filled with fear, and were dispersed and scattered throughout various places. But the queen fled to Saint Duthac★★ in Ross, where she was taken by William Earl of Ross, and brought to the king of England; and she was kept prisoner in close custody, till the battle of Bannockburn. Nigel of Bruce, however, one of the king's brothers, fled, with many

---

★ *In summer 1306 only a small proportion of Scots declared for King Robert. Many still supported the Balliol claim, many accepted the lordship of Edward I and in all probability a very large proportion would have willingly accepted the lordship of anyone who could offer them peace and stability.*
★★ *the sanctuary of Saint Duthac at Tain*

ladies and damsels, to Kyndrumie Castle★, and was there welcomed, with his companions. But, the same year, that castle was made over to the English through treachery, and Nigel, and other nobles of both sexes, were taken prisoners, brought to Berwick, and suffered capital punishment. The same year, Thomas and Alexander of Bruce, brothers of the aforesaid king, while hastening towards Carrick by another road, were taken at Lock Ryan, and beheaded at Carlisle − and, thus, all who had gone away and left the king, were, in that same year, either bereft of life, or taken and thrown into prison.

CXXI
Sundry troubles which fell upon King Robert

The Earl of Lennox and Gilbert of Haya, alone among the nobles, followed the aforesaid king, and became his inseparable companions in all his troubles. And though sometimes, when hard pressed by the pursuing foe, they were parted from him in body, yet they never departed from fealty and love towards him. But, soon after this, it came to pass that the aforesaid king was cut off from his men, and underwent endless woes, and was tossed in dangers untold, being attended at times by three followers, at times by two; and more often he was left alone, utterly without help. Now passing a whole fortnight without food of any kind to live upon, but raw herbs and water; now walking barefoot, when his shoes became old and worn out; now left alone in the islands; now alone, fleeing before his enemies; now slighted by his servants; he abode in utter loneliness. An outcast among the nobles, he was forsaken; and the English bade him be sought for through the churches like a lost or stolen thing. And thus he became a byword and a laughing-stock for all, both far and near, to hiss at. But when he had borne these things for nearly a year alone, God, at length, took pity on him; and, aided by the help and power of a certain noble lady, Christiana of the Isles, who wished him well, he, after endless toils, smart, and distress, got back, by a round-about way, to the earldom of Carrick. As soon as he reached that place, he sought out one of his castles, slew the inmates thereof, destroyed the castle, and shared the arms and other spoils among his men. Then, being greatly gladdened by such a beginning after his long

★ *Kildrummy Castle, Aberdeenshire*

spell of ill-luck, he got together his men, who had been scattered far and wide; and, crossing the hills with them in a body, he got as far as Inverness, took the castle thereof with a strong hand, slew its garrison, and levelled it with the ground. In this very way dealt he with the rest of the castles and strongholds established in the north, as well as their inmates, until he got, with his army, as far as Slenach★.

CXXII
Rout at Slenach

In the year 1307, John Comyn, Earl of Buchan, with many nobles, both English and Scots, hearing that Robert, king of Scotland, was, with his army, at Slenach, marched forward to meet him and give him battle. But when they saw the king, with his men, over against them, ready for the fray, they halted; and, on Christmas Day, overwhelmed with shame and confusion, they went back, and asked for a truce, which the king kindly granted. After the truce had been granted, the king abode there, without fear, for eight days; and he there fell into a sickness so severe, that he was borne on a pallet whithersoever he had occasion to be moved.

CXXIII
Death of King Edward I, King of England

The same year died Edward I, king of England, on the 5th of April, at Burgh-upon-Sands. This king stirred up was as soon as he had become a knight, and lashed the English with awful scourgings; he troubled the whole world by his wickedness, and roused it by his cruelty; by his wiles, he hindered the passage to the Holy Land; he invaded Wales; he treacherously subdued unto him the Scots and their kingdom; John of Balliol, the king thereof, and his son, he cast into prison; he overthrew churches, fettered prelates, and to some he put an end in filthy dungeons; he slew the people, and committed other misdeeds without end. He was succeeded by his son Edward II, who was betrothed to Elizabeth★★, daughter of Philip, king of France.

★ *Slaines*
★★ *The chronicler has misnamed Edward II's queen, Isabella, who would be instrumental, with Sir Roger Mortimer, in bringing about the depositon and murder of Edward II.*

CXXIV
Rout at Inverury

In the year 1308, John Comyn and Philip of Mowbray, with a great many Scots and English, were again gathered together, at Inverury. But when King Robert heard of this, though he had not yet got rid of his grievous sickness, he arose from his pallet, whereon he was always carried about, and commanded his men to arm him and set him on horseback. When this had been done, he too, with a cheerful countenance, hastened with his army against the enemy, to the battle-ground — although, by reason of his great weakness, he could not go upright, but with the help of two men to prop him up. But when the opposing party saw him and his ready for battle, at the mere sight of him they were sore afraid and put to flight; and they were pursued as far as Fivy, twelve leagues off. So when the rout was over, and the enemy were overthrown and scattered, King Robert, ravaged the earldom of Buchan with fire; and, of the people, he killed whom he would, and, to those whom he would have live, he granted life and peace. Moreover, even as, from the beginning of his warfare until the day of this struggle, he had been most unlucky in the upshot of every battle, so, afterwards, there could not have been found a man more fortunate in his fights. And, from that day, the king gained more ground, and became ever more hale himself; while the adverse party was daily growing less.

King Robert's destruction (Barbour calls it the 'herschip' or 'harrying)' of the county of Buchan, one of the main centres of power of the Comyn family, did more than just undermine the leadership of his Scottish opposition, it made clear the penalty for failing to accept his kingship.

CXXV
Victory over the Gallwegians, at the River Dee

The same year, at the Feast of Saint Peter and Saint Paul, Donald of the Isles gathered together an imposing host of foot, and marched up to the River Dee. He was met by Edward of Bruce, who overcame the said Donald and all the Gallwegians. In this struggle, Edward slew a certain knight named Roland, with many of the nobles of Galloway; and arrested their leader, the said Donald, who had taken to flight. After this he burnt up the island.

Galloway is not an island, but in the thirteenth and fourteenth centuries it was seen as having a particular identity of its own with different customs and even laws to the rest of the country; perhaps this is what Fordoun is implying by the use of the term 'island'.

CXXVI
Conflict of King Robert with the men of Argyll.

The same year, within a week after the Assumption of the Blessed Virgin Mary, the king overcame the men of Argyll, in the middle of Argyll, and subdued the whole land unto himself. Their leader, named Alexander of Argyll, fled to Dunstafinch Castle★, where he was, for some time, besieged by the king. On giving up the castle to the king, he refused to do him homage. So a safe-conduct was given to him, and to all who wished to withdraw with him; and he fled to England, where he paid the debt of nature★★.

CXXVII

In the year 1310, so great was the famine and death of provisions in the kingdom of Scotland, that, in most places, many were driven, by the pinch of hunger, to feed on the flesh of horses and other unclean cattle.

CXXVIII

In the year 1311, the aforesaid King Robert, having put his enemies to flight at every place he came to, and having taken their fortresses, and levelled them with the ground, twice entered England, and wasted it, carrying off untold booty, and making huge havoc with fire and sword. Thus by the power of God, the faithless English nation, which had unrighteously racked many a man, was now, by God's righteous judgement, made to undergo awful scourgings; and, whereas it had once been victorious, now it sank vanquished and groaning.

Once again Fordoun shows his clerical view of political events. King Robert takes his army into England and causes widespread destruction, but it is (in

★ *Dunstaffnage*
★★ *The 'debt of nature' – death*

Fordoun's view) the wicked behaviour of the English in the past that has roused God's anger – Robert is only the agent of their misery.

CXXIX
The town of Perth taken by King Robert

On the 8th of January 1313, the town of Perth was taken with the strong hand by that same King Robert; and the disloyal people, both Scots and English, were taken, dragged, and slain with the sword; and thus, 'Fordone, they drained the gall themselves had brewed.'

The king, in his clemency, spared the rabble, and granted forgiveness to those that asked it; but he destroyed the walls and ditches, and consumed everything else with fire. The same year, the castles of Buth, Dumfries, and Dalswinton, with many other strongholds, were taken with the strong hand and levelled with the ground. The same year, the town of Durham was, in part, burnt down by the Scots; Piers de Gaveston was killed by the Earl of Lancaster; and Edward*, the first-born of the King of England, was born at Windsor.

CXXX
Roxburgh Castle taken by James of Douglas

On Fasten's Even, in the year 1313, Roxburgh Castle was happily taken by the Lord James of Douglas, and, on the 14th of March, Edinburgh Castle, by the Lord Thomas Randolph, Earl of Moray; and their foes were overcome. The same year, the king entered the Isle of Man, took the castles thereof, and victoriously brought the land under his sway.

CXXXI
Conflict at Bannockburn

Edward II, king of England, hearing of these glorious doings of King Robert's, and seeing the countless losses and endless evils brought upon him and his by that king, gathered together, in revenge for the foregoing, a very strong army both of well-arms horsemen and of foot – crossbow-men and archers, well skilled in war-craft. At the head of

* *the future Edward III*

this body of men, and trusting in the glory of man's might, he entered Scotland in hostile wise; and, laying it waste on every side, he got as far as Bannockburn. But King Robert, putting his trust, not in a host of people, but in the Lord God, came, with a few men, against the aforesaid king of England, on the blessed John the Baptist's day, in the year 1314, and fought against him, and put him and his to flight, through the help of Him to whom it belongeth to give the victory. There, the Earl of Gloucester and a great many other nobles were killed; a great many were drowned in the waters, and slaughtered in pitfalls; a great many, of divers ranks, were cut off by divers kinds of death; and many – a great many – nobles were taken, for whose ransom not only were the queen and other Scottish prisoners released from their dungeons, but even the Scots themselves were, all and sundry, enriched very much. Among these was also taken John of Brittany, for whom the queen and Robert, bishop of Glasgow, were exchanged. From that day forward, moreover, the whole land of Scotland not only always rejoiced in victory over the English, but also overflowed with boundless wealth.

Once again, faith in the Almighty prevails over trust in men and their arms. Fordoun exaggerates when he says that the Scots enjoyed constant success in battle after Bannockburn, but they certainly achieved a remarkable level of consistent military success between 1312 and 1332 which gave them a level of martial dominance over the English which would not be repeated until the Bishop's Wars of the seventeenth century.

CXXXII
Edward crosses into Ireland

Edward of Bruce, King Robert's brother, entered Ireland, with a mighty hand, in the year 1315; and, having been set up as king there, he destroyed the whole of Ulster, and committed countless murders. This however, some little time after, brought him no good. In the year 1316, King Robert went to Ireland, to the southern parts thereof, to afford his brother succour and help. But, in this march, many died of hunger, and the rest lived on horse-flesh. The king, however, at once returned, and left his brother there. In the year 1317, the cardinals were plundered, in England, by Robert of Middleton, who was, soon after, taken, and drawn by horses, in London.

CXXXIII
The town of Berwick taken

In the year 1318, Thomas Randolph, Earl of Moray, destroyed the northern parts of England; and, on the 28th of March of the same year, the Scots took the town of Berwick, which had been, for twenty years, in the hands of the English. On the 14th of October of the same year was fought the battle of Dundalk, in Ireland, in which fell the lord Edward of Bruce, and a good many Scottish nobles with him. The cause of this way was this: Edward was a very mettlesome and high-spirited man, and would not dwell together with his brother in peace, unless he had half the kingdom to himself; and for this reason was stirred up, in Ireland, this war, wherein, as already stated, ended his life.

From Barbour down to the present day Scottish writers have depicted Edward Bruce as a headstrong and rash person; however this assessment is essentially based on the outcome of one battle, Dundalk (or Faughart). Edward's death in action obviously prevented him explaining his actions there and very little material exists relating to the fighting, certainly not enough to make a viable analysis of the conflict. There is any case a historiographical problem with both strategic and tactical analysis; historians are inclined to 'rate' individuals on the basis of their success in conflicts. The loss of one battle can be enough to consign kings and generals to the catalogue of militarily incompetent figures in history. Quite apart from the inescapable fact that our understanding of the approach to battle in the medieval period is considerably worse than just poor, we seldom have anything approaching a viable understanding of the tactical and adminis-trative pressures on the commanders involved. It is worth bearing in mind that Edward Bruce had been successful in many actions in the previous decade and more, and that his experience of fighting in Scotland, England and Ireland massively outweighed that of any person living today. The most significant source for his career is Barbour, who had a vested interest in showing King Robert in the best possible light; and last, but not least, we should remember that Edward lost this particular battle... but had he won it, he might have won his war and been the progenitor of a line of 'Bruce' kings of Ireland. Had this been the case would his followers now be described by historians as 'Scoto-Normans' or perhaps 'Franco-Scots'? Defeat in a battle should not, in general, be seen as an indicator of incompetence and even repeated defeats may be more a reflection of the greater resources of one combatant than of the competence of the other.

CXXXIV
Berwick besieged by the King of England

In the year 1319, on the day of the finding of the Holy Cross, Edward, king of England, besieged the town of Berwick; but, meeting with no success, he quickly retreated in great disorder. The same year, the Earl of Moray burnt up the northern parts of England, as far as Wetherby; and, at the end of the month of August, he pitched his tents at Boroughbridge.

CXXXV
Treachery of John of Soulis and his adherents

In the beginning of the month of August 1320, Robert, king of Scotland, held his parliament at Scone. There, the lord William of Soulis and the Countess of Stratherne were convicted of the crime of high treason, by conspiring against the aforesaid king; and sentence of perpetual imprisonment was passed upon them. The lords David of Brechin, Gilbert of Malerb, John of Logie, knight, and Richard Broune, esquire, having been convicted of the aforesaid conspiracy, were first drawn by horses, and, in the end, underwent capital punishment. The lords Eustace of Maxwell, Walter of Barclay, sheriff of Aberdeen, and Patrick of Graham, knights, Hamelin of Troupe, and Eustace of Retreve *(Rattray)*, esquires, were accused of the same crime, but were not found guilty in any way. It so happened, also, at the same time, that when Roger of Mowbray had been released from the trammels of the flesh★, his body was taken down thither, and convicted of conspiracy; where-upon it was condemned to be drawn by horses, hanged on the gallows, and beheaded. But the king had ruth★★, and was stirred with pity; so he yielded him up to God's judgment, and commanded that the body of the deceased should be handed over for burial by the Church, without having been put to any shame. The same year, on the 17th of March, our lord the Pope's legates came to the king of Scotland, at Berwick.

Dismembering the body of an accused who died before a sentence could be carried out was a normal judicial process throughout medieval Europe. Other than

★ *died*
★★ *mercy*

for treason offences, and not always for those, drawing, quartering and similar horrors do not seem to have been at all common in Scotland compared to France, England or Spain.

CXXXVI

In the year 1321, there was a very hard winter, which distressed men, and killed nearly all animals. The same year, the Earl of Moray destroyed the northern parts of England, and the bishopric of Durham, with famine, fire, and sword.

The repeated incursions of the Scots not only generated a stream of income for Robert, they denied the resources of several English counties – Northumberland, Cumberland, Westmorland, Durham, and to a lesser extent Yorkshire and Lancashire – to Edward II, thereby further undermining his authority.

CXXXVII
The King of Scotland crosses into England, and the King of England into Scotland

On the 1st of July 1322, Robert, king of Scotland, entered England, with a strong hand, and laid it waste for the most part, as far as Stanemore, together with the county of Lancaster. The same year, on the 12th of August, Edward II, king of England, entered Scotland with a great army of horse and foot, and a large number of ships, and got as far as the town of Edinburgh; for he sought to have a struggle and to come to blows with the aforesaid king. But the king of Scotland, wisely shunning an encounter for the nonce, skilfully drew away from his army all animals fit for food. So, after fifteen days, Edward, being sore pressed by hunger and starvation, went home again dismayed, having first sacked and plundered the monasteries of Holyrood in Edinburgh, and of Melrose, and brought them to great desolation. For, in the said monastery of Melrose, on his way back from Edinburgh, the lord William of Peebles, prior of that same monastery, one monk who was then sick, and two lay-brethren, were killed in the dormitory by the English, and a great many monks were wounded unto death. The Lord's Body was cast forth upon the high altar, and the pyx wherein it was kept was taken away. The monastery of Dryburgh was utterly consumed with fire, and reduced to dust; and a great many other holy places did the fiery flames consume, at the hands of the aforesaid king's forces. But God rewarded them therefore, and it brought them no good. For, the same year, on the 1st of October, King Robert marched into England in hostile wise, and utterly laid it waste, as far as York, sacking the monasteries, and setting fire to a great many cities and towns. But Edward II, king of England, came against him at Biland, with a great force, both of paid soldiers from France, and others hired from a great many places, and of natives of the kingdom itself; but he was put to flight at the above-named place, in the heart of his own kingdom, not without great slaughter of his men, and in no little disorder. Out of his army, John of Brittany, Henry of Stibly★, and other nobles, not a few, fled to the monastery of Rievaulx, and were there taken; and they were afterwards ransomed for sums untold. Thus, the king of Scotland, having gained a gladsome victory, went home again, with his men, in great joy and humour. The same year, on the 1st of October, Andrew of Barclay was taken, and, having been convicted of treachery, underwent capital punishment.

Henry de Sully was Constable of France. He fell prisoner to Sir James Douglas, who gave him to King Robert, who in turn released Henry without ransom as a diplomatic gesture to the king of France. Henry's release was an expensive transaction for the king, however, because Douglas obviously required compensation for the loss of what would inevitably be a very heavy ransom. The 'Emerald Charter' of extensive lands and privileges granted to Sir James was presumably his reward for cooperation with the king's diplomatic campaign.

CXXXVIII
Ambassadors sent by the King of Scotland to the Pope and the King of France

In the year 1325, ambassadors were sent by Robert, king of Scotland, to treat for a renewal of the friendship and alliance formerly struck up between the kings of France and Scotland, and to restore them in force forever, that they might last for all time unto them and their successors; and also that he might be at one, and come to a good understanding, with the holy Roman Church, which had, through the insinuations of

★ *Sully*

enemies, been somewhat irritated against the king and kingdom. So when all this business had been happily despatched, these messengers sped safely home again. In that year – on Monday the 5th of March, to wit, in the first week of Lent – David, King Robert's son, and the heir of Scotland, who succeeded his father in the kingdom, was born in the monastery of Dunfermline, after complines.

CXXXIX
The Queen of England brings hired soldiers into England

In the year 1326, the lady Elizabeth, queen of England, brought a great many hired soldiers from sundry parts of the world; and, after having taken her husband, King Edward, and thrown him into prison, she bade Hugh de Spensa *(Despenser)*, and his father, be hanged on the gallows, and be torn limb from limb. Because of this outbreak, a bishop was beheaded in London; and a great many earls, barons, and nobles were everywhere condemned to a most shameful death. The same year, Edward III, then fifteen years old, on his father being thrown into prison, was, though unwilling, crowned king of England, at Candlemas. That year, moreover, was, all over the earth, beyond the memory of living man, fruitful and plentiful in all things to overflowing The same year, the whole Scottish clergy, the earls and barons, and all the nobles, were gathered together, with the people, at Cambuskenneth, and, in presence of King Robert himself, took the oaths to David, King Robert's son and heir, and to Robert Stewart, the aforesaid king's grandson, in case that same David died childless. There, also, Andrew of Moray took to wife the lady Christina, that king's sister.

CXL
Messengers sent to the King of Scotland by the English

In the year 1327, the English sent messengers to the king of Scotland, under a show of wishing to treat for a secure peace. But though they met together more than once, they made no way. At length their double-dealing was laid bare, and the Scots entered the northern parts of England, with a strong hand, on the 15th of June, and wasted it with fire and sword. The same year, in the month of August, the Earl of

Moray and James of Douglas, with many Scottish nobles, invaded England, with arms in their hands, and after having brought great loss upon the English, pitched their tents in a certain narrow place named Weardale; while, over against them, and at the outlet of the road, as it were, over 100,000* English troops were posted round the Scots. There the armies lay, for eight days, in sight of each other, and daily harassed one another with mutual slaughter; but they shunned a hand-to-hand battle. At length, however, the Scots, like wary warriors, sought an opportunity of saving themselves; and, having struck down in death many of the foe, and taken a great many English and Hainaulters, they returned home safe and sound, by a round-about road, by night.

CXLI

The same year, a few days after their retreat, the king of Scotland besieged Norham Castle, and, soon after, Alnwick Castle, one after the other; and in that siege of Norham, William of Montealt, knight, John of Clapham, and Robert of Dobery, were killed through their own want of skill. The same year, on the 17th of March, ambassadors were sent by the king of England to the king of Scotland, at Edinburgh, to arrange and treat for a firm and lasting peace, which should abide for all time. So, after sundry negotiations, and the many and various risks of war incurred by both kingdoms, the aforesaid kings there came to an understanding together about an indissoluble peace; and the chiefs and worthies of either kingdom tendered their oaths thereto, which were to last unshaken for all time, swearing upon the soul of each king faithfully to keep all and sundry things, as they are more fully contained under certain articles of their instruments thereof, drawn up on either side as to form the peace. And, that it might be a true peace, which should go on without end between them and between their respective successors, the king of Scotland of his own free and unbiased will, gave and granted 30,000 Merks** in cash to the king of England, for the losses he himself had brought upon the latter and his kingdom; and the said king of England gave his sister, named Joan, to King Robert's son

---

* *This is a massive exaggeration and the author does not intend the figure of 100,000 to be taken literally; he merely wishes to impress on the reader the enormous size and power of the English army.*
** *A Merk, or Mark, was two thirds of a pound – 160 pennies or 13s 4d.*

and heir, David, to wife, for the greater security of peace, and the steady fostering of the constancy of love.

CXLII
Espousal of King David − Death of William of Lamberton, Bishop of Saint Andrews

On the 17th of July 1328, David, King Robert's son and heir, was, to the unspeakable joy of the people of either kingdom, married to Joan, sister of Edward III, king of England, at Berwick, in presence of Elizabeth, the girl's mother, then queen of England. The same year died William of Lamberton, bishop of Saint Andrews.

CXLIII
Death of King Robert of Bruce

On the 7th of June 1329, died Robert of Bruce, of goodly memory, the illustrious king of Scots, at Cardross, in the twenty-fourth year of his reign. He was, beyond all living men of his day, a valiant knight.

King Robert Bruce and his second wife from a Scottish Armorial of the reign of Queen Mary, illuminated between 1561 and 1565.

3

Excerpts from the *Lanercost Chronicle* (1296–1329)

Translated by H. Maxwell, 1913

*T*he compilers of the Lanercost Chronicle *saw the effects of war quite literally on their doorstep. Scottish armies passed through the North of England repeatedly and on at least one occasion King Robert used the abbey as his headquarters (as mentioned later). Odd errors of date, place or persons notwithstanding, the chronicle provides us with an invaluable view of Robert I's reign as seen by the communities of northern England. These excerpts are from the 1913 edition by H. Maxwell. Additions to the text in square brackets are by the translator, those in italics are mine.*

Robert murders Sir John Comyn of Badenoch and has himself installed as King at Scone early in 1306.

In the same year, on the fourth of the Ides of February, to wit, on the festival of St Scholastica virgin, Sir Robert Bruce, Earl of Carrick, sent seditiously and treacherously for Sir John Comyn, requiring him to come and confer with him at the house of the Minorite Friars in Dumfries; and, when he came, did slay him and his uncle Sir Robert Comyn in the church of the Friars, and afterwards took [some] castles of Scotland and their wardens, and on the Annunciation of the Blessed Virgin next following was made King of Scotland at Scone, and many of the nobles and commonalty of that land adhered to him.

53

When the King of England heard of this, he sent horse and foot to Carlisle and Berwick to protect the Border. But because the men of Galloway refused to join the aforesaid Robert in his rebellion, their lands were burnt by him, and, pursuing one of the chiefs of Galloway, he besieged him in a certain lake, but some of the Carlisle garrison caused him to raise the siege, and he retreated, after burning the engines and ships that he had made for the siege.

But those who were in garrison at Berwick, to wit, Sir Robert Fitzroger, an Englishman who was warden of the town, and Sir John Mowbray, Sir Ingelram de Umfraville, and Sir Alexander de Abernethy, Scotsmen, with their following, over all of whom Sir Aymer de Valence was in command — all these, I say, entered Scotland and received to the King of England's peace some of those who at first had been intimidated into rebellion with Sir Robert. Him they pursued beyond the Scottish sea★, and there engaged him in battle near the town of St John (which is called by another name Perth), killed many of his people, and in the end put him to flight.

Meanwhile the King of England, having assembled an army, sent my lord Edward, his son aforesaid (whom he had knighted in London together with three hundred others), and the Earl of Lincoln, by whose advice the said lord Edward was to act, in pursuit of the said Robert de Brus, who had caused himself to be called King. When they entered Scotland they received many people to peace on condition that they should in all circumstances observe the law; then marching forward to the furthest bounds of Scotland, where the said Robert might be found, they found him not, but they took all the castles with a strong hand. But they hanged those who had part in the aforesaid conspiracy, design and assistance in making him king, most of whom they caused first to be drawn at the heels of horses and afterwards hanged them; among whom were the Englishman Christopher de Seton, who had married the sister of the oft-mentioned Robert, and John and Humphrey, brothers of the said Christopher, and several others with them. Among those who were hanged were not only simple country folk and laymen, but also knights and clerics and prebendaries, albeit these protested that, as members of the Church, justice should be done to them accordingly. Then Sir Simon Fraser, a Scot, having been taken to London, was first drawn,

★ *the River Forth*

then hanged, thirdly beheaded, and his head set up on London Bridge beside that of William Wallace. They also took to England and imprisoned the Bishop of St Andrews, whom the King of England had appointed Guardian of Scotland, and who had entered into a bond of friendship with the said Robert, as was proved by letters of his which were found; also the Bishop of Glasgow, who had been principal adviser in that affair, and the Abbot of Scone, who assisted the aforesaid Robert when he was received into royal honour. Howbeit in the meantime Robert called de Brus was lurking in the remote isles of Scotland.

Throughout all these doings the King of England was not in Scotland, but his son, with the aforesaid army. But the King was slowly approaching the Scottish border with the Queen, by many easy stages and borne in a litter on the backs of horses on account of his age and infirmity; and on the feast of St Michael he arrived at the Priory of Lanercost, which is eight miles from Carlisle, and there he remained until near Easter. Meantime his kinsman, the Earl of Athol, who had encouraged the party of the said Robert to make him king, had been captured, and by command of the King was taken to London, where he was drawn, hanged and beheaded, and his head was set upon London Bridge above the heads of William Wallace and Simon Fraser, because he was akin to the King.

After this, on the vigil of St Scholastica virgin, two brothers of Robert de Brus, Thomas and Alexander, Dean of Glasgow, and Sir Reginald de Crawford, desiring to avenge themselves upon the people of Galloway, invaded their country with eighteen ships and galleys, having with them a certain kinglet of Ireland, and the Lord of Cantyre and other large following. Against them came Dougal Macdoual (that is the son of Doual), a chief among the Gallovidians, with his countrymen, defeated them and captured all but a few who escaped in two galleys. He ordered the Irish kinglet and the Lord of Cantyre to be beheaded and their heads to be carried to the King of England at Lanercost.

Thomas de Brus and his brother Alexander and Sir Reginald de Crawford, who had been severely wounded in their capture by lances and arrows, he likewise took alive to the King, who pronounced sentence upon them, and caused Thomas to be drawn at the tails of horses in Carlisle on the Friday after the first Sunday in Lent, and then to be hanged and afterwards beheaded. Also he commanded the other two to be hanged on the same day and afterwards beheaded; whose heads, with the heads of the four others aforesaid, were set upon the three gates of Carlisle, and the head of Thomas de Brus upon the keep of Carlisle. Nigel, the third brother of Robert, had been hanged already at Newcastle.

About the same time a certain cardinal named Peter came to England, sent a *latere* from my lord the Pope to establish peace between the King of France and the King of England; and it so happened that both my lord the King and my lord the said cardinal entered Carlisle on Passion Sunday. Then in the cathedral church on the Wednesday following my lord cardinal explained the object of his legation before a very great number of people and clergy, and showed them the excellent manner in which my lord the Pope and my lord the King of France had agreed, subject to the consent of the King of England — to wit, that my lord Edward, son and heir of the King of England, should marry Isabella, daughter of the King of France. When this had been said, up rose William of Gainsborough, Bishop of Worcester, and on the part of the King briefly informed my lord cardinal and all who had come thither of the manner of Sir John Comyn's assassination, praying that he would deign to grant some indulgence for his soul, and that he would pronounce sentence of excommunication upon the murderers; whereupon the legate liberally granted one year [of indulgence] for those who should pray for the said soul so long as he [the cardinal] should remain in England, and for one hundred days afterwards. Then straightaway having doffed his ordinary raiment and donned his pontificals, he denounced the murderers of the said Sir John as excommunicate, anathematised, and sacrilegious, together with all their abettors, and any who offered them counsel or favour; and expelled them from Holy Mother Church until they should make full atonement; and thus those who were denounced were excommunicate for a long time throughout all England, especially in the northern parts and in the neighbourhood where the murder was committed.

Following the death of his father, Edward II continues the war against Robert Bruce, but fails to apprehend him, July 1307.

On the vigil of St Peter ad Vincula he moved his army into Scotland in order to receive homage and fealty from the Scots, as he had forewarned them, having summoned by his letters all the chief men of the country to appear before him at Dumfries, there to render him the service due. Afterwards he divided his army into three columns to search for the oft-mentioned Robert; but, this time, as formerly, he was not to be found, so they returned empty-handed to England after certain guardians had been appointed in Scotland.

Edward makes a truce with the Scots to run until November 1309.

Meanwhile, taking advantage of the dispute between the King of England and the barons, Edward de Brus, brother of the oft-mentioned Robert, and Alexander de Lindsey and Robert Boyd and James de Douglas, knights, with their following which they had from the outer isles of Scotland, invaded the people of Galloway, disregarding the tribute which they took from them, and in one day slew many of the gentry of Galloway, and made nearly all that district subject to them. Those Gallovidians, however, who could escape came to England to find refuge. But it was said that the King of England desired, if he could, to ally himself with Robert de Brus, and to grant him peace upon such terms as would help him to contend with his own earls and barons. Howbeit, after the feast of St Michael some kind of peace and agreement was patched up between the King of England and his people, on condition that the king should do nothing important without the advice and consent of the Earl of Lincoln; but from day to day the king, by gifts and promises, drew to his side some of the earls and barons.

About the beginning of the following Lent an embassy was sent to the King of England by order of the Pope and at the instance of the King of France, desiring him to desist from attacking the Scots, and that he should hold meanwhile only what he possessed at the preceding feast of St James the Apostle; and likewise an embassy was sent to Robert de Brus desiring him to keep the peace, and that meanwhile he should enjoy all that he had acquired at the preceding feast of the same St James, and no more; and that the truce should endure until the festival of All Saints next to come. But Robert and his people restored nothing to the King of England of that which he had wrongously usurped between the said feast of St James and the beginning of Lent aforesaid; rather were they continually striving to get more.

Further truces are offered and accepted, but the Scots continue to hold the initiative; Edward had pressing domestic problems which prevented him from pursuing his Scottish war effectively and had little choice about accepting, or allowing his supporters to accept, truces which gave King Robert the opportunity to successfully conduct his campaigns against the Comyn and MacDougall factions, 1310–11.

But in the aforesaid parliament there was read a fresh sentence of excommunication pronounced against Robert de Brus and against all who should give him aid, counsel, or favour.

Now about the feast of All Saints, when the said truce was due to expire, the King of England sent Sir John de Segrave and many others with him to keep the march at Berwick; and to defend the march at Carlisle [he sent] the Earl of Hereford and Baron Sir Robert de Clifford, Sir John de Cromwell, knight, and others with them. But a little before the feast of St Andrew they made a truce with the oft-mentioned Robert de Brus, and he with them, subject to the King of England's consent, until the twentieth day after Christmas, and accordingly Robert de Clifford went to the king to ascertain his pleasure. On his return, he agreed to a further truce with the Scots until the first Sunday in Lent, and afterwards the truce was prolonged until summer; for the English do not willingly enter Scotland to wage war before summer, chiefly because earlier in the year they find no food for their horses.

About the feast of the Assumption the king came to Berwick with Piers, Earl of Cornwall, and the Earl of Gloucester and the Earl of Warenne, which town the King of England had caused to be enclosed with a strong and high wall and ditch; but the other earls refused to march with the king by reason of fresh dispute that had arisen. But he [the king] advanced with his suite further into Scotland in search for the oft-mentioned Robert, who fled in his usual manner, not daring to meet them, wherefore they returned to Berwick. So soon as they had retired, Robert and his people invaded Lothian and inflicted much damage upon those who were in the king of England's peace. The king, therefore, pursued with a small force, but the Earl of Cornwall remained at Roxburgh with his people to guard that district, and the Earl of Gloucester [remained at] Norham.

After the feast of the Purification the king sent the aforesaid Earl of Cornwall with two hundred men-at-arms to the town of St John

beyond the Scottish Sea, in case Robert de Brus, who was then marching towards Galloway, should go beyond the said sea to collect troops.
But the king remained on at Berwick. The said earl received to peace all
beyond the Scottish Sea, as far as the Mounth. After the beginning of
Lent the Earls of Gloucester and Warenne rode through the great Forest
of Selkirk, receiving the foresters and others of the Forest to peace.

The Scots start to carry the war into England, August/September 1312.

The said Robert, then, taking note that the king and all the nobles of
the realm were in such distant parts, and in such discord about the
said accursed individual [Piers], having collected a large army invaded
England by the Solway on Thursday before the feast of the Assumption
of the Glorious Virgin, and burnt all the land of the Lord of Gillesland
and the town of Haltwhistle and a great part of Tyneside, and after eight
days returned into Scotland, taking with him a very large booty in cattle. But he had killed few men besides those who offered resistance.

About the feast of the Nativity of the Blessed Virgin, Robert returned
with an army into England, directing his march towards Northumberland,
and, passing by Harbottle and Holystone and Redesdale, he burnt the
district about Corbridge, destroying everything; also he caused more
men to be killed than on the former occasion. And so he turned into
the valleys of North and South Tyne, laying waste those parts which he
had previously spared, and returned into Scotland after fifteen days; nor
could the wardens whom the King of England had stationed on the
marches oppose so great a force of Scots as he brought with him.
Howbeit, like the Scots, they destroyed all the goods in the land, with
this exception, that they neither burnt houses nor killed men.

Meanwhile the Northumbrians, still dreading lest Robert should
return, sent envoys to him to negotiate a temporary truce, and they
agreed with him that they would pay two thousand pounds for an
exceedingly short truce – to wit, until the Purification of the Glorious
Virgin. Also those of the country of Dunbar, next to Berwick, in
Scotland, who were still in the King of England's peace, were very
heavily taxed for a truce until the said date.

In all these aforesaid campaigns the Scots were so divided among
themselves that sometimes the father was on the Scottish side and the

son on the English, and vice versa; also one brother might be with the Scots and another with the English; yea, even the same individual be first with one party and then with the other. But all those who were with the English were merely feigning, either because it was the stronger party, or in order to save the lands they possessed in England; for their hearts were always with their own people, although their persons might not be so.

The monastic community at Lanercost learns about the Scots first hand, August 1312.

In the same year the said Robert de Brus, King of Scotland★, came with a great army in the month of August to the monastery of Lanercost, and remained there three days, making many of the canons prisoners and doing an infinity of injury; but at last the canons were set at liberty by himself.

The communities of northern England buy truces from King Robert, 1312–13.

When Robert de Brus heard of this discord in the south, having assembled a great army, he invaded England about the feast of the Assumption of the Blessed Virgin, and burnt the towns of Hexham and Corbridge and the western parts, and took booty and much spoil and prisoners, nor was there anyone who dared resist. While he halted in peace and safety near Corbridge he sent part of his army as far as Durham, which, arriving there suddenly on market day, carried off all that was found in the town, and gave a great part of it to the flames, cruelly killing all who opposed them, but scarcely attacking the castle and abbey. The people of Durham, fearing more mischief from them, and despairing of help from the king, compounded with them, giving two thousand pounds to obtain truce for that bishopric until the nativity of John the Baptist; which, however, the Scots refused to accept unless on condition that they might have free access and retreat

---

★ *This is the first instance of Robert receiving the title king in the* Lanercost Chronicle. *The writer is not aware of an earlier example in any other English account.*

through the land of the bishopric whensoever they wished to make a raid into England. The Northumbrians also, fearing that they would visit them, gave them other two thousand pounds to secure peace until the aforesaid date; and the people of Westmorland, Copland, and Cumberland redeemed themselves in a similar way; and, as they had not so much money in hand as would pay them, they paid a part, and have as hostages for the rest the sons of the chief lords of the country. Having achieved this, Robert returned to Scotland with his army.

King Robert attempts to recover Berwick, one of the most important Scottish towns before its capture by Edward I in 1296.

Now the oft-mentioned Robert, seeing that thus he had the whole March of England under tribute, applied all his thoughts to getting possession of the town of Berwick, which was in the King of England's hands. Coming unexpectedly to the castle on the night of St Nicholas, he laid ladders against the walls and began to scale them; and had not a dog betrayed the approach of the Scots by loud barking, it is believed that he would quickly have taken the castle and, in consequence, the town.

Now these ladders which they placed against the walls were of wonderful construction, as I myself, who write these lines, beheld with my own eyes. For the Scots had made two strong ropes as long as the height of the wall, making a knot at one end of each cord. They had made a wooden board also, about two feet and a half long and half a foot broad, strong enough to carry a man, and in the two extremities of the board they had made two holes, through which the two ropes could be passed; then the cords, having been passed through as far as the knots, they had made two other knots in the ropes on foot and a half higher, and above these knots they placed another log or board, and so on to the end of the ropes. They had also made an iron hook, measuring at least one foot along one limb, and this was to lie over the wall; but the other limb, being of the same length, hung downwards towards the ground, having at its end a round hole wherein the point of a lance could be inserted, and two rings on the sides wherein the said ropes could be knotted.

Having fitted them together in this manner, they took a strong spear as long as the height of the wall, placing the point thereof in the iron hole, and two men lifted the ropes and boards with that spear and placed the iron hook (which was not a round one) over the wall. Then they were able to climb up those wooden steps just as one usually climbs ordinary ladders, and the greater the weight of the climber the more firmly the iron hook clung over the wall. But lest the ropes should lie too close to the wall and hinder the ascent, they had made fenders round every third step which thrust the ropes off the wall. When, therefore, they had placed two ladders upon the wall, the dog betrayed them as I have said, and they left the ladders there, which our people next day hung upon a pillory to put them to shame. And thus a dog saved the town on that occasion, just as of old geese saved Rome by their gaggle, as saith St Augustine in *de Civitate Dei*, book iii Chapter 4, *de magnis*, and Ambrose in *Exameron in Opere Quintae Diei*.

Robert, having failed in his attempt on Berwick, marched with his army to the town of St John★, which was then still in the King of England's hands; and he laid siege thereto, and on Monday of the octave of Epiphany it was taken by the Scots, who scaled the walls by night on ladders, and entered the town through the negligence of sentries and guards. Next day Robert caused those citizens of the better class who were of the Scottish nation to be killed, but the English were allowed to go away free. But the Scottish Sir William Oliphant, who had long time held that town for the King of England against the Scots, was bound and sent far away to the Isles. The town itself the Scots utterly destroyed.

Robert demands payment for new truces, summer 1313.

After the feast of the Nativity of St John the Baptist, when the English truce on the March had lapsed, Robert de Brus threatened to invade England in his usual manner. The people of Northumberland, Westmorland and Cumberland, and other Borderers, apprehending this, and neither having nor hoping for any defence or help from their king (seeing that he was engaged in distant parts of England, seeming not to give them a thought), offered to the said Robert no small sum of money, indeed a very large one, for a truce to last till the feast of St Michael in the following year.

★ *Perth*

The major English-held garrisons in the south of Scotland become vulnerable and start to fall to the Scots, February/March 1314.

Now at the beginning of Lent the Scots cunningly entered the castle of Roxburgh at night by ladders, and captured all the castle except one tower, wherein the warden of the castle, Sir Gillemin de Fiennes, a knight of Gascony, had taken refuge with difficulty, and his people with him; but the Scots got posession of that tower soon afterwards. And they razed to the ground the whole of that beautiful castle, just as they did other castles which they succeeded in taking, lest the English should ever hereafter be able to lord it over the land through holding castles.

In the same season of Lent they captured Edinburgh Castle in the following manner. In the evening one day the besiegers of that castle delivered an assault in force upon the south gate, because, owing to the position of the castle there was no other quarter where an assault could be made. Those within gathered together at the gate and offered a stout resistance; but meanwhile the other Scots climbed the rocks on the north side, which was very high and fell away steeply from the foot of the wall. There they laid ladders to the wall and climbed up in such numbers that those within could not withstand them; and thus they threw open the gates, admitted their comrades, got possession of the whole castle and killed the English. They razed the said castle to the ground, just as they had done to Roxburgh Castle.

Having accomplished this success, they marched to Stirling and besieged that castle with their army.

The Scots are strong enough to ignore the truce when it suits them, but have the power to enforce it on the English, 1313.

On Tuesday after the octave of Easter, Edward de Brus, Robert's brother, invaded England by way of Carlisle with an army, contrary to agreement, and remained there three days at the bishop's manor house, to wit, at Rose, and sent a strong detachment of his army to burn the southern and western districts during those three days. They burnt many towns and two churches, taking men and women prisoners, and collected a great number of cattle in Inglewood Forest and elsewhere, driving them off with them on the Friday; they killed few men except those who made determined resistance; but they made attack upon the city of Carlisle because of the knights and country people who were assembled there. Now the Scots did all these wrongs at that time because the men of that March had not paid them the tribute which they had pledged themselves to pay on certain days. Although the Scots had hostages from the sons and heirs of the knights of that country in full security for covenanted sums, yet they did not on that account refrain from committing the aforesaid wrongs.

Edward raises an army and makes his way northward from Berwick to relieve Stirling Castle before the date agreed for its surrender, and also in the hope of bringing the Scots to battle, June 1314.

Thus before the feast of the Nativity of St John the Baptist, the king, having massed his army, advanced with the aforesaid pomp towards Stirling Castle, to relieve it from siege and to engage the Scots, who were assembled there in all their strength. On the vigil of the aforesaid Nativity the king's army arrived after dinner near Torwood; and, upon information that there were Scots in the wood, the king's advanced guard, commanded by Lord de Clifford, began to make a circuit of the wood to prevent the Scots escaping by flight. The Scots did not interfere until they [the English] were far ahead of the main body, when they showed themselves, and, cutting off the king's advanced guard from the middle and rear columns, they charged and killed some of them and put the rest to flight. From that moment began a panic among the English and the Scots grew bolder.

On the morrow – an evil, miserable and calamitous day for the English – when both sides had made themselves ready for battle, the English archers were thrown forward before the line, and the Scottish archers engaged them, a few being killed and wounded on either side; but the King of England's archers quickly put the others to flight. Now when the two armies had approached very near each other, all the Scots fell on their knees to repeat *Pater noster*, commending themselves to God and seeking help from heaven; after which they advanced boldly against the English. They had so arranged their army that two columns went abreast in advance of the third, so that neither should be in advance of the other; and the third followed, in which was Robert.

Of a truth, when both armies engaged each other, and the great horses of the English charged the pikes of the Scots, as it were into a dense forest, there arose a great and terrible crash of spears broken and of destriers wounded to the death; and so they remained without movement for a while. Now the English in the rear could not reach the Scots because the leading division was in the way, nor could they do anything to help themselves, wherefore there was nothing for it but to take to flight. This account I heard from a trustworthy person who was present as eye-witness.

In the leading division were killed the Earl of Gloucester, Sir John Comyn, Sir Pagan de Typtoft, Sir Edmund de Mauley and many other nobles, besides foot soldiers who fell in great numbers. Another calamity which befell the English was that, whereas they had shortly before crossed a great ditch called Bannockburn, into which the tide flows, and now wanted to recross it in confusion, many nobles and others fell into it with their horses in the crush, while others escaped with much difficulty, and many were never able to extricate themselves from the ditch; thus Bannockburn was spoken about for many years in English throats.

Utterly defeated the English army disintegrates and Edward is lucky to make his escape.

The king and Sir Hugh le Despenser (who, after Piers de Gaveston, was as his right eye) and Sir Henry de Beaumont (whom he had promoted to an earldom in Scotland), with many others mounted and on foot, to their perpetual shame fled like miserable wretches to Dunbar Castle, guided by a certain knight of Scotland who knew through what districts they could escape. Some who were not so speedy in flight were killed by the Scots, who pursued them hotly; but these, holding bravely together, came safe and sound through the ambushes into England. At Dunbar the king embarked with some of his chosen followers in an open boat for Berwick, leaving all the others to their fate.

In like manner as the king and his following fled in one direction to Berwick, so the Earl of Hereford, the Earl of Angus, Sir John de Segrave, Sir Antony de Lucy and Sir Ingelram de Umfraville, with a great crowd of knights, six hundred other mounted men and one thousand foot, fled in another direction towards Carlisle. The Earl of Pembroke left the army on foot and saved himself with the fugitive Welsh; but the aforesaid earls and others, who had fled towards Carlisle were captured on the way at Bothwell Castle, for the sheriff, the warden of the castle, who had held the castle down to that time for the King of England, perceiving that his countrymen had won the battle, allowed the chief men who came thither to enter the castle in the belief that they would find a safe refuge, and when they had entered he took them prisoners, thereby treacherously deceiving them. Many, also, were taken wandering round the castle and hither and thither in the country, and many were killed; it was said, also, that certain knights were captured by women, nor did any of them get back to England save in abject confusion. The Earl of Hereford, the Earl of Angus, Sir [John] de Segrave, Sir Antony de Lucy, Sir Ingelram de Umfraville and the other nobles who were in the castle were brought before Robert de Brus and sent into captivity, and after a lengthy imprisonment were ransomed for much money. After the aforesaid victory Robert de Brus was commonly called King of Scotland by all men, because he had acquired Scotland by force of arms.

About the same died King Philip of France.

Shortly afterwards, to wit, about the feast of St Peter ad Vincula, Sir Edward de Brus, Sir James of Douglas, John de Soulis and other nobles of Scotland invaded England by way of Berwick with cavalry and a large army, and, during the time of truce, devastated almost all Northumberland with fire, except the castles; and so they passed forward into the bishopric of Durham; but there they did not burn much, for the people of the bishopric ransomed themselves from burning by a large sum of money. Nevertheless, the Scots carried off a booty of cattle and what men they could capture, and so invaded the county of Richmond beyond, acting in the same manner there without resistance, for nearly all men fled to the south or hid themselves in the woods, except those who took refuge in the castles.

The Scots even went as far as the Water of Tees on that occasion, and some of them beyond the town of Richmond, but they did not enter that town. Afterwards, reuniting their forces, they all returned by Swaledale and other valleys and by Stanemoor, whence they carried off an immense booty of cattle. Also they burnt the towns of Brough and Appleby and Kirkoswald, and other towns here and there on their route, trampling down the crops by themselves and their beasts as much as they could; and so, passing near the priory of Lanercost, they entered Scotland, having many men prisoners from whom they might extort money ransom at will. But the people of Coupland, fearing their return and invasion, sent envoys and appeased them with much money.

Victory at Bannockburn does not give Robert the recognition of his kingship that is his prerequisite for peace and he continues to take his army into England, 1315.

Meanwhile the Scots occupied both north and south Tynedale – to wit Haltwhistle, Hexham, Corbridge, and so on towards Newcastle, and Tynedale did homage to the King of Scots and forcibly attacked Gillesland and the other adjacent districts of England.

At this time also the Scots again wasted Northumberland; but from the aforesaid Nativity of Our Lord until the Nativity of St John the Baptist the county of Cumberland alone paid 600 marks in tribute to the King of Scots.

The Scots, therefore, unduly elated, as much by their victory in the field as by the devastation of the March of England and the receipt of very large sums of money, were not satisfied with their own frontiers, but fitted out ships and sailed to Ireland in the month of May, to reduce that country to subjection if they could. Their commanders were my lord Edward Bruce, the king's brother, and his kinsman my lord Thomas Randolf, Earl of Moray, both enterprising and valiant knights, having a very strong force with them. Landing in Ireland, and receiving some slight aid from the Irish, they captured from the King of England's dominion much land and many towns, and so prevailed as to have my lord Edward made king by the Irish. Let us leave him reigning there for the present, just as many kinglets reign there, till we shall describe elsewhere how he came to be beheaded, and let us return to Scotland.

The Scots, then, seeing that affairs were going everywhere in their favour, invaded the bishopric of Durham about the feast of the Apostles Peter and Paul, and plundered the town of Hartlepool, whence the people took the sea in ships; but they did not burn it. On their return they carried away very much booty from the bishopric.

Also, a little later in the same year, on the feast of St Mary Magdalene, the King of Scotland, having mustered all his forces, came to Carlisle, invested the city and besieged it for ten days, trampling down all the crops, wasting the suburbs and all within the bounds, burning the whole of that district, and driving in a very great store of cattle for his army from Allerdale, Copland, and Westmorland. On every day of the siege they assaulted one of the three gates of the city, sometimes all three at once; but never without loss, because there were discharged upon them from the walls such dense volleys of darts and arrows, likewise stones, that they asked one another whether stones bred and multiplied within the walls. Now on the fifth day of the siege they set up a machine for castling stones next the church of Holy Trinity, where their king stationed himself, and they cast great stones continually against the Caldew gate and against the wall, but they did little or no injury to those within, except that they killed one man. But there were seven or eight similar machines within the city, besides other engines of war, which are called springalds, for discharging long darts, and staves with sockets for casting stones, which caused great fear and damage to those outside. Meanwhile, however, the Scots set up a certain great berefrai like a kind of tower, which was considerably higher than the city walls. On perceiving this, the carpenters of the city erected upon a tower of the wall against which that engine must come if it had ever reached the wall, a wooden tower loftier than the other; but neither that engine nor any other ever did reach the wall, because, when it was being drawn on wheels over the wet and swampy ground, having stuck there through its own weight, it could neither be taken any further nor do any harm.

Moreover the Scots had made many long ladders, which they brought with them for scaling the wall in different places simultaneously; also a sow for mining the town wall, had they been able; but neither sow nor ladders availed them aught. Also they made great numbers of fascines of corn and herbage to fill the moat outside the wall on the east side, so as they might pass over dry-shod. Also they made long bridges of logs running upon wheels, such as being strongly and swiftly drawn with ropes might reach across the width of the moat. But during all the time the Scots were on the ground neither fascines sufficed to fill the moat, nor those wooden bridges to cross the ditch, but sank to the depths by their own weight.

Howbeit on the ninth day of the siege, when all the engines were ready, they delivered a general assault upon all the city gates and upon the whole circuit of the wall, attacking manfully, while the citizens defended themselves just as manfully, and they did the same next day. The Scots also resorted to the same kind of stratagem whereby they had taken Edinburgh Castle; for they employed the greater part of their army in delivering an assault upon the eastern side of the city, against the place of the Minorite Friars, in order to draw thither the people who were inside. But Sir James of Douglas, a bold and cautious knight, stationed himself, with some others of the army who were most daring and nimble, on the west side opposite the place of the Canons and Preaching Friars, where no attack was expected because of the height [of the wall] and the difficulty of access. There they set up long ladders which they climbed, and the bowmen, whereof they had a great number, shot their arrows thickly to prevent anyone showing his head above the wall. But, blessed be God! they met with such resistance there as threw them to the ground with their ladders, so that there and elsewhere around the wall some were killed, others taken prisoners and others wounded, yet throughout the whole siege no Englishman was killed, save one man only who was struck by an arrow (and except the man above mentioned), and few were wounded.

Wherefore on the eleventh day, to wit, the feast of St Peter ad Vincula, whether because they had heard that the English were approaching to relieve the besieged or whether they despaired of success, the Scots marched off in confusion to their own country, leaving behind them all their engines of war aforesaid. Some Englishmen pursuing them captured John de Moray, who in the aforesaid battle near Stirling had for his share twenty-three English knights, besides esquires and others of meaner rank, and had taken very heavy ransom for them. Also they captured with the aforesaid John, Sir Robert Bardolf, a man specially ill-disposed to the English, and brought them both to Carlisle Castle; but they were ransomed later for no small sum of money.

In the octave of the Epiphany the King of Scotland came stealthily to Berwick one bright moonlit night with a strong force, and delivered an assault by land and by sea in boats, intending to enter the town by stealth on the waterside between Brighouse and the castle, where the wall was not yet built, but they were manfully repulsed by the guards and by those who answered to the alarm, and a certain Scottish knight,

Sir J. de Landels, was killed, and Sir James of Douglas escaped with difficulty in a small boat. And thus the whole army was put to confusion.

King Robert's armies penetrate as far south as Richmond, summer 1316.

About the feast of the Nativity of St John the Baptist the Scots invaded England, burning as before and laying waste all things to the best of their power; and so they went as far as Richmond. But the nobles of that district, who took refuge in Richmond Castle and defended the same, compounded with them for a large sum of money so that they might not burn that town, nor yet the district, more than they had already done. Having received this money, the Scots marched away some sixty miles to the west, laying waste everything as far as Furness, and burnt that district whither they had not come before, taking away with them nearly all the goods of that district, with men and women as prisoners. Especially were they delighted with the abundance of iron which they found there, because Scotland is not rich in iron. Now in that year there was such a mortality of men in England and Scotland through famine and pestilence as had not been heard of in our time. In some of the northern parts of England the quarter of wheat sold for forty shillings.

After the Scots had returned to their own country, their King Robert provided himself with a great force and sailed to Ireland, in order to conquer that country, or a large part thereof, for his brother Edward. He freely traversed nearly all that part of it which was within the King of England's dominion, but he did not take walled towns or castles.

Lancaster maintained that he was not obliged to perform military service beyond the borders of England. As a military tenant of the Crown it was his duty to provide troops at his king's request, therefore if he was called to Newcastle to perform that service he would obey the call, but moving from Newcastle into Scotland was another matter, September 1316.

After the feast of St Michael, the Earl of Lancaster with his adherents marched toward Scotland as far as Newcastle in compliance with the king's behest; but the king declined to follow him as they had agreed upon together, wherefore the earl marched back again at once; for neither of them put any trust in the other.

The Pope intervenes, the Scots make another attempt on Berwick.

After the feast of St Michael the Pope sent a bull to England wherein he advised a truce between England and Scotland to last for two years after the receipt of the said bull. Now the English received the said bull with satisfaction, both on account of the dissension between the king and the Earl of Lancaster and because of excessive molestation by the Scots arising out of the said dissension, and they hung the bull according to the Pope's command in the cathedral churches and other important places. But the Scots refused to accept it, and paid it no manner of respect, and therefore came deplorably under the sentence of excommunication delivered by the Pope and contained in the said bull.

In the middle of the said truce Pope Clement the Fifth died, and Pope John the Twenty-second was elected.

On the second day of the month of April, in mid-Lent, about midnight on Saturday, the Scots treacherously took the town of Berwick through means of a certain Englishman, Peter of Spalding, living in the town, who, being bribed by a great sum of money received from them and by the promise of land, allowed them to scale the wall and to enter by that part of the wall where he himself was stationed as guard and sentry. After they had entered and obtained full possession of the town, they expelled all the English, almost naked and despoiled of all their property; howbeit, in their entrance they killed few or none, except those who resisted them.

Also the castles of Wark and Harbottle, to which they had already laid siege, were surrendered to them in that season of Lent, because relief did not reach them on the appointed day. Also they took the castle of Mitford by guile, and subdued nearly the whole of Northumberland as far as the town of Newcastle, except those castles which have not been mentioned above. Howbeit the castle of the town of Berwick defended itself manfully against the town, but at length capitulated through want of victual.

The Scots continue their campaigns in northern England, May, 1317.

In the month of May the Scottish army invaded England further than usual, burning the town of Northallerton and Boroughbridge and sundry other towns on their march, pressing forward as far as the town of Ripon, which town they despoiled of all the goods they could find; and from those who entered the mother church and defended it against the Scottish army they exacted one thousand marks instead of burning the town itself.

After they had lain there three days, they went off to Knaresborough, destroying that town with fire, and, searching the woods in that district whither the people had fled for refuge with their cattle, they took away the cattle. And so forth to the town of Skipton in Craven, which they plundered first and then burnt, returning through the middle of that district to Scotland, burning in all directions and driving off a countless quantity of cattle. They made men and women captives, making the poor folks drive the cattle, carrying them off to Scotland without any opposition.

Excommunicated for the murder of Sir John Comyn, Bruce was desperate to have the interdict lifted, if not for the sake of his soul then for the sake of the political future of the Bruce family as kings. Unsurprisingly, Edward II's representatives at the Curia were assiduous in their campaign to keep the sentence in place, September 1318.

In the same year, about the feast of the Nativity of the Blessed Virgin, the Cardinals, who then were still in England, wrote to all the prelates of England that in every solemn mass on ordinary days as well as festivals, they should thrice denounce Robert de Brus, with all his counsellors and adherents, as excommunicate; and, by the Pope's authority, they proclaimed him infamous and bereft of all honour, and placed all his lands and the lands of all his adherents under ecclesiastical interdict, and disqualified the offspring of all his adherents to the second generation from holding any ecclesiastical office or benefice. Also against all prelates of Scotland and all religious men, whether exempt or not exempt from episcopal jurisdiction, who should adhere to the said Robert or show him favour they promulgated sentence of excommunication and interdict, with other most grievous penalties. Howbeit the Scots, stubbornly pertinacious, cared nothing for any excommunication, nor would they pay the slightest attention to the interdict. It is not to be wondered at, therefore, that afterwards the weighty vengeance of God, in the appearance of a true heir of the realm, visited so rebellious a people, whose head (I will not call him king, but usurper) showed such contempt for the keys of Holy Mother Church.

King Robert's armies sweep through northern England against an English force offers battle at Myton and is swiftly driven off, summer 1319.

Meanwhile my lord Thomas Randolf, Earl of Moray and Sir James of Douglas, not daring to encounter the King of England and the earl [of Lancaster], invaded England with an army, burning the country and taking captives and booty of cattle, and so pressed as far as Boroughbridge. When the citizens of York heard of this, without knowledge of the country people and led by my lord Archbishop William de Meltoun and my lord the Bishop of Ely, with a great number of priests and clerics, among whom were sundry religious men, both beneficed and mendicant, they attacked the Scots one day after dinner near the town of Myton, about twelve miles north of York; but, as men unskilled in war, they marched all scattered through the fields and in no kind of array. When the Scots beheld men rushing to fight against them, they formed up according to their custom in a single schiltrom, and then uttered together a tremendous shout to terrify the English, who straightway began to take to their heels at the sound. Then the Scots, breaking up their schiltrom wherein they were massed, mounted their horses and pursued the English, killing both clergy and laymen, so that about four thousand were slain, among whom fell the mayor of the town, and about one thousand, it was said, were drowned in the water of Swale. Had not night come on, hardly a single Englishman would have escaped. Also many were taken alive, carried off to Scotland and ransomed at a heavy price.

When the King of England, occupied in the siege of Berwick, heard of such transactions in his own country, he wished to send part of his forces to attack the Scots still remaining in England, and to maintain the siege with the rest of his people; but by advice of his nobles, who objected either to divide their forces or to fight the Scots, he raised the siege and marched his army into England, expecting to encounter the Scots. But they got wind of this and entered Scotland with their captives and booty of cattle by way of Stanemoor, Gilsland and those western parts. Then the king disbanded his army, allowing every one to return home, without any good business done.

But the excommunicate Scots, not satisfied with the aforesaid misdeeds, invaded England with an army commanded by the aforesaid two leaders, to wit, Thomas Randolf and James of Douglas, about the feast of All Saints, when the crop had been stored in barns, and burnt the whole of Gilsland, both the corn upon which the people depended for sustenance during that year and the houses wherein they had been able to take refuge; also, they carried off with them both men and cattle. And so, marching as far as Borough under Stanemoor, they laid all waste, and then returned through Westmorland, doing there as they had done in Gilsland, or worse. Then, after ten or twelve days, they fared through part of Cumberland, which they burnt on their march, and returned to Scotland with a very large spoil of men and cattle.

Howbeit, before the Nativity of our Lord, the wise men of both nations met, and by common consent arranged a truce between the kingdoms, to last for two years, and that truce was proclaimed on the march on the octave of the Nativity of our Lord.

The two-year truce expires and the Scots immediately resume their raiding policy in the hopes of forcing the English to accept a permanent peace, January 1322.

Now after the Epiphany, when the truce between the kingdoms lapsed, the Scottish army invaded England and marched into the bishopric of Durham, and the Earl of Moray remained at Darlington. But James of Douglas and the Steward of Scotland went forward plundering the country in all directions, one of them raiding towards Hartlepool and the district of Cleveland, the other towards Richmond. The people of Richmond county, neither having nor hoping to have any defender now as formerly, bought off the invaders with a great sum of money. This time the Scots remained in England a fortnight and more; and when the northern knights came to the Earl of Lancaster at Pontefract, where he usually dwelt, ready to fight against the Scots if he would assist them, he feigned excuse; and no wonder! seeing that he cared not to take up arms in the cause of a king who was ready to attack him.

King Edward tries to regain the initiative by invading Scotland, 1322.

The king mustered an army in order to approach Scotland about the feast of St Peter ad Vincula; hearing of which Robert de Brus invaded England with an army by way of Carlisle in the octave before the Nativity of St John the Baptist, and burnt the bishop's manor at Rose, and Allerdale, and plundered the monastery of Holm Cultran, notwithstanding that his father's body was buried there; and thence proceeded to waste and plunder Copeland, and so on beyond the sands of Duddon to Furness. But the Abbot of Furness went to meet him, and paid ransom for the district of Furness that it should not be again burnt or plundered, and took him to Furness Abbey. This notwith-standing, the Scots set fire to various places and lifted spoil. Also they went further beyond the sands of Level to Cartmel, and burnt the lands round the priory of the Black Canons, taking away cattle and spoil: and so they crossed the sands of Kent as far as the town of Lancaster, which they burnt, except the priory of the Black Monks and the house of the Preaching Friars. The Earl of Moray and Sir James of Douglas joined them there with another strong force, and so they marched forward together some twenty miles to the south, burning everything and taking away prisoners and cattle as far as the town of Preston in Amoundness, which also they burnt, except the house of the Minorite Friars. Some of the Scots even went beyond that town fifteen miles to the south, being then some eighty miles within England; and then all returned with many prisoners and cattle and much booty; so that on the vigil of St Margaret Virgin they came to Carlisle, and lay there in their tents around the town for five days, trampling and destroying as much of the crops as they could by themselves and their beasts. They re-entered Scotland on the vigil of St James the Apostle, so that they spent three weeks and three days in England on that occasion.

The King of England came to Newcastle about the feast of St Peter ad Vincula, and shortly afterwards invaded Scotland with his earls, barons, knights and a very great army; but the Scots retired before him in their usual way, nor dared to give him battle. Thus the English were compelled to evacuate Scottish ground before the Nativity of the Glorious Virgin, owing as much to want of provender as to pestilence in the army; for famine killed as many soldiers as did dysentery.

After the retreat of the King of England the King of Scotland collected all his forces, both on this side of the Scottish sea and beyond it, and from the Isles and from Bute and Arran, and on the day after the feast of St Michael he invaded England by the Solway and lay for five days at Beaumond, about three miles from Carlisle, and during that time sent the greater part of his force to lay waste the country all around; after which he marched into England to Blackmoor (whither he had never gone before nor laid waste those parts because of their difficulty of access), having learned for a certainty from his scouts that the King of England was there. The king, however, hearing of his approach, wrote to the new Earl of Carlisle, commanding him to muster all the northern forces, horse and foot, of his county and Lancaster, that were fit for war, and to come to his aid against the Scots. This he [Carlisle] did, having taken command of the county of Lancaster, so that he had 30,000 men ready for battle; and whereas the Scots were in the eastern district, he brought his forces by the western district so as to reach the king. But the Scots burnt the villages and manors in Blackmoor, and laid waste all that they could, taking men away as prisoners, together with much booty and cattle.

Now my lord John of Brittany, Earl of Richmond, having been detached with his division by the king to reconnoitre the army of the Scots from a certain height between Biland Abbey and Rievaulx Abbey, and being suddenly attacked and surprised by them, attempted by making his people hurl stones to repel their assault by a certain narrow and steep pass in the hill; but the Scots forced their way fiercely and courageously against them; many English escaped by flight and many were made prisoners, including the aforesaid earl. Justly, indeed, did he incur that punishment, seeing that it was he himself who had prevented peace being made between the realms.

When this became known to the King of England, who was then in Rievaulx Abbey, he, being ever chicken-hearted and luckless in war and having [already] fled in fear from them in Scotland, now took to flight in England, leaving behind him in the monastery in his haste his silver plate and much treasure. Then the Scots, arriving, immediately after, seized it all and plundered the monastery, and then marched on to the Wolds, taking the Earl [of Richmond] with them, laying waste that country nearly as far as the town of Beverley, which was held to ransom to escape being burnt by them in like manner as they had destroyed other towns.

Now when the aforesaid Earl of Carlisle heard that the king was at York, he directed his march thither in order to attack the Scots with him and drive them out of the kingdom; but when he found the king all in confusion and no army mustered, he disbanded his own forces, allowing every man to return home. The Scots on that occasion did not go beyond Beverley, but returned laden with spoil and with many prisoners and much booty; and on the day of the Commemoration of All Souls they entered Scotland, after remaining in England one month and three days. Wherefore, when the said Earl of Carlisle perceived that the King of England neither knew how to rule his realm nor was able to defend it against the Scots, who year by year laid it more and more waste, he feared lest at last he [the king] should lose the entire kingdom; so he chose the less of two evils, and considered how much better it would be for the community of each realm if each king should possess his own kingdom freely and peacefully without any homage, instead of so many homicides and arsons, captives, plunderings and raidings taking place every year. Therefore on the 3rd January [1323] the said Earl of Carlisle went secretly to Robert the Bruce at Lochmaben and, after holding long conference and protracted discussion with him, at length, to his own perdition, came to agreement with him in the following bond. The earl firmly pledged himself, his heirs and their adherents to advise and assist with all their might in maintaining the said Robert as King of Scotland, his heirs and successors, in the aforesaid independence, and to oppose with all their force all those who would not join in nor even consent to the said treaty, as hinderers of the public and common welfare. And the said Robert, King of Scotland, pledged himself upon honour to assist and protect with all his might the said earl and all his heirs and their adherents according to the aforesaid compact, which he was willing should be confirmed by six persons each [kingdom] to be nominated by the aforesaid king and earl. And if the King of England should give his assent to the said treaty within a year, then the King of Scots should cause a monastery to be built in Scotland, the rental whereof should be five hundred merks, for the perpetual commemoration of and prayer for the souls of those slain in the war between England and Scotland, and should pay to the King of England within ten years 80,000 merks of silver, and that the King of England should have the heir male of the King of Scotland in order to marry to him any lady of his blood.

On behalf of the King of Scotland my Lord Thomas Randolf, Earl of Moray, swore to the faithful fulfillment of all these conditions without fraud, and the said Earl of Carlisle in his own person, touching the sacred gospels; and written indentures having been made out, their seals were set thereto mutually.

Now the Earl of Carlisle made the aforesaid convention and treaty with the Scots without the knowledge and consent of the King of England and of the kingdom in parliament; nor was he more than a single individual, none of whose business it was to transact such affairs. But the said earl, returning soon after from Scotland, caused all the chief men in his earldom to be summoned to Carlisle, both regulars and laymen, and there, more from fear than from any liking, they made him their oath that they would help him faithfully to fulfill all the things aforesaid. But after all these things had been made known for certain to the King and kingdom of England, the poor folk, middle class and farmers in the northern parts were not a little delighted that the King of Scotland should freely possess his own kingdom on such terms that they themselves might live in peace.

Edward II is deposed by his wife Isabella and Sir Roger de Mortimer; the Scots claim that the deposition of Edward nullifies the truce and resume the offensive. The newly crowned Edward III, fifteen years old and firmly in the control of his mother and Mortimer, is sent northwards with an army to counter the Scots. Outmanoeuvred and very nearly captured in a night raid by Douglas, he disbands his army and the communities of northern England seek another round of truces from King Robert, 1327.

On the night of the king's coronation in London, the Scots, having already heard thereof, came in great force with ladders to Norham Castle, which is upon the March and had been very offensive to them. About sixteen of them boldly mounted the castle walls; but Robert de Maners, warden of the castle, had been warned of their coming by a certain Scot within the castle, and, rushing suddenly upon them, killed nine or ten and took five of them alive, but severely wounded. This mishap ought to have been a sign and portent of the ills that were to befall them in the time of the new king.

Howbeit, this did not cause them [the Scots] to desist in the least from their long-standing iniquity and evil habits; for, hearing that the King of England's son had been crowned and confirmed in the kingdom, and that his father, who had yielded to them their country free, together with a large part of the English march, had been deposed and was detained in custody, they invaded England, before the feast of St Margaret Virgin and Martyr, in three columns, whereof one was commanded by the oft-mentioned Earl of Moray, another by Sir James of Douglas, and the third by the Earl of Mar, who for many years previously had been educated at the King of England's court, but had returned to Scotland after the capture of the king, hoping to rescue him from captivity and restore him to his kingdom, as formerly, by the help of the Scots and of certain adherents whom the deposed king still had in England. My lord Robert de Brus, who had become leprous, did not invade England on this occasion.

On hearing reports of these events, the new King of England assembled an army and advanced swiftly against the Scots in the northern parts about Castle Barnard and Stanhope Park; and as they kept to the woods and would not accept battle in the open, the young king, with extraordinary exertion, made a flank march with part of his forces in a single day to Haydon Bridge, in order to cut off their retreat to Scotland. But, as the Scots continued to hold their ground in Stanhope Park, the king marched back to their neighbourhood, and, had he attacked them at once with his army, he must have beaten them, as was commonly said by all men afterwards. Daily they lost both men and horses through lack of provender, although they had gathered some booty in the country round about; but the affair was put off for eight days in accord with the bad advice of certain chief officers of the army, the king lying all that time between the Scots and Scotland; until one night the Scots, warned, it is said, by an Englishman in the king's army that the king had decided to attack them the next morning, silently decamped from the park, and, marching round the king's army, held their way to Scotland; and thus it was made clear how action is endangered by delay.

One night, when they were still in the park, Sir James of Douglas, like a brave and enterprising knight, stealthily penetrated far into the king's camp with a small party, and nearly reached the king's tent; but, in returning he made known who he was, killed many who were taken by surprise, and escaped without a scratch.

When the king heard that the Scots had decamped he shed tears of vexation, disbanded his army, and returned to the south; and Messire Jehan, the Count of Hainault's brother, went back with his following to his own country. But after the king's departure, the Scots assembled an army and harried almost the whole of Northumberland, except the castles, remaining there a long time. When the people of the other English marches saw this, they sent envoys to the Scots, and for a large sum of money obtained from them a truce to last till the following feast of Pentecost.

The English are forced to accept peace on Robert I's terms. The chronicler carefully attaches any blame to Edward II, and to Isabella and Roger Mortimer, excusing Edward III, not unreasonably, on account of his age. This would prove to be significant in the 1330s when Edward would renounce the 'Shameful Peace' sealed by the marriage of his sister, Joanna, to David, the son of King Robert, on the grounds that he had been a minor when the peace was agreed.

Acting on the pestilent advice of his mother and Sir Roger de Mortimer (they being the chief controllers of the king, who was barely fifteen years of age), he was forced to release the Scots by his public deed from all exaction, right, claim or demand of the overlordship of the kingdom of Scotland on his part, or that of his heirs and successors in perpetuity, and from any homage to be done to the Kings of England. He restored to them also that piece of the Cross of Christ which the Scots call the Black Rood, and likewise a certain instrument or deed of subjection and homage to be done to the Kings of England, to which were appended the seals of all the chief men of Scotland, which they delivered, as related above, to the king's grandsire, and which, owing to the multitude of seals hanging to it, is called 'Ragman' by the Scots. But the people of London would no wise allow to be taken away from them the Stone of Scone, whereon the Kings of Scotland used to be set at their coronation at Scone. All those objects the illustrious King Edward, son of Henry, had caused to be brought away from Scotland when he reduced the Scots to his rule.

Also, the aforesaid young king gave his younger sister, my lady Joan of the Tower, in marriage to David, son of Robert de Brus, King of Scotland, he being then a boy five years old. All this was arranged by the king's mother the Queen [dowager] of England, who at that time governed the whole realm. The nuptials were solemnly celebrated at Berwick on Sunday next before the feast of St Mary Magdalene.

The King of England was not present at these nuptials, but the queen mother was there, with the king's brother and his elder sister and my lords the Bishops of Lincoln, Ely and Norwich, and the Earl of Warenne, Sir Roger de Mortimer and other English barons, and much people, besides those of Scotland, who assembled in great numbers at those nuptials. The reason, or rather the excuse, for making that remission or gratuitous concession to the Scots (to wit, that they should freely possess their kingdom and not hold it from any King of England as over-lord) was that unless the king had first made peace with the Scots, he could not have attacked the French who had disinherited him lest the Scots should invade England.

The same King Edward of England granted other letters, wherein he declared that he expressly and wholly withdrew from every suit, action or prosecution arising out of processes or sentences laid by the Supreme Lord Pontiff and the Cardinal-legates, Sir Joceline the priest, and Luke the deacon, against the said Lord Robert, King of Scotland, and the inhabitants of his kingdom, and would henceforth be opposed to any renewal of the Pope's processes. In testimony whereof, *et cetera*. But it is to be observed that these notable acts were done in the sixteenth year of the king's age.

My lord Robert de Brus, King of Scotland, died a leper; he had made for himself, however, a costly sepulchre. His son, David, a boy of six or seven years, succeeded him. He had married the sister of the King of England, as had been explained above; but he was not crowned immediately, nor annointed, although his father had obtained [authority] from the [Papal] Court for such anointing of the Kings of Scotland in future.

The many sins of King Robert are, in the chronicler's eyes, at least to some extent balanced by the fact that he has spent a lot of money on a tomb, a sure sign of contrition and Christian faith.

Brass of Robert Bruce, Dunfermline Abbey. Above his shoulders are, on the left, the lion rampant of Scotland and, on the right, the saltire of the Bruce family.

4

The Acts of King Robert
(1306–1329)

*T*he documents known to have been issued by King Robert are hardly extensive, but are certainly large enough to deter a translation of the entire series, which runs to the better part of 600 items. The series is accessible in the sense that it can be obtained in print through libraries, but the fact that virtually all of the documents are in Latin is not conducive to easy reading. The sheer bulk of the series prevents its repetition here, and the usefulness of such an exercise would be limited to say the least. What follows is merely a small, but hopefully representative, sample of the nature of King Robert's correspondence. The majority of the documents fall into a relatively small number of categories and, unsurprisingly, there is a great deal of minor variation in the format of letters, grants and instructions, but there is a good deal of consistency, enough to make a translation of each item in full more than just a little repetitive and the reading of them less than riveting. These few samples are translated from volume five of the 'Regesta Regum Scottorum', edited by Dr A.A.M. Duncan. This volume is a veritable mine of material for those with an interest in the early fourteenth century, not only for the acta themselves but for the wealth of information in Dr Duncan's extensive introduction and text notes.

Charter to Walter de Bickerton, 20/03/1309

Robert, by the grace of God, King of Scots, to all good men throughout the land, greetings. Know that we have given, and by this our charter confirm, that we grant to Walter de Bickerton our thanage* of Downie** with its pertinents. To be held by Walter and his heirs from us and our heirs in fee and heritage, and in free barony with toll and teme, with pit and gallows and *infangthief***, by its correct boundaries, including meadows and pastures, in moor and marsh, in roads and paths, in wood and plain in pond and mill, in waters and fishings and with all legitimate liberties, easements and other things pertaining to them. Performing for ourselves and our heirs the service of one knight. Witnesses to these matters, Lord Bernard, our chancellor, William, Earl of Ross, James, Steward of Scotland, John de Menteith, Gilbert de Hay, Robert de Keith, Robert Boyd and William Wyseman, knights. *(Given)* at Dunfermline on the 20th March, the third year of our reign.

Charter to Malcolm Earl of Lennox, 02/11/1309

Robert, by the grace of God King of Scots, to all good men throughout his land, greetings. Know that we give, heritably, to Malcolm, Earl of Lennox, the office of Sheriff of Clackmannan, to do justice for all according to the laws and customs of *(our)* realm. Therefore we require that everyone of whatever station to be obedient to the orders of the said Malcolm and his heirs that become sheriffs of Clackmannan. Witnesses to this matter, Lord Gilbert, our chancellor, Gilbert de Hay, Robert de Kethe and William de Vipond, knights, *(Given)* at St Andrews, 2nd November, the fourth year of our reign.

Instruction to the King's officers in the sherrifdom of Forres, 19/06/1311

Robert by the grace of God King of Scots, to his Sheriff and bailies of Forres, greetings. It is our will that you immediately require the farmers of our thanage of Dyke and Brodie to repair and make good

---

* *thanage, a form of tenure predating knight service, found mostly in eastern Scotland north of the Forth. The tenure of thains was managerial rather than proprietorial; they held tenure of properties belonging to the king in exchange for produce or money renders, and/or for services − military, hunting, judicial − to the king and his administration.*
** *an estate, formerly Royal Demesne, in Angus*
*** *forms of criminal jurisdiction, including imprisonment and the death penalty, both for his tenants and for persons from outwith his estate caught redhanded*

without delay the millpond of Dalpottie which pertains to the mill of Forres which those farmers are obliged to do for the Priory and Convent of Pluscarden. Failure to enforce this instruction will may cause us to apportion the cost of making the repairs to you personally. Witnessed personally, *(given)* at Elgin, 19th June, the sixth year of our reign.

Robert by the grace of God King of the Scots to all good men throughout the land, greetings. With the advice and consent of our dearest brother, Edward King of Ireland and of the prelates, Earls and barons of our realm, give, and with this charter confirm to our dear nephew Thomas Randolph, Knight, the whole Earldom of Moray with its pertinents and the whole island of Man with all the privileges, liberties and easements as stipulated in this charter. For his service in the past, for his homage and his good and praiseworthy service in the future to us and our Kingdom. For us and our heirs, the said Edward, King of Ireland and the prelates, earls and barons confirm this charter in all things to be *(safeguarded)* against any claims or revocations by us or our heirs, Our great seal appended to this as confirmation and ratification and with the seals of the said lord Edward, King of Ireland and the said bishops, earls and barons and their successors and heirs for all time. Given at Cupar in Fife, the last day of September in the 11th year of our reign.

King Robert issued this charter to ensure that the earldom of Moray and the Isle of Man would be safeguarded against encroachment by Robert's successor. Still without legitimate issue at this time (1316) there was a very real possibility that Edward Bruce could come to the throne, hence his very prominent inclusion, not only as a witness, but also as a party to the agreement. Should Edward become king he might have been tempted to revoke some of the very extensive grants made to Sir Thomas by King Robert. King Robert was perhaps paying a price for Randolph's loyalty, not to himself, but to his successor.

Robert by the grace of God, King of the Scots to all good men throughout his realm, greetings. Know that we have given, and by this charter confirm, the gift of William de Fenton, knight, to God and the blessed Mary and the Abbey and monks of Cupar for all time the benefits of the whole land of Ardory in the tenement of Rethy with its pertinents. To be held by those monks and their successors at that Abbey in unrestricted tenure of all easements and liberties in perpetual alms. Given by the charter of William to those monks, with its rightful boundaries measured and attested to, saving our service. In testimony to this we have appended here our great seal. Witnesses, Bernard, Abbot of Abirbrothot, our chancellor, Alexander the Stewart, Gilbert de Hay, William Oliphaunt and Robert de Keith, Knights. At Abrebrethot, the seventh of October, the 11th year of our reign.

This is a 'confirmation'; a declaration that the transaction described — a gift, an exchange of lands — had been approved by the king.

Robert, by the grace of God, King of the Scots, to all good men throughout his realm, greetings. Know that we have given, and by this charter confirm to our dear and faithful James of Garioch, knight, for his homage and service the forest of Fordyce by the bounds stated below. Starting from the valley called Achinacradoc and descending along the burn to the mill of Kinaldy and from there along the Northern boundary of the aforesaid forest to the two great rocks below Thorrynadach and from there to Polnacroscell and from there descending to beside the river Don around the Shaws of Alton of Fyntreff and from there downward along the path to the spring called Tubirnacrag then up to Schencragoc and up to Carenleth and from Carenleth to the burn called Adenacloch and from there to Carenleth iuxta Kirkton of Dyce and from there by the path which leads to the said vill of Dyce then to the pond and then to the other *(next?)* pond at the midpoint of the road that leads from the said vill along the eastern edge of the said forest as far as the King's highway which leads to Aberdeen, and from there to the spring called Tubirnaldi and from there to the valley called Achynnasonee and from there to the valley which is called Achynaterman and from there by the Southern part of the said forest by the path that leads to Glencaren iuxta the vill of Huctereny and from there by *'unam reske'* to a Crucifix and a great stone at the King's highway near Huctereny, and from there out of the Eastern side of the said vill to the burn called Aldynalene and from there up that burn to the head of the burn of Glenconan and from there up to the top of the hill called Cragnathybo and from there down to the burn of Glenyn and by that burn to the ditch which leads to a great stone and along the same ditch to the Bishop's wall, and then along that wall to the old wagon-way which leads to the vill of Clentrethy Herhard and leads down to the marsh and from there as far as the spring under the Crag of Clentrethy and from the same spring up to Achinacragoc, where they *(the bounds)* start. To be held by the said James and his heirs from us and our heirs in fee and heritage by all its right boundaries and with all easements, liberties and all things properly pertaining to them for the service of a fifth part of a knight and for the customary Scottish Service when it is required. In confirmation of which we have attached our seal. Witnesses, Bernard, Abbot of Aberbrothoc, our Chancellor, Alexander the Stewart, Gilbert Hay, our Constable of Scotland and Robert Keith, our Marshal of Scotland.

Descriptions of properties were a feature of the judicial system; this one defines hunting area boundaries, but mostly they were carried out in order to calculate the various duties payable on the death of a landowner or to adjudicate boundary disputes. A jury of local men, presumably those referred to as 'worthy' – probis – in charters would be charged with making the necessary perambulations and making a report of their findings to the appropriate officer, usually the sheriff.

An exemption from a variety of services due to the Crown

Clerics were not liable for military service themselves, but their tenants were, and this liability is specifically retained.

Robert, by the grace of God King of the Scots, to Justices, Sheriffs, Provosts and their bailies and to all that receive these letters, greetings. Know that through our inspection of the charters of the good Lord David, former King of Scots and of others of our royal predecessors the religious men of the Abbey and Convent of Dunfermline are to be free of all tallages, carriages and other services of whatever kind apart from service in our army in defence of the realm, the said charter to be taken as the superior in all matters, both general and particular. It is our firm command that any thing done contrary to this charter is to be considered as being against our personal will. Given at Haddington, the 17th September in the 12th year of our reign.

The King makes a religious donation

Robert by the grace of God, King of Scots, to all good men throughout his realm, greetings. Know that we have given to God and the Blessed Virgin Mary and to Saints John the Apostle and the Evangelist and to the religious men of the Abbey and Convent of Inchaffray the patronage of the Church of Killin in Glendsochyrthe with all crops and other things that pertain to the said church in free alms. However the said Abbey and Convent shall install one Canon to celebrate divine *(services)* in the church of Strathfulane. As confirmation of these things we have appended our privy seal. Given at Clackmannan, 24th February, the 12th year of our reign.

By means of acts like this religious foundations could accrue extensive interests all over the country. When a church was founded it was normal to make an endowment of land to support the incumbent. By acquiring these lands and the rights attendant on them, an abbey or convent could divert the income to their own needs and use a portion of that income to pay a 'vicar', in place of the 'rector'.

A safe conduct for an English peace mission

Robert, by the grace of God, King of the Scots to all his bailies and faithful men to whom this letter may concern inside and outside his realm, greetings. Know that we have granted, on the part of ourselves and of all those in our faith a secure safe conduct for the representatives sent by the Prince Edward, by the grace of God King of the English to procure an armistice between the said lord King and his *(men)* on one side and us and ours on the other, to the number of fifty persons of whatever station without conditions. Further, the said representative has a safe conduct to go to Berwick-upon-Tweed and from there to wherever they wish in *(territory within)* my power, to negotiate with our council and have complete freedom to return *(to England)*. It is our further desire and command that the said representatives, and all the men in his party shall have liberty to return to England undisturbed and without interference with them, their horses, their harness or *(any)* other things or goods. This letter patent to be valid for one month from the Festival of the Purification of the Blessed Virgin Mary. Witnessed personally at Berwick on Tweed, 26th January the fifteenth year of our reign.

Seal of Robert Bruce, earl of Carrick.
Appended in 1301 to a charter in favour of the Abbey of Melrose.

5

Extracts from the Chamberlains' Rolls for 1328

*O*nly a very tiny proportion of the administrative documents of King Robert's reign have survived to the present day. This shortage is most commonly attributed to the physical effects of war, but we should bear in mind that these records were compiled 700 years ago, and that they are fragile, terribly vulnerable to damp, fire and vermin; these factors may be more significant than the years of intermittent conflict between Scotland and England. The most extensive group of Chamberlains' Roll material is for the year 1329. It includes records of the returns to the Crown from a few sheriffdoms, the income and expenditure of the various departments of the royal household (as addressed later) and a précis of the income of the vacant See of St Andrews*.

A translation of the whole series of these rolls would be a lengthy exercise of limited value; a good deal of it is repetitious in the extreme, but it is important to have some awareness of the wide variety of responsibilities carried by the king's administrators.

The financial and administrative structures of the Crown in medieval Scotland were less sophisticated than their equivalent in England, simply because they could be; however they were neither primitive nor ineffective.

---

* During an episcopal vacancy the temporal dues that would normally have gone to the bishop were passed to the Crown until a new bishop was elected and consecrated.

Chamberlain's account

The compotus of Robert de Peebles, Chamberlain of Scotland, given at Scone, 26th June, Year of Grace 1328. His receipts and expenditure from the 18th of March, Year of Grace 1327 to the present day.

Confirming the receipt of 20s 8d from the provosts of the Burgh of Inverkeithing, and of £4 13s 4d from the provosts of the Burgh of Crail and of £7 19s 8d from the provosts of Dundee and of 15s 11d from the provosts of the Burgh of Montrose and of £7 5s 5d from the provosts of Lanark and of 64s from the provosts of Perth and £36 15s 8½d from the provosts of Aberdeen and of £5 15s 11d from the provosts of Cullen and of £5 13s from the provosts of Banff and of £10 18s 1d from the provosts of Haddington and of £36 19s 8½d from the provosts of Edinburgh and of £8 15s 8d from the provosts of the Burgh of Inverness and of 50s from the provosts of the Burgh of Linlithgow and of 2s 9d from the provosts of Auchterarder.

These receipts totalling £141 10s 10d.

Towns which acquired a charter of their liberties and privileges from the Crown were 'Royal' or 'King's' Burghs, enjoying — at least in theory — a privileged position compared to the ecclesiastical and baronial burghs. Each of the king's burghs paid an annual rent to the king for the land on which the town stood and the trading privileges stated in its charter. The rent or 'farm' of the burgh was payable to the chamberlain rather than to the local sheriff. Burghs were largely independent of the shrieval system, administering their own internal judicial and commercial business.

Even as early as the thirteenth century, the burghs chose their own 'provosts' who were responsible for the wellbeing of the town generally.

Income From customs

Confirming the receipt of £4 15s 7d from the collector of the 'new custom' for the Burgh of Cupar and of £6 5s 5d from the customar of Inverkeithing and of £19 3s 2d from the customar of Perth and of £240 6s 8d from the customar of Berwick and of £126 12s from the customars of Aberdeen and of £48 13½d from the customars of Edinburgh.

These receipts totalling £465 4s ½d.

Income from sheriffdoms

Confirming the receipt of £137 2s 4½d from the Sheriff of Perth and of £46 from the Sheriff of Fife and of £34 2s 6d from William Bonner, constable of Kinghorn and of £130 13s 9d from the Sheriff of Inverness and of £9 5s 8d from Laurence de Wilmerton(?) constable of Crail and of £33 from Alan de Vipont Bailie of Kinross and of £92 8s 5d from the Sheriff of Forfar and of £86 8s 8d from the Sheriff of Kincardine and of £17 6s 8d from the Sheriff of Stirling and of 12s 4¼d from the Sheriff of Selkirk and of £12 11s 8d from the Sheriff of Selkirk and of £88 10s 10d from the Sheriff of Roxburgh and of £57 8s 5¾d from the sheriff of Berwick and of £80 17s 5¾d from the Sheriff of Banff and of £158 10d from the Sheriff of Aberdeen and of £254 4s 3d from the Sheriff of Edinburgh.

These receipts totalling £1221 3s 11½d.

The sheriffs carried the responsibility of representing the king in several guises, as tax and rent collector, as administrator of the king's justice, and of ensuring readiness among, and providing the leadership for, those liable for normal military service.

Accounts of the earldom of Carrick, 1328–29

The account of Malcolm, Bailie of the Earldom of Carick. He acknowledges, firstly, the receipt of £66 8s 7d , proceeds of the 'tenth penny*' from the earldom of Carrick, delivered to Dumbarton, and of £100 22½d collected before this compotus and of £133 9s 2d collected in the said earldom for the 'contribution for peace**' and of £115 3s 1½d of the 'farms' of the said earldom of Carrick collected over two years of this compotus and of £15 castle guard and escheats***

* *The 'tenth penny' was a tax granted by parliament to Robert I in exchange for his relinquishing the right to various traditional rights of carriage (of the king's goods) and requisition (of other peoples' goods).*
** *The contribution for peace was a sum of £20,000 promised by Robert I as part of the conditions of the Treaty of Berwick in 1328. In theory the money was to help repair the ravages of war in the north of England, in practice it seems to have been appropriated by Queen Isabella of England and Sir Roger Mortimer.*
*** *Castle guard was an obligation on landholders to provide manpower (or funds in lieu) to garrison their lord's castles. Should a landholder die without an heir their property would revert to the person from whom they had gained the land – it would be an 'escheat'.*

collected during the period of this compotus and of 13 'marts' (*beef carcasses*) received from the same sources.

These receipts totalling £430 7s 9d and 13 marts.

Farms of the King's lands in the sheriffdom of Stirling

Compotus of Reginald More, given at Scone, 21st of August, Year of Grace 1329. His income and costs from his last compotus, given at Dumbarton, until the present day.

He acknowledges receipt of £80 of the 'farms' of Skeoch, C'gorth, Auchenbouthy and Tulchys for the three terms of the period of this accounting and of the £4 annual rent of Raploch and of £170 4s 5d received by the chamberlain at Scone.

These receipts totalling £254 4s 5d.

A 'farm' in this context is the rent payable on the property. The property might contain any number of actual farms, each with one or more tenants renting from the 'farmer'. Royal rights (collection of taxes or customs for example) could be, and a great many estates were, 'farmed' out to men who paid a sum for the privilege and then recouped their expenditure − and hopefully a profit − from the office or by subletting the land.

The arms of the King of Scotland.
The drawing represents a lion within a bordure, pierced by ten fleurs-de-lys.

6

The Bruce family in English State records

Extracts from the Calendar of Documents
Relating to Scotland, volumes 1–3

Edited by J. Bain, 1881–88

Many aristocratic and noble families owned properties in more than one country and therefore owed allegiance to more than one king. The (mostly) peaceful relationship that existed between the kings of Scotland and England throughout the thirteenth century meant that this was not a serious problem – there was no real conflict in the duties due to the two kings. The long and close relationship between the Bruce family and Edward I is not really typical of the condition of the Scottish aristocracy; few Scottish lords were so deeply involved in English administrative matters or enjoyed such a close relationship with the king of England; nonetheless they did have commitments to him, and it is surely understandable that they were concerned to maintain their holdings outwith Scotland. Although it is seldom referred to, a similar situation faced those Scottish lords with holdings in Ireland, where the extension of Edward's lordship brought those lords increasingly under Edward's influence.

PAGE 12 – *24 June 1275*
The K. signifies to the Treasurer and Barons that of his special grace he has permitted Robert de Brus to pay his debts at Exchequer by equal moieties at Michaelmas and Easter next. Westminster.

This relates to Robert 'the Noble', grandfather of Robert I.

PAGE 20 — *12 May 1276*

The King to his Barons of Exchequer. As his late father gave Isabella de Brus in exchange for her share of the earldom of Chester, by charter, which the K. has inspected, the manors of Writele and Hatfelde in Essex, with the half hundred of Hatfelde, for service of a knight's fee only, and the demand from Robert de Brus her son and heir 100s. for his relief, as if he held a barony, the K. commands them, after inspecting the charter and satisfying the K. for the relief as therein, to free Robert from the 100s. and make an enrolment accordingly. Westminster.

'Relief' was a sum of money paid by the heir to the king or other 'superior' for entry to an estate; this was standard practice in both England and Scotland.

PAGE 27 — *29 Sept 1278*

Homage and fealty rendered to the K. by Alexander K. of Scotland; Robert de Brus earl of Carrick, swearing fealty on his behalf. Westminster.

Alexander III owed homage to the king of England for his honour of Tynedale, a fief of the English Crown. In order to avoid giving homage in person, which would be seen as degrading for a king, it was normal to appoint a senior noble to act as proxy. English kings had a similar obligation for their properties held from the kings of France.

PAGE 37 — *3 Nov 1278 to 16 Jan 1279*

Robert de Brus and Cristiana his wife hold the manors of Gamelesby and Glassanby of the K. by cornage.

PAGE 58 — *9 Sept 1280*

Robert de Brus *senior* came into the K.'s chancery at Carlisle on the morrow of the Nativity of the Blessed Mary, and restored to Bernard de Brus all his right in the manor of Exton in Rutland, which he (Robert) held according to the 'dictum of Kenileworthe', drawing thence 40s yearly in payment of 420 marks, for which Bernard redeemed the manor in terms of said 'dictum'; excepting 2 acres of meadow within the park of Bernardshille, which Robert retains for life, and also reserving to him as chief lord, the due services therefrom. Bernard acknowledged that he was still owing 120s; whereof he would pay Robert 40s yearly. Carlisle.

PAGE 62 – *10 Sept 1281*

The King guarantees a loan of 40s to Robert de Brus earl of Carrick. Windsor.

Even great landowners could be regularly embarrassed for relatively minor sums due to the perennial cash flow problems common to agricultural rentiers in any monetarised economy.

PAGE 62 – *13 Sept 1281*

Robert de Brus earl of Carrick in Scotland acknowledges a loan from K. Edward, at London, by the hands of Baruncin Gualteri and others, citizens and merchants of Lucca, of 40s good new and lawful sterlings, to be repaid at London at the next Parliament of St Michael. Dated Saturday next before the Feast of the Exaltation of the Holy Rood, AD 1281. London.

'Sterling' was a generic and international term for silver coins (pennies) of a specific weight and quality. A recoinage had lately taken place in England in an effort to remove poorer coins from circulation, hence the stipulation that the payment should be in 'good new lawful' currency.

PAGE 67 – *24 May 1282*

The K. having granted leave to Robert de Brus earl of Carrick to send his men to Ireland to buy wines, corn, and other victuals for his use, commands his bailiffs and lieges there to offer them no hindrance. Hertlebyre.

PAGE 71 – *29 April 1283*

The K. having committed to Robert de Brus earl of Carrick the custody of the castle and county of Carlisle, commands the Barons not to deliver them to any other till otherwise commanded. And should they have been so delivered, they are with the utmost haste to revoke the same. Given under the privy seal, 29th April, in the K.'s 11th year.

PAGE 71 – *2 May 1283*

The K. has committed to Robert de Brus earl of Carrick, the castle of Carlisle and the county of Cumberland, during pleasure; paying therefor yearly to the K. at his Exchequer as much as other sheriffs have been in use to pay for the same. Aberconwey in Snaudone.

Command to Archbishops and others to be attentive to Robert (as constable and sheriff of Carlisle) Also to William de Boyville to deliver the Castle with 'armatures etc.' and the county with 'rolls etc.' by a chyrograph. [Same place.]

PAGE 72 — *28 June 1283*
Geoffry de Neville, keeper of the K.'s forest *ultra* Trent, is commanded to give Robert de Brus earl of Carrick, 12 bucks in the forest of Inglewode by way of gift from the K. Rothelan.

PAGE 75 — *12 Aug 1284*
The K. commands his clerk, Hugh de Kendale, to give Elena widow of Geoffry de Lucy, dower from her husband's lands according to the extent made; Richard de Brus, to whom the K. had given the custody, having promised to ratify the same. Aber, 24th August, 12th of his reign.

PAGE 75 — *26 Sept 1284*
Richard de Brus, to whom the K. lately gave 12 live bucks and does in his forest of Essex, to stock his park, having with men taken one or two deer beyond the number, by misadventure, the K. pardons them the trespass. Overton.

PAGE 77 — *Hilary Term 1285*
The K. commands the Barons of Exchequer to respite the demand which they have made on Robert de Brus earl of Carrick, and Richard de Brus, or their tenants, concerning the assarts of Hathfeld, Writele, and the half hundred of Harlawe, till the next parliament after Easter, and to relax the distraint, if any made.

An assart was an area broken out of 'waste' or forest, i.e. new acreage under cultivation which had not been included as such in the original grant.

PAGE 77 — *Trinity Term 1285*
Robert de Brus earl of Carrick sheriff of Cumberland, had a day for his *compotus* on Saturday the Feast of the Translation of St Thomas the Martyr, and was absent the first, second, and third days. Therefore is amerced 15s, viz., for each day's default 100s and as to the fourth day, at the K.'s pleasure.

The compotus was the return made by sheriffs to the Crown, derived from rents and the issues of justice.

PAGE 78 — *15 Dec 1285*

The K. has pardoned to Robert de Brus lord of Annandale, and John de Seytone, his knight, their trespass in Inglewode Forest in taking a doe and a red deer 'priket' when hunting, beyond the ten does which the K. gave to Robert last year; for which doe and 'priket' the said Robert and John were indicted before the justices itinerant on pleas of the Forest in Cumberland; and the K. commands the justices to acquit them. Forde [Abbey].

PAGE 79 — *28 Dec 1285*

The K. pardons to Robert de Brus earl of Carrick, all his trespasses in the K.'s forest of Englewode to this date. Exeter. And commands William de Vescy justice of the Forest *ultra* Trent, if the Earl has been amerced before him or any of his servants for the said trespass, to quit him thereof, and cancel the record in his rolls. Exeter.

PAGE 79 — *1 Jan 1286*

The K. grants to Richard de Brus the custody of the manors of Ashby la Zuche in the county of Leicester, and of North Multone in the county of Devon, belonging to the late Roger la Zuche, till the heir's majority. Exeter.

PAGE 79 — *3 Jan 1286*

Robert de Brus, who remains in Scotland, appoints Master Adam de Crokedaike, and William de Cumbertrees, his attorneys for two years. Exeter.

Presumably this refers to Robert, son of Robert 'the Noble' and father of Robert I, since Robert the Noble was sheriff of Carlisle, and therefore unlikely to be able to spend so much time in Scotland. The high incidence of landownership in more than one country made the appointment of attorneys a necessity.

PAGE 83 — *12 July 1286*

Northumberland: – N. de Stapeltone [and three others], are appointed to hold an assize arraigned by William de Duglas, against Richard de

Brus and others, concerning the diversion of a water course in Dagenham. Westminster.

Richard de Bruce was the uncle of Robert I. The William Douglas of this document was probably William 'le Hardi', father of King Robert's great lieutenant Sir James, the original 'black' Douglas.

PAGE 85 – 26 Jan 1287
As Richard de Brus who held of the K. *in capite*, is dead, the escheator *citra* Trent is commanded to take his lands in the K.'s hand without delay. *Teste*, Edmund earl of Cornwall, the K.'s cousin. Westminster.

On 10th February thereafter the escheator is commanded to cause Richard's lands to be repledged to Robert de Brus his father till a month from Easter next, and then to take them again in the K.'s hand, unless otherwise commanded.

PAGE 85 – 6 Feb 1287
1   Inquisition [in virtue of writ of *diem extremum* to the K.'s escheator *citra* Trent, dated Westminster, 25th January previous] made at Writele in Essex, on Thursday next after the Purification of the Virgin Mary, in the K.'s 15th year, by Richard de Springefeud [and 11 others], who say, that Richard de Brus held nothing in said county of the K. *in capite*, but held the manor of Writele of Sir Robert de Brus his father, who enfeoffed him and the lawful heirs of his body for homage and a gold ring, value 2s, or 2s yearly. Richard died without lawful heirs, as he never married. The said manor is worth in all issues £139 17s 9d yearly.
2   Inquisition [under same writ] at Totynham, on the 8th February same year, by William Inzeale, Walter Thurkil, John of the Cross, William Lombe, Gilber Manger, Ashelon the miller, Geoffry the reeve, Walter grom, William Attemarke, John Attewode, William Arnolde, and Odo Inzeale; who say that the late Richard de Brus held nothing in the county of Mydilsexe of the K. *in capite*, but held some lands in Totynham by Sir Robert de Brus his father's gift, who enfeoffed him by charter, to be held by Richard and the lawful heirs of his body. And as he died without such, the lands should return to his said father. He held these lands, and also the third part of Kemeston manor in Bedford, by the service of half a knight's fee. The said lands of Totynham are worth in all issues £12 17s yearly. The jurors append their seals.

3   Inquisition [under same writ] regarding the lands of the late Richard de Brus, by [12 jurors] who say, that the deceased held nothing of the K. *in capite* in the county of Bedford; but held the third part of Kemestone manor of Sir Robert de Brus his father, who enfeoffed him (*ut supra*) by the service of a knight's fee. That the said land is worth 35*l.* yearly. That the land should revert to his father, as Richard died without heir of his body.

Lands belonging to those who died without an heir normally reverted to the king, and inquisitions would be held to determine the responsibilities that were attached to the properties. English kings had two officers (escheators) who administered those properties on behalf of the Crown.

PAGE 86 – *6 April 1287*
The K. to his cousin Edmund earl of Cornwall, his lieutenant in England. Robert de Brus complains that the lands of his late son Richard have been seized by the escheator, though they reverted to himself on his death without issue. The K. commands them to be restored. Bordeaux, 6th April, 15th year of his reign.

King Edward had allowed the properties of Richard to revert to his father, who had enfeoffed them to his son in the first place.

PAGE 88 – *8 October 1287*
Robert de Brus earl of Carrick, who remains in Scotland, appoints two attorneys for a year. Westminster.

PAGE 88 – *15 October 1287*
The K. to the Abbot of Holmcoltran. Writ of '*dedimus potestatem*' to receive the attorneys of Robert de Brus and Christiana his wife, who are staying in Scotland, in all their pleas in the English courts, for a year. Westminster, 15th Oct., 15th of his reign. *(Endorsed)* The attorneys are Master Adam de Crokd'[yk] and John Scirlock.

PAGE 94 – *28 April 1289*
Robert de Brus earl of Carrick, who stays in Scotland, appoints attorneys for a year. Westminster. *Teste*, Edmund [earl of Cornwall].

The said Robert and Cristiana his wife, who stay in Scotland, appoint two attorneys for a year. Westminster. *Teste ut supra.*

PAGE 96 — *3 October 1289*
The Guardians of Scotland accredit the Bishops of St Andrews and Glasgow, Robert de Brus the father, and John Comyn, to treat with the Ambassadors of the K. of Norway. Melros.

PAGE 109 — *(?) 1290*
Appeal by the seven Earls of Scotland and the community of the realm, against William bishop of St Andrews, and Sir John Comyn, conducting themselves as Guardians. They assert their privilege of placing the King of Scotland on the throne — complain of the Guardian's oppressions on Donald earl of Mar and the freemen of Moray — narrate the recognition of Robert de Brus of Annandale as next heir to the throne by Alexander II — admit the Count of Holland's right failing the line of Huntingdon — and relate the restoration by William the Lyon of the earldom of Mar to Morgund M'Gylochery.

PAGE 118 — *(?) May 1291*
Letter by a Competitor [not named] stating certain rights of the seven earls of Scotland, arguing that Richard I. could not release the homage of Scotland, and asking favour for himself.
[Palgrave attributes it to the elder de Brus]

The political situation in Scotland at this time would seem to make it very likely indeed that this letter was from Robert 'the Noble', his case for inheritance by primogeniture was not so strong as that of the only other really serious candidate, Sir John Balliol, so he tended to make more of traditional practices and relatively minor points of law. For a brief, lucid account of the process see R. Nicholson, Scotland, The Later Middle Ages *(Edinburgh, 1974).*

PAGE 120 — *5 June 1291*
Letters patent by the Count of Holland, Robert de Brus, John de Balliol, John de Hastings, John Comyn, the Earl of March, William de Vesci for his father, Nicholas de Soules and William de Ros, Competitors for the Crown, agreeing to be bound by the K.'s decision as Overlord. Append their seals. Norham, Tuesday next after the Ascension, 1291.
    (*Endorsed*) '*Scriptum per quod petentes jus in regno Scocie obligant se ad petendum et recipiendum jus suum coram Rege Anglie superiore domino Scocie,*

et per quod concedunt quod ipse Rex audiat et terminet jura sua in dicto regno, sicut ei qui est superior dominus Scocie, competit in hac parte.'

Edward's insistence on acceptance of his overlordship by all the candidates for the Scottish Crown as a condition of their candidature completely compromised his promise to maintain the independence of the country by effectively prejudging a constitutional issue in the absence of a Scottish king.

PAGE 121 – *10 June 1291*
Indenture dated Pentecost 1291, between Sir Robert de Brus lord of Annandale, and Sir John de Strivelyn of Moray, whereby the former leases to the latter all his land within the barony of Invirbervyn, within and without burgh; to be held by Sir John and his heirs of Sir Robert and his heirs for five years, for the yearly rent of 16*l.* sterling, payable at Dundee, and doing all other services except the King's aid and host. And he shall deliver the lands at the end of the lease in 'the same state or better' than he received them. They append their seals to counterparts at Berwick.

PAGE 125 – *Shortly before 12 August 1291*
Reasons or allegations propounded by Sir Robert de Brus for the purpose of proving that he is entitled to the kingdom of Scotland as nearest heir of the Royal blood.

PAGE 125 – *Shortly before 12 August 1291*
Further arguments by Sir Robert de Brus, closing with the repetition of the recognition by Alexander II, his bishops, earls, and barons, of his right of blood the writing attesting which under their seals remains in the Royal Treasury.

PAGE 126 – *Shortly before 12 August 1291*
Further arguments and examples adduced by Sir Robert de Brus in support of his plea as nearest in degree.

PAGE 127 – *12 August 1291*
Sir Robert de Brus's further arguments (drawn from the Pope's deposition of the K. of France) against female succession.

PAGE 131 — *13 August 1291*
The K. commands his bailiffs in Ireland and Scotland to permit the men of Robert de Brus earl of Carrick to buy corn, wine, and other victuals in Ireland and take them to Carrick. Chatton.

PAGE 135 — *12 January 1292*
Charter of *inspeximus* by the K. of one by Robert de Brus lord of Annandale, whereby the latter confirmed to the church of All Saints of Wrytel a grant by Richard of Great Badewe to that church at the instance of Friar Algucius its '*custos*,' of an acre and a half of pasture in the vill of Writel in frank almoigne for the safety of his soul, and an annual mass in the church on the anniversary of his death for ever. Witnesses [to Richard's grant], Master Adam de Crokedake seneschal of the said Sir Robert de Brus, and others; [to Robert de Brus's charter, dated at Hert on the morrow of the Nativity of St John Baptist, AD 1288], Sirs John de Setone, Henry de Graham, knights, Master Adam de Crokedake seneschal aforesaid and others. Westminster.

PAGE 147 — *20 August 1292*
The following (among others) have acquittance from summons to common pleas in Cumberland. Creyke. Alexander [de] Bonkil, Robert de Brus, David de Torthorald, the Abbot of Jedburgh, Walter de Corry, John de Seton.

Most landholders had to perform 'suit of court' as part of their obligation to their superior. This involved attendance at a particular court, usually three times a year, to take part in the administration of justice. The inconvenience of this burden meant that people often tried to evade it. All of the above would have had lands in Cumberland, but lived elsewhere. They are all Scottish lords with the possible exception of John de Seton.

PAGE 150 — *3 November 1292*
Geoffry de Moubray complains that Robert de Brus *senior* and Cristiana his wife, who hold 4 *carucates** and 600 acres of wood in Boulton and Bastingthwait as her dower in the plaintiff's heritage, have cut down 1000 oaks, value of each 4d, and made and carried off

---

* carucate, *a unit of landholding, normally about 100 acres and a quantity of grazing.*

marl from a rood of land in excess of her dower, and to his damage of 300*l*. The defendants say they have taken nothing but reasonable estovers for 'burning, building and enclosing', as entitled. The sheriff in person and a jury of 12 to hold an inquiry in the ground, and certify the justices at Newcastle-on-Tyne on the morrow of Hilary next.

Robert de Brus *senior* and Cristiana his wife complain that Geoffry de Moubray refuses to keep an agreement entered into between Adam de Gesemuthe her former husband, herself, and Robert de Moubray, Geoffry's uncle, whose heir he is, on the morrow of the Virgin's Nativity [9th Sept] 1261, – whereby Roger was to assign to Adam and Cristiana in dower the third of a vaccary and other tenements in Bolton – to their damage of 20*l*., and produce the writing. Geoffry by attorney pleads that as their writ is for damages, they cannot recover the freehold under it. Afterwards at Newcastle-on-Tyne, in the 5th week after Easter [29th March 1293], the plaintiffs are nonsuited and amerced for a false claim.

PAGE 158 – *25 September 1293*

Indenture attesting that on Friday next before Michaelmas 1293, the following articles were delivered to Sir Odoenus Uglacii and Master Weyland de Stiklawe for the use of 'the most serene lady' Lady Isabella de Brus*, Queen of Norway, by Sir Ralph de Ardena, Master Nigel Cambel, Lucas de Tany, and H[enry] de Stiklawe, the envoys of Sir Robert de Brus earl of Carrick. *(Followed by a list of delivered items.)* The aforesaid 'recipients' and 'deliverers' respectively affix their seals to counterparts at the city of Berghem, date aforesaid.

PAGE 159 – *(?) Sept 1293*

Robert de Brus and Cristiana his wife to the K. As they dwell in Scotland, beg him to allow them to appoint general attorneys and to command some one to take these.

PAGE 161 - *2 June 1294*

Pardon to Robert de Brus *senior* of his fine of 100 marks, for his trespass

---

* *Isabella Bruce was the sister of Robert I.*

in taking venison in Essex without the K.'s leave. Westminster, by the K. himself.

PAGE 163 — *20 April 1294*
Robert de Brus earl of Carrick, going to Ireland, has a conduct till Michaelmas next and for a year afterwards. Canterbury.

In common with a number of Scottish lords, particularly those with extensive lands in the western counties, the Bruces had interests in north-east Ireland.

PAGE 164 — *3 May 1295*
Mainprize by Thomas de Hellebek knight of Westmorland, Adam de Twynham of Hertford and Westmorland, John de Gledelawe of Essex, and Richard de Langwatby of Westmerland, that Adam de Crokdaik knight, and master William de Irby, executors of Robert de Brus's will, shall discharge all his debts to the K.

Refers to Robert 'the Noble'.

PAGE 165 — *(?) May 1295*
[From an official not named] to his 'reverend lord.' The writer in terms of the K.'s writ directed to him, which he returns under seal, has taken from Lady Cristiana widow of the late Sir Robert de Brus lord of Annandale, her oath not to marry without the K.'s consent, and also admitted her attorneys to receive her dower from the lands, knights fees, and advowsons★ of churches, which belonged to her late lord.

PAGE 165 — *(?) July 1295*
The K. to John de Langetone his chancellor. As Robert [de Brus] son and heir of Robert de Brus *senior* deceased who held *in capite* has done homage, he commands letters under the Great seal to be issued. Aberconway, 4th July (?).

The letters would be instructions to the sheriffs of the various counties in which the late Robert had held lands to pass those lands on to his heir.

★ *advowsons, the right to appoint priests to particular parishes; these posts were often given in exchange for a fee to the lord, or to provide an income for friends or family members.*

PAGE 166 – *4 July 1295*
On 5th of same month Master Andrew of St Alban, Robert de Brus's clerk, going beyond seas, has leave to appoint special attorneys.

PAGE 166 – *10 Aug 1295*
Recognizance by Robert de Brus lord of Writele of his debt to Adam del Crokdayk, executor of his father Robert de Brus's will, for 99*l*. 9s. 6d. payable in moieties at the Purification of the Virgin and Pentecost next. Westminster.

In moieties – in two equal instalments

PAGE 166 – *6 October 1295*
The K. commits to his liege Robert de Brus lord of Annandale the keeping of the castle at Carlisle. Canterbury.

PAGE 166 – *15 October 1295*
The K. confirms the grant by Christiana widow of Robert de Brus late lord of Annandale, to Adam del Crokdayk and his heirs in perpetuity, of the vill of Glassanby. Westminster.

PAGE 170 – *About 25 March 1296*
R. de Brus earl of Carrick and lord of Annandale prays Sire J. de Langeton the chancellor for a protection for Walter Cryps his baker, going with him to Scotland, as his name had been forgotten on the '*bylle*' last made. Sealed with his privy seal.

By this time the kingship of John I of Scotland was under threat from Edward. He had extracted homage and fealty from John as king of Scotland, and then forced him to 'rebel', thus giving Edward an opportunity to intervene militarily and enforce his will.

PAGE 217 – *31 August 1296*
The K. commands his escheator *ultra* Trent, to deliver to Cristiana widow of Robert de Brus of Annandale, the manors of Great Haddow in Essex, and Kemston in Bedford, assigned to her as dower with the assent of Robert de Brus★ his son and heir. Berwick-on-Tweed.

★ *Robert I*

PAGE 223 — *December 1296*

The K. for the great esteem he has for the good service of Robert de Brus earl of Carrick, commands the barons to 'atterm' his duties at Exchequer in the easiest manner for him, the attermement, always, however, remaining at the K.'s pleasure. Wartre.

PAGE 237 — *Beginning of July 1297*

Instrument assigning the reasons of the insurrection headed by the Bishop of Glasgow, the Earl of Carrick, and the Steward, and conditions of peace required by them.

Driven to resistance by the interference and demands of Edward I, John I eventually (1295) made an offensive/defensive alliance with France which he was not prepared to forswear. Edward brought an army to Scotland in 1296, quickly overcame the Scots and forced John's abdication. Confident that his lieutenants could complete the acquisition of Scotland, Edward turned his attention elsewhere. Early in 1297 there were a number of insurrections across the country, one led by William Wallace (a tenant of the Steward) and one by Sir Andrew Moray. The above mentioned fizzled out quickly, resulting in a capitulation at Irvine (as described later).

PAGE 237 — *7 July 1297*

Letters patent by Henry de Percy and Robert de Clifford attesting their having, on behalf of the K. of England, received to his peace the Bishop of Glasgow, Robert de Brus earl of Carrick, and James the Steward, and their followers. Done at Irewyn★.

PAGE 237 — *9 July 1297*

Robert de Brus earl of Carrick, James the Steward of Scotland, Alexander de Lindseye, John the brother of the Steward, and William de Douglas, confess their rebellion against the K., and place themselves in his will. Irvine.

PAGE 237 — *9 July 1297*

Robert bishop of Glasgow, James the Steward of Scotland, and Alexander de Lindseye, become guarantees for the Earl of Carrick's loyalty till he delivers his daughter Margerie as a hostage. Irvine.

★ *Irvine*

It seems odd that the guarantors of Robert's behaviour should be men who had been involved with him in the insurrection of 1297.

PAGE 240 – *29 July 1297*

The K. gives Robert de Brus *senior*, who is about to go beyond seas with him, in his service, respite of his debts at Exchequer during pleasure, and also freedom from distraint for his other debts. Westminster.

PAGE 241 – *1 Aug 1297*

John earl of Warenne to the K. He expects the Bishop of Glasgow, the Earl of Carrick, and the Steward of Scotland, on Thursday before St Laurence to perform their covenants with Sir Henry de [Percy]. The Earl of Stratherne has taken the traitor Macdof and his two sons. They shall receive their deserts when they arrive. Berwick.

PAGE 247 – *14 Nov 1297*

Powers conferred on J. bishop of Carlisle and Robert de Clifford to receive to the King's peace Robert de Brus earl of Carrick and his friends, as seems best to their discretion. By the Council. Westminster.

PAGE 252 – *4 June 1298*

The sheriff of Essex is commanded to levy from the goods and chattels of Robert de Brus, 295*l.* which he owes the K. by a prest, and 359*l.* 14s 1d, for divers debts. And to have the money at York on the morrow of St Margaret, to be paid the K. there. York.

PAGE 255 – *3 July 1298*

Robert de Brus earl of Carrick and lord of Annandale to Sir John de Langeton chancellor of England. On behalf of his 'bachelors' Sir John de Wigeton, Sir John de Seton, and Sir Walter Haket, who are with him in the King's service in Galloway, and are approaching the place where the King is, and whose late protection expired at the Nativity of St John Baptist last, he begs a renewal. Offers to do anything the Chancellor commands him. Turnebiry-en-Carrik.

PAGE 268 – *28 Dec 1298*

Memoranda as to troops for Scotland to be provided by the Earl of Carrick, Gibbon fitz Kan, Donkan Maddowell, Sir Richard Siward and others, from Carlisle, Galloway, Nithsdale, and the northern and mid-land counties. Total foot, 8100.

PAGE 272 − *13 July 1299*
Extent of Sir Robert de Brus's manor of Writtle before the sheriff of Essex (by twelve jurors); who say that the *messuage*★ with garden, pigeon house, *curtilage*★★ and vineyard is worth 30s; 1011 acres arable in *demesne*★★★ are worth £8 10s 4d at 4d an acre; 32 acres 'mowable' meadow, 64s; 60 acres pasture, 40s at 8d an acre; fixed rents £336 0s 7d; the market 2 Marks. Pleas and perquisite of the court and view of frankpledge, 100s; Pannage of the vill and '*lepselver*' 30s; grazing in the parks and underwood, pannage and nuts, £8; 26 virgates of customary land, whereof the labours are worth £26; 13 virgates '*firmar*' with said customary tenants who plough yearly 252 acres , value £6 6s at 6d an acre. They find 40 men to hoe for one day, value 20d. Also 112 labourers in autumn, fed by the lord, value 9s 4d. Also the farmers mow 36 acres in autumn, worth 9s at 3d an acre. Carriages there are worth 2s 2d. The tenants of Stane give 6 cocks and 6 hens at Christmas, worth 12d. The grazings of the enclosures of the vill are worth ½ Mark. They append their seals, Monday before St Margaret's day anno xxvii. Total of the manor £100 17s 5d.

This inquisition gives a good indication of the complexity of even a fairly minor barony and the many ways in which cash, labour and goods could be extracted from tenants.

★ messuage − *the main house of the estate*
★★ curtilage − *the immediate environs of that house*
★★★ demesne − *land of the estate kept 'in hand' by the lord instead of being let to tenants. Demesne farming was less common in Scotland than England, most Scottish landholders preferring to lease out virtually all of their estate. This property and the two that follow, which have not been included in full, generated an income in excess of £180 p.a., a very large sum in 1299, and it shows clearly why Scottish landholders were afraid of losing their English properties. The commonly expressed view that their English properties were inevitably more valuable than their Scottish holdings is not substantiated by the evidence − if it had been so, Scottish landlords would surely have been much more likely to live on their English properties and just collect the rents of their Scottish ones. The English properties of the Bruce family were quite extensive compared to those of most Scottish lords and Writele was by far the most valuable of those properties, but hardly rich enough to make the Bruces important players in English politics. The personal relationships involved (Robert 'the Noble' had been on crusade with Edward I and he and his son both served as sheriffs or constables of Carlisle) were probably more important.*

PAGE 273 – *18 July 1299*
Extent of the lands of Robert de Brus, taken before the sheriff of Huntingdon on Saturday next before the F. of St Margaret, anno xxvij.

PAGE 283 – *(?) Nov 1299*
Wages of esquires keeping Lochmaben pele: – For the wages of Philip de Slane, and 3 fellow esquires with 4 barbed horses, 5 hoblars with 5 unarmed horses, and 9 foot of Sir Alan fitz Warin's retinue, defending the pele of Lochmaben under Sir Robert de Clifford's orders while captain, against the assault made by the Earl of Carrick, from the 1st to 25th August, 25 days, and a *hoblar*★ and horse from 1st to 20th; each barbed horse 12d, each other 6d, and each footman 2d, 10*l*. 10s. To Alexander de Hilton [and 5 other squires] with 6 barbed horses, in garrison under Sir Ralph's orders, in Lochmaben pele, to escort victuals from Annan to the castle on account of the Scots, from 14th September to 19th October, 36 days, and another esquire from 14th to 29th September, wages *ut supra*, 11*l*. 6s.

The insurrections of the Scots forced Edward to spend huge sums maintaining garrisons across Scotland. To a limited extent these could be manned and provisioned from the resources of those parts of the country in Edward's control, but throughout the wars the drain on his English income would be enormous and would compromise his other operations.

PAGE 284 – *(?) Nov 1299*
Portage of victuals from ship to land, wages of a groom watching on the bank of the Annan while waiting for carriage, from 20th July till 17th August, 29 days at 1d *per diem*, mending sacks, groom's wages watching (*guarding*) wine on bank; and repairing a house in the '*clocherium*' of Annan to save the said victuals in case of the Earl of Carrick's attack, 2s; for hoops bought for the wine casks lying on the bank there, 4d; total, 16s 5d. Hire of 79 horses at 4d each, and 7 waggons at 12d each, carrying stores from Annan to Lochmaben between 10th July and 16th September, *vicissim*, 33s 4d.

★ hoblar/hobilar, *a light cavalry/mounted infantry soldier.*

PAGE 328 — *16 Feb 1302*

The K. having at the instance of Robert de Brus earl of Carrick, pardoned Ector Askeloc for the death of Cuthbert of Galloway and other offences in Cumberland and elsewhere in England and Scotland, and breaking prison at Carlisle, commands a pardon under the Great seal to be issued. Roxburgh.

Presumably Robert's request predated his resistance of Edward's occupation.

PAGE 330 — *6 April 1302*

Ph[ilip] K. of France to Robert de Brus earl of Carrick and John Comyn the son, Guardians of Scotland in the name of K. John, and to the bishops, abbots, priors, earls, barons, and other magnates, and the whole community, his dear friends, wishes health and hope of fortitude in adversity. He received with sincere affection their envoys John abbot of Jeddwurth★, and John Wissard knight, and fully understands their letters and messages anxiously expressed by the envoys. Is moved to his very marrow by the evils brought on their country through hostile malignity. Praises them for their constancy to their King and their shining valour in defence of their native land against injustice, and urges them to persevere in the same course. Regarding the aid which they ask, he is not unmindful of the old league between their King, themselves, and him, and is carefully pondering ways and means of helping them. But bearing in mind the dangers of the road, and dreading the risks which sometimes chance to letters, he has given his views by word of mouth to W[illiam] bishop of St Andrews, for whom he asks full credence. St Germain en Laye, 6th April.

PAGE 331 — *Shortly before 28 April 1302*

Attestation that Patrick Trumpe le fiz came to the K.'s peace in company with the Earl of Carrick, whose tenant he is; and he and his 'aunte Maulde de Carrigg,' who also came to the K.'s peace, claim right to land in the manor of Levington in Cumberland which has fallen to them by the death of Dame Sarre de Paveley who held it in dower; and praying that the K. would grant them the land at the request of...

★ *Jedburgh.*

Robert had obviously returned to Edward's peace shortly before this, possibly before the letter from Philip of France (above). His change of allegiance was probably a due to the success of the Scots, then fighting for the restoration of John I, which would not be in Robert's interest since it would greatly undermine his own chances of acquiring the Crown. The Scots had enjoyed considerable success for some time and the restoration of John was beginning to look like a real possibility. Although Robert had been active in the Balliol cause, the fact that he had not supported King John in the campaign of 1296, and of course his potential interest in gaining the throne for himself, would hardly have endeared him to a restored Balliol monarchy.

PAGE 331 – *28 April 1302*
The K. having of special favour granted to the tenants of his liege Robert de Brus earl of Carrick, their lands in England lately taken for their rebellion, commands his escheator to restore to Patrick de Trumpe and Matillidis de Carrick, two of their number, as attested by John de St John *senior*, their lands in Levyngton in Cumberland. Devizes.

PAGE 348 – *April 1303*
Galloway:– A letter close to the Earl of Carrick to come with all the men-at-arms he can. And from Carrick and Galloway, 1,000 men at his discretion.

PAGE 354 – *14 July 1303*
Letters patent of John Post, vallet of Sir John Buttetourte acknowledging receipt at Edinburgh, 14th July, anno xxxi, from Richard de Bremmesgrave from the K.'s store, for the use of Sir Robert de Brus earl of Carrick and the aforesaid Sir John, of a prest of their wages by the precept of Sir Aymer de Valence the K.'s lieutenant south of Forth, of 4 qrs wheat, and 18 qrs oats – one half to each.

PAGE 387 – *30 March 1304*
The K. to the Earl of Carrick. Credence for John Botetourte where he sends to him on business. Same to Sir John de St John, Sir John de Segrave, and Sir Robert de Clifford. St Andrews.

PAGE 388 – *4 April 1304*
Robert de Brus earl of Carrick, to Sir William de Hameltone. Begs him to command the K.'s escheators of Essex, Middelsex, and

Huntingdon, to take inquisitions without delay of his lands there on account of his father's death, 'who is with God'. For his love to do this quickly, as he wishes to go to the K. with the inquisitions and do homage. Done at Hatfeud in Essex, Saturday next after Easter.

Once more in King Edward's favour, Robert was, understandably, anxious to gain entry to the properties of his late father, who had been constantly in Edward's peace until his death.

PAGE 388 − *4 April 1304*
Robert de Brus earl of Carrick and lord of Annandale to the K. Informs him that he has been in London and in Essex where his lands lie, and is still there, endeavouring in every possible way to procure horses and armour for himself and his people, but 'on the faith and loyalty which he owes to God and the K.' assures him he has been quite unsuccessful in his attempts to borrow for the purpose, or get a penny of his rents. Wherefore he prays the K.'s pleasure in this emergency.

PAGE 390 − *15 April 1304*
Letter from the K. to the Earl of Carrick. Thanks him for sending his engines to Stirling, and asks him to forward the rod of the great engine if he possibly can, but will send to help him. Inverkethyn★.

The siege at Stirling was the final action of the pro-Balliol party, in fact the siege continued while the remaining Balliol supporters were negotiating a settlement with Edward. King Phillip of France had abandoned the Scots shortly before this as part of a peace settlement with England.

PAGE 400 − *25 May 1304*
Inquisitions into lands held by Earl of Carrick in England, totaling in excess of £200 p.a.

PAGE 403 − *14 June 1304*
The K. to Master William de Grenefeld his chancellor. As Robert de Brus earl of Carrick, son and heir of Robert de Brus deceased, has done homage and fealty, he commands letters under the Great Seal to be issued according to law and custom. Stirling.

★ *Inverkeithing, Fife*

PAGE 403 – *17 June 1304*

The K. commands that diligent search be made in the rolls and 'remembrances' of Exchequer for all debts due there by Robert de Brus earl of Carrick or his ancestors, and meanwhile that all these be respited. Stirling. [A certificate from Exchequer follows, dated York 8th July, that he owed debts of his ancestors: 518*l.* 5s 8d.]

How such a large debt was accrued is unclear; however there are several documents relating to loans at the English Exchequer to Robert, his father and grandfather. None of them are particularly large, and the outstanding debt may include 'relief' due on properties on account of the death of Robert I's father.

PAGE 411 – *31 August 1304*

Inquisition [under writ dated Linlithgow 12 of same month, commanding inquiry as to the privileges claimed by Robert de Brus earl of Carrick in Annandale, and that the jury be composed of men of the counties of Roxburgh and Dumfries] made at Dumfries on Monday next after the Decollation of St John Baptist in the K.'s 32nd year, before Mathew de Redeman and John de Luscy, by Richard le Mareschal, Mathew del Ecles, Dovenald fitz Cane, Fergous le Mareschal, Roland le Mareschal, Henry de Mondevyl, Dovenald Cambel, Walter de Twynham, knights; Michael Macgethe, Patrick Magylboythyn, Gilbert Macmonhathe, Cuthbert M'Cane, Walter Danande(?), Walter de Comestone, Thomas de Kyrkconevel, Thomas de Arbygelande, Hugh de Ur, Adam de Fauhope, Thomas Belle, Gy de Denhom, John de Hederstone, Richard del Fleckes, William de Fausyde, Peter de Hessewel, and John Aliores(?) jurors; who find that the Earl of Carrick has this liberty, viz', that no sheriff of Dumfries or other servant of the K. or his ancestors may enter the bounds of Annandale to make attachments, summonses, or distraints, nor have they done so for time beyond memory; but that the K. may choose a coroner from one of the Earl's homagers in Annandale, and issue writs to him direct, who shall represent and answer to the K. and his justices of Lothian at Dumfries; that the earl has the liberties by the 'title of antiquity' viz., from the time of William K. of Scotland and all his successors uninterruptedly to this day. They append their seals.

PAGE 421 — *26 October 1304*

The K. to master William de Grenefeld his chancellor. Sends him by the bearer an inquisition lately made regarding certain franchises and customs claimed by Robert de Brus earl of Carrick, in Annandale, commanding him and the rest of the Council to consider carefully the points and advise him thereon. Brustwyk.

On 6th November thereafter the K. encloses to the treasurer and Chancellor a petition by the Earl of Carrick on same subject, for consideration by the Council.

PAGE 446 — *Shortly before 1 April 1305*

Petition by Robert de Brus earl of Carrick, that the K. would give him the lands which Sir Ingram de Umfraville held in Carrick by grant of Sir John de St John after he came to the K.'s peace (and have again been taken in the K.'s hand), on the same terms as Sir John made to the earl in presence of many good people.

(Endorsed) 'Granted, except as to *demesnes*.'

The earl also prays an order on the Chamberlain of Scotland to allow him his expenses laid out on the castle and bailiary of Ayr.

(Endorsed) The K.'s pleasure is that he account to the Chamberlain who will pay him from the issues* of Scotland.

PAGE 446 — *1 April 1305*

The K. to John de Sandale chamberlain of Scotland. Wishing that his liege Robert de Brus earl of Carrick, should account for the time when he had the custody of the Castle of Ayr, and the sheriffdoms of Ayr and Lanark, he commands the Chamberlain and James de Dalilege to audit the compotus, and allow the earl his expenses as ascertained, out of the issues of Scotland. Westminster.

PAGE 459 — *Shortly after 15 September 1305*

The Earl of Carrick to place Kildrummy castle in the keeping of one for whom he shall answer.

A great deal has been made of this document by both Scottish and English historians who have suggested that Edward was doubtful of the loyalty of Robert.

---

* *issues — the rents and other income due to the Crown*

The phrase 'one for whom he shall answer' is in fact fairly common in instruc-tions of this nature, indeed it was used in an order to Aymer de Valence, Edward's cousin and trusted lieutenant for many years.

PAGE 462 – *26 October 1305*
Duncan de Ferendragh keeper of the forest of Buthyn is commanded to give John Comyn earl of Buchan, 6 hinds, and 25 oaks fit for timber. Westminster.

Robert de Brus earl of Carrick, keeper of the forest of Laundmorgun, is commanded to give John de Spauyding canon of Elgin, 20 oaks fit for timber.

The said Robert keeper of the forest of Kintorre is commanded to give the said Earl of Buchan 6 hinds, and 25 oaks fit for timber. Westminster.

PAGE 465 – *2 December 1305*
The K. to William de Grenefeld his chancellor. Having granted to his vallet Thomas de Umfraville the marriage of Alianora widow of Robert de Brus, a tenant in chief, he commands letters to be issued under the Great seal in his favour. Brustwick.

PAGE 468 – *1302-05*
Robert de Brus earl of Carrick and lord of Annandale asks a protection and respite of debts for John baron of Graystoc, who is going with him to Scotland in the K.'s service.

PAGE 471 – *8 February 1306*
The K. to the Treasurer and Barons of Exchequer. As the late Robert de Brus, formerly earl of Carrick, had his service with the K.'s army in Wales in the 5th and 10th years for one knight, as appears by inspection of the rolls of the marschalcy, he commands them to discharge Robert de Brus his son and heir, of the *scutage*★. Fromptone.

PAGE 473 – *10 April 1306*
Charter by the K. for his good service, to Humphrey de Bohun earl of Hereford and Essex, and Elizabeth his wife, the King's daughter, of the

★ scutage, *a payment in lieu of military service*

castle at Lochmaben, and all the lands of Robert de Brus formerly earl of Carrick, in Annandale, escheated to the K. for his felony in seditiously and treacherously slaying John Comyn of Badenaghe⋆ before the High Altar of the church of the Friars Minors of Dumfries, and thus committing sacrilege; to be held by them and the heirs of their bodies under the kings of England; and failing such issue to revert to the K. and his successors.

PAGE 474 − *15 April 1306*

The K. to John de Sandale chamberlain of Scotland. Having appointed Aymer de Valence his lieutenant and captain of the forces at Berwick-on-Tweed, to put down Robert de Brus, late earl of Carrick and his rebel accomplices, he commands that their pay run from the date when the horses of Aymer and his men are valued⋆⋆ by the Chamberlain, and meanwhile they shall receive from the Wardrobe on account, viz., Aymer 200*l.*; Henry de Grey, 50 marks; William le Latimer, 50*l.*; William la Zusche, 20 marks; Aymer la Zusche, 10*l.*; Richard Lovel, 10 marks; and Henry de Beaumont, 50 marks; to be afterwards deducted from their pay. Winchester.

Similar writ for Henry de Percy lieutenant and captain at Carlisle, 100 marks; Robert de Clifford, 100*l.*; Robert de Felton, 20 marks; John de St John, 50 marks; Thomas Paynel, 10*l.*

PAGE 475 − *1 May 1306*

The K. commits the lands in Totenham Middlesex, which were Robert de Brus's late earl of Carrick, to Walter de Bedewynde from Easter last, during his pleasure, for the rent of 12*l.* payable half yearly. *Teste*, the Treasurer.

Unsurprisingly, since he had by this time had himself installed as king (Scottish kings were not 'anointed' until the coronation of David II, Robert's successor) Robert was forfeited as a traitor and rebel.

PAGE 477 − *26 May 1306*

The K., for his good service, grants to Robert de Clifford and his heirs

⋆ *Badenoch*
⋆⋆ *It was standard practice for English kings to guarantee reimbursement for the horses of men-at-arms lost in wartime. Obviously these horses had to be valued to prevent fraud*

the manor of Hert in the bishopric of Durham, forfeited by Robert de Brus, late earl of Carrick, for his felony, rebellion, and sacrilege, and treacherous slaughter of John Comyn of Badenaghe, before the High Altar of the church of the Friars Minors of Dumfries; saving to the church of St Cuthbert of Durham and the bishop, their right, if any. Westminster.

PAGE 478 – *12 June 1306*

The K. to Aymer de Valence. Is well pleased to hear by his letter that he has burned Sir Simon Fraser's lands in Selkirk forest. Commands him to do the same to all enemies on his march, including those who turned against him in his war of the Earl of Carrick, and have since come to his peace as enemies and not been guaranteed; and to burn, destroy, and waste their houses, lands, and goods in such wise, that Sir Simon and others may have no refuge with them as heretofore. But to honour the loyal and spare them and their houses and goods.

The possession of Scotland was of little value to Edward if he could not draw the income due to the Scottish Crown so it was imperative that he offer 'good lordship' – stability and security – to those Scots in his peace in order to keep their support. Many Scots were prepared to accept Edward's rule as long as they could enjoy their properties in peace and many who had fought for the Balliol dynasty were opposed to Robert's usurpation of the crown.

PAGE 479 – *16 June 1306*

The K. to Aymer de Valence. Is greatly pleased with his good news from Scotland, and desires him to thank those with him for their exertions in his service and urge them so to continue. Hears by the letters of Sir Henry de Beaumont and Sir Alexander de Abernethy to John de Sandale the chamberlain of Scotland, that the Bishop of Glasgow is captured, at which he is almost as much pleased as if it had been the Earl of Carrick. Commands him instantly to send the Bishop well guarded to Berwick, till the K. gives orders about him, 'having no regard to his estate of prelate or clerk'. To do the same if he captures the Bishop of St Andrews, and above all to beware of treason and surprise by the enemy, and send news as often as he can. As to his request on behalf of Sir Alexander Cheveroill and Sir Giles D'Argentan for the lands of Sir Michel de Wymes and Sir David his son, he has as yet granted no lands except the earldom of Levenax★ to [Sir John de] Menetethe, for whom he has ordered the Chancellor and Chamberlain to prepare a charter, as one to whom he is much beholden for his good service, as Sir Aymer tells him, and he hears from others; and commands Sir Aymer to give him *seisin*. The request of Sir Alexander and Sir Giles is placed among the memoranda in the Wardrobe till he comes to Scotland, as others are, when all will be considered. St Albans. Under the Privy seal, 16th June, in the 34th year.

PAGE 480 − *28 June 1306*
The K. to Aymer de Valence. Referring to his orders to put to death all enemies and rebels already or hereafter taken, commands him, if he takes the Earls of Carrick, Athol, and Sir Simon Fraser, to see them safely guarded till he declares his pleasure on their fate. Stoke Goldington. Under the Privy seal, 28th June, in 34th year.

PAGE 486 − *4 August 1306*
John de Seton − taken in Richard Siward's castle of Tibbers, which he (John) was holding against the K. for Robert de Brus a traitor, and for aiding said Robert in killing John Comyn in the church of the Friars Minors of Dumfries, '*nequiter et contempnabiliter*' in contempt of God and most Holy Church, and against the K.'s peace, on Thursday next before 'Carneprevyum' this year; and likewise on same day at the capture of said Richard's person, then the K.'s sheriff of the county of Dumfries and constable of the castle, and at the capture of said castle, with said Robert − appeared before the justices, and these charges being sufficiently notorious and manifest to the K. and his court, he was sentenced to be drawn and hanged as above. No lands or chattels.

The said Bernard [de Mouhaut] − for being in the conflict between Aymer de Valence the K.'s lieutenant in Scotland, and Robert de Brus, on Sunday next after Midsummer day this year, and bearing arms against the K., fighting in the field between the town of St John of Perth and the town of Meffen *(Methven)*, and feloniously and wickedly slaying some of the K.'s liegemen there, and taken on the field, and slaying the aforesaid Roger de Tany the K.'s vallet in Selkirk forest, and burning and destroying churches in Scotland −

★ *Lennox*

appeared, and was also sentenced to be drawn and hanged. No lands or chattels.

The remainder of the prisoners, charged with killing the K.'s lieges at the said battle under Robert de Brus, and taken on the field, were all condemned to be hanged.

Inquisition being made as to their lands and chattels, it was found that none had any in England except John de Somerville, who had 100s of land in Hedgly in Northumberland, taken in the K.'s hand as a forfeit of war. The Chancellor of Scotland to be commanded as to his and the others lands there, which are to be taken in the K.'s hand, and the Chamberlain to be certified in due form.

In the early stages of the war several prisoners were executed, including Robert's brothers and close associates like Sir Christopher Seton, husband of Robert's sister Cristiana. In due course the growing success of the Scots inevitably meant that they in turn took prisoners; Englishmen and Scots in the allegiance of Edward II. The high numbers of those prisoners, and perhaps more importantly their high status, eventually forced the English to extend the normal practices of parole, exchange and ransom to the Scots. This in itself would have had a beneficial effect on the prestige of King Robert and a detrimental effect on the authority of Edward II. The exchange of prisoners and/or money implied a certain degree of recognition on the part of the English.

PAGE 487 – *9 August 1306*
Notarial instrument attesting that on 9th August 1306, William bishop of St Andrews acknowledged the verity of the following documents exhibited to him by Sirs John de Sandale, Robert de Cotingham, and John de Wincop(?)...

1 his oath of fealty to the K. of England, dated at Stirling, 4th May 1304, under his seal in red wax [recited at length].

2 his confederacy with Robert de Brus earl of Carrick, at Cambuskenneth on St Barnabas day same year, under seal [also recited].

3 Being also interrogated why he concealed the said confederacy with Robert de Brus on the day when he was admitted of the King's Council at Schene near Kingeston, in violation of his oath? He replied, that he had entirely forgotten that league, and therefore did not mention it.

4 Being asked by Sir John de Sandale why he, a trusted councillor of the K. of England, hastened to cross the Forth to Robert de Brus when

he was crowned? He replied, that he went to see him on account of grievous threats against his person and substance, and for no other reason; and now was heartily sorry, for he saw he had lost all.

5   Being asked by Sir Robert de Cotingham why he, so trusted by the K. as to have charge of the person of Andrew, son and heir of Sir James the Steward of Scotland, delivered him to Robert de Brus after the K. had commanded his return? Denied this.

6   He admitted that he had communicated Mass to Robert de Brus after Sir John Comyn's murder, because he, being in pontificals on Palm Sunday, the third day after the coronation, had done fealty for his temporalities and sworn allegiance on the Evangels. Done at Newcastle-on-Tyne in the Bishop's chamber there, before Sir John de Schefeld [and others], and Master John de Heselartone clerk, public imperial notary. Attested by Andrew de Tang clerk of York, notary public.

PAGE 492 — *28 September 1306*
Compotus of Walter of Gloucester the K.'s escheator *citra* Trent, from Michaelmas at the close of the 33rd year, to same date at the close of the 34th year.

The lands of Robert de Brus. Essex:– He accounts for 75*l*. 10s 9 ½d of the rents and issues of two parts of the manor of Writele which were Robert de Brus's earl of Carrick, a Scotsman and traitor to the K., from 9th February in the 34th year, on which day they fell to the K.'s hand by forfeiture of said Robert, till Michaelmas thereafter, when the K. leased them to Master Richard de Abyndone by his writ; and for 8*l*. 16s ½d for 6 qrs 1 bushel of meslin, 2qrs of rye, 7qrs 1 bushel of oats, 11 avers and 8 oxen of said Robert's found on the manor, and then sold as in the roll 'de particulis' delivered to the Treasury; and for 44*l*. 2s 9d of the crop of 294 acres and 1 rood of wheat and rye in said manor, sown by Robert before the seizure, and sold as aforesaid. And for 35*l*. 6s 1½d of rents and issues of the manor of Badewe forfeited as above, from the above date till Michaelmas aforesaid, when the manor and park were delivered to the K.'s writ to William de Hameltone in lease for 7 years; and for 13*l*. 16s 6½d for 4 qrs 7 bushels rye, 5 avers and 3 oxen found there; and the crop of 78 acres sown with rye there by Robert, sold in gross as in said roll. And for 57*l*. 11s 7d of rents and issues of the manor of Hatfeld forfeited as above, from the aforesaid date till Michaelmas, when the manor and half hundred except the dower of Alienora, widow of Robert de Brus, father of said Robert), were delivered in lease by the K.'s writ to the Prior of Hatfeld; and for 11*l*. 19s 2d for 9½ qrs of wheat, 1qr 2 bushels peas, 31 qrs 6 bushels of oats, 1qr 2 bushels of drowe★ 10 avers, 6 oxen of Robert's found there; and for 20*l*. of all kinds of winter crops sown by Robert, sold in gross.

Middlesex:– For two parts of the manor of Tottenham forfeited from the aforesaid 9th February till Easter thereafter, till they were delivered to the keeping of Walter de Bedewynde during the K.'s pleasure, by writ dated 1st May. No response, as there were no issues for said period.

Bedford:– For 32*l*. 13s 1d, rents and issues of the third part of the manor of Kemestone forfeited, from the said 9th February till Michaelmas there-after, when it was forfeited to Roger de Hegham for 7 years by the K.'s writ; and for 13*l*. 14s 8d for 5 avers and 13 oxen of Robert's found there; with the crop of 77½ acres of wheat, and 4½ acres of rye sown by him.

Huntingdon:– And for 9*l*. 7s 1d rents and issues of 2 parts of the manor of Caldecote, forfeited, for the aforesaid period; and for 75s 9d for 3 workhorses and 2 oxen of Robert's found there, and the crop of 17½ acres wheat sown by him, sold in gross – and 37s 9d of a rent in the vill of Huntingdon forfeited, for the terms of Easter and Michaelmas.

PAGE 494 – 20 October 1306

Letters patent by the K. granting to Humphrey de Bohun earl of Hereford and Essex, the forfeitures of the lands of all the rebels who held of Robert de Brus the King's enemy, of the castle of Lochmaben and Valley of Annan, on the day when he treacherously slew John Comyn, to hold to the Earl and his heirs for ever. Lanercost.

PAGE 496 – 24 November 1306

The K. sends to Walter bishop of Chester, the Treasurer, Malcolm de Innerpeffrei knight, who at the time of this last 'riote' of the Scots was the K.'s sheriff of Clakmanan and Auchterarder, but nevertheless was one of the first to join Sir Robert de Brus, and wickedly abetted the earls of Menteth and Strathern in aiding said Robert; also fought against the K. at the battle of Seint Johan de Perth, and has done all the damage he could; commanding that he be secured in some strong castle, not in irons, but body for body. Lanercost. Under the Privy seal.

★ *drag*

Whereon said Malcolm was at once delivered to the constable of the Tower of London, on 7th December.

Another writ follows regarding Sir Malcolm's two horses, which the K. permits him to make profit of at pleasure.

PAGE 497 — (?) November 1306

The memorial of Malise earl of Stratherne to the K. and Council, showing that he was compelled to join Robert de Brus through fear of his life.

It is perfectly possible that this is an agreed fiction between the earl and King Edward to 'explain' the earl's change of allegiance.

PAGE 502 — 29 January 1307

The K. to the Treasurer of Ireland. Having lately commanded Hugh Byset with as many well manned vessels as he can procure, to come to the Isles on the Scottish coast and join John de Menetethe in putting down Robert de Brus and his accomplices lurking there, and destroying their retreat, he commands the Treasurer to give every aid to High in equipping the fleet with the utmost dispatch, and to pay the wages of himself and his crews for 40 days from his setting sail. Sends William de Ponton to aid in and supervise the expedition. Lanercost.

PAGE 504 — 1 February 1307

The K. commands William de Mulcastre, sheriff of Cumberland, and James de Dalileye, to collect all the vessels and empty barges at Skinburness, Whitehaven, Workington, and elsewhere on that sea coast, victual and provide them with stout crews, and dispatch them towards Ayr in pursuit of Robert de Brus and his abettors, and destroy his retreat. They are to see to this personally. Lanercost.

The K. commands his lieges to give every aid to William le Getur, who with part of the fleet is in search of Robert de Brus; and if they can by keeping watch, arrest the persons of Robert or his abettors, the K. will be greatly bound to them.

PAGE 506 — 20 February 1307

The K. for a fine, pardons Adam de Middeltone his trespass in acquiring a *vaccary* in Heselspryngge in Cumberland from the late Cristiana de Brus, a tenant *in capite*, and demising the same to her for life without license, and confirms it to him and his heirs. Lanercost.

PAGE 507 – (?) *March 1307*

Ordinances by the K. and Council for better assuring the peace of Scotland.

Agreed that the Guardian take order as to trade(?) in burghs and towns... and the justices errant on their eyres be empowered to receive rebels desirous to come to the King's peace; and malefactors guilty of capital offences to be taken wherever they live by the people of the country; if not, that 'the hue and cry by horn be raised against them', and pursuit made till they submit or are taken dead or alive... The Guardian to make strict search regarding receivers of such attainted persons. The K. and Council order that all present at the death of Sir john Comyn, or of counsel and assent thereto, shall be drawn and hanged. Those... found in Scotland without the King's permission, or their resetters, shall be hanged or their heads cut off. All rebels in the war previous to the battle of Methven, or in the battle, or after, and who surrender, shall be sent to such prisons as the K. orders, and not released till the King's pleasure is taken. Those of Robert de Brus's party, or who advised in any way the rising against the King, by preaching to the people, are to be arrested, whether clerks or laymen, and imprisoned till the King's pleasure is known. The poor commons of Scotland, who have been forced to rise against the King in this war, shall be held to ransom as the Guardian shall see their offences require. This ordinance is in three parts, one to remain in the Wardrobe another with the Bishop of Chester the treasurer, and another with Sir Robert de la Warde seneschal of the Household.

(Endorsed) Lordonance... a Lanrecost par le Roi et son consail 'pour mielz asseurer e garder la terre Descoce, c., en lan &c xxxv.'

PAGE 508 – *13 March 1307*

The King to Aymer de Valence, guardian and his lieutenant in Scotland. As some persons, as he understands, interpret his late ordinance for settling Scotland as too harsh and rigorous, which was not his intention, he commands him to proclaim throughout Scotland that all who have been compelled by the abettors of Robert de Brus to rise against the K. in war, or to reset Robert innocently by his sudden coming among them, shall be quit of all punishment therefore. Carlisle. Similar to James de Dalylegh, escheator south of the Forth; to John de Westone, escheator north of the Forth; the coroner of Annandale; the sheriffs of Wigton, Roxburgh, Berwick, Edinburgh, Dumfries, Invernairn, Haddington, Linlithgow, Forres, Ughterardre*, Dumbarton, Kyncardyn, Deyngeval, Banf, Lanark, Elgin, Stirling, Clacmanan, Fife, Forfar, Perth, Inverness, Aberdeen, Crombathy, Ayr

Effectively, Edward was offering an amnesty to Scots who would abandon the cause of Robert I.

PAGE 511 — *12 February to 3 May 1307*
To same [Sir James de Dalileghe] for the wages of Sir John de Butetourte captain of divers knights, sergeants-at-arms, esquires, soldiers, and foot, in the valley of Nith, pursuing the said Robert [de Brus] and his accomplices the K.'s enemies, between 5th March and 23rd April [in all 1 baneret, 19 knights and 51 esquires. Besides the knights above named, there are Sirs Thomas de Bykenore, John le Strange, Edmon Foliot, John Leware, Edmund de Wylington, Warin de Bassingburne, pay *ut supra*]; and 7 Welsh archers of the K.'s in Sir John's company for 48 days. Total, 170*l* 11s.

PAGE 513 — *15 May 1307*
To some high official (*unknown*). The writer gives him the news of his neighbourhood. He hears that Sir Robert de Brus never had the good will of his own followers or the people at large or even half of them so much with them as now; and it now first appears that he has right, and God is openly for him, as he has destroyed all the K.'s power both among the English and the Scots, and the English force is in retreat to its own country not to return. And they firmly believe by the encouragement of the false preachers who come from the host that Sir Robert de Brus will now have his will. And these preachers are such as have been attached before the Guardian and the justices as abettors of war, and are at present freed on *mainprise* and carry themselves worse than before, boasting in their malice and deceiving the people thus by their false '*prechement*'. For he believes assuredly, as he hears

---

* Auchterarder, Fife. A very small sheriffdom, later incorporated into Fife.

from Sir Renaud de Chien, Sir Doncan de Ferendrauth, and Sir Gilbert de Glenkerni, and others who watch the peace both beyond and on this side of the Mountains, that if Sir Robert de Brus can escape any way 'saun dreytes', or towards the parts of the Roos *(Ros)*; he will find them all ready at his will more entirely than ever, unless the K. will be pleased to send more men-at-arms to these parts; for there are many people living well and loyally at his faith provided the English are in power, otherwise they see that they must be at the enemies will through default of the K. and his Council, as they say. And it would be a deadly sin to leave them so without protection among enemies. And may it please God to keep the K.'s life, for 'when we lose him, which God forbid' (say they openly), all must be on one side, or they must die or leave the country with all those who love the K., if other counsel and aid be not sent them. For these preachers have told them that they have found a prophecy of Merlin, how after the death of 'le Roi Coueytous'* the Scottish people and the Bretons shall league together, and have the sovereign hand and their will, and live together in accord till the end of the world. Begs his correspondent's pleasure in this and all other matters; and God keep him. Written at Forfar, 15th May.

Given the poor fortune of Robert I in the first few months of his campaign for the crown it is remarkable that – in the opinion of these officers at least – he enjoyed as much support in an area where there was relatively little in the way of Bruce lands. It would not be unreasonable to see this letter as an indication that the Edwardian administration was less than popular in the north-eastern parts of Lowland Scotland. Edward was by this time an old man who could not be expected to live much longer.

PAGE 523 – *July/August 1307*
Elizabeth de Brus** to the K. Complains that though he had commanded his bailiffs of Holderness to see herself and attendants honourably sustained, yet they neither furnish attire for her person or head, nor a bed, nor furniture of her chamber, saving on a robe of three 'garnementz' yearly, and for her servants one robe each for everything.

* 'the covetous King'
** *Elizabeth, daughter of the Earl of Ulster and the second wife of Robert I had been captured at Tain in 1306.*

Prays the K. to order amendment of her condition, and that her servants be paid for their labour, that she not be neglected; or that she may have a yearly sum allowed by the K. for her sustenance.

(Addressed) 'A Nostre Seigneur le Roi par Elizabeth de Brus.'

PAGE 1 – 5 Aug 1307
Letters patent by Hunfrai de Bohun earl of Hereford and Essex and constable of England, and Elizabeth his 'Compaigne', appointing Monsire William Poucy or Sire Aundreu de Kynbauton their constable of Plesitz, as attorneys to receive seisin of the manors of Wrytele, Badewe, Hatfeud, and Brounesho, and all other lands of Robert de Brus in Essex, which the K. has given them by charter. Append their seals. Done at Dumfries 5th August 1 Edw. II.

PAGE 9 – 22 June 1308
The K. having ordered that Elizabeth de Brus wife of Robert de Brus, late earl of Carrick, shall change her residence, commands the bailiff of Brustwyck to deliver her with her retinue and baggage by his vallet John de Bentelee to be conducted where the K. has instructed him. Marlborough.

PAGE 16 – After 11 March 1309
John of Argyll to the K. received his letters on 11th March for the tenor of which he greatly thanks 'his Majesty'. He was on sick-bed at their reaching him, and had been for half a year. Robert de Brus had approached his territories with 10,000 or 15,000 men, it was said, both by land and sea. He had no more than 800 to oppose him, 500 of these being in his pay to keep his borders, and the barons of Argyll gave him no aid. Yet, though he and his were few in respect of his power, Robert de Brus had asked a truce from him, which he granted for a short space, and received the like, till the K. sends him succours. He hears that Robert, when he came, was boasting saying that the writer had come to his peace at the report that many others would rise in his aid, which God and the writer know is not true. Should the K. hear this from others, he is not to believe it, for he is and will ever be ready to serve him to the utmost of his power. He has three castles to guard, and a lake 24 leagues long on which he has vessels properly manned, but is not sure of his neighbours.

So soon as the K. or his power arrives, he will be ready with lands, ships and others to aid him, if sickness does not prevent him; but if it unfortunately so chances, he will send his son with his forces to the K.

This letter is indicative of the problems facing those Scots who opposed the Bruce party. It is hardly credible that Robert I should be conducting operations with anything approaching 10,000 men let alone 15,000, however it is perfectly plausible that his armed strength should surpass the power of one magnate, especially if the support of the local baronage was not forthcoming. In all likelihood a truce was arranged, but it does seem rather more likely that the truce was offered by Robert to John rather than the other way around.

PAGE 19 – *21 August 1309*
Commission to Richard de Burgo earl of Ulster, to treat in the K.'s name with Robert de Brus respecting peace. Langley.

A settlement of the Scottish war was desirable to Edward for many reasons, but the terms on which he sought peace were not realistic from the point of view of Robert I. Edward's offers of peace were essentially based on 'pardons' for Robert and his supporters in exchange for their support of his kingship. Edward was in an impossible situation; his power was not sufficient to beat the Scots, but he could not abandon his supporters in Scotland or accept the damage to his prestige incurred by acceding to Robert's demands. Edward was not a particularly intelligent or realistic man; even after the defeat at Bannockburn his offers of peace were still based on acceptance of his lordship.

PAGE 44 – *13 June 1311*
The Bailiffs, good men, and community of the vill of Setone to the K. They declare their inability to join the town of Sydemuthe in providing two well-armed vessels to be sent to the port of Wolrikesford near Knaefergus in Ulster by the morrow of St John Baptist next, to sail with the fleet under John of Argyll the K.'s admiral, against the rebel Robert de Brus, as they have no vessel in their port, or money to fit one out. Append their seal at Seton on Sunday next after Holy Trinity, 4th year.

The burdens of military service could be quite onerous and were, almost inevitably, unwelcome both to those who had to serve in the field and to those who had to find the men — and in this case, ships — required. The reasons offered by the community of Seton may have been perfectly valid, but kings tended to be suspicious of excuses. King Edward's reaction to this particular petition does not seem to have survived.

PAGE 46 – 15 *October 1311*

Mandate by the K. to allow Richard de Horslee sheriff of Northumberland 12*l*. 12s paid to Adam of Konyngham, William Dirland, and David del Gley, prisoners in Newcastle, from 6th February 1309–10 till 24th June 1311 – 504 days at 2d each; 8s 9d to Fergus de Ardrossan, prisoner there, from 2nd to 25th January 1310–11 – 25 days, when liberated, at 3d a day; and 3 days after, going to the K. at Berwick-on-Tweed at 4d and his equipage; 101s 6d to William Giffard, Adam Pykard, and Gillecrist de Coquina, prisoners there, from 2nd January last till 24th June – 174 days, William at 3d and the two others at 2d daily; 48s 8d to Mary de Brus sister of Robert de Brus, prisoner, from 29th January till 24th June last – 146 days at 4d a day; and 48s to Sir William de Moref knight, prisoner there, from 1st February till Midsummer last – 144 days at 4d a day. Wyndsor.

As a general rule prisoners of war could expect to receive an allowance for their keep. The 4d per day allowed to Mary Bruce was slightly better than the 3d per day usually allowed for captive knights.

PAGE 49 – 6 *February 1312*

The K. commands the constable of Windsor castle to receive Elizabeth wife of Robert de Brus and her retinue, providing sufficient houses to accommodate them. John de Benteleye to be in attendance on her as hitherto. York.

As the daughter of Richard de Burgh, earl of Ulster and a close associate of the late king (Edward I) Elizabeth could hardly be kept in harsh confinement, and in any case, the Scots were, by this time, taking plenty of prisoners themselves and could no longer be denied the normal practices of prisoner exchanges and ransoms. Ill treatment of Scots in English hands might well lead to similar treatment of English people in captivity in Scotland.

PAGE 52 – *15 March 1312*
The K. commands the constable of Corfe castle to deliver William de Murreff of Sandford knight, a prisoner there, to Adam de Haliburton – lately made prisoner in Scotland by Robert de Brus, who demands a ransom of 400 marks for him – that he may be applied in aid of such ransom. York.

PAGE 55 – *14 July 1312*
[Anonymous] to the K. The writer says since he left him at York, Sir Robert de Brus had held a parliament at Ayr, and intended to send Sir Edward his brother, with the greater part of his forces, into England, while he himself attacked the castles of Dumfries, Buittle [Botyll], and Carlaveroc, remaining there, and sending his light troops to plunder the north for their support. The bearer will relate matters touching the K.'s dignity. Dunfres, 14th July.

PAGE 59 – *23 January 1313*
Allowed the clerk of the wardrobe 20 marks paid to Sir Adam Gordun knight of Scotland, by the hands of William Gurdun, his son, of his gift from the K. till otherwise provided; and 10*l.* paid to John de Bentle, for the expenses of Lady Elisabeth wife of Sir Robert de Brus, by Treasury precept; 28th January, 10 marks to Malise de Stratherne by his own hands, to account of his allowance from the K.

PAGE 63 – *1 July 1313*
Respite of 12*l.* paid to Elizabeth de Brus wife of Robert de Brus for expenses of herself and retinue for 12 weeks (6th year) at 20s a week... 6*l.* 16s 4d paid to William de Mouryue *(Moray)* knight, a Scottish prisoner in Corfe castle, from Pasch 4th year, till 15th March following, when liberated – 329 days at 4d a day; and 20s for his dress for same time.

PAGE 71 – *18 July 1314*
The K. commands the Prior of Sixhill to deliver Cristiana sister of Robert de Brus, widow of Christopher de Seton, to the sheriff of Lincoln to be brought to him at York. York.

The crushing defeat suffered by the English at Bannockburn did not bring the war to a close, but the many prisoners taken there forced Edward II to arrange an extensive prisoner exchange and to provide financial support for many of his supporters so that they could pay their ransoms.

PAGE 71 — *18 July 1314*

The K. orders that Robert bishop of Glasgow, Elizabeth wife of Robert de Brus, Donald de Mar, and other Scots in England, be brought to him at York. York.

PAGE 74 — *2 October 1314*

The K. sends Robert bishop of Glasgow, the Countess of Carrick wife of Robert de Brus, with his sister and daughter and Donald de Mar, to Carlisle castle, to be taken thence to a place arranged by the Earl of Essex and Hereford and the sheriff. York.

PAGE 81 — *26 April 1315*

Middlesex:– The K. commits to his clerk, Adam de Herewynton, all the forfeited lands of Robert de Brus in Tottenham, in lease from Easter last, during pleasure, paying 12*l.*, yearly at Exchequer. *Teste* the Treasurer.

PAGE 91 — *14 March 1316*

The K. commands the Chancellor to issue a commission in favour of Sir John de Castre of the same date as that appointing him warden of the castle and town of Carlisle, as he has been empowered to receive to the K.'s peace those people of Cumberland who have joined the Scots. Suleby.

Generations of historians, both Scottish and English, have written a great deal about Scottish lords in the service of English kings and in the main, they have chosen to see that service as evidence of the inconstant nature of the Scottish aristocracy and gentry. It is of course much more difficult to maintain patriotic sentiments if there is an enemy army on your doorstep. The communities of the north of England who sought 'the peace' of King Robert were not particularly disposed to, or amenable to, Scottish occupation; they were simply, like those Scots who had lived under Edwardian government in the preceding twenty years, accepting the inevitable.

PAGE 92 – *28 April 1316*
The K. authorises Master John Waleweyn and two others to give safe conducts to Robert de Brus and other Scots coming to England to treat for a truce. Westminster.

This Robert Bruce is not the king, but his illegitimate son, who would be killed at the battle of Dupplin Muir, 1332.

PAGE 93 – *28 April 1316*
Commission to Master John de Waleweyn and two others to treat with Robert de Brus and other Scots as to a peace or truce. Westminster.

PAGE 102 – *3 January 1317*
Warrant for letters in favour of Sir David de Betoigne, to whom the King has granted Robert de Brus's lands in Totenham, for the support of himself and children, he answering at Exchequer for the surplus beyond 10*l*. per annum. Clipston.

PAGE 107 – *17 June 1317*
Grant to David de Betoigne, for the support of himself and his children, of 12*l*. yearly at Exchequer, in place of the forfeited lands of Robert de Brus in Totenham, granted to him on 29th March last, afterwards given to another. Westminster.

PAGE 112 – *1317*
Petition to the K. that the Chancellor command the Abbot of Selby, collector of the late 10th and 12th penny per mark of church goods, granted for his Scottish war, to pay Roger Heiron 148*l*, for his horses lost at Stirling under '*billes*' sealed by the '*Chaumburlaynrye*' of Berwick.

In the absence of evidence to the contrary it seems reasonable to conclude that the horses in question were lost at Bannockburn – usually called the battle of Stirling. The various records normally kept of English armies in this period are generally assumed to have been lost in the aftermath of the battle, but this entry is an indication that the records were assembled at the time and possibly that some part of that record had survived to 1317. If the army horse rolls had been irretrievably lost in June 1314 Roger Heiron would not have been able to justify his claim for compensation.

PAGE 114 — *(?) June 1318*

The mayor and community of Hertilpolle shew the K. that Sir Robert de Brus has granted a truce to the whole bishopric of Durham except their town, which he intends to burn and destroy for their capturing a ship freighted with his '*armeours*' and victuals, and, as they are enclosing a great part of the town, and building a wall to the best of their power, they beg him to give them 100 marks owing him for victuals bought on their pier by one Robert de Musgrave, due at Easter next year.

(Endorsed) Let the money be assigned in aid of the work, and they must hurry it on, that the peril be anticipated.

In the years before Bannockburn King Robert had been able to force his ene-mies to accept truces on his terms. Since Edward was not in a position to protect his supporters in Scotland they had had to make whatever arrangements they could to preserve life and property. To a limited extent before summer 1314, and increasingly thereafter, Robert was able to impose a certain degree of lordship on the communities of northern England, even into Yorkshire due to Edward's inability to prevent Scottish incursions. King Robert, of course, hoped to enforce an acceptance of his kingship on Edward, via the truces and the blackmail paid by English communities, but those truces had an adverse effect on the prestige and authority of Edward II.

PAGE 121 — *26 April 1319*

Writ to the sheriff of Lancaster to obey as if it were the K. himself, Richard earl of Arundel, his lieutenant, sent to put down the Scots invasion, and aid him with the array of his county when required by the Earl or his deputies. Westminster.

PAGE 121 — *22 May 1319*

The advocate, echevins, consuls and community of Ypres to the K. In reply to his letters complaining that arms and provisions have been supplied to Robert de Brus and the insurgent Scots by some of their townsmen, they assure him that although they have no authority to restrain them from trade, which is the prerogative of their Count, they will use their utmost endeavours to dissuade them from holding any communication with the Scots. Given in 1319, Tuesday after Ascension Day.

PAGE 124 – *18 September 1319*

The K. to W. archbishop of York, and J. bishop of Ely, chancellor. Commands them instantly to raise the whole '*defensable*' foot of the county to attack the enemy, who have entered England, wherever found, and to proclaim that none will be excused muster on pain of life and limb. He has spies watching by day and night where they are drawing. Beleford.

Raising levies for the defence of the realm was the only form of active response that could be made to the Scots as long as Edward was not prepared to consider a political settlement. Unfortunately for the communities of northern England hurriedly assembled conscripts were not an adequate response to the highly motivated forces of King Robert. A steady stream of defeats in the field did nothing to bolster confidence in Edward or his lieutenants. In the 1290s and early 1300s the Scots had discovered that levied farmers were no match for trained, disciplined, and above all, confident soldiers – in the 1310s and 1320s the English learned the same lessons.

PAGE 129 – *22 December 1319*

[Fragment of] document [by Robert de Brus] declaring the conditions of the truce concluded between the Bishop of Ely chancellor, Aymer de Valence earl of Pembroke and Bartholomew de Badelesmere steward of the household, on behalf of Edward II, and himself, for 2 years from St Thomas's day, referring to the surrender of Herbotel(?) castle before Michaelmas, the property of vessels that might chance to be wrecked on the Scottish coasts, and no new fortresses to be made within the sheriffdoms of Berwick, Roxburgh, or Dumfries. The Earl of Moray has sworn on the granter's soul to keep these conditions. Berwick-on-Tweed, 22nd December, 14th of his reign.

PAGE 131 – *20 January 1320*

The K. authorises (under certain circumstances), the redelivery to Robert de Brus, or destruction, of the castle of Herbottel, according to the conditions of the late truce with him. York.

The fact that Edward was obliged to even consider the loss of a castle in his own kingdom at the demand of King Robert was sufficiently damaging to his status and authority that he gave instructions that if the castle had to be demolished it should be done as secretly as possible.

PAGE 133 — *17 November 1320*
Safe conduct for certain persons coming from Robert de Brus to treat about peace. Westminster.

PAGE 134 — *11 December 1320*
The K. empowers the Archbishop of York to release from excommunication those Scots who shall be received to his peace by the Earl of Athol and others. Windsor.

Similar to the Bishop of Carlisle, and for such as shall be received by Andrew de Hartcla.

This was part of the process of 'rehabilitating' those Scottish nobles who had been involved in the de Soulis conspiracy and had survived its discovery. All the supporters of Robert had been excommunicated and that excommunication had to be lifted if the individuals concerned were to be accepted into Edward's peace. The de Soulis conspiracy of 1320 was an attempt to depose Robert I. Barbour suggests that de Soulis was to be king in his place, but de Soulis had no claim to the throne and in fact the intended replacement for King Robert was Edward Balliol, son of John I who had recently been received into the peace of Edward II. The conspiracy indicates that many Scots still viewed the Balliol family as the legitimate heirs to the crown despite the military triumphs of King Robert. It might be the case that there was a body of opinion in Scotland that believed there could be no permanent peace as long as Robert held the throne.

PAGE 134 — *28 December 1320*
The K. commands the Mayor and bailiffs of York to deliver John de Anand, William de Nesbet, Adam de Roule, Scotsmen, with some Flemings, Germans, and others, made prisoners in a wreck off Ledbrestone on the Yorkshire coast, in possession of three letters under Robert de Brus's seal of the *coket** of Berwick, to the sheriff of York. Marlborough.

The sheriff is commanded to liberate the Scotsmen and their goods under the provisions of the truce, and to retain the other prisoners. Marlborough.

---

* *The* coket *was the seal used to denote that duty had been paid on goods for export in a particular burgh.*

A truce might be in place, but Edward II refused to recognise the independence of the Scots in general and the authority of King Robert, nonetheless, some observance of the terms of the truce was necessary due to the military dominance of the Scots.

PAGE 136 – *12 January 1321*
Safe conduct for Sir John de Pilmor monk of Coupar, coming from Sir Robert de Brus to the K.Yeshampstede.

PAGE 136 – *19 January 1321*
Commission to W. archbishop of York, and others to treat for a peace with Robert de Brus. Westminster.

PAGE 136 – *26 January 1321*
Safe conduct by Robert [I] king of Scots, for the envoys of the K. of England to the number of 50 persons, of whatever state or condition, coming to Berwick-on-Tweed, or elsewhere within his kingdom, to treat with his Council and return – to last for a month after the instant Candlemas. Berwick-on-Tweed, 26th January, 15th year of his reign.

PAGE 137 – *20-24 February 1321*
On this day the Bishop of Hereford delivered in Exchequer eight bulls of Pope John XXII, the third of them the process against R. de Brus by the Cardinals, the fourth the citation of some Scottish bishops to the Roman Court, the fifth to the Prelates of England, excommunicating the invaders of England and their '*fautors*', the sixth directing the Archbishop of York, and the Bishops of Durham and Carlisle, to proclaim Robert de Brus excommunicated for the death of John Comyn; the remaining two directed to the Cardinals that they might proceed with the censures and sentences against Robert de Brus in England, notwithstanding their return to Rome. These last delivered to the keeper of the Privy seal, to be taken with the K. to France, on 24th February.

Edward may have lost the war in terms of actions in the field, but the political and diplomatic campaigning continued unabated. Throughout the conflict Edward's representatives in the courts of Europe generally and at the Curia in particular endeavoured to maintain that the Anglo-Scottish conflict was no more than a local rebellion against the lawful superior of Scotland rather than a

war between nations. The success of the Scots had forced Edward to effectively
(but tacitly) recognise the Scots as bona fide combatants, but the 'official line'
was still that the Scots were in a state of rebellion rather than conducting a war
between sovereign states.

PAGE 137 – *27 February 1321*

The K. empowers David earl of Athol, [and four others], to receive to
his peace a number of Scotsmen who came to England with Sir
Alexander de Moubray knight, a Scotsman, on the same conditions, if
they are of good repute and not claimants of English lands.
Westminster.

PAGE 138 – *25 August 1321*

The K. orders the castle of Herbotel to be destroyed, according to the
terms of the treaty with the Scots. Westminster.

PAGE 138 – *25 August 1321*

The K. orders the sheriff of Northumberland in person and others, to
assist in the destruction of Herbotel castle, and that it be done as
secretly as possible. Westminster.

PAGE 141 – *20 May 1322*

The K. appoints Sir Robert de Leyburne knight, Admiral of the fleet
on the western sea of Scotland, with power to receive the Scots to his
peace. York.

PAGE 141 – *3 July 1322*

The K. orders Andrew de Harcla earl of Carlisle to levy forces in
Cumberland, Westmorland, and Lancaster to repel the Scots. York.

PAGE 142 – *5 August 1322*

The K. sends the Bishop of Norwich the chancellor, a petition from
the burgesses of Lancaster, for his attention. Goseford.

(*Enclosure*) The burgesses of Lancaster shew the K. that by grant of
his '*besael*' K. John, they have common pasture and estovers in
Whernemor forest, i.e. dead wood for burning, and live wood for
building, as they need. That the Scots lately came and burned their
town and castle so entirely that nothing is left. And Sir John Travers the

K.'s warden in these parts, prevents them taking estovers to repair their burgages, and they pray remedy.

PAGE 144 – *17 September 1322*
The K. to the Archbishop of Canterbury. Tells him he is in good health, and has just returned from his expedition to Scotland as far as Edinburgh on the Scottish sea. Having taken the road on the sea coast to do more damage, he found neither 'man nor beast' and will winter on the March for its safety. Thanks him for his letters and his diligence in raising his people to oppose 'these evil Flemings'. As soon as he hears them he will send his navy to clear the seas. Begs him to send in all haste the money granted in aid of the Scottish war. Newcastle-on-Tyne, September 17. *(A draft.)*

PAGE 148 – *c.1322*
Petition [by the dwellers on the Marches] to the K. relating their dire sufferings for the last eight years and still, at the hands of the Scots, which have become unendurable, and nothing but the K.'s presence with the whole power of England will abate them, or they must leave the country. They have nothing but their naked bodies for his service. They ask that the commission to Andrew de Harcla warden of Carlisle, be changed, as it is quite insufficient for the defence of the Border. Assure the K. that it is useless to spend money on wardens of the March who are unable to keep down the enemy, and he must come himself with a strong force. Refer him to the bearer for news of the counties of Cumberland and Westmoreland. [No date.]

(Endorsed) The Council thinks that Sir Andrew de Harcla warden of Carlisle and neighbourhood, should be instructed to harass the enemy in every way, at the advice of the best men of the country.

Unable to maintain sufficient force in the north of England to deter the Scots, Edward could do little more than make encouraging noises to his subjects. His commission to Sir Andrew was undoubtedly well intentioned, but was hardly a realistic response to the military situation. Sir Andrew could – and did – harass the Scots in the hope of disrupting their operations, but he could hardly be expected to seize and retain the initiative against the Scots with the very limited resources at his disposal.

PAGE 148 – *19 January 1323*

Writ of Privy seal sending to the Treasurer and Barons, and others the K.'s Council at York, the transcript of an endenture between Andrew de Harcla earl of Carlisle and Robert de Brus, which appears to the K. fraught with great danger; wherefore he has ordered William le Latymer to remain in command of the forces at York for its safety. Stowe Park.

(Enclosure) Agreed between Sir Robert de Bruys on one part and the Earl of Carlisle on the other – (1) That each realm shall have its own national king; (2) that they shall aid him *(Brus)* to maintain Scotland against all its gainsayers; (3) in like manner the K. *(Brus)* and the Earl and adherents shall maintain the realm of England at the judgement *(dit)* of 12 persons sworn, or the majority *(6 elected by the K. and 6 by the Earl)*; and the great lords shall be bound to perform their decree in all points, to the common good of both realms. If the K. of England assents to these conditions within a year, and the K. of Scotland has his realm secured to him and his heirs, the latter will found an abbey in Scotland of 500 marks sterling rent, for the souls of those slain in war, and, moreover, within 10 years will pay 40,000 marks sterling, – 4,000 yearly. The K. of England shall also have the marriage of the K. of Scotland's heir male, as advised by the aforesaid 12 persons. If the Ks. agree, they shall not be bound to receive in either realm any one who has been against them, or to restore his lands, except of their free grace. The Earl of Morreve has sworn on the K. of Scotland's soul to maintain all who adhere to him, and make no peace unless they are included. The Earl of Carlisle has sworn in like manner.

Sir Andrew's initiative may have been based on a realistic appraisal of the political and military realities of the situation, but Edward could hardly be expected to allow his senior officers to make treaty arrangements with the enemy without his express permission and Sir Andrew's career was terminated by his execution for treason.

PAGE 149 – *21 March 1323*

Letter, Robert K. of Scotland, to Sir Henry de Sully chivaler, complaining that in the K. of England's letter, of which Sir Henry has sent him a transcript, he is not named a principal, but included with the least of his subjects. Will not agree to a truce on these terms; but if properly addressed, will do so willingly. Sends the transcript, which he cannot think he has read. Asks safe conduct for his envoys Sir Alexander de Seton and Sir William de Mountfichet knights, and Master Walter de Twynham clerk. Will not remain at Berwick beyond Wednesday in Easter week, so asks a speedy reply. Written at Berwick, 21st March, at the hour of *tierce*, in reply to his letter received the night before.

The identification of king with country and the inescapable fact that Robert had usurped the throne inevitably meant that a formal acknowledgement of his kingship was fundamental to Robert's conditions for a peace settlement. He was more than ready to offer reasonable terms to Edward, but not to compromise on questions of his status and authority.

PAGE 155 – *15 July 1324*
Safe conduct for William bishop of St Andrews, and Thomas Randolf earl of Moray, envoys of Robert de Brus for a final peace, with a retinue of 50 horsemen each. Porchester.

PAGE 155 – *15 July 1324*
Protection and safe conduct for Roger de Fauside, a Scotsman, and two horsemen, with their grooms, coming to England on his private affairs, but only for two turns, till Pentecost next. Porchester.

A state of war between England and Scotland did not obviate the necessity for those with interests in both countries to conduct their business whether private or commercial. Despite the repeated entreaties of King Edward trade between the business communities of both countries continued in a reduced and clandestine form throughout the series of conflicts from 1286 until the 'final peace' of 1328.

PAGE 155 – *23 September 1324*
Protection and safe conduct for six envoys (in addition to the Bishop of St Andrews and the Earl of Moray) coming from Robert de Brus to treat for peace. Porchester.

PAGE 157 – *1324*
Six poor women of Ripon shew the K. that their husbands are hostages in Scotland for the commune of Ripon, who, when the Scots lately

came there and would have burned the town, church, and franchise, made a fine to prevent them, delivering these hostages, till a day fixed, and swore on the saints to relieve them long before; but the commune and franchise now do nothing, suffering them to languish and die. The K. lately commanded the Sheriff of York to give relief, who could not, as Ripon is within franchise; and though the petitioners have long sued the Archbishop [of York], he does nothing. Wherefore they pray relief or their husbands will die in prison. [No date.]

(Endorsed) Let a formal letter be sent to the Archbishop of York lord of the liberty of Ripon, that, if the complaint is true, he compels the men of the town and liberty to have the prisoners released according to their agreement.

However much he may have resented it, the hard facts of the military situation during the 1320s forced Edward to accept the local truces extracted from English communities by Robert and his lieutenants. These arrangements were common enough throughout northern England that Edward had to pardon those who made such truces without his sanction. Wholesale forfeiture of those who entered Robert's peace would have further destabilised his authority.

PAGE 158 – *3 May 1325*
The K. permits Bernard de Brus to grant his manor of Conynton (which he holds *in capite* through the forfeiture of Robert de Brus) to Robert de Brus clerk, to be regranted by him to Bernard and Agnes his wife for life, with remainder to Bernard son of Bernard and the heirs of his body, whom failing, to the right heirs of Bernard *senior*. For a fine of 5 marks. Wynton.

PAGE 158 – *3 May 1325*
Similar grant to Bernard de Brus to enfeoff Bernard his son and Matillidis his wife in the manor of Exton, held of the K. *in capite* as of the Honour of Huntingdon, and the heirs of their bodies, whom failing to the right heirs of Bernard *(the father)*. For a fine of 15 marks. Wynton.

PAGE 167 – *26 June 1327*
The K. commands the sheriff of Salop to make diligent search for James Turmyn and others banded with him, who lately joined the

Scots with Dunald de Mar, a rebel, and have returned to the Welsh Marches, where they are plotting against the K., and put them in prison. Tudhou.

Similar to the Mayor of Shrewsbury.

Donald Earl of Mar had been brought up in England and seems to have had a genuine regard for Edward II. The deposition of Edward seems to have been the catalyst for Donald's defection to the Scots. Although there seems to have been some doubt as to the value of his new allegiance, Donald remained in the peace of the kings of Scotland until his death at the battle of Dupplin Muir in 1332.

PAGE 167 – *4 July 1327*
Anonymous letter to the K., addressed '*Trescher et tree amex Seignur et neveu*' [probably from the Earl Mareschal his uncle], telling him that 'this Friday' when the writer was going to bed, news was brought that the Scots were at Appelby, and he and his forces watched all night, looking out for them. Begs instructions, and to be excused joining him as ordered, this Saturday, for he must be on watch again to-night. If he hears of them, he will send out scouts on horseback to spy, and has ordered all the empty houses about, to be set on fire *(alumer)* to warn the people and the country. He will come if he please to order him.

PAGE 167 – *12 July 1327*
Indenture between Robert K. of Scotland and Henry de Maundeville seneschal of Ulster, whereby the K. grants a truce to the people of Ulster for a year, from St Peter's day in the 'Goule de Aust', for 100 '*cendres*' of wheat and 100 '*cendres*' of barley, Scottish measure, delivered free in the haven of Wlringfrith★, one half at Martinmas and the other at Whitsunday following. The Irish of Ulster who adhere to the Scottish K. being included in the truce. The seals of the K. and the said Henry appended. Glendouyn.

Despite the death of Edward Bruce and the defeat of his forces at the battle of Faughart King Robert was able to continue to exert his influence in Ireland sufficiently to have Irish people in his peace included in a truce despite the superiority over Ireland claimed by English kings.

★ *Lough Larne*

PAGE 173 — *9 August 1328*

The K. to the 'magnificent prince Sir Robert, by the grace of God K. of Scots, his dearest friend, greeting and embraces of sincere affection,' Begs his favourable consideration for his well beloved John de Torthorald, who claims certain lands and tenements in Scotland, and is about to proceed thither in quest of his heritage. York.

The peace treaty of 1328 finally acknowledged Robert as the legitimate king of Scotland, hence the use of his title. The treaty was unpopular in England generally and with Edward III in particular, who would later claim that since he had been a minor at the time he was not bound by the provisions of the treaty and was therefore within his rights to support the efforts of Edward Balliol to seize the Scottish Crown.

PAGE 174 — *12 September 1328*

The K. at the request of his brother David son of the K. of Scotland, and Johanna his wife the K.'s sister, pardons Adam son of Richard of West Swynburne for adhering to the Scots in the late and his own reign, and riding with them in war on the English Marches. St Botulph's.

The marriage of David to Joanna was part of the treaty arrangements of 1328. By marrying his son into the royal house of England Robert was trying to safeguard the rights of his son in the traditional manner of medieval European diplomacy. In a sense he was successful; if Robert had been captured in battle, as David would be at Neville's Cross, he would undoubtedly have been executed. The value to Edward III of David as a prisoner was very limited unless Edward accepted him as the king of Scotland. Such recognition, even if it was just in terms of negotiations with David's supporters, seriously undermined the position of Edward Balliol. If even his patron was prepared to do business with the Scots 'King Edward of Scotland' would retain little credibility beyond his own household.

PAGE 174 — *3 November 1328*

Warrant to the Chancellor to issue letters in favour of Gilbert de Umfraville son and heir of the late Robert de Umfraville, though only 19 years of age, as the K. has granted him all his lands on account of the losses of his ancestors, in 'abatement' of their castles and destruction of their lands, in the service of the State; except the dower lands of

Elizabeth, late countess of Angus, in Northumberland and the franchise of Redesdale, held by Sir Roger Mauduyt till Gilbert's majority. Winchester.

Inspeximus and confirmation in favour of Hugh de Tenpliton of various charters and letters patent granted by the late K. in the 16th *(year)* of his reign, of Balylug, Tobyr *juxta* Dunlone, the manor of Martry, lands in the barony of Kenlyn in Meath, &c., forfeited by Walter son of Walter de Say for his rebellion in company of Robert de Bruys, Edward de Bruys, and other Scottish felons in Ireland. Gloucester.

The K. consents to receive from Robert K. of Scots, 5,000 marks on account of 10,000 due on St John Baptist's day next; the balance to be paid at Martinmas following. Eltham.

The K. signifies the above arrangement to the Treasurer and Barons of Exchequer.

Part of the peace arrangements of 1328 required King Robert to provide a 'contribution for peace' amounting to £20,000 — an enormous sum for the fourteenth century. Several writers have made a connection between this money and the destruction of northern England by the Scots.

The K. sends the Chancellor two letters from Sir Robert de Brus, 'Roi Descoce,' commanding him to consider them with the Council, and do what is expedient. Canterbury.

(Enclosures) The K. of Scotland [who is not named] reminds Edward of his former request on behalf of the Abbot of Abirbrothoc for restoration of Hautwisille church, to which he had promised to give a final answer at London in three weeks after last Easter. Begs him earnestly, for veneration of St Thomas of Canterbury, in whose honour his ancestors, Ks. of Scotland, founded the monastery and endowed it with this church, and considering that he himself has restored and daily is restoring their benefices to English churchmen, to satisfy the present incumbent otherwise, and give back the church. Given at Cardros, 3rd May.

(2) The same to same. Complaints that Scottish merchants are charged 3d on each pound of their goods on entering or leaving English ports by sea or land, by the collectors of the custom called 'Maletots'. Begs him therefore to give the same privileges to these Scottish merchants as he would wish English merchants to enjoy in Scottish ports; and to reply in writing with his decision. Cardros. 3rd May.

A number of clergymen had been driven out of their benefices over the preceding thirty years and more, in some cases because they were English, in some cases because they had been appointed to vacancies by Edward I or Edward II in areas outwith their control or to areas from which their administration had been driven, and some who simply did not change sides at the right time. The property of religious houses was to be restored regardless of the country in which that property lay, but the physical reclamation of those properties might not be easily achieved without Crown intervention.

PAGE 178 – *26 June 1329*

The K. acknowledges receipt, by the hands of Master Thomas de Gartone controller of his household, of 5,000 marks from David K. of Scotland, due at St John Baptist's day last part, under the peace with the late K. Robert of good memory. Rochester.

PAGE 180 – *16 November 1329*

Pardon to Gilbert de Colewen for joining the Scots in their country, and fighting against the late K.; and restoration of his escheated lands in Shap in Westmoreland. Kenilworth.

PAGE 183 – *30 December 1330*

The K. requests David K. of Scots to make restitution of their lands and possessions in Scotland to Thomas Wake lord of Lidel and Henry de Beaumont earl of Buchan, as he understands that Henry de Percy only has received his, in terms of the treaty with the late Robert K. of Scotland. Westminster.

PAGE 184 – *10 Jan 1331*

Receipt by the K. for 5,000 marks sterling in part payment of 10,000 due on St John Baptist's day next by David K. of Scotland, in full satisfaction of the 30,000 due under the treaty with the late K. Robert. Westminster.

Two other receipts for 3,000 and 2,000 marks from he said K. David, and one for the entire 10,000 marks. *Ibid.*

PAGE 184 – *12 January 1331*
The K. to David K. of Scotland. Recommends to him certain merchants of the Society of the Bardi of Florence, who are going with their goods to Scotland, and begs him to pay them the 10,000 marks (the balance of the 30,000 due under the treaty with the late K. of Scotland), which he has assigned to them. Westminster.

The majority of the money paid by the Scots would seem to have been appropriated by Isabella, widow of Edward II, and her partner, Sir Roger Mortimer.

PAGE 187 – *13 May 1331*
Petition to the K. by Sir John de Grymestede, who was taken prisoner by the Scots when with the late K. at the battle of Strivelyn, and held to ransom for 100 marks, in part payment of which he had to sell 10*l.* of timber in his '*demesne*' wood of Grymstede, then within the regard of Clarindone Forest, but now deafforested by the perambulation. He was fined 10*l.* by the lieutenant of Sir Hugh de Despenser, then justice of the Forest, and is now impeaced *(apesche)* for same before Sir Robert de Ufford and other justices errant in Wyltes, and begs the K. to pardon it. [No date.]

The K. commands that the prayer be granted. Haveryng atte Boure, 13th May

Capture on the battlefield had wider implications than simply procuring a sum of money to gain release. The administration of estates might deteriorate in the lord's absence, neighbours might identify an opportunity to further their own interests at the expense of their absent neighbour or the money demanded might be more than the estates of the captive could easily bear, resulting in 'asset stripping' and the sale of land.

7

Why was there a battle at Stirling in 1314?

*B*ecause *of its place in the Scottish psyche, Bannockburn has attracted more than its fair share of attention from historians, and yet it is little understood as an event, despite, or perhaps on account of, the efforts of both scholars and cinematographers. The massive amount of print that has been devoted to locating the different parts of the battle has not served to make a clearer picture of the engagement, and given the disparities between the near-contemporary accounts available to us it should come as no surprise that there is no great unanimity of opinion among interested parties today. If the accounts of Bannockburn that Thomas Grey claims to have studied when he was a prisoner of the Scots (c.1355) were to come to light now they might radically alter our perceptions of the battle even if they did not materially contradict the existing sources, simply by giving us a better description of the actions of the troops involved or of the structure of the armies. Equally, such a new source could utterly contradict one existing source without necessarily compromising any of the others. If some newly discovered contemporary Scottish account were to agree with the English chronicler Geoffrey Baker (writing c.1345) that the all the Scots fought on foot – even King Robert himself – where would that put Keith's cavalry attack on the English archers? Our current understanding of the course of the battle is heavily dependent on this manoeuvre, though the only source for its occurrence is Barbour (c.1370). The scant nature of the material with regard to the deployment, number and precise location of the armies and the separate engagements is therefore a considerable barrier to any realistic appraisal of the conduct of the battle.*

If we cannot be sure of very much concerning the battle itself, we can hopefully make some observations about the motivation and opportunities of the two protagonists, Robert I and Edward II. For King Robert, the war with England was the remaining great political issue of the day, but for King Edward the campaign of 1314 was one element amid a number of pressing concerns.

The decay of English power in Scotland throughout Edward's reign had not occurred simply because of regal indifference; his commitments in France and repeated disagreements with his magnates rather monopolised his attentions and when he did try to conduct operations against the Scots in 1310–11 he made very little impact on the situation. If Edward was to preserve an English presence in Scotland he obviously needed to act, but why at this particular time and place?

The continuing success of the Scots throughout 1313–14[1] and in particular his failure to relieve even those garrisons which could be supplied by sea obliged Edward to take some positive action, if only to encourage his remaining supporters and garrisons, and his victory over his domestic opposition in the parliaments of 1313[2] gave him the freedom of action to prosecute a major war. The announcement of a campaign to 'recover' Scotland would enhance his own reputation and, perhaps, serve to cast any continuing baronial opposition in a rather unpatriotic light. In order to protect and further his position in Scotland Edward had to demonstrate that he was an effective source of good lordship. He had to give tangible proof that his Scottish supporters could rely on his willingness and ability to provide protection and stable government, which until June 1314, he was self-evidently failing to do, given that the English control in such areas as could still reasonably be described as 'occupied' was diminishing and the vulnerability of castles as garrisons was increasing; he had simply lost the capacity to operate freely within the country.

Military action was obviously the only possible avenue open to Edward if he was going to avoid the massive blow to his prestige that would ensue from the 'loss' of Scotland. The damage to his prestige brought about by regular Scottish raiding across his border was coupled with material loss to the communities of northern England and therefore gain to his enemy – a situation that Edward could not countenance indefinitely, although he seems to have regarded the plight of his northern counties as being less pressing than other concerns[3].

The loss of territory and resources to the Scots was not the only challenge to Edward's authority. The increasing power of Robert I automatically detracted from Edward's status among his own subjects, who would see the loss of the war in Scotland, for which they had contributed service and taxes, as being the direct responsibility of the king, and foreign opinion can hardly have been impressed

*by a king who could not protect his subjects within his own traditional bound-
aries let alone suppress a rebellion in a recently acquired 'province'.*

*A campaign against the Scots would hold a number of attractions for
Edward, particularly in terms of reinforcing his personal and political authority,
but most importantly, if he could bring them to battle and achieve a notable victory, he could reverse the whole trend of the war. The occupation forces were still
considerable at the close of 1313, but their situation had been deteriorating
steadily for some time. If the power of King Robert could be broken in a large
general engagement Edward would be able to take the initiative as his father
had done ten years previously, when he had been able to force the Scots to the
negotiating table without a fight by astute political manoeuvring and a massive
demonstration of military strength[4].*

*In 1314, however, there was no viable basis for a peaceful, political settlement
and war must have seemed the only real option for Edward. The problem lay in
the difficulty of forcing battle on the Scots who had been studiously avoiding
such an eventuality since the battle of Falkirk. In 1314 the Scots made an
opportunity for just the sort of action the English wanted.*

*By Easter 1314 the commander of the garrison at Stirling Castle, Sir Philip
de Mowbray, had entered into an agreement with the Scots, that he would surrender the castle if not relieved by the feast of Saint John[5], 24 June. Traditionally
the pact is seen as a rash act by Edward Bruce, unsanctioned by the king, but
these arrangements were a normal practice of fourteenth-century war; indeed
Dundee had recently fallen to King Robert under similar circumstances[6].*

*The loss of any major castle would have been a severe blow in itself, but the
location of Stirling, traditionally the gateway to the North, made its possession
vital if Edward was to have any influence north of the Forth or a viable administration in northern central Scotland. In addition to the obvious material loss if
the castle were to be surrendered, there would be serious damage to Edward's
credibility if he did not respond vigorously to the challenge to his authority
implied by what was effectively an invitation to battle. If he did not act to save
Stirling why should anyone believe he would act to save any other garrison in
Scotland?*

*Edward, confident of the superior strength of an English army, with some
personal experience of fighting in Scotland[7] and the services of several competent
lieutenants[8] was well placed to embark on an offensive aimed at restoring his
fortunes in Scotland. Having successfully freed himself from the constrictions of
the Lords Ordainer, he could scarcely afford any damage to his prestige in
England[9] and his improved status might be considerably enhanced by the per-*

formance of a chivalric, 'kingly' act — achievement of victory in battle over the Scots. Additionally, as Dr McKisack suggests, he might be able to take his victorious army south to confront his domestic opposition, headed by the powerful magnate Thomas Earl of Lancaster.

There were, of course, risks involved in adopting a combat strategy. If Edward's call to arms did not generate a force large enough to carry out the operation[10] his personal and regal status would be diminished among those who did appear and the credibility of his Scottish administration would be severely, perhaps irretrievably, compromised. Aware of the precarious nature of his support in Scotland Edward was not sparing in his efforts to ensure that he raised as large and powerful a force as possible with as much logistical support as he could enlist[11] to avoid the potential humiliation of having to withdraw through failure of supply without compelling the Scots to fight. Edward probably gave little consideration to the prospect of tactical, as opposed to strategic, defeat. In seven years of campaigning Robert I had never brought his troops to a large-scale, conventional battle against a major English army, and regardless of the debate on force size[12] this was certainly perceived as a large army by the standards of the day[13].

Edward may not have really expected to have to fight at all; given that he would command probably a much larger and, ostensibly, better army than his enemy he might be able to intimidate the Scots sufficiently to make them desert in large enough numbers to make combat an impossible choice for the Scots, thereby undermining Robert's credibility as defender of his subjects.

A variety of factors, then, influenced Edward to mount a powerful expedition against the Scots in 1314, and the compact to surrender Stirling Castle provided a specific issue which effectively defined the primary operational objective of the campaign. Successfully fulfilling the strategic and political objectives would depend on achieving a tactical victory. To gain that victory Edward needed to concentrate his army in order to deploy it properly, and a number of factors should be considered in relation to his choice of an appropriate site on which to camp prior to the main engagement.

Although the English expected to take the offensive on the morning of 24 June the possibility of a night attack by the Scots was not ruled out[14], and if the flanks and rear of the English camp could be protected by streams adequate to the army's demand for water Edward would be well placed to advance in the morning on the Scots, who lay to the west on higher ground, in a position to threaten the flank of an English approach to Stirling.

The 700 years of criticism regarding Edward's conduct of the battle of Bannockburn should not be accepted too easily. On arriving in the battle area he had probed his enemy's positions and found a suitable area in which to concentrate his troops, and had effected the technical relief of Stirling Castle. It simply did not occur to him that his army might be attacked openly in its own lines by an enemy whose usual policy was to avoid field actions. It is in fact difficult to construct a different viable course of action for Edward to follow. His options were essentially limited to two approaches to the Scots; either to concentrate and deploy to the east of the contour line running south–south-east from Stirling toward Skeoch, where his troops would find water and night security, or to attempt a flanking movement to the west of the Scots, where the rough terrain would reduce the effectiveness of the cavalry, impede the concentration of the army and its subsequent deployment, and even possibly facilitate a night attack on the English camp. Edward might then have been able to threaten the Scots from the west, perhaps forcing them to make a poor redeployment, but at the risk of exposing his own flank and lines of communications to a counterstroke. Edward had several experienced soldiers on hand to advise him, and although he may have found them personally distasteful on account of their close relationship with his father, it is surely unreasonable to assume that Edward enlisted these men[15] in order to ignore them; and if anyone identified a better plan[16] than Edward's no trace of it has survived. The only clear record of a tactical disagreement between Edward and any of his officers relates to choices of action on the morning of 24 June, not the previous evening.[17]

A remarkably similar set of factors affected the position of King Robert. There is some doubt as to whether he intended to offer battle on a grand scale but it is difficult to escape the conclusion that he considered a combat strategy viable. It would seem that he was as much concerned with the quality of his force as with its size[18] and by not confronting Edward's advance from Berwick, Robert may have let him keep his army intact, but he also ensured that the English force would be tired in comparison with his own. However great an investment Edward devoted to his logistical effort the strain of a week on the march from Berwick would have weakened his army whereas the Scots could remain in one location waiting for an enemy that they knew must approach Stirling. As long as Robert could feed his troops without moving them around the country he would be able to keep them fresh for battle and train them in the area in which he intended to fight, but was it really in his interests to fight at all? His policy of almost continual low-level warfare had been steadily, if unspectacularly, successful in reducing the presence of the occupiers to the point where it had no real power north of the Clyde and Forth and its remaining garrisons in the south were looking increasingly insecure following the loss of the important castles of Edinburgh and Roxburgh[19]. In general, the war was going well for the Scots, but it was going slowly. Fighting under King Robert's banner had been going on for seven years and there had been a war for more than a decade before that. Wars are not fought on thin air, and the burden of taxation and military service must have weighed heavily on King Robert's subjects. If Robert could inflict a serious battlefield defeat on the English the progress of his campaign of evicting the occupation and anti-Bruce forces would probably be accelerated and he could perhaps expect to draw some of his Scottish opponents into his own camp. Even if he did not offer battle Robert might further his cause if he could humiliate Edward by consistently outmanoeuvring his army until he had to retire, but this would be a risky strategy. If Edward could cross the Forth without major damage to his army he would be able to cause huge material damage to Robert's supporters. This would have grave implications for Robert's status. If he was to secure his own position beyond the level of rule by right of conquest he had to demonstrate 'good lordship' by providing protection and stability to the people under his rule, which he would be manifestly failing to do if Edward could march his army into northern Scotland.

Robert stood to enhance his prestige in a variety of ways if he could achieve a convincing battlefield victory. To defeat one's enemy in battle was to perform a kingly deed, and a victory over the English would be a tremendous boost to the reputation of a king whose path to the throne was at least dubious and probably murderous. His standing would be improved and his authority confirmed if he could shake off any lingering suggestions that he was little more than the usurper[20] of English propaganda. A vigorously pursued insurgent war served Robert very well up to a point, but if he was to gain credibility in foreign courts — particularly the papal and French courts — his diplomats would need to have more ammunition than the occasional capture of town or castle to convince foreign powers of the validity of Robert's rule. He might be able to conduct operations south of the Forth but he could not retain the castles he captured and nobody at the court of King Philip would have been likely to be terribly impressed by any Scottish town, so whether it was in Scottish or English hands would be of limited consequence; but the defeat of a major English army might well have positive implications for France if it affected Edward's capacity to defend his Angevin inheritance. If Edward were to be killed in action or taken prisoner the whole tenor of the complex relationship between the countries of northern Europe could be radically altered — a regency administration (whether on behalf of Edward II or his two-year-old son) would be too preoccupied with internal affairs to be able to wield much power in Scotland, France, Ireland or the Low Countries.

Robert's decision to keep open the combat option in June 1314 is, arguably, consistent with the development of his strategy since his capture of Aberdeen in 1308[21]. Although Robert is largely associated with insurgency campaigning, his wars were conducted to acquire and retain territory[22] or (as in the north of England) to deny its resources to his enemy – both essentially 'persisting' rather than 'raiding' strategies[23]. Although he had mounted campaigns against the Comyns and the MacDougalls Robert had not been yet been obliged to fight any major actions against the English to further his war aims, but if he wanted to make the most of his successes in the south and east of Scotland he would have to demonstrate that his acquisition of territory was intended to be permanent and to do that he would have to show his willingness to defend his 'right' in battle.

The risks were, of course, enormous. If Edward fell prisoner to the Scots the price of his liberty would be huge, but at least he could be confident of recovering that liberty. If Robert were to be captured he could be confident of the block if he were lucky and the rope if he were not, so he had to be sure of his ability to win, but also to be sure of his capacity to sustain a minor defeat and still be able to continue his war. If he were to offer battle to an English army, which would almost inevitably be numerically and qualitatively[24] superior to his own he would need to be able to force the development of actions to suit his own forces, and because strategic factors forced Edward to approach Stirling, Robert was in a position to choose the ground on which the battle – if there was going to be one – would take place. The ground he chose[25] gave him a sheltered route of withdrawal, security from observation, good observation of the enemy and a deployment area which would be difficult to attack with cavalry but from which it would be possible to execute an attack on foot very quickly if he saw a promising opportunity. His choice of position was good enough that it was not compromised by the deployment of the English through the night of the 23 June so Robert could continue to mask his intentions from his enemy until his attack the next day was almost fully developed, thus negating the normal tactical and strategic advantage of the defence. The same capacity to predict and prepare for the operations of the enemy which Robert had exploited brought Edward to a situation where the Scots might be able to engage his army under unusually advantageous conditions.

Throughout the campaign of 1314 it seems reasonable to conclude that both Robert and Edward considered the combat option at Stirling in 1314 as a possible or preferred course of action in pursuit of their 'persisting' strategies in relation to the control of central Scotland in the immediate future and as part of *their general war aims. To Edward, Stirling represented the furthest stronghold of his Scottish domain, to Robert it was one of the obstacles preventing him from converting completely to a 'persisting' strategy in central Scotland, and so in a strategic sense it was a frontier town whose value was denied to both sides as long as town and castle were in opposing hands. Edward self-evidently failed to achieve his objectives and suffered a major defeat which disempowered him militarily and politically at home, and weakened his status abroad.*

However much it added to his prestige, and however much it improved his general regal and military status, Bannockburn was not a completely decisive victory for Robert politically; even such a dramatic defeat was not enough of a blow to England to force recognition of his rule and the war would continue for another fourteen years.

Whether the battle is seen as the turning point in the war or as a confirmation of its general trend, the fact that a battle occurred specifically at Stirling on 23–24 June 1314 should not be seen as an inevitability; but two administrations pursuing 'persisting' strategies for the same territory must obviously clash, and a similar set of circumstances applied to another locality, such as Berwick, might have provoked a battle near the Tweed rather than the Forth. Neither Edward or Robert could accept the existence of the other's power, and while Robert could happily afford to win without making a major demonstration of armed strength Edward could not afford to give up his 'right'[26] in Scotland without a struggle, so Robert would probably be forced to offer battle eventually, and the possession of Stirling Castle became an issue at time when both kings felt strong enough to advance their cause through the test of battle.

8

The more we know, the more we know we don't know

The Scots and the English at war in the fourteenth century (1290-1329)

*I*t is, unfortunately, only the truth to say that our knowledge of the three
*actions that comprise the battle of Bannockburn is sparse and that such
sources as are available contradict one another almost as much as they agree.
This shortage of material is compounded by a general scarcity of information
about the nature of both armies but particularly the Scots. Our understanding of
the conditions and extent of military service obligations is limited to a general
agreement that the primary weapon of Scottish troops was the spear, and that
their armies were weakened by the inadequacy of the mounted and missile elements, heavy cavalry and archers[1].*

*Beyond the traditional burden of forty days' service in defence of the realm
and further service (or payment in lieu) for castleguard[2] we have no hard information regarding the organisation of troops raised other than the rather
optimistic-sounding numerical distribution into units and sub-units attributed
to William Wallace[3], but it is unrealistic to assume that an army perhaps 10,000
strong could be administered adequately in the four or five Scottish battlefield
formations to be seen on a plan of Bannockburn. That a unit of 1,500 or 2,000
men could be controlled in action by one commander is not in question[4], but
such a formation needs to have recognisable subdivisions capable of manoeuvre
both independently and as part of its parent formation if it is to have the flexibility to negotiate the battlefield as a useful part of the army[5]. The only piece of
information which might be worth consideration in this area is Barbour's
description of Sir Thomas Randolph's command in his action on 23 June, which*

is put at 500 strong. This obviously conflicts both with the overall army size given in The Bruce *− 40,000 − and with the more acceptable modern estimates of 5,000 to 10,000. If Moray was a senior lieutenant, why was his command as small as 500 men? Possibly this force was a part of Moray's command, a battalion within his brigade effectively. Equally, it may represent the troops in Randolph's immediate following, his friends, his tenants and others owing him army service, but these are not mutually exclusive possibilities. This puts a lot of weight on one very minor note in what is primarily a work of art but it is hard to envisage a practical approach to arranging ration parties in a force of such magnitude, let alone training or battlefield manoeuvres without a more sophisticated level of command structure than simply 'the army'. An administrative subdivision, or more likely a hierarchy of subdivisions each with a nominal basic 'unit' size of 500 or so, is commonplace throughout history from Roman cohorts to the present day. The overall strength of the army as a whole is open to question, but any force of several thousand would have been a community as large as any town in Scotland and would have had needs that were just as extensive, so some form of administration simply must have existed if men were to be trained, and we are in no doubt that King Robert had concentrated his forces in good time in order to train them in the area in which they would operate.*

Subdivision of the army was of course necessary for tactical purposes; commanders may need to dispose their troops in any number of ways, and the army must be able change its distribution and alignment in reasonable order and very quickly.

This crucial flexibility is only possible where the constituent parts of an army are sufficiently rehearsed in their roles; it is not, however, exclusively the province of regular troops, but a good deal of practice is required for the troops to act competently and confidently. In the period between Edward's summoning his troops and his arrival at Bannockburn Robert had plenty of time[6] to bring his forces to a very high degree of efficiency (by medieval standards) in battle drills[7] as well as time to study the ground and identify threats and opportunities[8]. It is impossible to draw any conclusions about the nature of combat drill beyond giving some thought to the experience and expectations of the individual combatant, i.e. what were the chances of surviving the battle if one were posted in the front rank? If one were simply stuck in the front rank until one became a casualty the competition to be in the rearmost rank would be extreme unless service in the front rank was perceived as being much less hazardous to the soldiers of Robert I than it seems to us. Alternatively, if advance after contact was carried out by the passage of one rank through another the risk of injury would be more evenly spread and it might be easier to maintain the momentum necessary to disrupt the enemy and prevent his re-organisation.

Edward's troops would also have attained some degree of articulation, but most of their existence as an army was spent mustering[9] for the campaign and marching into Scotland, and while it is true that some degree of training could be achieved on the march, there would be likely to be some disparity in the state of preparedness between the two forces. The speed with which the Scots were able to deploy and engage, and the inability of the English to react adequately, was the proof of the pudding.

We are aware that two decades of war in Scotland had built up a certain level of military experience among both Scots and English[10], which was coupled, by this time, with a growing tradition of success in battle for the former, but we hardly even know how the troops were equipped. It would seem that considerable quantities of arms were imported from Germany and from England (some re-exported from Ireland) to Scotland[11] but there would seem to be no information on the types or quantity of these shipments readily available. Were they chiefly quality armaments for wealthy paladins whose requirements could not be met locally or was it 'munition' weaponry issued to those who could not supply their own needs? The latter would seem the more likely if the demands of Scottish armies were large enough to be beyond the manufacturing capacity of Scottish society, but the former becomes more probable if the most up-to-date armour could not be produced in adequate quantities by Scottish craftsmen. The issue of 'munition' armour would imply a system for its distribution and even perhaps for its retrieval and storage against future eventualities. The discovery of a Scots arms depot by Edward Balliol after the battle of Dupplin Moor would suggest that the State was purchasing equipment for common issue by 1332, so it may well have been doing so twenty years before. Certainly the import of arms indicates that the prosecution of a lengthy war made demands beyond the normal bounds of Scotland's economy[12], and it is a fair assumption that some portion of the spoils of Robert's war in England found its way back to English merchants involved in the arms trade[13]. Without some analysis of that trade it is difficult to make any very useful observations concerning the details of soldier's kit in the fourteenth century but the return on the trade must have been considerable to make it worthwhile for merchants to risk shipping expensive goods into a war zone.[14]

For want of information to the contrary it seems fair to assume the same sort of equipment scales for Scottish soldiers as we can observe in contemporary illustrations and descriptions of English troops of the same status, if only because of the common sources of supply. The selection of arms borne by the opposing armies is an issue in itself; there is no reason to accept the convention that Scottish archers used a shorter bow than their English counterparts, nor to assume that they should be recruited exclusively from the 'forest' area of southern Scotland, but both of these questionable assumptions are incorporated into virtually every account of the battle[15] since the nineteenth century.

A similar tradition is attached to the Scottish cavalry force. Because Barbour describes them as being mounted on 'lecht' horses Keith's unit has been almost invariably described as a light cavalry force[16] although the same source tells us twice at least (once in the line before the reference to 'lycht' horses)[17] that the members of the unit were 'armit wele' — meaning well armoured rather than armed — in 'stele'. Keith's troops fought in a heavy cavalry role, seeking a conventional contact engagement. The term 'lycht' could just as easily mean high-spirited as 'light'.

Superficially, this would seem to support the contention that these troops are the 'gentry' of the Scottish army, but close order combat was a perfectly viable option for any mounted troops facing unsupported light infantry so the question of equipment scale is not addressed by tactical analysis.

The suggestion that Keith's attack is a fiction of Barbour's making and simply could not have occurred due to the power of the longbow as demonstrated at Dupplin Moor and Halidon is not sustainable. The power of the longbow is legendary, perhaps in more ways than one. It may well have been possible for a good archer to get two or even three arrows in the air at a time but the value of having the arrows arrive consistently on target and the rate of expenditure of a very bulky, cumbersome, expensive and probably very limited supply of ammunition would suggest a rather more sedate pace of shooting. The effect of massed archery was awesome but could not be maintained for long due to the combination of ammunition shortage[18] and the rapid exhaustion of the archers themselves. The deformities consistent with archery practice from childhood as identified in archaeological investigations of the Mary Rose arise from the strain of repeatedly performing a task so demanding that it causes damage to the body similar to that associated with competitive weightlifting, so the archer could not ply his trade indefinitely.

Archery was an established part of the fabric of English armies[19] and had proven its value on the battlefield at Falkirk[20], but it was not yet fully developed in the combined arms role that would be winning dramatic victories in Scotland and France within a generation. Even in the heyday of archers, their survival on the battlefield was only possible when they were deployed in conjunction with close combat infantry to prevent being overrun[21]. The archers might take the 'steam' out of the enemy's advance but could not depend on stopping him in his tracks and they needed protection from those enemy troops who survived the arrow storm[22].

The question of how Scottish spearmen could withstand the charge of English men-at-arms seems to be a puzzle of mechanics. Each mounted heavy cavalryman galloping at twenty or twenty-five miles an hour and weighing somewhere in the region of three-quarters of a ton would seem to require an absolute minimum of fifteen or even twenty spearmen to counter his enormous weight if the animal simply charged into them[23]. Assuming that the cavalryman is charging and is supported by several more ranks of similarly equipped soldiers in a sort of equestrian rugby scrum the cavalry force must become virtually unstoppable by mere infantry unless the first dozen or more ranks of spearmen are willing to sacrifice their lives 'soaking up' the impetus of the enemy horses.

The initial premise does not bear examination however. When cavalry advance to contact it is crucial to have the front rank arrive 'on target' at the same time in order to provide an intimidating aspect and maximise the shock of impact. For this reason and because of the virtual impossibility of achieving a common speed at the gallop (even for troops that have been regularly exercised as units) it has been, since classical times, the practice of heavy cavalry to charge at the trot, reducing the likely speed of the rider to perhaps ten to fifteen miles an hour[24] at best. The impact of second and subsequent ranks of the unit might drive the front rank on to the spears of the enemy, but cavalry units do not travel 'nose to tail', if only to prevent a 'pile-up' should a front-rank animal fall or be shot. The physical effect of second and subsequent ranks at the first onset of combat would therefore be minimal at best. Their effectiveness would normally become apparent as soon as the opposing infantry broke ranks, but if the infantry did not break, only the front rank of the cavalry would have any chance of engaging at all, assuming they could persuade their mounts to come to contact in the first place. On the other hand, if the rear ranks of cavalry did press forward the front rankers might find themselves hoisted on to the spear points of the opposition. That riders intended this very thing is hard to support[25]. In fact, throughout history there are very few instances of cavalry breaking confident infantry. If we accept that men go into action believing that the chances of their survival are greater than the chances of their being killed or seriously wounded then it is fair to assume that although they might be willing to be courageous they were not likely to be suicidal. Nor, even though the king would have to pay for it[26], would they lightly risk an expensive, highly trained *horse whose services might well be required to remove its owner from the battle area very quickly.*

Horses are, by and large, reasonably intelligent creatures, which means they can be trained to do a number of things, but how can they be trained to throw themselves bodily on to a 'hedge of spears'? Whilst it might be possible to encourage the beast to try it once, there would be a very real barrier to achieving it a second time due to the likely demise of the horse. The horses could be blinkered to reduce their view of the battlefield, but blinkers are to prevent the horse being distracted from the sides — if the horse were blinkered to the front it would have problems moving forward at all let alone at speed. When confronted by an, apparently, immovable object bristling with spears a considerable proportion of horses will shy, rear, sit down or just slow to a halt, greatly reducing the potential impact of the cavalry unit on its dismounted opponents[27]. There are very few examples from the medieval period of unsupported cavalry defeating formed spearmen and the will of the horse would seem to have been the same impediment to overwhelming formed foot in this period as it was in others. While accepting that examples from different periods in history are apt to be of questionable value at best, it is worth bearing in mind that there are many examples from the Napoleonic wars of formed infantry successfully resisting cavalry even after they had run out of ammunition[28]. If a unit equipped with bayonet-armed muskets and arrayed in two or three ranks could prevail against regular cavalry in the early nineteenth century there would seem to be no good reason to be surprised that a (probably) much deeper formation equipped with long spears should be able to do the same against the cavalry of the early fourteenth century.

Success in battle is dependent on a huge variety of factors and the greatest barrier to tactical analysis after any engagement is the difficulty of acquiring adequate relevant information on which to base any deductions or observations concerning the development of the battle. At a distance of 700 years that information is likely to be thin on the ground, and we must depend on a very small amount of material none of which is directly from eyewitnesses[29]. Because the accounts conflict there is a tendency to attempt reconstructions that include all of these accounts, and if two should contradict one another to decide that one of them is 'confused'. This is particularly true of those events portrayed by Barbour, which do not surface in other sources[30]. To some extent this is simply a product of a different political perspective, but it is also a product of the fact that Barbour was creating an artwork, not a history. Adherence to the principles of his art in order to build a fine romance was more important than making a sober, factual assessment of the life and times of Robert I.

The scarcity of documentary evidence has not been usefully offset by analysis of the terrain. Efforts to locate the battle bear a passing resemblance to pinning tails onto donkeys and the debate has, at times, been heated but never very informative. Much of the confusion around the tactical course of the actions has been generated by the desire to depict the battle on a map showing precise deployments and manoeuvres. The creation of the map symbols themselves is an example of this. In an effort to clarify our understanding of an event of which the location is unknown, involving armies whose sizes are unknown, we draw a map and place upon it markers whose size − as map symbols − bears no relationship whatsoever to the physical size of the formation that the markers represent.

Study of the Ordnance Survey maps of the area, regardless of vintage, can also lead us astray. The contour line is a cartographer's device and a fine invention, but it only shows the course of an imaginary line at a given height above sea level. A steep rise or fall in the ground of five or six feet might easily affect the course of battle quite dramatically but be far too insignificant to be shown on a map. More to the point, campaigners in medieval Scotland were not issued with maps, contour or otherwise, so their approaches to battle were not influenced by the map board in the way that modern commanders (and historians) are.

Better understanding of the battle has been hampered a good deal by endeavours to 'explain' an occurrence that seems to conflict with the normal practice of medieval war − the defeat of armoured cavalry by footmen.

To provide an explanation for that defeat, historians have looked for factors to offset what is generally perceived as the enormous combat superiority of the horseman. To reduce the speed and agility of the cavalry it is only necessary to place the fighting on boggy ground[31], and there was certainly some to be found in the area. This might vindicate the reputation of the English gentry at war but it equally raises a question about the ability of Scottish spearmen to maintain the cohesion of a close-order formation, perhaps consisting of several sub-units and as much as 2,000 strong, negotiating a marsh while carrying (and using) long spears against the enemy. More crucially, if the softness of the ground was an issue on the day we might expect that at least one of the contemporary writers would mention it. These bogs and swamps seem to have entirely escaped their notice and instead they are at pains to stress the hardness of the field. This is the factor that made an impression on the chroniclers. The defeat of unsupported cavalry was not in itself revolutionary; actions in Scotland and abroad had demonstrated the strength of disciplined infantry in both large and small engagements. Many of these victories were a product of offering or forcing defensive battle in terrain that negated the advantages of the mounted soldier[32], but at Bannockburn the infantry moved to attack a cavalry force on a 'hard playne field'[33] traditionally the pre-ferred arena for the deployment of horsemen. A rough, wet or otherwise difficult battleground would offer very real advantages to an infantry force in defence against an enemy superior in cavalry, but would not be so convenient for the delivery of an attack because of the disruptive effect it would have on the align-ment of the units and on the 'dressing' of the individuals within those units. The weakness of unformed or disrupted infantry in the face of mounted troops is unquestioned[34] so the ability to keep their dressing was absolutely paramount to the survival of spearmen. The 'hedgehog' effect of the spear points could only be maintained if the unit could keep good order. As long as the unit remained sta-tionary this would not be a problem, but rough ground would soon allow gaps to appear in the ranks once the unit started to manoeuvre. If the cavalry could exploit these gaps and penetrate the formation the infantryman would be ham-pered by the length of his spear due to the difficulty of fighting to the left or right without tripping or injuring his neighbours, but the horseman would be advan-taged by his superior height and actively assisted by a very aggressive horse trained to participate in the fight rather than simply carry his rider. In these cir-cumstances the weight and strength of the horse and the value of its armour would come into their own and the effect was devastating.

Disruption of the opposition's infantry was almost a prerequisite of successful cavalry action but was not necessarily dependent on terrain. It could be induced in a number of ways, but most commonly in northern Europe by missile com-bat[35]. Although archers were a normal part of English armies the process of artic-ulation was not well developed and consequently there was no 'habitual' posture for the English army of 1314 to adopt[36]. The failure to deploy appropriately and enable the components of the army to function in a properly co-ordinated fash-ion robbed Edward of the opportunity to take control of the battle either by attacking the Scots or by assuming a defensive position too difficult for them to approach. He had taken precautions against sudden attacks on his flanks and at the rear through his choice of camp-ground but had not given sufficient consider-ation to receiving a frontal attack that could deny him any room for manoeuvre. Contemporary sources are quite clear that the battlefield was very constricted and that the advance of the Scots prevented the complete deployment of the English army[37]. If the chroniclers are accurate in this — and it is difficult to find a locality in the generally accepted battle area that does not fit the description — the English troops in contact with the enemy must obviously have been forced backwards into their own supports, causing greater confusion and disorder as *they were pushed further and further back into and through their wagon lines until the army was completely disrupted and incapable of effective action*[38].

The simplest and most popular[39] 'explanation' for the English defeat has been the sheer incompetence of Edward and, by implication, of his lieutenants. Edward certainly failed to deploy his army in the most effective manner to receive a Scottish attack, but the likelihood of such an attack, other than a disruptive night raid[40], would have seemed remote indeed to the English, who had come to Stirling expecting to take the battle to the Scots[41], always assuming that the Scots would stand and fight at all. The greatest difficulty experienced by various English commanders in fighting the Scots was in bringing about a general engagement in the first place, so not unnaturally Edward concentrated his army in order to attack in force the next day assuming that the Scots were still disposed to accept battle. The site Edward (or his officers) chose was eminently suitable for his purpose whether it lay between the Pelstream and the Bannock burns or between the Bannock burn and the River Forth. By drawing the army onto a piece of ground bounded by burn or river on three sides he provided his force with night protection from harassment raids and with running water for men and animals, a matter of some importance at the end of a long summer's day of marching. The two minor engagements on the evening of 23 June failed in their efforts to force the Scots to abandon their position blocking the road through the new park[42], scene of the famous feat of arms by the king, or to achieve an act of chivalry through the 'relief' of Stirling Castle by a force of 300 men-at-arms[43]. The technical relief of the beleaguered garrison had already been achieved through the arrival of the English army within 'eight leagues' of the castle. The failure of these two operations was unexpected, but since every contact with the enemy has a reconnaissance value, Edward and his staff could hardly help but develop some picture of the location and condition of the enemy, even though the terrain and the success of the Scots in both engagements would have prevented them getting much idea of Robert's tactical posture.

If the Scots were going to stand and fight Edward would want an area of hard flat ground on which to array his troops and from (or on) which to develop his attack. This area would also have to accommodate the camp, and, if we accept Barbour's account of the conversation between Edward and D'Umfraville there must also have been enough room to the rear of the camp to allow the army to deploy between the camp and the River Forth[44]. D'Umfraville suggested that the English army should retire behind their encampment, expecting that the Scots troops would not be sufficiently well disciplined to keep to their ranks when *tempted by the prospect of looting the English baggage train and camp. Edward chose not to take the advice, but if we accept Barbour's story it surely indicates that the English army was deploying for combat and facing west toward the Scottish line of battle, and with 'good' ground — flat and hard — between the two forces.*

Given his tactical and strategic situation, the nature of the terrain, the material needs of his army and the considerable experience of fighting the Scots that Edward shared with his senior subordinates it is difficult to identify a better course of action for the English army than the one they chose. An approach on Stirling from the west side of the Roman road from Falkirk would have meant advancing through terrain ideal for the defence, either immediately with a force of tired men and beasts or on the following day when English intentions would have been too easily observed by the enemy.

Their tactical crisis arose from the Scots' adopting an unlikely course of action — they attacked before Edward could develop his own manoeuvre, denying him any opportunity for a forward concentration while the constricted area of the battlefield prevented him from making an effective flank attack or from conducting an orderly withdrawal. The streams and marshes which had protected Edward's army from night attacks also protected the flanks of the advancing Scots from appropriate English countermeasures. If the Lanercost chronicler is correct in his claim that the English army had crossed[45]:

a great ditch called Bannock burn into which the tide flows, and now wanted to cross it in confusion, many nobles and others fell into it with their horses in the crush, while others escaped with difficulty, and many were never able to extricate themselves from the ditch.

Edward's army must have deployed further north and west than is generally accepted. The precise location of the main battle is not really the issue, but the chronicler's comments clearly indicate the constricted nature of the field, that the Scots attacked, that the English were driven backwards, the precipitate nature of the English withdrawal and its rapid degeneration into a rout.

The defeat of Edward's army was caused by the one contingency that he (nor apparently his staff) had not considered — a Scottish attack on the morning of 24 June. To criticise his deployment in the light of the actions of 23 June is more misleading than the simple application of hindsight. Both of these actions were initiated by English units and both essentially demonstrated the inability of unsupported cavalry to defeat formed infantry; they obviously were not

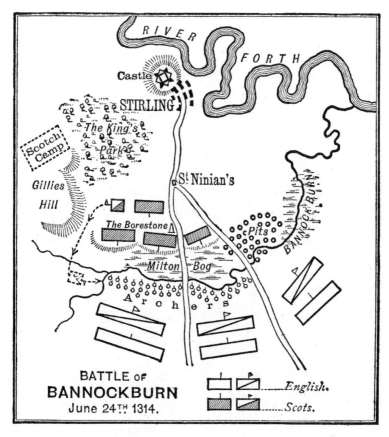

The battle of Bannockburn as envisaged by Sir Charles Oman (after S.R. Gardiner). Gardiner and Oman's interpretations were for many years the 'received history' of the battle, although neither bears examination in the light of the documentary evidence.

construed as an indication that the Scots might take the initiative the next morning and force a general engagement in open terrain.

Despite the undoubted success of his conduct of the campaign King Robert has attracted a good deal of criticism from historians[46] for choosing to fight at all. Certainly superficial number crunching would suggest that with his less heavily equipped and numerically inferior force he was running an inordinately high risk, but numbers are not necessarily a decisive factor in battle, and there seems to be no special reason to assume that the Scots were poorly kitted out compared to their English counterparts. With more than twenty years experience of war, it is reasonable to assume that Robert had a good idea of the capacities of his troops and of the enemy. He may not have been committed to a general engagement after the actions of 23 June[47] but it would be unreasonable to believe that he was

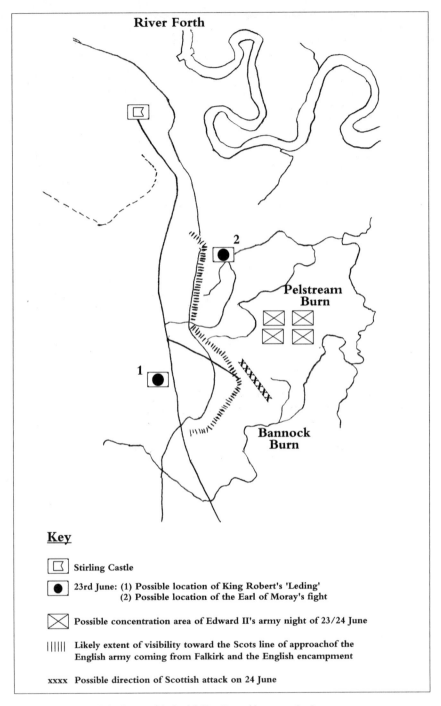

River Forth

**Pelstream
Burn**

2

1

**Bannock
Burn**

Key

Stirling Castle

23rd June: (1) Possible location of King Robert's 'Leding'
(2) Possible location of the Earl of Moray's fight

Possible concentration area of Edward II's army night of 23/24 June

|||||| Likely extent of visibility toward the Scots line of approach of the English army coming from Falkirk and the English encampment

xxxx Possible direction of Scottish attack on 24 June

A sketch map of the battlefield at Bannockburn on 23/24 June 1314.

not alert to the possibility of offering battle if he could identify a good attacking opportunity. Edward's choice of encampment provided just such an opening.

Although the two cavalry actions of 23 June furnished the English with some idea of the location of the Scots it seems clear that the 'reconnaissance battle' had gone in Robert's favour. English cavalry had failed to penetrate his lines and he enjoyed a commanding position, which allowed him to deploy at leisure unobserved by the enemy. Intelligence provided by a defector[48] gave him some insight into the condition of the opposing force and he concluded that an aggressive combat option was the most appropriate course of action. The success of the two actions on the 23 June must obviously have been a boost to the confidence of the Scots as a whole, but it was also presumably a vindication of the methodology of Robert. The strength of formed infantry against unsupported cavalry had been adequately demonstrated on previous occasions but for infantry to advance from high ground to offer battle was an innovative manoeuvre; sufficiently so for the English commander not to perceive it as a threat[49] and be willing to give ground to the advancing Scots, confident that he would achieve a useful tactical victory and perhaps enhance his chivalric reputation.

It is conceivable that when the Scots emerged on to the field they were on the left flank of the English army[50] although this would mean that the English had deployed facing north, which in turn would suggest that they had completely lost touch with the general location of the Scots army in the hours of darkness and that seems less than likely given the shortness of a mid-summer night in Scotland.

If we can be sure that the Scots advanced on the English we cannot be very confident as to the manner of their deployment. When historians use the term 'schiltrom' they generally mean a ring formation of spearmen, like a hedgehog as Barbour tells us, but we should be careful not to assume that this was the only 'unit-tactical' option available to the Scots. Any unit which is well enough drilled that it can successfully manoeuvre as a 'ring' — whether round, oval or a hollow square — is not going to find movement in column or in line a great test of its abilities. The advantage of the 'ring' is that it cannot be (in minor tactical terms) outflanked, but as an attacking formation it would be very slow moving, would only dominate a very small front relative to the number of men in the unit and would be particularly vulnerable to archery. The advantage of an advance in line lay in the better rate of movement and greater dominance of the forward edge of the battle area due to the greater proportion of the unit taking part in the action; the disadvantage lay in the vulnerability of its flanks and rear. If the Scots adopted a linear formation they would have to completely dominate the breadth of the field to preserve the integrity of their deployment; if the English could evade the Scots and redeploy in their rear and counterattack while the Scots were heavily engaged to their front the superiority of English numbers could be effective. If the Scots advanced in 'hollow square' schiltroms they would have secure flanks and rear so long as they were not exposed to archery but would have a reduced capacity to prevent the useful redeployment of English troops due to the smaller frontage of rings compared to lines. The linear unit with a frontage of 200 yards and say 1,500 strong — seven or eight ranks — when deployed into a ring is likely to be only seventy or eighty yards across assuming the troops are dressed in the close order necessary to make spear formations effective, a density in the region of one man per square yard in the first two ranks at least.

A succession of linear formations advancing, perhaps in echelon as suggested by the Lanercost Chronicle, would certainly have the capacity to 'cork the bottle in which they [the English] had inserted themselves' as McKenzie describes the situation[51] although this does not necessarily locate the action between the Bannock burn and the River Forth as definitively as he seems to have believed[52] since so much of the area west of the fifty foot contour running south–east from Stirling Castle would have provided similar tactical conditions. If the key to Scottish success in the combat phase of the battle lies in the exertion and maintenance of pressure all along the English front line, preventing an organised resistance or withdrawal, it would seem likely that the advantages of a linear approach would outweigh the disadvantages.

There is a popular picture of the battle, wherein rings or ovals of Scottish spearmen stand rigidly in serried ranks — the front rank kneeling perhaps — to receive the onslaught of English knights, but this would hand the tactical initiative to the English who would be able to withdraw and reform at will to construct a more measured attack making better use of the available resources which is surely at odds with everything we can observe about the course of the engagement.

Not all of Robert's army were spearmen; there were also archers[53] and cavalry[54]. The archers seem to have functioned primarily as skirmishers rather than line-of-battle missile troops and the English archers dismissed them quickly, but not quickly enough to give themselves time to cause serious damage to the spear units before the intervention of Sir Robert Keith's force[55]. Even if the Scottish archers were driven off without doing any appreciable damage to the English army, they had fulfilled their battlefield role successfully by attracting English shooting toward a less crucial and less vulnerable target[56] than the densely packed spear formations during the closing stages of Robert's deployment and the initial phase of his attack.

For traditional, romantic reasons Bannockburn is dear to Scottish hearts as the victory of 'the boys' over 'the toffs' — ill-armed amateurs making a desperate *stand against a massive but incompetent imperialist power; and it would not be a popular step to suggest that this image could or should be replaced with one of two well-organised and equipped armies conducting a systematic battle of manoeuvre, in the course of which one commander identifies an opportunity, (dawn 24 June) conceives and successfully executes a decisive attack in a perfectly orthodox manner on a perfectly conventional battlefield.*

Exactly where that battlefield lay has been the subject of much academic debate, none of which has produced a generally acceptable conclusion. The profusion of swamps alluded to by so many scholars seems not to have made much impression on contemporary writers. The site recognised by the National Trust might not impress them much either. With such a scarcity of valid material it is perhaps rash to even tentatively offer a location; however it seems even more rash to reject both the Lanercost chronicler's clear statements that the English army concentrated, camped and deployed on the north side of the Bannock burn and Grey's 'en un plain deueres leau de Forth outre *Bannockburn' (on a plain before the water of Forth {and} beyond Bannockburn). A deployment on this area would provide the water needed for men and animals and the night security desirable when making camp in the vicinity of the enemy, be close enough to the castle to allow practical communication with the garrison, give open ground to the front of the army and still leave enough space to the west, allowing the army to withdraw behind its encampments, and enough space to the north to accommodate the concentration of English archers on the left flank of the Scots and their subsequent dispersal by Keith's cavalry as described by Barbour, assuming that the 'open' (left) flank of the Scots had become exposed since their advance on the English front was no longer being screened by the unnamed burn that flows into the Forth 200 or 300 yards upstream of Cambuskenneth Abbey.*

As Professor Barrow has pointed out, the name of the battle has itself been a source of confusion. The desire to associate the terms 'battle' and 'burn' led Oman to see this action as an opposed river crossing, a preposterous proposition that just cannot be reconciled with the documentary evidence, but because of his reputation, Oman is still seen as a credible authority – indeed his view of the engagement has recently resurfaced[57], achieving a spurious credibility through its repetition.

Considering how much study has been devoted to two days in June 1314, it really is remarkable how little we know about them. The last word on the subject should be the observation of two great historiographers, Sellars & Yeatman: 'The fact that the English were defeated has so confused historians that many false theories are prevalent about the Bannockburn campaign.'

9

The people of
King Robert

A good deal of northern and western Scotland, the mountainous parts, is little changed in appearance since the fourteenth century. Some terms used in medieval documents have changed their popular meaning; today a forest is an area of woodland, but 700 years ago the connotation was 'wilderness' or 'the great outdoors'. The armies that fought King Robert's wars passed over mountains and through forest when they had to, but most campaigning took place in the most densely populated and agriculturally productive parts of the country. The prosperity of the whole community rested on farming and the export of produce, so it is worth examining Scottish society if only to see what the Scottish people were fighting for in their wars with the English. The wars may have been fomented by powerful landowners, but they could not be conducted without the support of the community as a whole. The social administration of Scotland in the days of King Robert would seem not to have differed too greatly from conditions in England before the reforms of Edward I. The king's laws and policies were implemented by a network of sheriffs and lords, assisted by their bailies and sergeants, who between them maintained law and order, administered justice, collected taxes, rents and customs, and carried the responsibility of leading the men within their jurisdiction in times of national emergency – usually war. These local potentates were supported by a wider group of minor nobles and, increasingly, successful commoners and burgesses exploiting the land market. Essentially rentier landowners ('middling folk'), retaining little if any land directly under their own management, relying instead on the rental income of their properties, provided the membership of criminal and civil juries in addition to their immediate landholding rights, which might themselves involve a degree of criminal jurisdiction. Effectively, the king provided for the needs of the men (and, to a lesser degree, women) who carried out his government by means of salaried office in some cases, and by grants of land, temporary or heritable, in others. Naturally, the proportion of the society that comprised the social and economic élite was only a tiny fraction of the population as a whole; for the vast majority of King Robert's subjects the reality of life was farmwork; in all likelihood nine out of ten people spent some part of their life doing it, and without question the entire economy was dependent on it.

Popular histories of Scotland (and some scholarly ones as well) offer a grim picture of universally impoverished peasant farmers living in the thrall of (probably rapacious) lordly nobles and gentry in a primitive agricultural — largely pastoral — economy. The instability of medieval Scotland: wars with England, domestic wars, plagues among the people, epidemics among sheep, cattle and even chickens, conspiring with poor climate and soil conditions, worked to prevent any real improvement in the wealth of the society. This is not a view supported to any great degree by the archaeological evidence, nor really by the documentary record of the period. Much of our perception of agricultural Scotland before the eighteenth century is coloured by the fact that so much of the 'pre-improvement' landscape is only described to us by the 'improvers' themselves — in their estate plans and in their diaries, letters and most importantly in their publications. Improving landlords had an agenda to pursue. Part of the justification for improvement inevitably lay in criticising the practices of the past. The commercial success that usually accompanied improvement demonstrated its validity in terms of increased production, but the prejudices of the improvers have helped to further obscure the realities of life for the majority of Scottish people in the medieval period. In the eighteenth and nineteenth centuries the mania for agricultural improvement swept away almost all of the traces of earlier farm practice in the race to replace the 'old ways' with modern, scientific methods.

The work of historians, unsurprisingly, tends to focus more on the actions and fortunes of the great and good. This is an unfortunate, if inevitable, consequence of trying to unravel the story of medieval Scotland as a political entity, as the narrative of a succession of kings and the kingdom they ruled.

Any study of the kingdom is bound to be preoccupied primarily with the leaders of men. In consequence there is a tendency to overlook the men that they led. The lives of the vast majority of medieval Scots are completely lost to us in terms of detailed biographical data of individuals. Scotland has no equivalent of the Paxton letters to shed light on the lives of the lower gentry and their servants. There is no shortage of evidence of the existence of the lower gentry and the peasant classes. The gentry figure in the witness lists of their lords' charters, the peasants as part of the stock referred to in those charters. Concerning the gentry we can ascertain a good deal from documentary evidence, primarily charters granting feudal land tenure. The granting or confirmation of a charter tells us about the land that the recipient of the charter is to enjoy and the rights that go with it. The charter will also make clear the services that the recipient must perform in order to fulfil his contractual obligations. The rental of the property due to the superior depended on custom and the relationship between lord and vassal, rather than any concept of the real commercial value of the contract.

In a feudal society all land was in theory owned by the king. The landholder's 'property' strictly speaking was merely rented, but on a perpetual and heritable lease, and at a fixed rate. Unsurprisingly, the holders of these leases were more enthusiastic about the perpetual and heritable aspects of the contract than they were about the inherently impermanent nature of a lease. As far as they were concerned they owned their land with free and secure title so long as they performed the stipulated services appropriate to that property.

The great landowners, as royal vassals, leased their estates from the king in order to lease them out to their own vassals and dependants who in turn let them to farming tenants. At some point in this chain of contracts, the nature of the payment, 'reddendo', changed from an 'honourable' rent of money and military service to a 'dishonourable' one of labour and produce. Once land was granted heritably, the tenant would naturally seek the erosion of any obligations due to the feudal superior, and the easiest – though in the long term most damaging – way for the superior to reward or influence his tenantry would often be to reduce those obligations. Among the gentry and aristocracy the 'rent' could be a purely symbolic payment – a pair of 'white gloves' or a hawk. Some of these rents are rather more astute than first glance would indicate. The fairly commonplace inclusion of expensive produce – such as a pound of pepper or cumin – was effectively a hedge against inflation. Fixing payment as the weight rather than the cash value of an expensive imported product must have paid dividends when the value of Scottish currency as foreign exchange collapsed in the later fourteenth and fifteenth centuries.

Military service was similarly 'hedged' against inflation. The quality of equipment needed to be able to perform knight service rose steadily in the thirteenth century, but because army service was assessed in days of service rather than a cash equivalent, the increasing cost of military service in general and knight service in particular fell on those who served it rather than those who received it. During the thirteenth century the demand for military service dwindled due to the long period of peace with England and stability at home, but the militarisation of society that was engendered by the war of Edward I in 1296 can be seen in the (relatively) large number of King Robert's charters that stipulate military service as an important part — sometimes the sum total — of service due to the king for the property.

The rents of tenant farms were generally of a much more realistic economic nature than the token payments levied for estate holdings, but the cost of appropriate military kit and the regularity of military service being demanded were obviously much less. The level of labour service attached to property diminished as commutation for cash payments became commonplace through the thirteenth century. The amount of unpaid labour that an individual had to perform on a lord's estate was an indicator of a person's status in the society. The term 'class' would have been incomprehensible to medieval Scots, but they were keenly aware of status. The rising incomes of the labouring classes allowed them to reduce their level of 'unfree' obligations, leading to a rapid decline in number of people living in serfdom. Landowners were not in a hurry to give up rights of ownership for their workers nor to lose labour services incidental to land they rented out, but the convenience of operating in a fiscal economy — even if rents were actually paid in produce — encouraged tenants to buy out their lord's rights if they felt they could make sufficiently profitable use of their time in pursuit of their own agenda to make it cost effective to either supply a hired hand to work the required days or negotiate the commutation of the labour into a cash settlement.

The extent to which a tenant enjoyed freedom from labour services on his landlord's property was an indication of the extent of his personal liberty, but it is important to bear in mind that our information really relates to the property in question, not to the person who worked that property. Labour service to be provided by a tenant was part of his rent and did not necessarily imply that the tenant was not personally free. The social position of the tenant was not an issue in this. When Sir Ingram de Guines became a tenant (with three others) of property at Lamberton, he became liable for his share of the ploughing and harvest services due from that property to the manor of Ayton in just the same way that any non-noble tenant would become liable for the services attached to the property he or she leased. The involvement of members of the baronial class in the agricultural land market as tenants of farms (or of mills) as well as landlords shows that farming was seen as a potentially lucrative venture. Interest in *agriculture was not limited to the peasants and the baronage. Successful burgesses bought farmland to lease not only for the profits of farming but to acquire an improved status in the community that would allow them to join what in later times would be called the gentry.*

Not everyone fitted perfectly into our picture of the feudal pyramid. The general pattern of farm tenants and cottars *paying rent to a lord was not absolutely universal. Proprietary farm touns existed, the toun being the property of a number of 'heritors', whose children, as the name implies, would inherit their rights in the property. The inhabitants of such a toun were not necessarily much better off than their tenant neighbours, but they obviously enjoyed security of tenure and freedom from labour services,* heriots, merchets *and the other trappings of feudal inferiority.*

The economic advance of the lower orders of Scottish society throughout the thirteenth and fourteenth centuries is unmistakable, and the changes in servile status that allowed farmers to expand their enterprises are both cause and product of an improving economy. The charter terms of servi, neyf, bondi, rustici *and* nativi *may have been definitive terms to medieval Scots, but if so this information has not been recorded. The inclusion of some or all of these terms in land transactions may sometimes be little more than the preservation of legal formulae which had largely fallen into* desuetude. *We might be better to regard these people as sitting tenants with a security of tenure that their children would inherit rather than a completely servile class* thirled *to the plough. Neyfs or* nativi *might be* thirled *to the land but they were not necessarily without rights or protection. A landlord at Arbuthnott refrained from removing a serf – Gillandres the lame – when he discovered that he was a long-standing adherent of the local bishop. The social standing of servile status is impossible to clearly ascertain. Professor Duncan has identified examples of 'free' men marrying 'villein' heiresses in order to obtain a landholding. Perhaps the land was as much* thirled *to the* villein *as the* villein *was* thirled *to the land. The implication surely is that while the lord might own the land and the people who farmed that land, the land was not much use to the lord without labour. If the neyfs could not prosper in their relationship with their lord they might easily desert him for another. In the climate of a declining population the 'new' lord, keen to ensure that all of his lands were in production, would be unlikely to enquire too closely into the technical 'liberty' of someone in search of a farm lease.*

The lack of personal liberty did not need to be a sign of abject poverty. In 1247 a burgess of Berwick purchased a neyf for twenty Merks. This large sum is explained by the fact that the neyf in question was the 'grieve' of Prenderguest in Berwickshire and therefore a man accustomed to considerable responsibilities. As the 'manager' of the property he would have far too much opportunity to improve his financial situation at the expense of his employer/owner if he was not adequately 'looked after'. The grieve may have been a 'slave' in the strictest sense, but he was not necessarily poor.

The aristocracy may have been keen to protect their 'property rights' over other human beings, but precisely what these rights meant in practical terms may not have been particularly clear to them, let alone us. The economic developments of the twelfth and thirteenth centuries and the extension of personal liberty in the fourteenth century may have made it genuinely difficult for both landlord and tenant to be sure of their rights and responsibilities. This may have been complicated by changes in lordship. A newly infeft lord would be unlikely to want to cause bad feeling among the tenants by demanding more of them than the previous incumbent — he would need the support of these men if his lordship was going to be successful. Perhaps more importantly, the arrival of a new lord might be a good opportunity for the tenants to play down their responsibilities to the estate, claiming traditions that their previous lord would not have recognised. Quite why servile status should have started to disappear in Scotland as early as it did is open to question, but the influx of French, English, Flemish and German merchants and artisans who settled there must have had some impact. The incomers were personally 'free' in the sense that they did not physically belong to another human and in the sense that they were not obliged to give extensively of their time to tending a lord's fields. These people did not come to Scotland to be poor; they came because of the potential rewards of operating in a rapidly modernising 'frontier' economy. The success stories among the immigrants would surely encourage the local Scots to aspire to the liberties and wealth of their new neighbours and to acquire a greater degree of personal liberty.

Some quite modest landowners held their property directly from the king, and even some small tenants, though few as humble as the group of 'King's husbandmen' who petitioned for an improvement in their tenure status in 1305. These smallholders were seeking the same tenure rights as their counterparts in England, who had longer leases, which shows that Scottish husbandmen were aware of the different conditions in another country and were not shy of approaching the king to secure an improvement in their own status. Only a tiny proportion of smallholders were direct tenants of the king, of course, but most landowners would have this sort of tenant and it is reasonable to assume that baronial tenants would be likely to want any improvement in the conditions of royal smallholders to be extended to themselves.

Below the smallest tenants there was a class of landless men who depended on labouring in other men's fields for their daily bread. This pool of labour was vital for the economy. Landless men had the most time available to perform it, but terms like 'cottar' or 'husbandman' should not be seen as strict social stratifications; day labouring was potentially an important part of the income of smallholders as it still is in many parts of the country today. Labour wages could also supplement the incomes of people who were not strictly members of the rural economy. Eyemouth in Berwickshire was founded as a trading port and fishing settlement to serve the priory of Coldingham, but of the fish bones recovered by excavation, the vast majority seem to have been caught in the summer months. This suggests that the villagers found harvest-time employment on nearby farms since the inhabitants of the village were mostly landless cottars.

Their lack of arable land is further indicated by a rental, rather later than the reign of King Robert admittedly (c.1430, but there is no reason to assume any great degree of economic change in the intervening century), in which the nineteen cottar *holdings are assessed rentals comprising money and fish, but no agricultural produce. Even within a small settlement like Eyemouth there was some variety in the tenure of the inhabitants. Beside the* cottars *there were four freeholders, presumably farmers whose products could be processed in a local mill that had not been mentioned in the previous rental taken about 1300. The main 'internal' enterprises of the township were fishing and brewing (four breweries existed c.1300 – surely more than enough for the inhabitants of a village with only twenty-five houses, nine of them unoccupied!); however the line between farmer and tradesman was not a hard and fast one. If the fishermen were involved in agriculture, the freeholders could be involved in the commercial activity of the village. The trading carried out for Coldingham would have called for labour and thus provided opportunities. The prior's interest in fishing was commercial. In c.1270 the priory had three fishing boats and two other smaller boats, still needing four oarsmen apiece.*

The rapid (by medieval standards) development of the economy in the thirteenth century changed the nature of Scottish society, but it also made Scotland an attractive proposition to its expansionist neighbour, Edward I of England. The lengthy wars of independence he engendered probably hastened the decline of servile status through the widespread disruption of the community that can be expected of any war. If we reject the proposition that medieval Scotland was an uncommonly primitive and poverty-stricken society, we should be equally careful not to exaggerate the prosperity of that community. Almost without exception, visitors to Scotland paint a pretty bleak picture of both the land and the people. A French knight who appears in The Bruce *describes Perth — one of the most important, largest and wealthiest of Scottish 'burghs' as a 'wrechyt hamillet', which at the very least tells us how Barbour (who had travelled to London and Paris) thought a foreigner might see what in Scottish terms was a rather grand place.*

The perceived prevalence of runrig *tends to give us an unrealistic picture of a standard format of farming practice in medieval Scotland; the arable divided into long rigs allocated to individuals, an infield under continual cultivation which gets all the manure, outlying pastures intermittently cultivated and a head dyke to separate the two. The reality of agricultural practice was rather more diverse. The precise nature of each farm depended on its situation, local traditions and conditions. An area of good arable land might be set to less profitable pasture if the area in question was prone to military activity, because flocks and herds can obviously be moved more easily than standing crops or stored produce. The purpose of* runrig *may well have been to 'collectivise' labour, tools and 'plant' in the shape of draught animals, a development that is unlikely to have been uniform either in time or form so we should not be surprised at regional or local variations in agricultural activity. References to* runrig *are common from the fifteenth century (Professor Barrow has identified a late twelfth-century righolder in 'Ballebotlia' toun). The term 'infieldland' first appears in a fifteenth-century tack for Abirbrothy in Angus, but 'infields' were common throughout the east of Scotland. This field would receive the bulk of the manure and was sometimes referred to as 'mukkitland'. Mukkitland would be more or less continuously cultivated and in marginal areas the exhaustion of the infield beyond the capacity of dung to repair the damage would lead to the abandonment of the toun and the incorporation of its grazing into other farms.*

If we accept that runrig *was the common approach, we should remember the exceptions — desmesne farming was not generally an important feature of land use in medieval Scotland but it was not unknown. Unless the formation of rigs was going to be a major improvement in the drainage of the field there would be no reason to adopt rigs if there was no reason to divide productivity on an individual basis. And why should a* cottar *with perhaps as little as two or three acres subdivide his field into narrow plots given the labour involved in digging and maintaining deep furrows which would effectively reduce the size of his field?*

When we consider the buildings in which people lived and worked, we again find a more sophisticated situation than we might expect. Unfortunately the most common materials used for construction — turf and wattle and daub — do not generally survive well. Roman turf fortifications have been successfully excavated, but they were massive constructions built under professional supervision; the less substantial dwellings of medieval Scottish peasants have simply dissolved due to weather erosion or almost all trace of them has disappeared under more recent construction. Chiefly due to the continuous occupation of farm locations, an unrepresentatively large proportion of the medieval archaeological work carried out in Scotland has been urban. The majority of the buildings investigated in both rural and urban settings have been wattle and daub constructions, but there is a considerable variety in the construction styles. The nature of the materials did not mean that the houses were all hovels. The bishops of St Andrews owned a manor house at Stobo, near Peebles, to which they could retreat; it is fair to assume that it was reasonably comfortable. Robert I built himself a manor house at Cardross, so presumably a manor could be at least as comfortable and even perhaps as prestigious as a castle. Self-evidently it could be a fit home for a king, even one as conscious of prestige as Robert I.

On a less exalted level, a successful merchant like John Mercer or Eleanor Monkton would presumably like to enjoy the fruits of his or her labour. The appearance of someone's home – especially if it is his or her place of business – is an indicator of status. An Inverness burgess who had expensive plank cladding added to his house had it installed only on the wall facing the street where it could make an impression on the people of the town. An excavation at Inverness has revealed clay walls 'supported by vertical oak planks or staves', wattle and clay-daub, and plank walls set into sill-beams all contemporary and in the same location. Similar work in Aberdeen showed an equal variety of construction methods, and also some houses built on stone sill work, which suggests a certain degree of permanency. This might well be a result of increasing prosperity and a considerable amount of redevelopment in the fourteenth century, but may just be a reflection of local fashion. Householders in the towns built according to taste and pocket – presumably rural freeholders (at least) did the same. Excavation at Springwood Park, Kelso, has indicated sturdy cruck[13]-built houses with stone walls to about one metre and a thatched roof to an apex of roughly three metres. Heather and turf were common roofing materials, but heather is scarce in Roxboroughshire and in an area of good agricultural land straw would be more likely.

The more marginal the land, the greater reliance on beasts rather than crops, and the declining population of the fourteenth century would have made these marginal fields uneconomic in terms of return on labour. The fact that people were willing to invest such a lot of effort into poorer soil areas is indicative of the profitability of agriculture, but the reversion of these lands to pasture in the years after the plagues of the mid-fourteenth century should remind us that marginal farmland was not typical farmland. Another, though unexplored, factor in the reversion to pasture or abandonment of farms in the later fourteenth century may have been the succession of 'good years' when crops were relatively heavy across much of Scotland. This would inevitably reduce the 'real' price of food with consequences for farms that were only marginally profitable in normal market conditions.

Where occupation of a medieval farm has been continuous to the present day — and this must be the vast majority of them — development has obviously hidden the past. This is not a completed pattern. The expanding use of very large prefabricated buildings around established farmsteads since the 1960s undoubtedly compounds the problem. Because of the rather insubstantial nature of wattle and daub construction many medieval sites probably go unrecognised as such. Enclosures and earthworks of the medieval landscape can be mistakenly associated with the outlines of prehistoric ring-houses that they happen to enclose.

While it is true that most people lived in small farm touns of wattle and daub construction, there were people who did not. At least one stone-built village, (Lour, Peebleshire) and one planned village (Midlem, Roxburghshire) have been identified. The discovery of two substantial 'Hall houses' at Rait and Morton would suggest a rising non-noble landowning class who could afford to invest in comfort as well as security. A nucleated village at Camphill, enclosed with ditch and rampart, indicates a degree of insecurity among the inhabitants, but it also suggests that they considered the effort of building these defences a worthwhile investment. That they had the resources to invest in such a project would further suggest that they were right

One of the functions of burgh administration was to set 'fair' prices for necessities. The most important of these products were bread and ale. The pricing or 'assize' of bread and ale was effectively set by the price of wheat and of barley. Oats do not seem to have been the subject of assizes save in times of dearth. The value of oats as a cash crop for landlords in east-coast Scotland by early modern times has been amply demonstrated by T.C. Smout and A.S. Fenton '…hardly a family north of the Tay not shipping grain or meal either coastwise or abroad'. If the chief means of turning agricultural activity into cash lay in the cultivation of oats there are questions to be asked about productivity. The traditional Scots proverb: 'Ane tae gnaw and ane tae saw and ane tae pay the laird with a'' *is difficult to accept at face value. If a good return on oats was three grains for* each one sown, how could farmers recover from abnormal contingencies? If the production of a farm was sufficient to provide rent, seed and sustenance, and nothing more, there would be no money to make good the inevitable accumulated shortfall caused by accidental damage, unseasonable weather conditions or the passage of armies. Even the most minor crop failure would permanently undermine the economy and viability of the farm. This did of course happen from time to time. Whole settlements could go out of use but that is comparatively rare. Desertion of a site is not necessarily a product of environmental factors. The village of Mow in Berwickshire disappeared because the landowners sold off small pieces of arable land with extensive grazing rights to Kelso Abbey until there was not enough to service the flocks of the villagers. Changes in the weather, soil exhaustion, market forces and depopulation due to war and plague caused the abandonment of farms and villages, but chiefly from marginal lands. If a return of three for one was the norm of cereal productivity farm failure and abandonment would be much more commonplace. Possibly that level of return represents the minimum return necessary to survive and not the normal expectation of yield. It is of course important to bear in mind that what might seem to us an insignificant difference in yield between one year and another might be of considerable import to a medieval farmer; the difference between three for one and three and a half for one represents a margin of greater than fifteen per cent, hardly trifling.

The poverty that early visitors to Scotland describe was very real. The vast majority of people lived what would seem to us a life of unrelieved squalor. For the poorer members of the community a poor harvest would mean a spell of serious deprivation at best and starvation at worst. The life of the medieval farmer in Scotland was not an easy one, but the same applies to farmers all over Europe. Scottish peasants may have been poor, but perhaps no more so than their equivalents elsewhere. Their personal freedom may have been a little more developed than the condition of the lower orders in other parts of Christendom, but it did not make them wealthier. On the other hand the peasants' revolts of England, France and Germany have no counterparts in medieval Scotland; so perhaps the ordinary men and women of that society were better off than it would seem to us.

10

Storys that suthfast wer... have doubill plesance in heryng

*N*o other medieval king is the subject of so ambitious a literary project as *The Bruce. To reject it as source material is to ignore the largest single block of evidence relating to the career of King Robert. At first glance the text may seem a little daunting, but it is in fact very accessible with only a modicum of effort. To (hopefully) make the process easier I have included, beside the main body of the text, a small number of words and phrases which struck me as being more than just a challenge to the average reader and these are reproduced as endnotes (p.383). Some short passages have been turned into 'standard' English (translated is hardly the word) and, again hopefully, this will provide a little guidance for those reading the text in its entirety – something I cannot recommend too highly! By far the best study of* The Bruce *is unquestionably that of Dr A.A.M. Duncan, published by Canongate, 1995, which includes a full English version of the complete text with very extensive and lucid explanatory footnotes.*

Is Barbour's primary interest the education or the entertainment of his audience? We should be in no doubt that Barbour himself wanted his epic poem to be regarded as a viable guide to the life and kingship of Robert I, and to the careers of his lieutenants. Certainly, it was Barbour's intention that his work should be seen as an authoritative guide to the events of King Robert's wars with both internal and external enemies. It was not however his intention to provide a conventional chronicle account, but to create an artwork depicting these events in an accessible fashion for a Scots-speaking aristocratic audience.[1]

The scarcity of Scottish writings of any description for the early fourteenth cen-tury has made the study of The Bruce *a vital source for Scottish medievalists. The romantic approach of Barbour has, unsurprisingly, led to some suspicion of his historical viability. This is not completely unjustified. Barbour's tendency to hagiography of King Robert and of Sir James Douglas in particular, his dra-matic style and his frequent — though far from universal — condemnation of the English are factors that make acceptance of the narrative as a whole more than just difficult. We should bear in mind that these factors were also vital to the popularity of the work in its primary function — the entertainment of an audi-ence already familiar with the bones of the narrative.*

A romantic style does not necessarily preclude historical accuracy any more than a scholarly style per se guarantees it. The popularity[2] of an accessible his-tory should not surprise us. The demand for 'easy' history is at least as strong now as it has been at any time; a glimpse at the history section of any bookshop will confirm this. Like the authors of most 'popular' histories, Barbour was not above enhancing the actions of his hero-figures in the interests of producing an exciting, even inspiring, account. Perhaps the key word here is 'inspiring'. Unlike other romance writers, Barbour is not relating fabulous exploits of myth-ical heroes in far-away places beyond the experience of his audience. The closeness of Barbour to the events he depicted would have precluded too much in the way of eulogising if he was to retain his credibility. The exploits of Barbour's heroes might be swollen almost, but not quite, beyond recognition but the deeds of other men, such as Gilbert Hay or Robert Boyd, would require inclusion if their descendants were not to be offended[3]. Unity of purpose among the Scots was dear to Barbour's heart and the inclusion of cherished ancestors' exploits in the narrative would help to produce a sympathetic audience. This audience, although presumably well-informed about King Robert and his wars and — one would think — sympathetic in the extreme to the Scottish cause, would not be favourably impressed with tales that contradicted their own knowledge of the events in question or with tales that defied belief.

Barbour did not, of course, set out to write a misleading account any more than anyone sets out to produce a poor artwork. The primary function of enter-taining the audience would be lost if the audience's attention was not seized and retained. In order to retain this attention, the account would need to be credible as well as dramatic. In order to demonstrate his credibility, Barbour would need to avoid wrongly ascribing actions to individuals whose descendants might well be in the audience but still ensure that his central characters gathered the lions' share of the glory.

Inevitably the political considerations of his own time are reflected in Barbour's work. The ill feeling that characterised the relationships between the descendants of Robert I, James Douglas and Walter the Steward were a cause for concern[4]. Barbour's unreserved commitment to the inheritance of the throne by virtue of descent from Robert I would have done him no harm at the court of Robert II[5]. Robert II was Barbour's patron, so it is hardly surprising that his father, Walter, who had died when Robert was a small child, should receive some attention. As Professor Duncan points out (The Bruce, 1997, p.30) the references to Walter the Steward (Husband of Marjory Bruce and father of Robert II) have the appearance of 'much made from very little'. Praise for the martial exploits of Walter:

Book XVIII
Stewart Walter that gret bounte
Set ay on hey chevalry

*The paladin, Walter Stewart
intent on great chivalry*

and the general popularity of Walter at the time of his death (at Bathgate, of an unidentified illness):

Book XIX
Then men mycht her men gret and cry
And mony a knycht and mony a lady
Mak in apert rycht evill cher

*Then men might hear men sob and sigh
And many a Knight and many a lady
be of right miserable cheer*

would have done no harm to Robert II's prestige among the gentry and aristocracy for whose entertainment and edification the poem was written. His description of Walter's piety:

Book XIX
Quhen all wes doyn him ilkdeill
That Crystyn man nedyt till have
As gud Crystyn the gast he gave

When he had done everything
That Christian men should do
He died as a good Christian ought

may have been pure convention, but it was desirable anyway to show any 'patriotic'
Scot in a devout light, demonstrating the moral superiority of the Scottish cause.

In addition to being 'politically correct' — patriotic — Barbour's hero was of
course the grandfather of Robert II and anything that increased the prestige of
King Robert would enhance that of his successors.

The intended entertainment value of The Bruce cannot be viably denied.
The construction of the poem clearly shows that it was written as a performance
piece, but we should be wary of assuming that Barbour was deliberately engaged
in what we might describe as 'myth-making'. Barbour himself tells us of his
intention to write an accurate account of King Robert's wars:

Book I
Now God gyff grace that I may swa
Tret it and bryng till ending
That I say nocht bot suthfast thing

Now God give grace that I may so
Treat this and bring it to an end
That I say nothing but truthful things

So Barbour's avowed intention was to faithfully record the events of his time. In
the strictest sense his tale is, of course, propaganda for the Bruce cause which he
identified with the 'national' interest. His commitment to:

Book I
Put in wryt a suthfast story

Put in writing a truthful story

was not going to prevent him from 'simplifying' matters to help his audience
identify with individuals or to avoid confusion:

Book I
That the lord off Anandyrdale
Robert the Bruys erle of Carryk

This is a reference to King Robert's grandfather, Robert the Noble. This Robert was never the Earl of Carrick, a title brought to the Bruce family by the marriage of Robert (father of Robert I and son of Robert the Noble) to Marjory Countess of Carrick. This information may have slipped past Barbour, but it is not unreasonable to see this as a device to simplify the story. Three Robert Bruces – grandfather, father and son – had too much potential for confusing the audience. Ignoring the existence of the king's father was in any case desirable on account of his steadfast support for Edward! If the career of King Robert's father were to be rehearsed in public, his behaviour might reflect badly on the ruling dynasty. The constancy of King Robert's struggle with the English (and with his domestic enemies before c.1312) is the core element in Barbour's story. For that reason if no other Barbour avoids any discussion of Robert's career in Edward I's household and government[6]. Is this myth-making or 'economy with the truth'? A chapter on the service performed for Edward would scarcely have helped to show Robert in a positive light and it would be hard to convey the realities of political life in a performance poem because political life itself bores so many people rigid. The entertainment value of stirring martial tales might be severely limited if they were preceded by a blow-by-blow description of events during the interregnum accompanied by a defence and justification of Robert's changes of allegiance. In any case, many, if not most, of Barbour's audience would have had parents or grandparents who had served Edward (or his son or his grandson) when it was incumbent on them to do so[7]. Barbour's work was intended to unite (primarily) the nobility behind a popular monarchy, not to make ammunition for dissent.

The exception to this is Thomas Randolph, Earl of Moray. His desertion of King Robert, his active involvement on the side of the English, his capture and eventual reversion to the Bruce cause and his rise to prominence as the chief of Robert's lieutenants[8] is described in some detail. Whether valid or not this is a demonstration of the ability of King Robert to win the hearts of decent men. The lengths he went to to recover Randolph's loyalty[9] and the trust that reposed in him shows the 'kingly' nature of Bruce as a wise judge who can command the respect, obedience and love of his subjects, and is magnanimous in victory.

Barbour was perfectly willing to be economical with truth. The de Soulis conspiracy is dealt with swiftly and sharply – as it was in 1320 – and no mention is made of Edward Balliol, on whose behalf the coup was to be carried out. Any reference to the Balliol claim could lend it an undeserved (in Barbour's view) credibility. The Balliol line died out in the 1360s[10] but Barbour was not going to encourage any form of historical rehabilitation of their cause. Rather than provoke difficult questions about the legitimacy of deposing and appointing kings or about the finer aspects of inheritance through primogeniture, Barbour simply ignores Balliol. His adoption of de Soulis (Book XIX, l.28) as the candidate to replace Robert on the throne effectively denies the possibility of any legitimist counterclaim to the Bruce kingship. Any claim for a de Soulis 'right' to the crown would have been very tenuous indeed, so Barbour was attempting to depict anti-Bruce sentiment as a marginal element; unrealistic but potentially damaging to a complacent Scotland enjoying the fruits of peace:

Book XIX

Than wes the land a quhile in pes,

Bot covatys, that can nocht ces

To set men apon felony

To ger thaim cum to senyoury

Then was the land a while in peace

But covetousness, which cannot cease

To drive men into felony

To bring them to power

The extent to which Barbour was myth-making is rather dependent on what exactly we mean by a myth. In the sense that Barbour is depicting heroic characters to inspire the potential 'flowers of chivalry' of his own day and hopefully generations to come then certainly he was actively constructing an image of the past with a practical social function. The audience that enjoyed the poem learned the history of their nation but they also gained a wealth of tales of adventure to equal the tales of bravery and daring of any other European country. When Scottish 'lordingis' met their counterparts abroad they would be able to hold their own in the undoubtedly competitive arena of war stories.

Traditionally, tales of dashing exploits are viewed with some suspicion; the repeated instances of Bruce overcoming three enemies for instance[11]. Even the most sympathetic audience would struggle to accept these encounters at face value. If Barbour did not intend these interludes to be believed why should he include them at all? Partly because they reflect a number of literary traditions and partly because they indicate the nature of the king and his most war-like lieutenant. Barbour gives his audience two descriptions of his hero's chivalry. The formal identification of the king or Douglas with the heroes of antiquity is one aspect and examples of specific deeds at times and places that we can iden-

tify from other sources is the other. The latter are the tales that Scottish 'lordingis' abroad would regale their hosts with, embroidered and exaggerated to suit the occasion.

It is important to bear in mind that Barbour was writing in a rather different political climate to the one in which his heroes operated. Although war with England was the primary issue of Barbour's day to an even greater extent than it had been in Bruce's, there were huge differences in the nature of the conflict. After the mid-fourteenth century English invasions no longer really threatened Scottish independence. English kings might claim suzerainty over their northern neighbours, but their inability to enforce their will militarily had been more than adequately demonstrated[12] by 1350. The cause of the 'disinherited' – those lords who had opposed Robert I and had been deprived of their estates – had quite literally died out in the 1340s[13]. The martial classes of Barbour's Scotland could afford to adopt the attitudes of chivalry more than Robert I's supporters could. If captured, the former might be crippled by the burden of their ransom, but the latter might well have been hanged. This situation did not persist beyond the early stages of Bruce's war. The success of the Scots soon led to exchanges and ransoms for the fighting men, though political prisoners[14] were not exchanged until after Bannockburn.

Fortunately for Barbour there was a fine example of the chivalrous knight to illustrate martial values in the shape of Sir James Douglas. The adventures of Douglas provide ample material for a 'flower of chivalry' to grace Barbour's narrative. The king provides the core of the tale and is frequently shown performing valiant deeds, but usually as a matter of necessity rather than of choice. The deeds themselves need not be conventionally chivalric, but they are an expression of the king's determination. The king orders a night attack on Perth and Barbour highlights the significance of his personal participation by having a French knight praise his valour and chivalric integrity:

Book IX
'A lord, quhat sall we say
Off our lordis of Fraunce that thai
With gud morsellis fayrcis thar pawnce
And will bot ete and drink and dawnce
Quhen sic a knycht and sa worthy
As this throu his chevalry
Into sic perell has him set
To win a wrechyt hamillet.'[15]

'O Lord, what shall we say
Of our Lords of France that they
With good morsels fill their paunch
And will but eat and drink and dance
When such a knight, and so worthy
As this (one) through his chivalry
In to such peril has put himself
To win a wretched hamlet.'

As a wise prince he cannot be seen to be risking his life needlessly on a regular basis. When he does, it is acceptable for his comrades to remonstrate with him:

Book XII
The lordis off his company
Blamyt him as thai durst gretumly
That he him put in aventur

The lords of his company
Blamed (scolded) him as much as they dared
For putting himself in such danger

*Douglas on the other hand was a private individual, however great a lord, and could therefore risk his life as he saw fit in pursuit of a glittering martial reputation. As Dr Edington has pointed out '...he marched to the beat of more than a single drum' (*Image and Identity, *1998, p.77). The Douglas elements allow Barbour to incorporate a thread to his work that is not entirely chivalric but is completely martial. The king may be forced by military realities to adopt forms of warfare outwith the conventional practice of the day, but he would undoubtedly behave in a more chivalrous fashion if circumstances allowed. When faced with the prospect of a surprise night attack on sleeping enemies as the only militarily useful choice, he is quite prepared to make that choice; victory is more important to him than the niceties of chivalry:*

Book V
For thai ly traistly but dreding,
Off us or off our her-cummyng,
And thocht we slepand slew thaim all
Repruff tharoff na man sall

For werrayour na fors suld ma
Quhether he mycht ourcum his fa
Throu strenth or throu sutelte
Bot that gud faith ay haldyn be

For they lie, trusting, without knowledge
of us or our here-coming (approach)
And though we slew them in their sleep
No man should disapprove of that
because a warrior should not care
Whether he might overcome his foe
Through strength or through subtlety
So long as he keeps good faith

Douglas may be a chivalric hero, but the realities of war are not lost on him. In the later part of his career he led several expeditions into England which Barbour makes little of because there were no acts of chivalry to report, but in the more desperate atmosphere of the campaigns before Bannockburn each skirmish has a significance in establishing Douglas's ferocious reputation. Douglas arranges ambushes at Arran (Book IV) and in Douglasdale (Book VI), he performs an act of war whose object is the horror and fear it will provoke among his enemies (Book VI) but he exhibits the 'gentle' face of chivalry in his conduct toward the ladies of the Bruce party in their flight after Methven and Dalry:

Book II
Bot of all that ever thai war
Thar was nocht ane amang thaim thar
That to the ladyis profyt was
Mar then James of Douglas

But of all those who were ever there
There was not one among them there
That to the lady's profit (helpful) was
More than James of Douglas

If Douglas was imbued with knightly values, he was not immune to human frailties. His relationship with the king's most trusted counsellor, Moray, was tinged with a degree of rivalry, of which Robert was quite aware – Barbour has him say to Sir Robert Keith:

Book XVII
'Certis thou wrocht as wis
That has discoveryt the fryst to me,
For giff thou had discoveryt the (thee)
To my nevo the Erle Thomas
Thou should displese the lord Douglas,
And him alsua in the contrer'

'Surely you have done wisely
in relating this to me first
For if you had told this
To my nephew, Earl Thomas
You would displease Lord Douglas
and him [Thomas] if the contrary [and vice versa]'

As with Bruce himself, some aspects of Douglas's career are left unexplored. His apparent attempt[16] to come into the 'peace' of Edward II is, not surprisingly, ignored. The sheer quantity of material relating to Douglas and the fact that Barbour gives his entire life story (which is more than he does for his other subjects, including the king) strongly suggests that he had access to a 'life' of the 'Good Sir James' that no longer exists[17].

The generally sound dating (usually by saints' feast days) and chronology of the narrative confirms Barbour's use of sources. How critically he investigated these sources is open to question since none of them are available to us. The fact that he consulted sources at all surely indicates that Barbour intended his narrative to be taken as a valid representation of the events of King Robert's wars. No one could accuse Barbour of impartiality, but objectivity was never really part of his agenda; his intention was always to write a Scottish account to celebrate Scottish feats of arms. The purpose of history to Barbour's society was not to describe events in an unbiased manner but to justify the position of the Bruce party and to build around that party a solid association with the national cause. To some extent it is a rebuttal of English suzerainty propaganda as well as a chance to present the Scots in a favourable light. It steadfastly maintains the rights of the Scots as a nation and the rights of Robert Bruce and his heirs to the kingship of that nation. If Barbour was writing history, it was a very partial history, and both he and at least the more knowledgeable members of his audience knew it.

A hero is hardly worthy of the name if he does not suffer before he triumphs, and Barbour's hero was no exception. The problems that confront the king are rehearsed thoroughly. When things go badly for him Barbour expounds on his difficulties because perseverance is a knightly, chivalrous trait as well as a kingly one. The greater the adversity the greater the achievement. The eventual triumphs of King David and Judas Maccabeus – two Old Testament paragons of knighthood – are paralleled by the king's travels around Scotland pursued by his enemies and rejected by the people:

Book II
He durst nocht to the planys ga
For all the commounys went him fra
That for thar liffis war full fayn
To pass to the Inglis pes agayn

He dared not go to the plains
For all the commons left him
They were obliged – for their lives
To accept the English peace [rule] again

The failure of the 'commounys' to stand by the king is explained by accepting that only a lord with power can protect his people and thereby earn their obedience:

Book II
Sa fayris ay commounly
In commouns may nane affy
Bot he that may thar warrand be
Sa fur thai then with him, for he
Thaim fra thar fais mycht nocht warand
Thai turnyt to the tother hand,
Bot threldome that men gert thaim fele
Gert thaim ay yarne that he fur wele

So goes it always
That none may trust the commoners
But he that can their protector be
So they left him, for he
Could not protect them from their foes
They turned to the other hand [side]
But slavery, that men cannot bear,
But slavery, that men cannot bear well

The people abandon Bruce (although one wonders how many of the people had sided with him in the first place) because he cannot give them 'good lordship', but he retains their sympathy because of the 'oppression' of the English administration. The king's own problems force him to adopt a disguise to travel the country and he is able to hear how popular he is from someone who does not know who he is:

Book VII

Quod the gud-wyff, 'I sall you say,
The King Robert the Bruys is he,
That is rycht lord off this countre
His fayis now haldis him in thrang,
Bot I think to se or ocht lang
Him lord and king our all the land
That na fayis sall him withstand'

Said the good-wife, 'I shall tell you
The King Robert the Bruce is he
That is rightful lord of this country
His foes now hold down
But I expect to see, before very long
Him lord and king over all the land
and no foes will him withstand'

Barbour is making it clear to the audience that the 'national' cause and fortunes of King Robert were of interest to more than just the upper classes. Although chivalry is obviously a vital part of the motivation of the gentry Barbour gives plenty of examples of men of non-gentle birth performing valiant acts. These scenes are important in a number of ways. They show the involvement of the people in acts of war, thus showing their support for their aristocratic leaders and their own independence. They also indicate to an aristocratic audience the value of the people they lead. Other countries produced soldiers from the commons, but Scotland produced valiant commoners like Thomas Dickson (Book V) who could perform noble (chivalrous) feats of arms. Only the finest 'flowers of chivalry' would be able to lead such independently minded commons, so self-evidently any member of the Scottish aristocracy would be bound to be chivalric.

Chivalric behaviour was not the sole preserve of the Scots. Sir Giles d'Argentan performs the ultimate act of chivalry by returning to a lost battle so that he can give up his life with his honour intact and Barbour treats him accordingly, having him say to Edward II:

Book XIII

'Havys gud day for agayne will I,
Yeit fled I never sekyrly
And I cheys her to bid and dey
Than for to lyve schamly and fley'

'Have a good day, for again [return] will I
I never yet fled safely [away]
And I choose to stay here and die
[rather] than live shamefully and fly'

Sir Aymer de Valence – a regular opponent of King Robert – is shown in a chivalrous light at the battle of Loudon. He challenges Robert to face him openly in battle:

Book VIII

He said his worschip suld be mar
And mar be turnyt in nobillay
To wyn him in the playne away
With hard dintis in evyn fechtying

He said his [Robert's] honour would be more
and be more steeped in nobilty
should he achieve victory in the open plain
with hard blows in fair fighting

King Robert accepts the challenge and de Valence attacks in the traditional manner:

Than as man off gret noblay
He held towart his trist his way

Then, like a man of great noblesse
He made his way toward his tryst

Making his way straight to the King:

> And the formest off his mengne
> Enbrasyt with the scheldis braid
> And rycht sarraly togydder raid
> With heid stoupand and speris straucht
> Rycht to the king thar wayis raucht
> That met thaim with sa gret vigour
> That the best and off maist valour
> War laid at erd at thar meting

> *And the foremost of his retinue*
> *Bearing their broad shields*
> *close-ordered, together rode*
> *With head stooped and spears levelled*
> *Made their way straight to the King*
> *Who met them with such great vigour*
> *That the best and most valorous*
> *Were laid to earth at their meeting*

Sir Aymer fulfils his challenge and is defeated by King Robert, but his chivalric and military reputation is undamaged. There is no chivalric disgrace in an 'honourable' defeat and Sir Aymer is a worthy opponent for the king. Barbour cannot glorify his hero if his hero's enemies are incompetent or cowardly.

The liberty of the people and the rights of Robert as king were deliberately conflated by Barbour to construct an ethos of 'fredome' from 'thryldome'. Whether 'national' – the defence of the traditions and practices of the past[18] – or personal, the struggle of the king and James Douglas to regain their inheritances was a 'just' war.

Taking up arms to restore an inheritance unjustly denied was of itself a knightly or chivalrous act, so the story of Bruce and Douglas and their successful enforcement of their 'rights' placed them among the heroes of classical and scriptural eras who had achieved their ambitions despite great adversity.

Barbour did not, strictly speaking, write a 'romance'. The nature of the events he portrays is, however romantic, a true relation of the reign of Robert I as far as Barbour was concerned. By chance, history gave his narrative features of a romance. The stories of Bruce and Douglas both come to 'positive' conclusions in terms of romance literature. The king died of natural causes, his 'right'

recognised by his enemy[19], his kingdom enjoying the fruits of peace and recon-
ciled with God despite his excommunication for the murder of John Comyn at
a church altar. Douglas, a stranger to peace, meets his death in battle with
'Goddis fayis' (God's foes) while trying to rescue one of his comrades. If
Robert was the equivalent of the Biblical King David, Douglas was another
Hector. The 'fabulous' exploits of the king are to be seen in the same way as
Barbour's discussions of people and events in ancient or mythological times.
They serve to fill the spaces between the more exciting and vivid passages in
much the same way as a modern 'war movie' must have a narrative to connect
the 'action' scenes. A change of pace is necessary from time to time to keep the
attention of any audience.

Did Barbour see his work as entertainment or information? The wealth of
detail, the careful chronology, the identification of individuals indicate a desire to
convey information well beyond the requirements of 'Storys [that] to rede ar
delatibill' (Book I). The careful observance of the literary styles that he was
familiar with and the inclusion of classical tales – usually as parables to illus-
trate the actions of his principal subjects – show his intention to provide his
audience with a compelling entertainment. He was not afraid of chronology; he
uses dates (sparingly before Book X, and not at all thereafter) to add to the cred-
ibility of his narrative; '...forouth the Sanct Jhonys mes' (Book X), but is
not beyond moving the season of the year for the sake of a better (more dra-
matic) story. King Robert had taken to the hills after the battle of Dalry on 14
August 1306[20], but according to Barbour his party:

Book III
Wandryt emang the hey montanys
Quhar he and his oft tholyt paynys
For it wes to the wynter ner

Wandered among the high mountains
Where he and his often suffered pains
For it was near to winter

To differentiate between good history and a good story is to impose a distinction
that would have been lost on most of Barbour's audience. He was not simply
creating a narrative, he was contributing to the development of what Dr Mason
(People and Power in Scotland, *Edinburgh, 1992, p.51) has called a 'usable*
past'; on the other hand he is clear in his mind that:

Book I
Storys that suthfast wer
And thai war said on gude maner
Have doubill plesance in heryng

Stories that are truthful
if they are told well
are doubly pleasing to hear

because of…

the suthfastnes
That schawys the thing rycht as it wes,
And suth thyngis that ar likand
Till mannys heryng ar plesand

the truthfulness
That shows a thing just as it was
For true things that are exciting
Are pleasant to men's hearing

He is telling the audience that he believes that a true story will 'lest ay furth in memory' (last much longer in memory) better than tales, however amusing, that are 'nocht bot fabill' (no more than fable) but he is also telling them that the deeds of real men in the not very distant past are more exciting than the exploits of the ancient heroes and that they themselves are a part of a noble martial tradition as worthy and honourable as any other. The Bruce *is exactly what Professor Duncan calls it, a romance-biography, the stirring account of a hero-king in a romantic form and with a rosy hue.*

II

The Bruce – John Barbour (1306-1329)

Book headings for *The Bruce*

I   The origins of the succession crisis of 1291–1292 and of the War of Independence; Bruce falls out of favour with Edward I

II   Bruce seizes the throne and is defeated at Methven

III   The king is forced to take to the hills and eventually makes his way to Rathlin, northern Ireland

IV   The queen is captured and the king launches a new campaign in the southwest

V   The king's adventures in Carrick and the Douglas 'larder'

VI   The king campaigns in the southwest and Douglas attacks Douglas Castle

VII   The king is pursued and has a narrow escape, and goes on to fight Aymer de Valence, earl of Pembroke at Glentrool

VIII   The king conquers Kyle and defeats de Valence at Loudon Hill

IX   Douglas campaigns in the southeast while the king heads to the northeast to attack the Comyn lords of Buchan and Badenoch before moving on Perth

X   The king returns to the west to defeat John of Lorne while Douglas and Randolph carry the war into Lothian, capturing Roxburgh and Edinburgh castles and the Pele at Linlithgow

XI   An agreement is entered into for the surrender of Stirling Castle; the Scots and the English gather their forces for battle

XII   The armies meet near Bannockburn on the evening, 23 June; the divisions of Moray and the king are engaged; the king kills de Bohun; the Scots elect to attack the following morning and Moray leads his division into the fight

XIII   Douglas's division joins the battle, followed by that of the king and by the cavalry under Keith; the English rout after a hard struggle and Edward II is pursued to Dunbar; King Robert attacks Northumberland

XIV   The invasion of Ireland and the battle of Dundalk

XV   Moray defeats the English at Connor and Douglas defeats them in Teviotdale

XVI   The king joins his brother in Ireland and wins a great victory, while Douglas defeats the English at Lintalee

XVII   Berwick falls to the Scots; the English attempt to recover the town, but are driven off and pursued into Yorkshire where Douglas and Moray win another great battle

XVIII   Edward Bruce is defeated and killed in Ireland; the English invade Scotland but are defeated by a scorched earth policy; they are forced out of Scotland and pursued to York

XIX   The de Soulis conspiracy; Edward III attempts an invasion of Scotland and is utterly defeated in the Weardale campaign of 1327

XX   The English are forced to sue for peace; the death of the king; Douglas takes the king's heart on crusade, where he is killed in battle and Moray dies by poison

The Bruce

BOOK I

Storys to rede ar delatibill[1]
Suppos that thai be nocht bot fabill[2],
Than suld storys that suthfast[3] wer
And thai war said on gud maner
Have doubill plesance in heryng.
The first plesance is the carping[4]
And the tother the suthfastnes
That schawys the thing rycht as it wes,
And suth thyngis that ar likand
Till mannys heryng ar plesand[5].
Tharfor I wald fayne set my will
Giff my wyt mycht suffice thartill
To put in wryt a suthfast story
That it lest ay furth in memory
Swa that na tyme of lenth it let
Na ger it haly be foryet.
For auld storys that men redys
Representis to thaim the dedys
Of stalwart folk that lyvyt ar[6]
Rycht as thai than in presence war.

And certis thai suld weill have prys
That in thar tyme war wycht and wys
And led thar lyff in gret travaill,
And oft in hard stour off bataill
Wan gret price off chevalry
And war voydyt off cowardy,
As wes King Robert off Scotland
That hardy wes off hart and hand,
And gud Schir James off Douglas[7]
That in his tyme sa worthy was
That off hys price and hys bounte
In ser landis renownyt wes he.
Off thaim I thynk this buk to ma,
Now God gyff grace that I may swa
Tret it and bryng till endyng
That I say nocht bot suthfast thing.
Quhen Alexander the king wes deid
That Scotland haid to steyr and leid,
The land sex yer and mayr perfay
Lay desolat eftyr hys day

Till that the barnage[8] at the last
Assemblyt thaim and fayndyt fast
To cheys a king thar land to ster
That off auncestry cummyn wer
Off kingis that aucht that reawte
And mayst had rycht thair king to be.
Bot envy that is sa feloune
Maid amang thaim gret discencioun,
For sum wald haiff the Balloll king
For he wes cummyn off the offspryng
Off hyr that eldest syster was,
And other sum nyt all that cas
And said that he thair king suld be
That war in als ner degre
And cummyn war of the neyst male
And in branch collaterale.
Thai said successioun of kyngrik
Was nocht to lawer feys lik,
For thar mycht succed na female
Quhill foundyn mycht be ony male
How that in lyne evyn descendand.
Thai bar all otherwayis on hand,
For than the neyst cummyn off the seid
Man or woman suld succeid.
Be this resoun that part thocht hale
That the lord off Anandyrdale[9]
Robert the Bruys erle off Carryk[10]
Aucht to succeid to the kynryk.[11]
The barounys thus war at discord
That on na maner mycht accord
Till at the last thai all concordyt
That thar spek suld be recordyt
Till Edward off Yngland king[12]
And he suld swer that but fenyeyng
He suld that arbytre disclar
Off thir twa that I tauld off ar
Quhilk succeid to sic a hycht,
And lat him ryng that had the rycht.

This ordynance thaim thocht the best,
For that tyme wes pes and rest
Betwyx Scotland and Ingland bath,
And thai couth nocht persave the skaith[13]
That towart thaim wes apperand.
For that at the king off Ingland
Held swylk freyndschip and cumpany
To thar king that wes swa worthy,
Thai trowyt that he as gud nychtbur
And as freyndsome compositur[14]
Wald have jugyt in lawte
But othir-wayis all yheid the gle.
A! Blind folk full off all foly,
Haid ye umbethocht you enkrely
Quhat perell to you mycht apper
Ye had nocht wrocht on that maner.
Haid ye tane keip how at that king
Alwayis foroutyn sojournyng
Travayllyt for to wyn senyhory
And throu his mycht till occupy
Landis that war till him marcheand
As Walis was and als Ireland[15],
That he put to swylk thrillage[16]
That thai that war of hey parage[17]
Suld ryn on fute as rebaldaill[18]
Quhen he wald our folk assaill.
Durst nane of Walis in bataill ride
Na yhet fra evyn fell abyd
Castell or wallyt toune within
That he ne suld lyff and lymmys tyne[19],
Into swilk thrillage thaim held he
That he ourcome throu his powste[20].
Ye mycht se he suld occupy
Throu slycht that he ne mycht throu
    maistri.
Had ye tane kep quhat was thrillag
And had consideryt his usage
That gryppyt ay but gayne-gevyng,

Ye suld foroutyn his demyng
Haiff chosyn you a king that mycht
Have haldyn weyle the land in rycht.
Walys ensample mycht have bene
To you had ye it forow sene,
And wys men sayis he is happy
That be other will him chasty,
For unfayr thingis may fall perfay
Als weill to-morn as yhisterday.
Bot ye traistyt in lawte[21]
As sympile folk but mavyte,
And wyst nocht quhat suld efter tyd.
For in this warld that is sa wyde
Is nane determynat that sall
Knaw thingis that ar to fall,
But God that is off maist poweste
Reservyt till his majeste
For to knaw in his prescience
Off alkyn tyme the movence.
On this maner assentyt war
The barounis as I said you ar,
And throuch thar aller hale assent
Messengeris till hym thai sent,
That was than in the Haly Land
On Saracenys warrayand.
And fra he wyst quhat charge thai had
He buskyt hym but mar abad
And left purpos that he had tane
And till Ingland agayne is gane,
And syne till Scotland word send he
That thai suld mak ane assemble,
And he in hy suld cum to do
In all thing as thai wrayt him to.
Bot he thocht weile throuch thar debat
That he suld slely fynd the gate
How that he all the senyhoury[22]
Throu his gret mycht suld occupy.
And to Robert the Bruys said he,

'Gyff thou will hald in cheyff off me[23]
For evermar, and thine ofspryng,
I sall do swa thou sall be king.'
'Schyr,' said he, 'sa God me save
The kynryk yharn I nocht to have
Bot gyff it fall off rycht to me,
And gyff God will that it sa be
I sall als frely in all thing
Hald it as it afferis to king,
Or as myn eldris forouth me[24]
Held it in freyast reawte.'[25]
The tother wreyth him and swar
That he suld have it never mar
And turnyt him in wreth away.
Bot Schyr Jhon the Balleoll perfay[26]
Assentyt till him in all his will,
Quharthrouch fell efter mekill ill.
He was king bot a litill quhile[27]
And throuch gret sutelte and ghyle[28]
For litill enchesone or nane[29]
He was arestyt syne and tane[30],
And degradyt[31] syne wes he
Off honour and off dignite,
Quhether it wes throuch wrang or rycht
God wat it that is maist off mycht.
Quhen Schyr Edward the mychty king
Had on this wys done his likyng
Off Jhone the Balleoll, that swa sone[32]
Was all defawtyt and undone,
To Scotland went he[33] than in hy,
And all the land gan occupy
Sa hale that bath castell and toune
War intill his possessioune
Fra Weik anent Orknay[34]
To Mullyr Snuk in Gallaway[35],
And stuffyt all with Inglismen.
Schyrreffys and bailyheys[36] maid he then,
And alkyn other officeris

That for to govern land afferis[37]
He maid off Inglis nation,
That worthyt than sa rycht fellone
And sa wykkyt and covatous
And swa hawtane and dispitous[38]
That Scottismen mycht do na thing
That ever mycht pleys to thar liking.
Thar wyffis wald thai oft forly
And thar dochtrys dispitusly[39]
And gyff ony of thaim tharat war rath[40]
Thai watyt hym wele with gret scaith[41],
For thai suld fynd sone encheson
To put hym to destruccione.
And gyff that ony man thaim by
Had ony thing that wes worthy,
As hors or hund or other thing
That war plesand to thar liking,
With rycht or wrang it have wald thai[42],
And gyf ony wald thaim withsay
Thai suld swa do that thai suld tyne
Othir land or lyff or leyff in pyne,
For thai dempt thaim efter thar will[43],
Takand na kep to rycht na skill.
A! Quhat thai dempt thaim felonly[44],
For gud knychtis[45] that war worthy
For litill enchesoune or than nane
Thai hangyt be the nekbane.
Alas that folk that ever wes fre,
And in fredome wount for to be,
Throu thar gret myschance and foly
War tretyt than sa wykkytly
That thar fays thar jugis war[46],
Quhat wrechitnes may man have mar.
A! Fredome is a noble thing
Fredome mays man to haiff liking.
Fredome all solace to man giffis,
He levys at es that frely levys.
A noble hart may haiff nane es

Na ellys nocht that may him ples
Gyff fredome failyhe, for fre liking
Is yharnyt our all other thing.
Na he that ay has levyt fre
May nocht knaw weill the propyrte
The angyr na the wrechyt dome
That is couplyt to foule thyrldome,
Bot gyff he had assayit it.
Than all perquer he suld it wyt,
And suld think fredome mar to prys
Than all the gold in warld that is.
Thus contrar thingis evermar
Discoveryngis off the tother ar,
And he that thryll is has nocht his.
All that he has enbandounyt is
Till hys lord quhatever he be.
Yheyt has he nocht sa mekill fre
As fre wyll to leyve or do
That at his hart hym drawis to.
Than may clerkis questioun
Quhen thai fall in disputacioun
That gyff man bad his thryll owcht do,
And in the samyn tym come him to
His wyff and askyt him hyr det,
Quhether he his lordis neid suld let,
And pay fryst that he awcht, and syne
Do furth his lordis commandyne,
Or leve onpayit his wyff and do
Thai thingis that commaundyt is him to.
I leve all the solucioun
Till thaim that ar off mar renoun
Bot sen thai mak sic comperyng
Betwix the dettis off wedding
And lordis bidding till his threll,
Ye may weile se thoucht nane you tell
How hard a thing that threldome is.
For men may weile se that ar wys
That wedding is the hardest band

206

That ony man may tak on hand,
And thryldome is weill wer than deid[47],
For quhill a thryll his lyff may leid[48]
It merrys him body and banys[49],
And dede anoyis him bot anys[50].
Schortly to say, is nane can tell
The halle condicioun off a threll.
Thusgat levyt thai and in sic thrillage
Bath pur and thai off hey parag[51],
For off the lordis sum thai slew
And sum thai hangyt and sum thai drew,
And sum thai put in hard presoune[52]
Foroutyn caus or enchesoun,[53]
And amang other off Douglas
Put in presoun Schyr Wilyam[54] was
That off Douglas was lord and syr,
Off him thai makyt a martyr.
Fra thai in presoune him sleuch
His land that is fayr inewch
Thai the lord off Clyffurd[55] gave.
He had a sone, a litill knave,
That was than bot a litill page,
Bot syne he wes off gret vaslage.[56]
Hys fadyr dede he vengyt sua
That in Ingland I underta
Wes nane off lyve that hym ne dred,
For he sa fele off harnys sched
That nane that lyvys thaim can tell.
Bot wonderly hard thing fell
Till him or he till state wes brocht.
Thair wes nane aventur that mocht
Stunay hys hart na ger him let
To do the thing that he wes on set,
For he thocht ay encrely
To do his deid avysily[57].
He thocht weill he was worth na seyle[58]
That mycht of nane anoyis feyle,
And als for till escheve gret thingis

And hard travalys and barganyngis,
That suld ger his price doublyt be.
Quharfor in all hys lyvetyme he
Wes in gret payn and gret travaill,
And never wald for myscheiff faill
Bot dryve the thing rycht to the end
And tak the ure that God wald send.
His name wes James of Douglas,
And quhen he herd his fader was
Put in presoune so fellounly,
And at his landis halyly
War gevyn to the Clyffurd perfay
He wyst nocht quhat to do na say,[59]
For he had na thing for to dispend
Na thar wes nane that ever him kend
Wald do sa mekill for him that he
Mycht sufficiantly fundyn be.
Than wes he wonder will off wane,
And sodanly in hart has tane
That he wald travaile our the se
And a quhile in Parys[60] be,
And dre myscheiff quhar nane hym kend
Til God sum succouris till hym send.
And as he thocht he did rycht sua,
And sone to Parys can he ga
And levyt thar full sympylly,
The-quhether he glaid was and joly,
And till swylk thowlesnes he yeid
As the cours askis off youtheid,
And umquhill into rybbaldaill.
And that may mony tyme availl,
For knawlage off mony statis
May quhile availye full mony gatis
As to the gud erle off Artayis[61]
Robert befell in his dayis
For oft fenyeyng off rybbaldy
Availyeit him and that gretly.
And Catone sayis us in his wryt

That to fenyhe foly quhile is wyt.
In Parys ner thre yer dwellyt he,
And then come tythandis our the se[62]
That his fadyr wes done to ded.[63]
Then wes he wa and will of red,
And thocht that he wald hame agayne
To luk gyff he throu ony payn
Mycht wyn agayn his heritage[64]
And his men out off all thryllage.
To Sanct Androws he come in hy,
Quhar the byschop full curtasly[65]
Resavyt[66] him and gert him wer
His knyvys forouth him to scher,
And cled him rycht honorabilly
And gert ordayn quhar he suld ly.
A weile gret quhile thar dwellyt he.
All men lufyt him, for his bounte,
For he wes off full fayr effer
Wys curtais and deboner.
Larg and luffand als[67] wes he,
And our all thing luffyt lawte.[68]
Leawte to luff is gretumly,
Throuch leawte liffis men rychtwisly.
With a vertu and leawte
A man may yeit sufficyand be,
And but leawte may nane haiff price
Quether he be wycht or he be wys,
For quhar it failyeys na vertu
May be off price na off valu
To mak a man sa gud that he
May symply callyt gud man be.
He wes in all his dedis lele,
For him dedeynyeit nocht to dele
With trechery na with falset.
His hart on hey honour wes set,
And hym contenyt on sic maner
That all him luffyt that war him ner.
Bot he wes nocht sa fayr that we

Suld spek gretly off his beaute.
In vysage wes he sumdeill gray[69]
And had blak har as Ic hard say,[70]
Bot off lymmys he wes weill maid
With banys gret and schuldrys braid,
His body wes weyll maid and lenye
As thai that saw hym said to me.
Quhen he wes blyth he wes lufly
And meyk and sweyt in cumpany,
Bot quha in battaill mycht him se
All othir contenance had he.
And in spek wlispyt he sumdeill,[71]
Bot that sat him rycht wonfre weill.
Till gud Ector of Troy mycht he[72]
In mony thingis liknyt be.
Ector had blak har as he had
And stark lymmys and rycht weill maid,
And wlispyt alsua as did he,[73]
And wes fullfillyt of leawte
And wes curtais and wys and wycht
Bot off manheid and mekill mycht
Till Ector dar I nane comper
Off all that ever in warldys wer.
The-quhethyr in his tyme sa wrocht he
That he suld gretly lovyt be.
He dwellyt thar quhill on a tid
The King Edward with mekill prid[74]
Come to Strevillyne with gret mengye[75]
For till hald thar ane assemble.[76]
Thidderwart went mony baroune,[77]
Byschop Wilyame off Lambyrtoun[78]
Raid thiddyr als and with him was
This squyer James of Douglas.
The byschop led him to the king
And said, 'Schyr, heyr I to you bryng
This child that clemys your man to be,
And prays you par cheryte[79]
That ye resave her his homage[80]

208

And grantis him his heritage.'
'Quhat landis clemys he?' said the king.
'Schyr, giff that it be your liking
He clemys the lordschip off Douglas,
For lord tharoff hys fader was.'
The king then wrethyt him encrely
And said, 'Schyr byschop, sekyrly
Gyff thou wald kep thi fewte
Thoue maid nane sis speking to me.
His fadyr ay wes my fay feloune
And deyt tharfor in my presoun
And wes agayne my majeste
Tharfor hys ayr I aucht to be.
Ga purches land quharever he may
For tharoff haffys he nane, perfay.
The Clyffurd sall thaim haiff for he
Ay lely has servyt to me.'[81]
The bischop hard him swa answer
And durst than spek till him na mar,
Bot fra his presence went in hy
For he dred sayr his felouny
Swa that he na mar spak tharto.
The king did that he com to do
And went till Ingland syn agayn
With mony man off mekill mayn.
Lordingis, quha likis for till her,[82]
The romanys now begynnys her[83]
Off men that war in gret distres
And assayit full gret hardynes
Or thai mycht cum till thar entent.
Bot syne our Lord sic grace thaim sent
That thai syne throu thar gret valour
Come till gret hycht and till honour,
Magre thar fayis everilkane[84]
That war sa fele that ay till ane
Off thaim thai war weill a thousand,
Bot quhar God helpys quhat may withstand.
Bot and we say the suthfastnes

Thai war sum tyme erar may then les,
Bot God that maist is off all mycht
Preservyt thaim in his forsycht
To veng the harme and the contrer
At that fele folk and pautener[85]
Dyd till sympill folk and worthy
That couth nocht help thaim self. For-thi
Thai war lik to the Machabeys[86]
That as men in the bibill[87] seys
Throw thar gret worschip and valour
Faucht into mony stalwart stour
For to delyver thar countre
Fra folk that throu iniquite
Held thaim and thairis in thrillage.
Thai wrocht sua throu thar vasselage
That with few folk thai had victory
Off mychty kingis as sayis the story,
And delyveryt thar land all fre,
Quharfor thar name suld lovyt be.
Thys lord the Bruys I spak of ayr[88]
Saw all the kynryk swa forfayr,
And swa troublyt the folk saw he
That he tharoff had gret pitte.
Bot quhat pite that ever he had
Na contenance tharoff he maid,
Till on a tym Schyr Jhone Cumyn[89]
As thai come ridand fra Strevillyn[90]
Said till him, 'Schyr, will ye nocht se
How that governyt is this countre.
Thai sla our folk but enchesoune[91]
And haldis this land agayne resoune,
And ye tharoff suld lord be.
And gyff that ye will trow to me
Ye sall ger mak you tharoff king,
And I sall be in your helping
With-thi ye giff me all the land
That ye haiff now intill your hand.
And gyff that ye will nocht do sua

Ne swylk a state upon you ta,
All hale my land sall youris be
And lat me ta the state on me
And bring this land out off thyrllage,
For thar is nother man na page
In all this land than thai sall be
Fayn to mak thaim selvyn fre.'
The lord the Bruis hard his carping
And wend he spak bot suthfast thing,
And for it likit till his will
He gave his assent sone thartill
And said, 'Sen ye will it be swa
I will blythly apon me ta
The state, for I wate that I have rycht,
And rycht mays oft the feble wycht.'[92]
The barounys thus accordyt ar,
And that ilk nycht writyn war
Thair endenturis, and aythis maid[93]
To hald that thai forspokyn haid.
Bot of all thing wa worth tresoun,
For thar is nother duk ne baroun
Na erle na prynce na king off mycht
Thocht he be never sa wys na wycht
For wyt worschip price na renoun,
That ever may wauch hym with tresoune.
Was nocht all Troy with tresoune tane
Quhen ten yeris off the wer wes gane?
Then slayn wes mony thousand
Off thaim without throu strenth of hand,
As Dares in his buke he wrate,
And Dytis that knew all thar state.
Thai mycht nocht haiff beyn tane throu
    mycht,
Bot tresoun tuk thaim throu hyr slycht.
And Alexander the conqueroure
That conqueryt Babilonys tour
And all this warld off lenth and breid
In twelf yher throu his douchty deid

Wes syne destroyit throu pusoune
In his awyne hous throu gret tresoun,
Bot or he deit his land delt he;
To se his dede wes gret pite.
Julius Cesar als, that wan
Bretane and Fraunce as douchty man,
Affryk, Arrabe, Egipt, Surry[94]
And all Europe halyly[95],
And for his worschip and valour
Off Rome wes fryst made emperour,
Syne in his capitole wes he
Throu thaim of his consaill preve
Slayne with punsoune rycht to the ded,
And quhen he saw thar wes na rede
Hys eyn with his hand closit he
For to dey with mar honeste.
Als Arthur that throu chevalry
Maid Bretane maistres and lady
Off twelf kinrikis that he wan,
And alsua as a noble man
He wan throu bataill Fraunce all fre,
And Lucius Yber vencusyt he[96]
That then of Rome wes emperour,
Bot yeit for all his gret valour
Modreyt his syster son him slew,
And gud men als ma then inew
Throu tresoune and throu wikkitnes,
The Broite beris tharoff wytnes.
Sa fell of this conand-making,
For the Cumyn raid to the king
Off Ingland and tald all this cas
Bot I trow nocht all as it was
Bot the endentur till him gaf he
That soune schawyt the iniquite.
Quharfor syne he tholyt ded,
Than he couth set tharfor na rede.
Quhen the king saw the endentur
He wes angry out of mesur,

And swour that he suld vengeance ta
Off that Bruys that presumyt swa
Aganys him to brawle or rys
Or to conspyr on sic a wys.
And to Schyr Jhon Cumyn said he
That he suld for his leawte
Be rewardyt and that hely,
And he him thankit humyly.
Than thocht he to have the leding
Off all Scotland but gane-saying
Fra at the Bruce to dede war brocht.
Bot oft failyeis the fulis thocht,
And wys mennys etling
Cummys nocht ay to that ending
That thai think it sall cum to,
For God wate weill quhat is to do.
Off hys etlyng rycht swa it fell
As I sall efterwartis tell.
He tuk his leve and hame is went,
And the king a parlyament
Gert set tharefter hastely
And thidder somounys he in hy
The barounys of his reawte,[97]
And to the lord the Bruce send he
Bydding to cum to that gadryng[98]
And he that had na persavyng
Off the tresoun na the falset
Raid to the king but langer let,
And in Lundon hym herberyd he
The fyrst day off thar assemble,
Syne on the morn to court he went.

The king sat into parleament
And forouth hys consaile preve
The lord the Bruce thar callyt he
And schawyt hym the endentur.
He wes in full gret aventur
To tyne his lyff, bot God of mycht
Preservyt him till hyer hycht,
That wald nocht that he swa war dede.
The king betaucht hym in that steid
The endentur the seile to se,
And askyt gyff it enselyt he?
He lukyt the seyle ententily
And answeryt till him humyly
And sayd, 'How that I sympill be
My seyle is nocht all tyme with me.[99]
Ik have ane other it to ber.
Tharfor giff that your willis wer
Ic ask you respyt for to se
This letter and tharwith avysit be
Till tomorn that ye be set,
And then foroutyn langer let
This letter sall I entyr heyr
Befor all your consaill planer,
And thartill into borwch draw I
Myn herytage all halily.'[100]
The king thocht he wes traist inewch
Sen he in bowrch hys landis drewch,
And let hym with the letter passe
Till entyr it as forspokin was.

BOOK II

The Bruys went till his innys swyth,[1]
Bot wyt ye weile he wes full blyth
That he had gottyn that respyt.

He callit his marschall till him tyt
And bad him luk on all maner
That he ma till his men gud cher,

For he wald in his chambre be
A weile gret quhile in prevate,
With him a clerk foroutyn ma.
The marschell till the hall gan ga
And did hys lordys commanding.
The lord the Bruce but mar letting
Gert prevely bryng stedys twa,[2]
He and the clerk foroutyn ma
Lap on foroutyn persavyng,
And day and nycht but sojournyng
Thai raid quhill on the fyften day
Cummyn till Louchmaben[3] ar thai.
Hys broder Edward[4] thar thai fand
That thocht ferly Ic tak on hand
That thai come hame sa prevely.
He tauld hys brodyr halyly
How that he thar soucht was
And how that he chapyt wes throu cas[5].
Sa fell it in the samyn tid
That at Dumfres rycht thar besid
Schir Jhone the Cumyn sojornyng maid.
The Brus lap on and thidder raid[6]
And thocht foroutyn mar letting
For to quyt hym his discovering.
Thidder he raid but langer let
And with Schyr Jhone the Cumyn met
In the Freris at the hye awter,
And schawyt him with lauchand cher
The endentur, syne with a knyff
Rycht in that sted hym reft the lyff[7].
Schyr Edmund Cumyn als wes slayn
And othir mony off mekill mayn.
Nocht-for-thi yeit sum men sayis
At that debat fell other-wayis,
Bot quhat-sa-evyr maid the debate
Thar-throuch he deyt weill I wat.
He mysdyd thar gretly but wer
That gave na gyrth to the awter,

Tharfor sa hard myscheiff him fell
That Ik herd never in romanys tell
Off man sa hard frayit as wes he
That efterwart com to sic bounte.
Now agayne to the king[8] ga we
That on the morn with his barne[9]
Sat intill his parleament,
And eftyr the lord the Bruys he sent
Rycht till his in with knychtis kene
Quhen he oft-tyme had callit bene
And his men efter him askit thai,
Thai said that he sen yhysterday[10]
Dwelt in his chambyr ythanly[11]
With a clerk with him anerly.[12]
Than knokyt thai at his chamur thar
And quhen thai hard nane mak answar
Thai brak the dur, bot thai fand nocht.
The-quhethir the chambre hale thai socht.
Thai tald the king than hale the cas
And how that he eschapyt was.
He wes off his eschap sary
And swour in ire full stalwartly
That he suld drawyn and hangit be.
He manansyt as him thocht, bot he
Thoucht that suld pas ane other way
And, quhen he as ye herd me say
Intill the kyrk Schyr Jhone haid slain,
Till Louchmabane he went agayne
And gert men with his lettres ryd
To freyndis apon ilk sid
That come to hym with thar mengye,[13]
And his men als assemblit he
And thocht that he wald mak him king.
Our all the land the word gan spryng
That the Bruce the Cumyn had slayn,
And amang other, lettres ar gayn
To the byschop off Androws towne
That tauld how slayn wes that baroun.

The letter tauld hym all the deid,
And he till his men gert reid
And sythyn said thaim, 'Sekyrly
I hop Thomas prophecy[14]
Off Hersildoune sall veryfyd be
In him, for swa Our Lord help me
I haiff gret hop he sall be king
And haiff this land all in leding.'
James off Douglas that ay-quhar
Allwayis befor the byschop schar
Had weill hard all the letter red,
And he tuk alsua full gud hed
To that the byschop had said.
And quhen the burdys doun war laid
Till chamyr went thai then in hy,
And James off Douglas prevely
Said to the byschop, 'Schyr, ye se
How Inglismen throu thar powste
Dysherysys me off my land,[15]
And men has gert you understand
Als that the erle off Carryk
Clamys to gevern the kynryk,
And for yon man that he has slayn
All Inglismen ar him agayn
And wald disherys hym blythly,
The-quhether with hym dwell wald I.
Tharfor, schir, giff it war your will
I wald tak with him gud and ill.
Throu hym I trow my land to wyn
Magre[16] the Cliffurd and his kyn.'
The byschop hard and had pite[17]
And said, 'Swet son, sa God help me
I wald blythly that thou war thar
Bot at I nocht reprovyt war.
On this maner weile wyrk thou may.
Thou sall tak Ferrand my palfray,
For thar is na hors in this land
Sa swytht na yeit sa weill at hand.

Tak him as off thine awyne hewid[18]
As I had gevyn tharto na reid,
And gyff his yhemar oucht gruch[19]
Luk that thou tak him magre his,[20]
Swa sall I weill assonyeit be.
Mychty God for his powste
Graunt that he that thou pasis to
And thou in all tyme sa weill to do
That ye you fra your fayis defend.
He taucht him siluer to dispend[21]
And syne gaiff him gud day
And bad him pas furth on his way,
For he ne wald spek till he war gane.
The Douglas then his way has taine
Rycht to the hors, as he him bad,
Bot he that him in yhemsell had
Than warnyt him dispitously,
Bot he that wreth him encrely
Fellyt hym with a swerys dynt,[22]
And syne foroutyn langer stynt
The hors he sadylt hastely,
And lap on hym delyverly
And passyt furth but leve-taking.
Der God that is off hevyn king
Sauff hym and scheld him fra his fayis.
All him alane the way he tais
Towart the towne off Louchmabane,
And a litill fra Aryk stane[23]
The Bruce with a gret rout he met
That raid to Scone for to be set
In kingis stole and to be king.
And quhen Douglas saw hys cummyng
He raid and hailsyt hym in hy
And lowtyt him full curtasly,
And tauld him haly all his state
And quhat he was, and als how-gat
The Cliffurd held his heritage,
And that he come to mak homage

Till him as till his rychtwis king,
And at he boune wes in all thing
To tak with him the gud and ill.
And quhen the Bruce had herd his will
He resavyt him in gret daynte
And men and armys till him gaff he.
He thocht weile he suld be worthy
For all his eldris war douchty.
Thusgat maid thai thar aquentance
That never syne for nakyn chance
Departyt quhill thai lyffand war.
Thair frendschip woux ay mar and mar,[24]
For he servyt ay lelely,[25]
And the tother full wilfully
That was bath worthy wycht and wys
Rewardyt him weile his servys
The lord the Bruce to Glaskow raid
And send about him quhill he haid
Off his freyndis a gret menyhe,
And syne to Scone in hy raid he
And wes maid king but langer let,
And in the kingis stole wes set
As in that tyme wes the maner.
Bot off thar nobleis, gret affer,
Thar service na thar realte
Ye sall her na thing now for me,
Owtane that he off the barnage
That thidder come tok homage
And syne went our all the land
Frendis and frendschip purchesand
To maynteym that he had begunnyn.
He wyst or all the land war wonnyn
He suld fynd full hard barganyng
With him that wes off Ingland king,
For thar wes nane off lyff sa fell
Sa pautener na sa cruell.
And quhen to King Edward wes tauld
How at the Bruys that wes sa bauld

Had brocht the Cumyn till ending,
And how he syne had maid him king,
Owt off his wyt he went weill ner,
And callit till him Schir Amer[26]
The Vallang that wes wys and wycht
And off his hand a worthy knycht,
And bad him men off armys ta
And in hy till Scotland ga,
And byrn and slay and rais dragoun[27],
And hycht all Fyfe[28] in warysoun
Till him that mycht other ta or sla
Robert the Bruce that wes his fa.
Schir Aymer did as he him bad,
Gret chevalry with him he had,
With him wes Philip the Mowbray,
And Ingram the Umfravill perfay
That wes bath wys and averty
And full off gret chevalry,
And off Scotland the maist party
Thai had intill thar cumpany,
For yheit then mekill off the land
Wes intill Inglismennys hand.
Till Perth then went thai in a rout,
That then wes wallyt all about[29]
With feile towris rycht hey bataillyt[30]
To defend giff it war assaylit,
Tharin dwellyt Schyr Amery
With all his gret chevalry.
The King Robert wyst he wes thar
And quhatkyn chyftanys with him war
And assemblyt all his mengye.
He had feyle off full gret bounte
Bot thar fayis war may then thai
Be fyften hunder as Ik herd say,[31]
The-quhether he had thar at that ned
Full feill that war douchty off deid
And barounys that war bauld as bar.
Twa erlis[32] alsua with him war,

Off Levynax and Atholl[33] war thai.
Edward the Bruce wes thar alsua,
Thomas Randell and Hew de le Hay
And Schyr David the Berclay
Fresale, Somerveile, and Inchmertyn.
James off Douglas thar wes syne
That yheyt than wes bot litill off mycht,
And othir fele folk forsye in fycht
Als was gude Cristell of Setoun
And Robert Boyd of greit renoun,
And uther feill of mekill micht
Bot I can nocht tell quhat thai hycht.[34]
Thocht thai war quheyn thai war worthy
And full off gret chevalry,
And in bataill in gud aray
Befor Sanct Jhonystoun[35] com thai
And bad Schyr Amery isch to fycht,
And he that in the mekill mycht
Traistyt off thaim that wes him by
Bad his men arme thaim hastily.
Bot Schir Ingram the Umfravill
Thocht it war all to gret perill
In playne bataill to thaim to ga
Or-quhill thai war arayit sa,
And till Schyr Amer said he,
'Schir, giff that ye will trow to me,[36]
Ye sall nocht ische thaim till assaile
Till thai ar purvayt in bataill,
For thar ledar is wys and wycht
And off his hand a noble knycht,
And he has in his cumpany
Mony a gud man and worthi
That sall be hard for till assay
Till thai ar in sa gud aray,
For it suld be full mekill mycht
That now suld put thaim to the flycht,
For quhen folk ar weill arayit
And for the bataill weill purvait

With-thi that thai all gud men be,
Thai sall fer mar be avise
And weill mar for to dreid then thai
War sumdele out off aray.
Tharfor ye may, schyr, say thaim till
That thai may this nycht and thai will
Gang herbery thaim and slep and rest,
And to-morn but langer lest
Ye sall isch furth to the bataill,[37]
And fecht with thaim bot gyf thai faile.
Sa till thar herbery went sall thai
And sum sall went to the forray,
And thai that dwellis at the logyng
Sen thai cum out off travelling
Sall in schort tyme unarmyt[38] be.
Then on our best maner may we
With all our fayr chevalry
Ryd towart thaim rycht hardyly.
And thai that wenys to rest all nycht
Quhen thai se us arayit to fycht
Cummand on thaim sa sudanly,
Thai sall affrayit be gretumly,
And or thai cummyn in bataill be
We sall speid us swagat that we
Sall be all redy till assembill.
Sum man for erynes will trymbill
Quhen he assayit is sodanly
That with avisement is douchty.'
As he avisyt have thai done,
And till thaim utouth send thai sone
And bade thaim herbery thaim that nycht
And on the morn cum to the fycht.
Quhen thai saw thai mycht no mar
Towart Meffayn[39] then gan thai far
And in the woud thaim logyt thai.
The thrid part went to the forray,
And the lave sone unarmyt war
And skalyt to loge thaim her and thar

Schyr Amer then but mar abaid
With all the folk he with him haid
Ischyt inforcely to the fycht,
And raid intill a randoun rycht
The straucht way towart Meffen[40].
The king that wes unarmyt then
Saw thaim cum swa inforcely,
Then till his men gan hely cry,
'Till armys, swyth, and makis you yar,
Her at our hand our fayis ar.'
And thai did swa in full gret hy
And on thar hors lap hastily.
The king displayit his baner
Quhen that his folk assemblyt wer
And said, 'Lordingis now may ye se
That yone folk all throu sutelte
Schapis thaim to do with slycht
That at thai drede to do with mycht.
Now I persave he that will trew
His fa, it sall him sum-tyme rew.
And nocht-for-thi, thocht thai be fele
God may rycht weill our werdis dele
For multitud mais na victory,
As man has red in mony story
That few folk has oft vencusyt ma.
Trow we that we sall do rycht sua.
Ye ar ilkan wycht and worthy[41]
And full of gret chevalry,
And wate rycht weill quhat honour is.
Wyrk yhe then apon swylk wys
That your honour be savyt ay.
And a thing will I to you say,
That he that deis for his cuntre
Sall herbryit intill hevyn be.'
Quhen this wes said thai saw cumand
Thar fayis ridand ner at the hand
Arayit rycht avisely
Willfull to do chevalry.

On athir syd thus war thai yhar
And till assemble all redy war.
Thai straucht thar speris on athir syd[42]
And swa ruydly gan samyn ryd
That speris al to-fruschyt war[43]
And feyle men dede and woundyt sar,
The blud out at thar byrnys brest,
For the best and the worthiest
That wilfull war to wyn honour
Plungyt in the stalwart stour
And routis ruyd about thaim dang.
Man mycht haiff seyn into that thrang
Knychtis that wycht and hardy war
Under hors feyt defoulyt thar
Sum woundyt and sum all ded,
The gres woux off the blud all rede.
And thai that held on hors in hy
Swappyt out swerdis sturdyly
And sa fell strakys gave and tuk
That all the renk about thaim quouk.
The Bruysis folk full hardely
Schawyt thar gret chevalry
And he him selff atour the lave
Sa hard and sa hevy dyntis gave
That quhar he come thai maid him way.
His folk thaim put in hard assay
To stynt thar fais mekill mycht
That then so fayr had off the fycht
That thai wan feild ay mar and mar.
The kingis small folk ner vencusyt ar,
And quhen the king his folk has sene
Begouth to faile, for propyr tene
His assenyhe gan he cry[44]
And in the stour sa hardyly
He ruschyt that all the semble schuk.
He all till-hewyt that he ourtuk
And dang on thaim quhill he mycht drey.
And till his folk he criyt hey,

'On thaim, on thaim, thai feble fast[45],
This bargane never may langer last.'
And with that word sa wilfully
He dang on and sa hardely
That quha had sene him in that fycht
Suld hald him for a douchty knycht.
But thocht he wes stout and hardy
And othir als off his cumpany,
Thar mycht na worschip thar availye
For thar small folk begouth to failye
And fled all skalyt her and thar.
Bot the gude at enchaufyt war
Off ire abade and held the stour
To conquyr thaim endles honour.
And quhen Schyr Amer has sene
The small folk fle all bedene
And sa few abid to fycht
He releyt to himm mony a knycht[46]
And in the stour sa hardyly
He ruschyt with hys chevalry
That he ruschyt his fayis ilkane.
Schyr Thomas Randell[47] thar wes tane
That then wes a young bacheler[48]
And Schyr Alexander Fraseyr
And Schyr David the Breklay
Inchmertyne and Hew de le Hay
And Somervell and other ma.
And the king him selff alsua
Wes set imtill full hard assay
Throu Schyr Philip the Mowbray
That raid till him full hardyly
And hynt hys rengye[49] and syne gan cry,
'Help! Help! I have the new-maid king.'
With that come gyrdand in a lyng
Crystall off Seytoun quhen he swa
Saw the king sesyt with his fa,
And to Philip sic rout he raucht
That thocht he wes of mekill maucht

He gert him galay disyly,
And haid till erd gane fullyly
Ne war he hynt him by his sted,
Then off his hand the brydill yhed.
And the king his enssenye gan cry,
Releyt his men that war him by
That war sa few that thai na mycht
Endur the fors mar off the fycht.
Thai prikyt then out off the pres,
And the king that angry wes
For he his men saw fle him fra
Said then, 'Lordingis, sen it is swa
That ure rynnys agane us her,[50]
Gud is we pas of thar daunger
Till God us send eft-sonys grace.
And yeyt may fall giff thai will chace
Quyt thaim corn-but sumdele we sall.'
To this word thai assentyt all
And fra thaim walopyt ovyr-mar[51].
Thar fayis alsua wery war
That off thaim all thar chassyt nane,
Bot with presoneris that thai had tane
Rycht to the toune thai held thar way,
Rycht glaid and joyfull off thar pray.
That nycht thai lay all in the toun,
Thar wes nane off sa gret renoun
Na yeit sa hardy off thaim all
That durst herbery with-out the wall,
Sa dred thai sar the gayne-cummyng
Off Schyr Robert the douchty king.
And to the king off Ingland[52] sone
Thai wrate haly as thai haid done,
And he wes blyth off that tithing
And for dispyte bad draw and hing
All the presonneris thocht thai war ma.
Bot Schyr Amery did nocht sua
To sum bath land and lyff gaiff he
To leve the Bruysis fewte

And serve the king off Ingland
And off him for to hald the land
And werray the Brus as thar fa.
Thomas Randell wes ane off tha
That for his lyff become thar man.
Off other that war takyn than
Sum thai ransounyt[53], sum thai slew
And sum thai hangyt and sum thai drew.
In this maner rebutyt was
The Bruys that mekill murnyn mais
For his men that war slayne and tane,
And he wes als sa will off wane
That he trowit in nane sekyrly[54]
Outane thaim off his cumpany,[55]
That war sa few that thai mycht be
Fyve hunder[56] ner off all mengye.
His broder alwayis wes him by
Schyr Edward that wes sa hardy,
And with him wes a bauld baroun[57]
Schyr Wilyam the Boroundoun.
The erle off Athole als wes thar,
Bot ay syn thai discomfyt war
The erle off the Levenax wes away
And wes put to full hard assay
Or he met with the king agayn,
Bot always as a man off mayn
He mayntemyt him full manlyly.
The king had in his cumpany
James alsua of Douglas
That wycht wys and averty was,
Schyr Gilbert de le Hay alsua
Schir Nele Cambell and other ma
That I thar namys can nocht say,
As utelawys[58] went mony day
Dreand in the Month thar pyne,
Eyte flesch and drank water syne.
He durst nocht to the planys ga[59]
For all the commounys went him fra[60]

That for thar liffis war full fayn
To pas to the Inglis pes agayn.[61]
Sa fayris ay commounly,
In commounys may nane affy[62]
Bot he that may thar warand be.[63]
Sa fur thai then with him, for he
Thaim fra thar fais mycht nocht warand
Thai turnyt to the tother hand,
Bot threldome that men gert thaim fele
Gert thaim ay yarne that he fur wele.
Thus in the hyllis levyt he[64]
Till the mast part off his menye[65]
Wes revyn and rent, na schoyn thai had
Bot as thai thaim off hydis mad.
Tharfor thai went till Aberdeyne[66]
Quhar Nele the Bruys come and the
    queyn.[67]
And other ladyuis fayr and farand
Ilkane for luff off thar husband
That for leyle luff and leawte
Wald partenerys off thar paynys be.[68]
Thai chesyt tyttar with thaim to ta
Angyr and payne na be thaim fra,
For luff is off sa mekill mycht
That it all paynys makis lych,
And mony tyme mais tender wychtis
Off swilk strenthtis and swilk mychtis
That thai may mekill paynys endur
And forsakis nane aventur
That evyr may fall, with-thi that thai
Tharthrou succur thair liffys may.
Men redys, quhen Thebes wes tane
And Kyng Aristas men war slane
That assailyt the cite,
That the wemen off his cuntre
Come for to fech him hame agayne
Quhen thai hard all his folk wes slayne,
Quhar the King Campaneus

Throu the help off Menesteus
That come percas ridand tharby
With thre hunder in cumpany
That throu the kingis prayer assailyt
That yeit to tak the toun had failyeit.
Then war the wiffys thyrland the wall
With pikkis, quhar the assailyeis all
Entryt and dystroyit the tour
And slew the pupill but recour.
Syn quhen the duk his way wes gayne
And all the kingis men war slayne
The wiffis had him till his cuntre
Quhar wes na man leiffand bot he.
In wemen mekill comfort lyis
And gret solace on mony wis,
Sa fell yt her, for thar cummyng
Rejosyt rycht gretumly the king.
The-quhether ilk nycht himselvyn wouk
And rest apon daiis touk.
A gud quhile thar he sojournyt then
And esyt wonder weill his men
Till that the Inglis-men herd say
That he thar with his menye lay
All at ese and sekyrly.
Assemblit thai thar ost in hy[69]
And thar him trowit to suppris[70]
Bot he that in his deid wes wys
Wyst thai assemblyt war and quhar,

And wyst that thei sa mony war
That he mycht nocht agayne thaim fycht.
His men in hy he gert be dycht
And buskyt of the toun to ryd,
The ladyis raid rycht by his syd.
Then to the hill thai raid thar way,
Quhar gret defaut off mete had thai.[71]
Bot worthy James off Douglas
Ay travailland and besy was[72]
For to purches the ladyis mete[73]
And it on mony wis wald get,
For quhile he venesoun thaim brocht,
And with his handys quhile he wrocht
Gynnys to tak geddis and salmonys[74]
Trowtis elys and als menounys,[75]
And quhill thai went to the forray,
And swa thar purchesyng maid thai.
Ilk man traveillyt for to get
And purches thaim that thai mycht ete.
Bot off all that ever thai war
Thar wes nocht ane amang thaim thar
That to the ladyis profyt was
Mar then James of Douglas,
And the king oft comfort wes
Throu his wyt and his besynes.
On this maner thaim governyt thai
Till thai come to the hed off Tay.

BOOK III

The lord off Lorne wonnyt thar-by
That wes capitale ennymy
To the king for his emys sak
Jhon Comyn, and thocht for to tak
Vengeance apon cruell maner.
Quhen he the king wyst wes sa ner[1]

He assemblyt his men in hy,
And had intill his cumpany
The barounys off Argyle alsua.
Thai war a thousand weill or ma
And come for to suppris the king
That weill wes war of thar cummyng.

Bot all to few with him he had
The-quhethir he bauldly thaim abaid,
And weill ost at thar fryst metyng
War layd at erd but recoveryng.
The kingis folk full weill thaim bar
And slew and fellyt and woundyt sar,
Bot the folk off the tother party
Faucht with axys sa fellyly,
For thai on fute war everilkane,
That thai feile off thar hors has slayne,
And till sum gaiff thai woundis wid.
James off Douglas wes hurt that tyd[2]
And als Schyr Gilbert de le Hay.
The king his men saw in affray
And his ensenye can he cry
And amang thaim rycht hardyly
He rad that he thaim ruschyt all
And fele off thaim thar gert he fall.
Bot quhen he saw thai war sa feill
And saw thaim swa gret dyntis deill
He dred to tyne his folk, forthi
His men till him he gan rely
And said, 'Lordyngis, foly it war
Tyll us for till assembill mar,
For thai fele off our hors has slayn,
And giff yhe fecht with thaim agayn
We sall tyne off our small mengye
And our selff sall in perill be.
Tharfor me thynk maist avenand
To withdraw us us defendand
Till we cum out off thar daunger,
For our strenth at our hand is ner.'
Then thai withdrew thaim halely
Bot that wes nocht full cowartly
For samyn intill a sop held thai
And the king him abandonyt ay
To defend behind his mengye,
And throu his worschip sa wrouch he

That he reskewyt all the flearis[3]
And styntyt swagat the chassaris
That nane durst out off batall chas,
For alwayis at thar hand he was.
Sa weile defendyt he his men
That quha-sa-ever had seyne him then
Prove sa worthely vasselage
And turn sa oft-sythis the visage
He suld say he aucht weill to be
A king off a gret reawte.
Quhen that the lord off Lorne saw
His men stand off him ane sik aw
That thai durst nocht folow the chase
Rycht angry in his hart he was,
And for wondyr that he suld swa
Stot thaim him ane but ma
He said, 'Me think Marthokys sone
Rycht as Golmakmorn was wone
To haiff fra Fyn all his mengne,
Rycht swa all his fra us has he.'
He set ensample thus mydlike,
The-quhethir he mycht mar manerlik
Lyknyt hym to Gaudifer de Larys[4]
Quhen that the mychty Duk Betys[5]
Assailyeit in Gadyrris[6] the forrayours,
And quhen the king thaim maid rescours
Duk Betys tuk on him the flycht
That wald ne mar abid to fycht.
Bot Gaudifer the worthi
Abandonyt him so worthyly
For to reskew all the fleieris
And for to stonay the chasseris
That Alysander to erth he bar
And alsua did he Tholimar
And gud Coneus alsua
Danklyne alsua and othir ma,
Bot at the last thar slayne he wes.
In that failyeit the liklynes,

220

For the king full chevalrusly
Defendyt all his cumpany
And wes set in full gret danger
And yeit eschapyt haile and fer.
Twa brethir war in that land[7]
That war the hardiest off hand
That war intill all that cuntre,
And thai had sworn iff thai mycht se
The Bruys quhar thai mycht him our-ta
That thai suld dey or then hym sla.
Thar surname wes Makyne Drosser,
That is al-so mekill to say her
As the Durwarth sonnys[8] perfay.
Off thar covyne the thrid had thai
That wes rycht stout ill and feloune.
Quhen thai the king off gud renoune
Saw sua behind his mengne rid
And saw him torne sa mony tid,
Thai abaid till that he was
Entryt in ane narow place
Betwix a louch-sid and a bra[9]
That wes sa strait Ik underta
That he mycht nocht weill turn in his
    sted.
Then with a will till him thai yede
And ane him by the bridill hynt,
Bot he raucht till him sic a dynt
That arme and schuldyr flaw him fra.
With that ane other gan him ta
Be the lege and his hand gan schute
Betwix the sterap and his fute,[10]
And quhen the king feld thar his hand
In his sterapys stythly gan he stand
And strak with spuris the stede in hy,
And he lansyt furth delyverly
Swa that the tother failyeit fete,
And nocht-for-thi his hand wes yeit
Undyr the sterap magre his.

The thrid with full gret hy with this
Rycht till the bra-syd he yeid
And stert behynd hym on his sted.
The king wes then in full gret pres,
The-quhether he thocht as he that wes
In all hys dedys avise
To do ane outrageous bounte,
And syne hyme that behynd him was
All magre his will him gan he ras
Fra behynd him, thocht he had sworn,
He laid hym evyn him beforn,
Syne with the swerd sic dynt hym gave
That he the heid till the harnys clave.
He rouschit doun off blud all rede
As he that stound feld off dede.
And then the king in full gret hy
Strak at the tothir vigorusly
That he efter his sterap drew
That at the fyrst strak he him slew.
On this wis him delyverit he
Off all thai felloun fayis thre
Quhen thai of Lorne has sene the king
Set in hym selff sa gret helping
And defendyt him sa manlely,
Wes nane amang thaim sa hardy
That durst assailye him mar in fycht,
Sa dred thai for his mekill mycht.
Thar wes a baroune Maknauchtan
That in his hart gret kep has tane
To the kingis chevalry
And prisyt him in hert gretly,
And to the lord off Lorne said he,
'Sekyrly now may ye se
Be tane the starkest pundelan[11]
That evyr your lyfftyme ye saw tane,
For yone knycht throu his douchti deid
And thro his outrageous manheid
Has fellyt intill litill tyd

Thre men off mekill prid,
And stonayit all our mengye swa
That eftyr him dar na man ga,
And tournys sa mony tyme his stede
That semys off us he had na dred.'
Then gane the lord off Lorn say,
'It semys it likis ye perfay
That he slayis yongat our mengye.'
'Schyr,' said he, 'sa Our Lord me se,
To sauff your presence it is nocht swa,
Bot quhether-sa he be freynd or fa
That wynnys prys off chevalry
Men suld spek tharoff lelyly,
And sekyrly in all my tyme
Ik hard never in sang na ryme
Tell off a man that swa smertly
Eschevyt swa gret chevalry.'[12]
Sic speking off the king thai maid,
And he eftyr his mengye raid
And intill saufte thaim led
Quhar he his fayis na-thing dred,
And thai off Lorne agayn ar gayn
Menand the scaith that thai haiff tayn.
The king that nycht his wachis set[13]
And gert ordayne that thai mycht et,
And bad conford to thaim tak
And at thar mychtis mery mak.
For disconford, as then said he,
Is the werst thing that may be,
For throu mekill disconforting
Men fallis oft into disparing,
And fra a man disparyt be
Then utraly vencusyt is he,
And fra the hart be discumfyt
The body is nocht worth a myt.
'Tharfor,' he said, 'atour all thing
Kepys you fra disparyng,
And think thouch we now harmys fele

That God may yeit releve us weill.
Men redys off mony men that war
Fer harder stad then we yhet ar
And syne Our Lord sic grace thaim lent
That thai come weill till thar entent.
For Rome quhilum sa hard wes stad
Quhen Hanniball thaim vencusyt had
That off ryngis with rich stane
That war off knychtis fyngeris tane
He send thre bollis to Cartage[14]
And syne to Rome tuk his viage[15]
Thar to distroye the cite all.
And thai within bath gret and small
Had fled quhen thai saw his cummyng
Had nocht bene Scipio the king,
That or thai fled wald thaim haiff slayn,
And swagat turnyt he thaim agayn.
Syne for to defend the cite
Bath servandis and threllis mad he fre,
And maid thaim knychtis everilkane,[16]
And syne has off the templis tane
The armys that thar eldrys bar,
In name off victory offeryt thar.
And quhen thai armyt war and dycht
That stalwart karlis war and wycht
And saw that thai war fre alsua,
Thaim thocht that thai had lever ta
The dede na lat the toun be tane,
And with commoune assent as ane
Thai ischit off the toune to fycht
Quhar Hannyball his mekill mycht
Aganys thaim arayit was.
Bot throu mycht off Goddis grace
It ranyt sa hard and hevyly
That thar wes nane sa hardy
That durst into that place abid,
Bot sped thaim intill hy to rid,
The ta part to thar pailyounys,

The tother part went in the toune is.
The rayne thus lettyt the fechtyn,
Sa did it twys tharefter syne.
Quhen Hannibal saw this ferly
With all his gret chevalry
He left the toune and held his way,
And syne wes put to sik assay
Throu the power off that cite
That his lyff and his land tynt he.
Be thir quheyne that sa worthily
Wane sik a king and sa mychty,
Ye may weill be ensampill se
That na man suld disparyt be,
Na lat his hart be vencusyt all
For na myscheiff that ever may fall,
For nane wate in how litill space
That God umquhile will send grace.
Had thai fled and thar wayis gane
Thar fayis swith the toune had tane.
Tharfor men that werrayand war
Suld set thar etlyng ever-mar
To stand agayne thar fayis mycht
Umquhile with strenth and quhile with slycht,
And ay thynk to cum to purpos,
And giff that thaim war set in chos
To dey or to leyff cowartly,
Thai suld erar dey chevalrusly.
Thusgat thaim comfort the king
And to comfort thaim gan inbryng
Auld storys off men that wer
Set intyll hard assayis ser
And that fortoun contraryit fast,
And come to purpos at the last.
Tharfor he said that thai that wald
Thar hartis undiscumfyt hald
Suld ay thynk entently to bryng
All thar enpres to gud ending,

As quhile did Cesar the worthy[17]
That traveillyt ay so besyly
With all his mycht folowing to mak
To end the purpos that he wald tak,
That hym thocht he had doyne rycht nocht
Ay quhill to do him levyt ocht.
Forthi gret thingis eschevyt he
As men may in his story se.
Men may se be his ythen will,
And it suld als accord to skill
That quha tais purpos sekyrly
And folowis it syne ententily
Forout fayntice or yheit faynding,[18]
With-thi it be conabill thing,
Bot he the mar be unhappy
He sall eschev it in party,
And haiff he lyff-dayis weill may fall
That he sall eschev it all.
For-thi suld nane haff disparing
For till eschev a full gret thing,
For giff it fall he tharoff failye
The fawt may be in his travailye.
He prechyt thaim on this maner
And fenyeit to mak better cher[19]
Then he had mater to be fer,
For his caus yeid fra ill to wer,
Thai war ay in sa hard travaill,
Till the ladyis began to fayle
That mycht the travaill drey na mar,
Sa did other als that thar war.
The Erle Jhone wes ane off tha
Off Athole that quhen he saw sua
The king be discumfyt twys,
And sa feile folk agayne him rys,
And lyff in sic travaill and dout,
His hart begane to faile all-out
And to the king apon a day

He said, 'Gyff I durst you say,
We lyff into sa mekill dreid,
And haffis oftsys off met sic ned,
And is ay in sic travailling
With cauld and hunger and waking,
That I am sad off my selvyn sua
That I count nocht my liff a stra.
Thir angrys may I ne mar drey,
For thoucht me tharfor worthit dey
I mon sojourne, quharever it be.
Levys me tharfor par cheryte.'
The king saw that he sa wes failyt
And that he ik wes for-travaillyt.
He said, 'Schyr erle, we sall sone se
And ordayne how it best may be.
Quharever ye be, Our Lord you send
Grace fra your fais you to defend.'
With that in hy to him callyt he
Thaim that till him war mast preve.
Then amang thaim thai thocht it best
And ordanyt for the liklyest
That the queyne and the erle alsua
And the ladyis in hy suld ga
With Nele the Bruce till Kildromy[20],
For thaim thocht thai mycht sekyrly
Dwell thar quhill thai war vittaillit weile[21]
For swa stalwart wes the castell
That it with strenth war hard to get
Quhill that tharin war men and mete.
As thai ordanyt thai did in hy,
The queyne and all hyr cumpany
Lap on thar hors and furth thai far.
Men mycht haiff sene quha had bene thar
At leve-takyng the ladyis gret[22]
And mak thar face with teris wet,
And knychtis for thar luffis sak
Bath bsich and wep and murnyng mak,[23]
Thai kyssyt thar luffis at thar partyng.

The king umbethocht him off a thing,
That he fra thine on fute wald ga
And tak on fute bath weill and wa,
And wald na hors-men with him haiff,
Tharfor his hors all haile he gaiff
To the ladyis that myster had.
The queyn furth on hyr wayis rade
And sawffly come to the castell
Quhar hyr folk war ressavyt weill
And esyt weill with meyt and drynk,
Bot mycht nane eys let hyr to think
On the king that wes sa sar stad
That bot twa hunder with him had,
The-quhethir thaim weill comfortyt he ay.
God help him that all mychtis may.
The queyne dwelt thus in Kyldromy,
And the king and his cumpany
That war twa hunder and na ma
Fra thai had send thar hors thaim fra
Wandryt emang the hey montanys,
Quhar he and his oft tholyt paynys,[24]
For it wes to the wynter ner,
And sa feile fayis about him wer
That all the countre thaim werrayit.
Sa hard anoy thaim then assayit
Off hunger cauld with schowris snell
That nane that levys can weill it tell.
The king saw how his folk wes stad
And quhat anoyis that thai had,
And saw wynter wes cummand ner,
And that he mycht on na maner
Dre in the hillys the cauld lying
Na the long nychtis waking.
He thocht he to Kyntyr[25] wald ga
And swa lang sojournyng thar ma
Till wynter wedder war away,
And then he thocht but mar delay
Into the manland till aryve

224

And till the end his werdis dryv.
And for Kyntyr lyis in the se
Schyr Neil Cambel befor send he
For to get him navyn and meite,
And certane tyme till him he sete
Quhen he suld meite him at the se.
Schir Nele Cambell with his mengye
Went his way but mar letting
And left his brother with the king,
And in twelf dayis sua traveillit he
That he gat schippyne gud plente
And vittalis in gret aboundance.
Sa maid he nobill chevisance
For his sibmen wonnyt tharby
That helpyt him full wilfully.
The king efter that he wes gane
To Louch Lomond[26] the way has tane
And come on the thrid day,
Bot tharabout na bait fand thai
That mycht thaim our the water ber.
Than war thai wa on gret maner
For it wes fer about to ga,
And thai war into dout alsua
To meyt thar fayis that spred war wyd.
Tharfor endlang the louchhis syd[27]
Sa besyly thai socht and fast
Tyll James of Douglas at the last
Fand a litill sonkyn bate[28]
And to the land it drew fut-hate,
Bot it sa litill wes that it
Mycht our the watter but a thresum flyt.
Thai send tharoff word to the king
That wes joyfull off that fynding
And fyrst into the bate is gane,
With him Douglas, the thrid wes ane
That rowyt thaim our deliverly
And set thaim on the land all dry,
And rowyt sa oftsys to and fra

Fechand ay our twa and twa
That in a nycht and in a day
Cummyn out-our the louch ar thai,
For sum off thaim couth swome full weill[29]
And on his bak ber a fardele.[30]
Swa with swymmyng and with rowyng
Thai brocht thaim our and all thar thing.
The king the quhilis meryly
Red to thaim that war him by
Romanys off worthi Ferambrace[31]
That worthily our-cummyn was
Throu the rycht douchty Olyver[32],
And how the duk-peris wer
Assegyt intill Egrymor[33]
Quhar King Lavyne[34] lay thaim befo
With may thousandis then I can say,
And bot ellevyn within war thai
And a woman, and war sa stad
That thai na mete thar-within had
Bot as thai fra thar fayis wan.
Yheyte sua contenyt thai thaim than
That thai the tour held manlily
Till that Rychard off Normandy
Magre his fayis warnyt the king
That wes joyfull off this tithing,
For he wend thai had all beyne slayne.
Tharfor he turnyt in hy agayne
And wan Mantrybill and passit Flagot,
And syne Lavyne and all his flot[35]
Dispitusly discumfyt he,
And deliveryt his men all fre
And wan the naylis and the sper
And the crowne that Jhesu couth ber,
And off the croice a gret party
He wan throu his chevalry.
The gud king apon this maner
Comfort thaim that war him ner
And maid thaim gamyn and solace

Till that his folk all passyt was.
Quhen thai war passit the water brad
Suppos thai fele off fayis had
Thai maid thaim mery and war blyth.
Nocht-for-thi full fele syth
Thai had full gret defaut of mete,
And tharfor venesoun to get
In twa partys ar thai gayne.
The king himselff wes intill ane
And Schyr James off Douglas
Into the tother party was.
Then to the hycht thai held thar way
And huntyt lang quhill off the day
And soucht schawys and setis set[36]
Bot thai gat litill for till ete.
Then hapnyt at that tyme percas
That the erle of the Levenax was
Amang the hillis ner tharby,
And quhen he hard sa blaw and cry
He had wonder quhat it mycht be,
And on sic maner spyryt he
That he knew that it wes the king,
And then foroutyn mar duelling
With all thaim off his cumpany
He went rycht till the king in hy,
Sa blyth and sa joyfull that he
Mycht on na maner blyther be
For he the king wend had bene ded,
And he wes alsua will off red
That he durst nocht rest into na place,
Na sen the king discumfyt was
At Meffan he herd never thing
That ever wes certane off the king.
Tharfor into full gret daynte
The king full humyly haylist he,
And he him welcummyt rycht blythly
And askyt him full tenderly,
And all the lordis that war thar

Rycht joyfull off thar meting war,
And kyssyt him in gret daynte.
It wes gret pite for til se
How thai for joy and pite gret
Quhen that thai with thar falow met
That thai wend had bene dede, forthi
Thai welcummyt him mar hartfully,
And he for pite gret agayne
That never off metyng wes sa fayne.
Thocht I say that thai gret sothly
It wes na greting propyrly,
For I trow traistly that gretyng
Cummys to men for mysliking,
And that nane may but angyr gret
Bot it be wemen, that can wet
Thair chekys quhenever thaim list with
   teris,
The-quhethir weill oft thaim na thing
   deris,
But I wate weill but lesyng
Quhatever men say off sic greting
That mekill joy or yeit pete
May ger men sua amovyt be
That water fra the hart will rys
And weyt the eyne on sic a wys
That is lik to be greting,
Thocht it be nocht sua in all thing,
For quhen men gretis enkrely
The hart is sorowful or angry,
Bot for pite I trow gretyng
Be na thing bot ane opynnyng
Off hart that schawis the tendernys
Off rewth that in it closyt is.
The barounys apon this maner
Throu Goddis grace assemblyt wer.
The erle had mete and that plente
And with glad hart it thaim gaiff he,
And thai eyt it with full gud will

That soucht na nother sals thar-till
Bot appetyt, that oft men takys,
For rycht weill scowryt war thar stom-
    akys.
Thai eit and drank sic as thai had
And till Our Lord syne lovyng maid,
And thankit him with full gud cher
That thai war mete on that maner.
The king then at thaim speryt yarne
How thai sen he thaim seyne had farne,
And thai full petwysly[37] gan tell
Aventurs that thaim befell
And gret anoyis and poverte.
The king tharat had gret pite
And tauld thaim petwisly agayne
The noy, the travaill and the payne
That he had tholyt sen he thaim saw.
Wes nane amang thaim hey na law
That he ne had pite and plesaunce
Quhen that he herd mak remembrance
Off the perellys that passyt war,
Bot quhen men oucht at liking ar
To tell off paynys passyt by
Plesys to heryng petuisly,
And to rehers thar auld disese
Dois thaim oftsys comfort and ese,
With-thi tharto folow na blame
Dishonour wikytnes na schame.
Efter the mete sone rais the king
Quhen he had levyt hys speryng,
And buskyt him with his mengye
And went in hy towart the se
Quhar Schyr Nele Cambell thaim mete
Bath with schippis and with meyte
Saylys ayris and other thing[38]
That wes spedfull to thar passyng.
Then schippyt thai foroutyn mar
Sum went till ster and sum till ar,

And rowyt be the ile of But.
Men mycht se mony frely fute
About the cost, thar lukand
As thai on ayris rais rowand,
And nevys that stalwart war and squar,
That wont to spayn gret speris war,
Swa spaynyt aris that men mycht se
Full oft the hyde leve on the tre.
For all war doand, knycht and knave,
Wes nane that ever disport mycht have
Fra steryng and fra rowyng
To furthyr thaim off thar fleting.
Bot in the samyn tyme at thai
War in schipping, as ye hard me say,
The erle off the Levenax was,
I can nocht tell you throu quhat cas
Levyt behynd with his galay
Till the king wes fer on his way.
Quhen that thai off his cuntre
Wyst that so duelt behynd wes he
Be se with schippys thai him socht,
And he that saw that he wes nocht
Off pith to fecht with thai traytouris[39]
And that he had na ner socouris[40]
Then the kingis flote, forthi
He sped him efter thaim in hy,
Bot the tratouris hym folowyt sua
That thai weill ner hym gan ourta
For all the mycht that he mycht do.
Ay ner and ner thai come him to,
And quhen he saw thai war sa ner
That he mycht weill thar manance her
And saw thaim ner and ner cum ay,
Then till his mengye gan he say,
'Bot giff we fynd sum sutelte
Ourtane all sone sall we be.
Tharfor I rede but mar letting
That outakyn our armyng[41]

We kast our thing all in the se,
And fra our schip swa lychtyt be
We sall row and speid us sua
That we sall weill eschaip thaim fra,
With that thai sall mak duelling
Apon the se to tak our thing
And we sall row but resting ay
Till we eschapyt be away.'
As he divisyt thai have done
And thar schip thai lychtyt sone
And rowyt syne with all thar mycht,
And scho that swa wes maid lycht
Raykyt slidand throu the se.
And quhen thar fayis gan thaim se
Forouth thaim alwayis mar and mar,
The thingis that thar fletand war[42]
Thai tuk and turnyt syne agayne,[43]
And leyt thai lesyt all thar payne.
Quhen that the erle on this maner
And his mengye eschapyt wer,
Eftyr the king he gan him hy
That then with all his cumpany
Into Kyntyr aryvyt was.
The erle tauld him all his cas,
How he wes chasyt on the se
With thaim that suld his awyn be,
And how he had bene tane but dout
Na war it that he warpyt out
All that he had him lycht to ma
And swa eschapyt thaim fra.
'Schyr erle,' said the king, 'perfay,
Syn thou eschapyt is away
Off the tynsell is na plenyeing.[44]
Bot I will say the weile a thing,
That thar will fall the gret foly
To pas oft fra my cumpany,
For fele sys quhen thou art away
Thou art set intill hard assay,

Tharfor me thynk best to the
To hald the alwayis ner by me.'
'Schyr,' said the erle, 'it sall be swa.
I sall na wys pas fer you fra
Till God giff grace we be off mycht
Agayne our fayis to hald our stycht.'
Angus[45] off Ile that tyme wes syr
And lord and ledar off Kyntyr,
The king rycht weill resavyt he
And undertuk his man to be,
And him and his on mony wys
He abandounyt till his service,
And for mar sekyrnes gaiff him syne
His castell off Donavardyne[46]
To duell tharin at his liking.
Full gretumly thankyt him the king
And resavyt his service.
Nocht-forthi on mony wys
He wes dredand for tresoun ay,[47]
And tharfor, as Ik hard men say,
He traistyt in nane sekyrly
Till that he knew him utraly[48]
Boy quhatkin dred that ever he had
Fayr contenance to thaim he maid,
And in Donavardyne dayis thre
Foroutyne mar then duellyt he.
Syne gert he his mengye mak thaim yar
Towart Rauchryne be se to far[49]
That is ane ile in the se,
And may weill in mydwart be
Betuix Kyntyr and Irland,
Quhar als gret stremys ar rynnand
And als peralous and mar
Till our-saile thaim into schipfair
As is the rais of Bretangye[50]
Or Strait off Marrok into Spanye.[51]
Thair schippys to the se thai set,
And maid redy but langer let

Ankyrs rapys bath saile and ar
And all that nedyt to schipfar.
Quhen thai war boune to saile thai went,
The wynd wes wele to thar talent.
Thai raysyt saile and furth thai far,
And by the Mole thai passyt yar
And entryt sone into the rase
Quhar that the stremys sa sturdy was
That wavys wyd wycht brakand war
Weltryt as hillys her and thar.
The schippys our the wavys slayd
For wynd at poynt blawand thai had,[52]
Bot nocht-forthi quha had thar bene
A gret stertling he mycht haiff seyne
Off schippys, for quhilum sum wald be
Rycht on the wavys as on a mounte
And sum wald slyd fra heycht to law
Rycht as thai doune till hell wald draw,
Syne on the wav stert sodanly,
And other schippys that war tharby
Deliverly drew to the depe.
It wes gret cunanes to kep
Thar takill intill sic a thrang
And wyth sic wavis, for ay amang
The wavys reft thar sycht of land
Quhen thai the land wes rycht ner-hand,
And quhen schippys war sailand ner
The se wald rys on sic maner
That off the wavys the weltrand hycht
Wald refe thaim oft off thar sycht.
Bot into Rauchryne nocht-forthi
Thai aryvyt ilkane sawffly,
Blyth and glaid that thai war sua
Eschapyt thai hidwys wavis fra.
In Rauchryne thai aryvyt ar
And to the land thai went but mar
Armyt apon thar best maner.

Quhen the folk that thar wonnand wer
Saw men off armys in that cuntre
Aryve into sic quantite
Thai fled in hy with thar catell
Towart a rycht stalwart castell
That in the land wes tharby.
Men mycht her wemen hely cry
And fle with cataill her and thar.
Bot the kingis folk that war
Deliver of fute thaim gan our-hy
And thaim arestyt hastely
And brocht thaim to the king agayne
Swa that nane off thaim all wes slayne.
Then with thaim tretyt swa the king
That thai to fulfill his yarnyng
Become his men everilkane,
And has him trewly undertane
That thai and tharis loud and still
Suld be in all thing at his will,
And quhill him likit thar to leynd
Everilk day thai suld him send
Vittalis for thre hunder men,[53]
And thai as lord suld him ken,
Bot at thar possessioune suld be
For all his men thar awyn fre.
The cunnand on this wys was maid,
And on the morn but langer baid
Off all Rauchryne bath man and page
Knelyt and maid the king homage,[54]
And tharwith swour him fewte
To serve him ay in lawte,
And held him rycht weill cunnand,
For quhill he duelt into the land
Thai fand meit till his cumpany
And servyt him full humely.

BOOK IV

In Rawchryne leve we now the king
In rest foroutyn barganyng,
And off his fayis a quhile speke we
That throu thar mycht and thar powste
Maid sic a persecucioune
Sa hard, sa strayt and sa feloune
On thaim that till hym luffand wer
Or kyn or freynd on ony maner
That at till her is gret pite.
For thai sparyt off na degree[1]
Thaim that thai trowit his freynd wer
Nother off the kyrk na seculer,[2]
For off Glaskow Byschop Robert
And Marcus off Man thai stythly speryt
Bath in fetrys and in presoune,
And worthy Crystoll off Seytoun
Into Loudoun betresyt was
Throu a discipill off Judas
Maknab, a fals tratour that ay
Wes off his dwelling nycht and day
Quhom to he maid gud cumpany.
It wes fer wer than tratoury
For to betreys sic a persoune
So nobill and off sic renoune,
Bot tharoff had he na pite,
In hell condampnyt mocht he be.
For quhen he him betrasyt had
The Inglismen rycht with him rad
In hy in Ingland to the king,
That gert draw him and hede and hing
Foroutyn pete or mercy.
It wes gret sorow sekyrly
That so worthy a persoune as he
Suld on sic maner hangyt be,
Thusgat endyt his worthynes.
Off Crauford als Schyr Ranald wes

And Schyr Bryce als the Blar
Hangyt intill a berne in Ar.
The queyn and als Dame Marjory[3],
Hyr dochter that syne worthily
Wes coupillyt into Goddis band
With Walter Stewart off Scotland,
That wald on na wys langar ly
In the castell off Kyldromy
To byd a sege, ar ridin raith
With knychtis and squyeris bath
Throu Ros rycht to the gyrth off Tayne.[4]
Bot that travaill thai maid in vayne,
For thai off Ros that wald nocht ber
For thaim na blayme na yeit danger
Out off the gyrth thame all has tayne
And syne has send thaim everilkane
Rycht intill Ingland to the king,
That gert draw all the men and hing,
And put the ladyis in presoune
Sum intill castell sum in dongeoun.
It wes gret pite for till her
The folk be troublyt on this maner.
That tyme wes in Kyldromy
Wyth men that wycht and hardy
Schyr Neile the Bruce and I wate weile
That thar the erle was off Adheill.
The castell weill vittalyt thai
And mete and fuell gan purvay
And enforcyt the castell sua
That thaim thocht na strenth mycht it ta.
And quhen it to the king was tauld
Off Ingland how thai schup till hauld
That castell, he wes all angry
And callyt his sone till hym in hy
The eldest and aperand ayr
A young bacheler and stark and fayr

Schyr Edward callyt off Carnauerane[5],
That wes the sterkast man of ane
That men fynd mycht in ony countre
Prynce of Walys that tyme wes he.
And he gert als call erlys twa
Glosyster and Harfurd war tha
And bad thaim wend into Scotland
And set a sege with stalwart hand
To the castell off Kyldromy.
And all the halderis halyly
He bad distroy for-owtyn ransoun
Or bryng thaim till him in presoune.
Quhen thai the commaundment had tane
Thai assemblyt ane ost onane
And to the castell went in hy
And it assegyt vigorusly
And mony tyme full hard assaylyt.
Bot for to tak it yeit thai failyt
For thai within war rycht worthy
And thaim defendyt douchtely
And ruschyt thair fayis oft agayne
Sum beft sum woundyt sum alslayne
And mony tymys ische thai wald
And bargane at the barrais hald
And wound thar fayis oft and sla.
Schortly thai thaim contenyt sua
That thai withoute disparyt war
And thocht till Ingland for to far
For thai sa styth saw the castell
And with that it wes warnyst weill
And saw the men defend thaim sua
That thai nane hop had thaim to ta,
Nane had thai done all that sesoune
Gyff it ne had bene fals tresoun
For thar with thaim wes a tratour.
A fals lourdane a losyngeour[6]
Hosbarne[7] to name maid the tresoun,
I wate nocht for quhat enchesoun

Na quham with he maid that conwyn
Bot as thai said that war within
He tuk a culter hate glowand[8]
That yeit wes in a fyr brynnand
And went him to the mekill hall
That then with corn wes fyllyt all
And heych up in a mow it did,[9]
Bot it full lang wes nocht thar hid
For men sayis oft that fyr na prid
But discovering may na man hid,
For the pomp oft the prid furth schawis
Or ellis the gret boist that it blawis,
Na thar may na man fyr sa covyr
Than low or rek sall it discovyr.
Sa fell it her, for fyr all cler
Son throu the thak-burd gan apper
Fyrst as a stern syne as a mone
And weill bradder tharefter sone
The fyr out syne in bles brast
And the rek rais rycht wondre fast.
The fyr our all the castell spred
That mycht na force of man it red.[10]
Than thai within drew to the wall
That at that tyme wes bataillit all
Within rycht as it wes withoute
That bataillyne withoutyn dout
Savit thar lyvis, for it brak
Bles that thaim wald ourtak.
And quhen thar fayis the myscheiff saw
Till armys went thai in a thraw
And assaylyt the castell fast
Quhar thai durst come for fyris blast,
Bot thai within that myster had
Sa gret defence and worthy mad
That thai full oft thar fayis rusit
For thai nakyn perall refusyt,
Thai travaillyt for to sauff thar lyffis
Bot werd that till the end ay dryvis

The warldis thingis sua thaim travaillyt
That thai on twa halfys war assailyt,
In with fyr that thaim sua broilyit
And utouth with folk that thaim sua toilyit
That thai brynt magre thaim the yat
That, for the fyre that wes sua hate
Thai durst nocht entyr sua in hy,
Tharfor thar folk thai gan rely
And went to rest for it wes nycht
Till on the morn that day wes lycht.
At sik myscheiff as ye her say
War thai within, the-quhethyr ay
Thai thaim defendyt douchtely
And contenyt thaim sa manlily
That or day throu mekill payn
Thai had muryt up thar yat agayn.
But on the morn quhen day wes lycht
And sone wes ryssyn schynand brycht
Thai without in hale bataill
Come purvayt redy till assaill,
Bot thai within that sua war stad
That thai vitaill na fewell had
Quhar-with thai mycht the castell hald
Tretyt fyrst and syne thaim yauld
To be in-till the kingis will,
Bot that to Scottis men wes ill
As sone eftyr weill wes knawin.
For thai war hangyt all and drawyn.
Quhen this cunnand thus tretyt wes
And affermyt with sekyrnes[11]
Thai tuk thaim of the castell sone
And in-till schort tyme has done
That all a quarter of Snawdoun[12]
Rycht till the erd thai tumyllyt doun
Syne towart Ingland went thar way.
Bot quhen the king Edward hard say
How Neill the Bruce held Kildromy
Agayne his sone sa stalwartly,

He gadryt gret chevalry
And towart Scotland went in hy,
And as in-till Northummyrland
He wes with his gret rout ridand
A sekness tuk him in the way
And put him to sa hard assay
That he mycht nocht ga na ryd.
Him worthit magre his abid
In-till ane hamillet tharby
A litill toun and unworthy,
With gret payne thidder thai him brocht.
He wes sa stad that he ne mocht
His aynd bot with gret paynys draw
Na spek bot giff it war weill law
The-quhether he bad thai suld him say
Quhat toun wes that that he in lay.
'Schyr,' thai said, 'Burch-in-the-sand
Men callis this toun in-till this land.'
'Call thai it Burch, als,' said he.
My hop is now fordone to me
For I wend never to thole the payne
Of deid till I throu mekill mayn
The burch of Jerusalem had tane,
My lyff wend I thar suld be gayne.
In burch I wyst weill I suld de
Bot I wes nother wys na sle
Till other burch kep to ta.
Now may I na wis forther ga.'
Thus pleynyeit he off his foly,
As he had mater sekyrly
Quhen he covyt certante
Off that at nane may certan be,
The-quhether men said enclosit he had
A spyryt that him answer maid
Off thingis that he wald inquer.
Bot he fulyt foroutyn wer
That gaiff throuth till that creatur,
For feyndys ar off sic natur

232

That thai to mankind has invy
For thai wate weill and witterly
That thai that weill ar liffand her
Sall wyn the sege quharoff thai wer
Tumblyt throuch thar mekill prid.
Quharthrou oft-tymys will betid
That quhen feyndys distrenyeit ar
For till aper and mak answar
Throu force of conjuracioun
That thai sa fals ar and feloun
That thai mak ay thar answering
Into doubill understanding
To dissaiff thaim that will thaim trow.
Insample will I set her now
Off a wer as I herd tell
Betwix Fraunce and the Flemyngis fell.
The erle Ferandis modyr was
Nygramansour, and Sathanas
Scho rasyt and him askyt syne
Quhat suld worth off the fechtyn
Betwix the Fraunce king and hyr sone,
And he, as all tyme he wes wone,
Into dissayt maid his answer
And said till hyr thir thre vers her,
'Rex ruet in bello tumilique carebit honore
Ferrandus comitissa tuus mea cara Minerva
Parisius veniet magna comitante caterva.'
This wes the spek he maid perfay
And is in Inglis toung to say,
'The king sall fall in the fechting
And sall faile honour off erding,
And thi Ferand Mynerve my der
Sall rycht to Parys went but wer,
Folowand him gret cumpany
Off nobill men and off worthy.'[13]
This is the sentence off this saw
That the Latyn gan hyr schaw.
He callyt hyr his Mynerve

For Mynerve ay wes wont to serve
Him, till scho leffyt, at his divis
And for scho maid the samyn service
His Mynerve hyr callyt he,
And als throu his sutelte
He callyt hyr der hyr till dissaiff
That scho the tyttar suld consaiff
Off his spek the undyrstanding
That mast plesyt till hyr liking.
This doubill spek sua hyr dissavit
That throu hyr feill the ded ressavit,
For scho wes off hyr answer blyth
And till hyr sone scho tald it swyth,
And bad him till the batell sped
For suld victory haiff but dred.
And he that herd hyr sermonuyng
Sped him in hy to the fechting
Quhar he discomfyt wes and schent
And takin and to Paris sent,
Bot in the fechting nocht-forthi
The king, throu his chevalry,
Wes laid at erd and lawit bath,
Bot his men helpyt him weill rath.
And quhen Ferandis moder herd
How hyr sone in the bataill ferd
And at he wes sua discomfyt,
Scho rasyt the ill spyryt als tyt
And askyt quhy he gabyt had
Off the answer that he hyr mad,
And he said he had said suth all.
'I said ye that the king suld fall
In the bataill, and say did he,
And failyeid erding, as men may se.
And I said that thi sone suld ga
To Paris, and he did rycht sua,
Folowand sic a mengye
That never in his lyff-tyme he
Had sic a mengye in leding.

Now seis thou I maid na gabbing.'
The wyff confusyt wes perfay
And durst no mar than till him say
Thusgat throu doubill understanding
That bargane come till sic ending
That the ta part dissavyt was.
Rycht sagat fell yt in this cas.
At Jerusalem trowit he
Gravyn in the burch to be,
The-quhethyr at Burch-into-the-sand
He swelt rycht in his awn land.
And quhen he to the ded wes ner
The folk that at Kildromy wer
Come with presoneris that thai had tane,
And syne to the king ar gane
And for to comfort him thai tald
How thai the castell to thaim yauld
And how thai till his will war brocht,
To do off thame quhatever he thocht,
And askyt quhat men suld off thaim do.
Than lukyt he angyrly thaim to
And said grynnand[14], 'Hangis and drawys.'
That wes wonder off sik sawis,
That he that to the ded wes ner
Suld answer apon sic maner
Foroutyn menyng and mercy.
How mycht he traist on Hym to cry
That suthfastly demys all thing
To haiff mercy, for his criying,
Off him that throu his felony
Into sic point had na mercy.
His men his maundment[15] has done
And he deyt thatefter sone
And syne wes brocht till berynes.
His sone syne king efter wes.
To the King Robert agayne ga we
That in Rauchryne with his menye
Lay till wynter ner wes gane

And off that ile his mete has tane
James off Douglas wes angry
That thai langar suld ydill ly
And to Schyr Robert Boid said he,
'The pure folk off thys countre
Ar chargit apon gret maner[16]
Off us that idill lyis her,[17]
And ik her say that in Arane[18]
Intill a styth castell off stane
Ar Inglis men that with strang hand
Haldys the lordschip off the land
Ga we thidder, and weill may fall
Anoy thaim in sum thing we sall.'
Schir Robert said, 'I grant thar-till,
Till her mar ly war litill skill.
Tharfor till Aran pas will we,
For I knaw rycht weill the countre
And the castell rycht sua knaw I
We sall cum thar sua prevely
That thai sall haiff na persavyng
Na yeit witting off our cumyng,
And we sall ner enbuschyt be
Quhar we thar outecome may se.
Sa sall it on na maner fall
Na scaith thaim on sum wis we sall.'
With that thai buskyt thaim on-ane
And at the king thar leiff has tane
And went thaim furth syne on thar way.
Into Kyntyr sone cummyn ar thai,
Syne rowyt alwayis by the land
Till that the nycht wes ner on hand,
Than till Arane thai went thar way
And saufly thar aryvyt thai,
And in a glen thar galay drewch
And syne it helyt weill ineuch.
Thar takyll ayris and thar ster
Thai hyde all on the samyn maner
And held thar way rycht in the nycht

Sua that or day wes dawyn lycht
Thai war enbuschyt the castell ner
Armyt apon thair best maner
And thoucht thai wate war and wery
And for lang fastyng all hungry
Thai thocht to hald thaim all preve
Till that thai weill thar poynt mycht se.
Schir John the Hastingis at that tid
With knychtis off full mekill prid
And squyeris and yemanry,[19]
And that a weill gret cumpany,
Wes in the castell off Brathwik[20]
And oftsys quhen it wald him lik
He went huntyng with his menye
And sua the land abandounyt he
That durst nane warne to do his will.
He wes into the castell still
The tyme that James off Douglas
As Ik haiff tald enbuschit was.
Sa hapnyt that tyme throu chance
That with vittalis and purvyaunce
And with clething and with armyng
The day befor in the evynning
The undyr-wardane arivyt was
With thre batis weill ner the place
Quhar that the folk I spak off ar
Prevely enbuschyt war.
Syne fra tha batis saw thai ga
Off Inglismen thretty and ma
Chargit all with syndry thingis.
Sum bar wyne and sum armyngis,
The remanant all chargit wer
With thingis off syndry maner,
And other syndry yeid thaim by
As thai war maistrys ydilly.
Thai that enbuschyt war that saw
All foroutyn dreid or aw
Thar buschement on thaim thai brak

And slew all that thai mycht ourtak.
The cry rais hidwysly and hey
For thai that dredand war to dey
Rycht as bestis gan rar and cry.
Thai slew thaim foroutyn mercy.
Sua that into the samyne sted
Weill ner fourty thar war dede.
Quhen thai that in the castell war
Hard the folk sa cry and rar
Thai ischyt furth to the fechting,
Bot quhen the Douglas saw thar
    cummyng
His men till him he gan rely
And went till meit thaim hastily.
And quhen thai off the castell saw
Him cum on thaim foroutyn aw
Thai fled foroutyne mar debate
And thai thaim folowit to the yate
And slew of thaim as thai in past,
Bot thai thair yate barryt fast
That thai mycht do at thame na mar.
Tharfor thai left thaim ilkane thar
And turnyt to the se agayne
Quhar that the men war forouth slayn.
And quhen thai that war in the batis
Saw thar cummyng and wyst howgatis
Thai had discumfyt thar menye
In hy thai put thaim to the se
And rowyt fast with all thar mayne,
Bot the wynd wes thaim agayne
That sua hey gert the land-bryst rys
That thai moucht weld the se na wis.
Then thai durst nocht cum to the land,
Bot held thaim thar sa lang hobland
That off the thre batis drownyt twa
And quhen the Douglas saw it wes sua
He tuk armyng and cleything
Vittalis wyne and other thing

That thai fand thar and held thar way
Rycht glaid and joyfull off thar pray.
Quhen this James off Douglas
And his menye throu Goddis grace
War relevyt with armyng
And with vittaill and clething
Syne till a strenth thai held thar way
And thaim full manly governyt ay
Till on the tend day that the king
With all that war in his leding
Aryvyt into that countre
With thretty small galayis and thre.
The king aryvyt in Arane
And syne to the land is gane
And in a toune[21] tuk his herbery,
And speryt syne specially
Gyff ony man couth tell tithand
Off ony strang man in that land.
'Yhis,' said a woman, 'Schyr perfay
Off strang men I kan you say
That ar cummyn in this countre,
And schort quhile syne throu thar bounte
Thai haff discomfyt our wardane
And mony off his men has slane,
Intill a stalwart place her-by
Reparis all thar cumpany.'
'Dame,' said the king, 'wald thou me wis
To that place quhar thar repair is
I sall reward the but lesing,
For thai ar all off my dwelling
And I rycht blythly wald thaim se
And sua trow I that thai wald me.'
'Yhis,' said scho, 'Schir I will blythly
Ga with you and your cumpany
Till that I schaw you thar repair.'
'That is ineuch my sister fayr,
Now ga we forth-warth,' said the king.
Than went thai furth but mar letting

Folowand hyr as scho thaim led
Till at the last scho schawyt a sted
To the king in a wode glen
And said, 'Schir, her saw I the men
That yhe sper after mak logyng.
Her I trow be thar reparyng.'
The king then blew his horn in hy
And gert the men that wer him by
Hald thaim still and all preve
And syne agayn his horn blew he.
James off Douglas herd him blaw
And he the blast alsone gan knaw
And said, 'Sothly yon is the king,
I knaw lang quhill syne his blawyng.'
The thrid tym thar-with-all he blew
And then Schir Robert Boid it knew
And said, 'Yone is the king but dreid
Ga we furth till him better speid.'
Than went thai till the king in hy
And hm inclynyt curtasly,
And blythly welcummyt thaim the kimg
And wes joyfull of thar meting
And kissit thaim and speryt syne
How thai had farne in thar outyne,
And thai him tauld all but lesing.
Syne lovyt thai God off thar meting,
Syne with the king till his herbery
Went bath joyfull and joly.
The king apon the tother day
Gan till his preve menye say,
'Ye knaw all weill and ye may se
How we are out off our cuntre
Banyst throu Inglismennys mycht
And that that suld be ouris of rycht
Throu thar maistrys[22] thai occupy,
And wald alsua foroutyne mercy
Giff thai haid mycht destroy us all.
Bot God forbeid it suld sa fall

Till us as thai mak manassyng
For than war thar na recoveryng,
And mankind biddis us that we
To procur vengeance besy be.
For ye may se we haiff thre thingis
That makkis us oft monestingis
For to be worthi wis and wycht
And till anoy thaim at our mycht.
Ane is our lyffis saufte
That on na wys suld sauft be
Gyff thai had us at thar liking
The tother that makys us eggyng
Is that thai our possessioune
Haldis strenthly agayn resoun.
The thrid is the joy that we abid
Giff that it happyn as weill may tid
That we wyn victour and maistry,
Till ourcum thar felony.
Therfor we suld our hartis rais
Sua that na myscheyff us abais
And schaip us alwayis to that ending
That beris in it mensk and loving.
And tharfor lordingis gyff ye se
Amang you giff that it speidfull be
I will send a man in Carrik
To spy and sper our kynrik
How it is led and freynd and fa.
And giff he seis we land may ta
On Turnberys snuke he may
Mak a fyr on a certane day
And mak takynnyng till us that we
May thar aryve in saufte.
And giff he seis we may nocht sua,
Luk on na wys the fyr he ma.
Sua may we thar-throu haiff wittring
Off our passage or our dwelling.'
To this spek all assentyt ar,
And than the king withoutyn mar

Callyt ane that wes till him preve
And off Carrik his countre,
And chargyt him in les and mar
As ye hard me divis it ar
And set him certane day to mai
The fyr giff he saw it war sua
That thai had possibilite
To maynteyme wer in that cuntre.
And he that wes rycht weill in will
His lordis yharnyng to fulfill
As he that worthy wes and leile
And couth secreis rycht weill conseil
Sad he wes boune intill all thing
For to fulfill his commaunding,
And said he suld do sa wisely
That na repruff suld efter ly
Syne at the king his leiff has tane
And furth apon his way is gane.
Now gais the messynger his way
That hat Cuthbert as I herd say.
In Carrik sone aryvyt he
And passyt throu all the countre,
Bot he fand few tharin perfay
That gud wald off his maister say,
For fele off thaim durst nocht for dreid,
And other sum rycht into deid
War fayis to the nobill king,
That rewyt syne thar barganyng.
Baith hey and law the land wes then
All occupyit with Inglismen
That dispytyt atour all thing
Robert the Bruce the douchty king.
Carrik wes giffyn then halyly
To Schir Henry the lord Persy
That in Turnberyis castell then
Was with weill ner three hunder men,
And dauntyt sagat all the land
That all wes till him obeysand.

237

This Cuthbert saw thar felony,
And saw the folk sa halely
Be worthyn Inglis baith rich and pur
That he to nane durst him discur,
But thocht to leve the fyr unmaid,
Syne till his maister went but baid
And all thar convyne till him tell,
That wes sa angry and sa fell.
The king that intill Arane lay
Quhen that cummyn wes the day
That he set till his messinger
As Ik divisit you lang er
Eftyr the fyr he lokyt fast
And als sone as the none wes past
Him thocht weill he saw a fyr
Be Turnbery byrnand weill schyr,
And till his menye it gan schaw.
Ilk man thocht weill that he it saw,
Then with blyth hart the folk gan cry,
'Gud king, speid you deliverly
Sua that we sone in the evynnyng
Aryve foroutyn persayving.'
'I grant,' said he. 'Now mak you yar,
God furthyr us intill our far.'
Then in schort time men mycht thaim se
Schute all thar galayis[23] to the se
And ber to se baith ayr and ster
And other thingis that myster wer,
And as the king apon the sand
Wes gangand up and doun, bidand
Till that his menye redy war,
His ost come rycht till him thar,
And quhen that scho him halyst had
A preve spek till him scho made
And said, 'Takis gud kep till my saw,
For or ye pas I sall you schaw
Off your fortoun a gret party,
Bot our all specially

A wyttring her I sall you ma
Quhat end that your purpos sall ta,
For in this land is nane trewly
Wate thingis to cum sa weill as I.
Ye pas now furth on your viage
To venge the harme and the outrag
That Inglismen has to you done,
Bot ye wat nocht quhat-kyne forton
Ye mon drey in your werraying.
Bot wyt ye weill withoutyn lesing
That fra ye now haiff takyn land
Nane sa mychty na sa strenthth off hand
Sal ger you pas out off your countre
Till all to you abandounyt be.
Within schort tyme ye sall be king
And haiff the land at your liking
And ourcum your fayis all,
Bot fele anoyis thole ye sall
Or that your purpos end haiff tane,
Bot ye sall thaim ourdryve ilkane.
And that ye trowis this sekyrly
My twa sonnys with you sall I
Send to tak part of your travaill,
For I wate weill thai sall nocht faill
To be rewardyt weill at rycht
Quhen ye are heyit to your mycht.[24]
The king that herd all hyr carping
Thankit hyr in mekill thing,
For scho confort him sumdeill,
The-quhethir he trowyt nocht full weill
Hyr spek, for he had gret ferly
How scho suld wyt it sekyrly,
As it wes wounderfull perfay
How ony mannys science may
Knaw thingis that ar to cum
Determinabilly, all or sum,
Bot giff that he inspyrit war
Off Him that all thing evermar

238

Seys in his presciens
As it war ay in presens,
As was David and Jeremy[25]
Samuell, Joell and Ysai,[26]
That throu His haly grace gan tell
Fele thingis that efter fell,
Bot the prophetis sa thyn ar sawyn
That nane in erd now is knawin.
Bot fele folk ar sa curyous
And to wyt thingis covatous
That thai, throu thar gret clergy
Or ellys throu thar devilry,
On thir twa maneris makis fanding
Off thingis to cum to haiff knawing.
Ane of thaim is astrologi,
Quhar-throu clerkys that ar witty
May knaw conjunctiones of planetis,
And quhethir that thar cours thaim settis
In soft segis or in angry,
And off the hevyn all halyly
How that the dispositioun
Suld apon thingis wyrk her doun
On regiones or on climatis,
That wyrkys nocht ay-quhar agatis
Bot sumquhar les and sumquhar mar
Eftyr as thar bemys strekyt ar
Othir all evyn or on wry.
Bot me think it war gud maistri
Till ony astrolog to say
'This sall fall her and on this day.'
For thoucht a man his lyff haly
Studyit sua in astrology
That on sternys his hewid he brak,
The wys man sayis he suld nocht mak
All his lyff certane dayis thre,
And yeit suld he ay doute quhill he
Saw how that it come till ending.
Than is that na certane demyng.

Or gyff thai men that will study
In the craft off astrology
Knaw all mennys nacioun
And knew the constellacioun
That kyndlik maneris gyfis thaim till
For till inclyne to gud or ill,
How that thai throu science of clergi
Or throu slycht off astrology[27]
Couth tell quhatkyn perell apperis
To thaim that haldys kyndlik maneris,
I trow that thai suld faile to say
The thingis that thaim happyn may.
For quhethir-sa men inclynyt be
To vertu or to mavyte[28]
He may rychtg weill refreynye his will
Othir throu nurtur or thru skill
And to the contrar turne him all.
And men has mony tyme sene fall
That men kyndly till ivill gevyn[29]
Throu thar gret wit away has drevyn
Thar ill and worthin off gret renoun
Magre the constellacioun,
As Arestotill[30] giff as men redis
He had folowyt his kyndly dedis,
He had bene fals and covatous
Bot his wyt maid him vertuous.
And sen men may on this kyn wys
Wyrk agayne that cours that is
Principaill caus off thar demyng
Me think thar dome na certane thing.
Nygromancy the tother is
That kenys men on syndry wys
Throu stalwart conjuracionys
And throu exorcizacionys
To ger spyritis to thaim apper
And giff answeris on ser maner,
As quhilum did the Phitones
That quhen Saul abaysyt wes

239

Off the Felystynys[31] mycht,
Raysyt throu hyr mekill slycht
Samuelis spyrite als tite,
Or in his sted the ivill spyrite
That gaiff rycht graith answer hyr to,
Bot off hyr selff rycht nocht wyst scho.
And man is into dreding ay
Off thingis that he has herd say,
Namly off thingis to cum, quhill he
Knaw off the end the certante.

And sen thai ar in sic wenyng
Foroutyne certante off witting,
Me think quha sayis he knawis thingis
To cum he makys gret gabingis.
Bot quhether scho that tauld the king
How his purpos suld tak ending
Wenyt or wist it witterly,
It fell efter halyly
As scho said, for syne king wes he
And off full mekill renomme[32].

BOOK V

Thys wes in ver quhen wynter tid
With his blastis hidwys to bid
Was ourdryvyn and byrdis smale
As turturis and the nychtyngale
Begouth rycht sariely to syng
And for to mak in thar singyng
Swete notis and sounys ser
And melodys plesand to her
And the treis begouth to ma
Burgeans and brycht blomys alsua
To wyn the helynd of thar hevid
That wykkyt wynter had thaim revid,
And all gressys beguth to spryng.
Into that tyme the nobill king
With his flote and a few mengye[1]
Thre hunder I trow thai mycht be,
Is to the se oute off Arane
A litill forouth evyn gane.
Thai rowit fast with all thar mycht
Till that apon thaim fell the nycht
That woux myrk apon gret maner
Sua that thai wyst nocht quhar thai wer
For thai na nedill had na stane,
Bot rowyt alwayis intill ane

Sterand all tyme apon the fyr
That thai saw brynnand lycht and schyr.
It wes bot aventur thaim led
And thai in schort tyme sa thaim sped
That at the fyr aryvyt thai
And went to land but mair delay.
And Cuthbert that has sene the fyr
Was full of angyr and off ire,
For he durst nocht do it away
And wes alsua doutand ay
That his lord suld pas to se.
Tharfor thar cummyng waytit he
And met thaim at thar aryving.
He wes wele sone brocht to the kimg
That speryt at him how he had done,
And he with sar hart tauld him sone
How that he fand nane weill luffand
Bot all war fayis that he fand,
And that the lord the Persy
With ner thre hunder in cumpany
Was in the castell thar besid
Fullfillyt of dispyt and prid
Bot ma than twa partis off his rowt
War herberyt in the toune without,

240

'And dyspytyt you mar, schyr king,
Than men may dispyt ony thing.'
Than said the king in full gret ire,
'Tratour, quhy maid thou than the fyr?'
'A schyr,' said he, 'Sa God me se
The fyr wes nevyr maid for me,
Na or the nycht I wyst it nocht,
Bot fra I wyst it weill I thocht
That ye and haly your menye
On hy suld put you to the se,
For-thi I come to mete you her
To tell perellys that may aper.'
The king wes off his spek angry
And askyt his pryve men in hy
Quhat at thaim thocht wes best to do.
Schyr Edward fryst answert tharto
His brodyr that wes sua hardy,
And said, 'I say you sekyrly
Thar sall na perell that may be
Dryve me eftsonys to the se.
Myne aventur her tak will I
Quhethir it be esfull or angry.'
'Brother,' he said, 'sen thou will sua
It is gud that we samyn ta
Dissese or ese or payne or play
Eftyr as God will us purvay.
And sen men sayis that the Persy
Myn heritage will occupy,
And his menye sa ner us lyis
That us dispytis mony wys,
Ga we and venge sum off the dispyte,
And that may we haiff done als tite
For thai ly traistly but dreding
Off us or off our her-cummyng,
And thocht we slepand slew thaim all
Repruff tharoff na man sall
For werrayour na fors suld ma
Quhether he mycht ourcum his fa

Throu strenth or throu sutelte,
Bot that gud faith ay haldyn be.'
Quhen this wes said thai went thar way,
And to the toune sone cummyn ar thai
Sa prevely but noyis making
That nane persavyt thar cummyng.
Thai skalyt throu the toun in hy
And brak up duris sturdely
And slew all that thai mycht ourtak,
And thai that na defence mocht mak
Full petously gan rar and cry,
And thai slew thaim dispitously
As thai that war in full gud will
To venge the angyr and the ill
That thai and thairis had thaim wrocht.
Thai with sa feloun will thaim soucht
That thai slew thaim everilkan
Owtane Makdowell him allan[2]
That eschapyt throu gret slycht
And throu the myrknes off the nycht.
In the castell the lord the Persy
Hard weill the noyis and the cry,
Sa did the men that within wer
And full effraytly gat thar ger,
Bot off thaim wes nane sa hardy
That ever ischyt fourth to the cry.
In sic effray thai baid that nycht
Till on the morn that day wes lycht,
And than cesyt into party
The noyis the slauchtyr and the cry.
The king gert be departyt then
All hale the reff amang the men
And dwellyt all still thar dayis thre.
Syk hansell to that fokk[3] gaiff he
rycht in the fyrst begynnyng
Newlingis at his aryvyng.
Quhen that the king and his folk war
Aryvyt as I tauld you ar,

Aquhile in Karryk leyndyt he
To se quha fa or frende might be,
Bot he fand litill tendyrnes,
And nocht-forthi the puple wes
Enclynyt till him in party,
Bot Inglismen sa angrely
Led thaim with daunger and with aw
That thai na freyndschip durst him
    schaw.
Bot a lady off that cuntre
That wes till him in ner degre
Of cosynage wes wonder blyth
Off his aryvyng and alswyth
Sped hyr till him in full gret hy
With fourty men in cumpany
And betaucht thaim all to the king
Till help him in his werraying,
And he resavyt thaim in daynte
And hyr full gretly thankit he,
And speryt tythandis off the queyne
And off his freyndis all bedene
That he had left in that countre
Quhen that he put him to the se.
And scho him tauld sichand full sar
How that his brothyr takyn war
In the castell off Kyldromy
And destroyit sa velanysly[4]
And the erle off Athall alsua
And how the queyn and other ma
That till his party war heldand
War tane and led in Ingland
And put in feloun presoune,
And how that Cristole off Setoun
Wes slayn, gretand scho tauld the king[5]
That sorowful wes off that tithing
And said quhen he had thocht a thraw
Thir wordis that I sall you schaw.
'Allace,' he said, 'For luff off me

And for thar mekill lawte
Thai nobill men and thai worthy
Ar destroyit sa velanysly,
Bot and I leyff in lege-powyste
Thar deid rycht weill sall vengit be.
The king the-quhether off Ingland
Thocht that the kynrik off Scotland
Was to litill to thaim and me
Tharfor he will it myn all be.
Bot off gud Cristole off Setoun
That wes off sa nobill renoun
That he suld dey war gret pite
Bot quhar worschip mycht provyt be.'
The king sichand thus maid his mayn
And the lady hyr leyff has tayn
And went hyr hame till hyr wonnyng
And fele sys confort the king
Bath with silver and with mete
Sic as scho in the land mycht get.
And he oft ryot all the land
And maid all his that ever he fand
And syne drew him till the hycht
To stynt better his fayis mycht.
In all that tym wes the Persy
With a full sympill cumpany
In Turnberys castell lyand,
For the King Robert sua dredand
That he durst nocht isch furth to fayr
Fra thine to the castell off Ayr
That wes then full off Inglismen,
Bot lay lurkand as in a den
Tyll the men off Northummyrland
Suld cum armyt and with strang hand
Convoy him till his cuntre.
For his saynd till thaim send he,
And thai in hy assemblyt then
Passand I weyne a thousand men
And askyt avisement thaim amang

242

Quhether that thai suld dwell or gang,
Bot thai war skownrand wonder sar
Sa fer into Scotland for to far,
For a knycht, Schyr Gawter the Lile[6]
Said it wes all to gret perile
Sua ner thai schavalduris[7] to ga.
His spek discomfort thaim sua
That thai had left all thar vyage
Na war a knycht off gret corage
That Schyr Roger off Sanct Jhon hycht
That thaim confort with all his mycht,
And sic wordis to thaim gan say
That thai all samyn held thar way
Till Turnbery, quhar the Persy
Lap on and went with thaim in hy
In Ingland his castell till
Foroutyn distroublyne or ill.
Now in Ingland is the Persy
Quhar I trow he a quhile sall ly
Or that he schap hym for to fayr
To werray Carryk ony mar,
For he wyst he had na rycht
And als he dreid the kyngys mycht
That in Carrik wes travailland
In the maist strenth off the land,
Quhar Jamys off Douglas on a day
Come to the king and gan him say,
'Schyr, with your leyve I wald ga se
How that thai do in my contre
And how my men demanyt ar,
For it anoyis me wonder sar
That the Clyffurd sa pesabylly
Brukys and haldys the senyoury
That suld be myn with alkyn rycht
Bot quhile I lyff and may haiff mycht
To lede a yowman or a swayne
He sall nocht bruk it but bargayne.'
The king said, 'Certis I can nocht se

How that thou yeit may sekyr be
Into that countre for to far
Quhar Inglismen sa mychty ar
And thou wate nocht quha is thi freynd.'
He said, 'Schyr, nedways I will wend
And tak that aventur will giff
Quhether-sa it be to dey or lyff.'
The king said, 'Sen it is sua
That thou sic yarning has to ga
Thou sall pas furth with my blyssing,
And giff the hapnys ony thing
That anoyis or scaithfull be
I pray the sped the sone to me
And tak we samyn quhatever may fall.'
'I grante,' he said and thar-with-all
He lowtyt and his leve has tane[8]
And towart his countre is he gane.
Now takis James his viage
Towart Douglas his heritage
With twa yemen foroutyn ma.
That wes a symple stuff to ta
A land or castell to wyn,
The-quhether he yarnyt to begyn
Till bring purpos till ending
For gud help is in gud begynnyng
For gud begynnyng and hardy
Gyff it be folowit wittily
May ger oftsys unlikly thing
Cum to full conabill[9] ending.
Sua did it her, bot he wes wys
And saw he mycht on nakyn wys
Werray his fa with evyn mycht
Tharfor he thocht to wyrk with slycht,
And in Douglasdaile his countre
Apon ane evynnyng entryt he.
And than a man wonnyt tharby,
That wes off freyndis weill mychty
And ryche off mobleis and off cateill[10]

And had bene till his fadyr leyll,
And till himselff in his youthed
He haid done mony a thankfull deid,
Thom Dicson wes his name perfay.
Till him he send and gan him pray
That he wald cum all anerly
For to spek with him prevely,
And he but daunger till him gais.
Bot fra he tauld him quhat he wais
He gret for joy and for pite
And him rycht till his hous had he,
Quhar in a chambre prevely
He held him and his cumpany,
That nane of him had persaving.
Off mete and drynk and other thing
That mycht thaim eys thai had plente.
Sa wrocht he throu sutelte
That all the lele men off that land
That with his fadyr war dwelland
This gud man gert cum ane and ane
And mak him manrent everilkane,
And he himselff fyrst homage maid.
Douglas in hart gret glaidschip haid
That the gud men off his cuntre
Wald suagate till him bundyn be.
He speryt the convyne off the land
And quha the castell had in hand
And thai him tauld all halily,
And syne amang thaim prevely
Thai ordanyt that he still suld be
In hiddillis and in prevete[11]
Till Palme Sonday that wes ner-hand
The thrid day efter folowand
For than the folk off that countre
Assemblyt at the kyrk wald be,
And thai that in the castell wer
Wald als be thar thar palmys to ber
As folk that had na dreid off ill

For thai thocht that all was at thar will.
Than suld he cum with his twa men,
Bot for that men suld nocht him ken
He suld ane mantill[12] have auld and bar
And a flaill as he a thresscher war.
Under the mantill nocht-forthi
He suld be armyt prevely,[13]
And quhen the men off his countre
That suld all boune befor him be
His ensenye mycht her hym cry,
Then suld thai full enforcely
Rycht ymyddys the kirk assaill
The Inglismen with hard bataill
Sua that nane mycht eschap thaim fra,
For thar-throuch trowyt thai to ta
The castell that besid wes ner.
And quhen this that I tell you her
Wes divisyt and undertane
Ilkane till his hous hame is gane
And held this spek in prevete
Till the day off thar assemble.
The folk apon the Sonounday
Held to Saynct Bridis kyrk[14] thar way,
And thai that in the castell war
Ischyt out bath less and mar
And went thar palmys[15] for to ber,
Outane a cuk and a portere.[16]
James off Douglas off thar cummyng
And quhat thai war had witting,
And sped him till the kyrk in hy,
Bot or he come, to hastily
Ane of his cryit, 'Douglas, Douglas.'
Thomas Dikson, that nerrest was
Till thaim that war off the castell
That war all innouth the chancell,
Quhen he 'Douglas' sua hey hard cry
Drew out his swerd and fellegy
Ruschyt amang thame to and fra,

244

Bot ane or twa foroutin ma
Than in hy war left lyand,
Quhill Douglas come rycht at hand
And then enforcyt on thaim the cry,
Bot thai the chansell sturdely
Held and thaim defendyt wele
Till off thar men war slayne sumdell.
Bot the Douglace sa weill him bar
That all the men that with him war
Had confort off his wele-doyng,
And he him sparyt nakyn thing
Bot provyt sua his force in fycht
That throu his woschip and his mycht
His men sa keynly helpyt than
That thai the chansell on thaim wan.
Than dang thai on sua hardyly
That in schort tyme men mycht se ly
The twa part dede or then deand[17]
The lave war sesyt sone in hand
Sua that off thretty levyt nane
That thaine war slayne ilkan or tane.
James off Douglas quhen this wes done
The presoneris has he tane alsone
And with thaim off his cumpany
Towart the castell went in hy
Or noyis or cry suld rys,
And for he wald thaim sone suppris
That levyt in the castell war
That war bot twa foroutyn mar,
Fyve men or sex befor send he
That fand all opyn the entre
And entryt and the porter tuk
Rycht at the yate and syne the cuk.
With that the Douglas come to the yat
And entryt in foroutyn debate
And fand the mete all redy graid
And burdys set and claithis laid
The yhattis then he gert sper

And sat and eyt all at layser,
Syne all the gudis turssyt thai
That thaim thocht thai mycht haiff away,
And namly wapnys and armyng
Silver and tresour and clethyng.
Vittalis that mycht nocht tursyt be[18]
On this maner destroyit he,
Als quheyt and flour and meill and malt
In the wyne-sellar gert he bring
And samyn on the flur all flyng
And the presonaris that he had tane
Rycht tharin gert he heid ilkane,
Syne off the tounnys the hedis outstrake[19]
A foul melle thar gane he mak,
For meile[20] and malt and blud and wyne
Rane all togidder in a mellyne
That was un semly for to se.
Tharfor the men off that countre
For sua fele thar mellyt wer
Callit it 'the Douglas lardner.'[21]
Syne tuk he salt as Ic hard tell
And ded hors and fordid the well,
And brynt all outakyn stane,
And is furth with his menye gayne
Till his resett, for him thocht weill
Giff he had haldyn the castell
It had bene assegyt raith
And that him thocht to mekill waith,
For he had na hop of reskewyng.
And it is to peralous thing
In castell assegyt to be
Quhar want is off thir thingis thre,
Vittaill or men with thar armyng
Or than gud hop off rescuyng,
And for he dred thir thingis suld faile
He chesyt furthwart to travaill
Quhar he mycht at his larges be
And sua dryve furth his destane.

245

On this wise wes the castell tan
And slayne that war tharin ilkan.
The Douglas syne all his menye
Gert in ser placis departyt be,
For men suld les wyt quhar thai war
That yeid departyt her and thar.
Thaim that war woundyt gert he ly
Intill hiddillis all prevely,
And gert gud lechis till thaim bring
Quhill that thai war intill heling,
And himselff with a few menye
Quhile ane quhile twa and quhilis thre
And umquhill all him allane
In hiddillis throu the land is gane.
Sa dred he Inglismennys mycht
That he durst nocht wele cum in sycht
For thai war that tyme all-weldand
As maist lordis our all the land.
Bot tithandis that scalis sone
Off this deid that Douglas has done
Come to the Cliffurd his ere in hy,
That for his tynsaill wes sary
And menyt his men that thai had slane,
And syne has to his purpos tane
To big the castell up agayne.
Tharfor as man off mekill mayne
He assemblit gret cumpany,
And till Douglas he went in hy
And biggyt up the castell swyth[22]
And maid it rycht stalwart and styth
And put tharin vittalis and men.
Ane of the Thyrlwallys[23] then
He left behind him capitane
And syne till Ingland went agayne.
Into Carrik lyis the king
With a full symple gadryng,
He passyt nocht twa hunder men.
Bot Schyr Edward his broder then

Wes in Galloway weill ner him by,
With him ane other cumpany
That held the strenthis off the land,
For thai durst nocht yeit tak on hand
Till our-rid the land planly.
For off Valence Schyr Amery
Was intill Edynburgh lyand
That yeyt was wardane of the land
Underneyth the Inglis king,
And quhen he herd off the cummyng
Off King Robert and his menye
Into Carryk and how that he
Had slain off the Persyis men
His consaile he assemblit then,
And with assent off his consaill
He sent till Ar him till assaill
Schyr Ingrame the Umfravill that wes
    hardy
And with him a gret cumpany.
And quhen Schyr Ingram cummyn wes
    thar
Him thocht nocht speidfull for till far
Till assaile him into the hycht,
Tharfor he thocht to wyrk with slycht
And lay still in the castell than
Till he gat speryng that a man
Off Carrik, that wes sley and wycht
And a man als off mekill mycht
As off the men off that cuntre,
Wes to the King Robert mast preve
As he that wes his sibman ner,[24]
And quhen he wald foroutyn danger
Mycht to the kingis presence ga,
The-quhether he and his sonnys twa
War wonnand still in the cuntre
For thai wald nocht persayvit be
That thai war speciall to the king.
Thai maid him mony tyme warnyng

Quhen that thai his tynsaill mycht se,
Forthi in thaim affyit he.
His name can I nocht tell perfay,
Bot Ik haiff herd syndry men say
Forsuth that his ane e wes out[25]
Bot he sa sturdy wes and stout
That he wes the maist doutit man
That in Carrik lyvyt than.
And quhen Schyr Ingrame gat wittering
Forsuth this wes na gabbing,
Efter him in hy he sent
And he come at his commandment.
Schyr Ingrame that was sley and wis
Tretyt with him than on sic wys
That he maid sekyr undertaking
In tresoun for to slay the king,
And he suld haiff for his service
Gyff he fullfillyt thar divice
Weill fourty pundis worth off land[26]
Till him and till his ayris ay lestand.
The tresoun thus is undertane,
And he hame till his hous is gane
And wattyt opertunyte
For to fulfill his mavyte.
In gret perell than was the king
That off this tresoun wyst na thing,
For he that he traistit maist of ane
His ded falsly has undertane,
And nane may betreys tyttar than he
That man in trowis leawte.
The king in him traistyt, forthi
He had fullfillyt his felony
Ne war the king throu Goddis grace
Gat hale witting of his purchace,
And how and for how mekill land
He tuk his slauchter apon hand.
I wate nocht quha the warnyng maid,
Bot on all tym sic hap he had

That quhen men schup thaim to betrais
He gat witting tharoff allwayis
And mony tyme as I herd say
Throu wemen that he wyth wald play
That wald tell all that thai mycht her,
And sua myvht happyn that it fell her,
Bot how that ever it fell perde
I trow he sall the warrer be.
Nocht-forthi the tratour ay
Had in his thocht bath nycht and day
How he mycht best bring till ending
His tresonabill undretaking,
Till he umbethinkand him at the last
Intill his hart gan umbecast
That the king had in custome ay
For to rys arly ilk day
And pas weill fer fra his menye
Quhen he wald pas to the preve,
And sek a covert him allane
Or at the maist with him ane.
Thar thocht he with his sonnys twa
For to supprise the king and sla
And syne went to the wod thar way,
Bot yeit off purpos failit thai,
And nocht-forthi thai come all thre
In a covert that wes preve
Quhar the king oft wes wont to ga
His preve nedys for to ma.
Thair hid thai thaim till his cumming,
And the king into the mornyng
Rais quhen that his liking was
And rycht towart that covert gais
Quhar lyand war the tratouris thre
For to do thar his prevete.
To tresoun tuk he then na heid
Bot he wes wont quharever he yeid
His swerd about his hals to ber
And that availlyt him gretli ther

For had nocht God all thing weldand[27]
Set help intill his awine hand
He had bene ded withoutyn dreid.
A chamber page thar with him yeid,
And sua foroutyn falowis ma
Towart the covert gan he ga.
Now bot God help the noble king
He is ner-hand till his ending,
For that covert that he yeid till
Wes on the tother sid a hill
That nane of his men mycht it se.
Thiddirwart went this page and he
And quhen he cummyn wes in the schaw
He saw thai thre cum all on raw
Aganys him full sturdely.
Than till his boy he said in hy,
'Yon men will slay us and thai may.
Quhat wapyn has thou?' 'Ha, Schyr, perfay
Ik haiff bot a bow and a wyr.'[28]
'Giff thaim me smertly bath.' 'A, Schyr
Howgaite will ye that I do?'
'Stand on fer and behald us to.
Giff thou seis me abovyn be
Thou sall haiff wapynnys gret plente,
And giff I dey, withdraw the sone.'
With thai wordis foroutyn hone
He tyte the bow out off his hand,
For the tratouris war ner cummand.
The fader had a swerd but mar,
The tother bath swerd and hand-ax bar,
The thrid a swerd had and a sper.
The king persavt be thar affer
That all wes as men had him tauld.
'Tratour,' he said, 'thou has me sauld.
Cum na forthyr bot hald the thar.
I will thou cum na forthermar.'
'A, Schyr, umbethinkis you,' said he,
How ner that I suld to you be.

Quha suld cum ner you bot I?'
The king said, 'I will sekirly
That thou at this tyme cum nocht ner.
Thou may say quhat thou will on fer.'
Bot he with fals wordis flechand
Was with his twa sonnys cummand.
Quhen the king saw he wald nocht let
Bot ay come on fenyeand falset
He taisyt the wyre and leit it fley[29]
And hyt the fader in the ey
Till it rycht in the harnys ran
And he bakwart fell doun rycht than.
The brother that the hand-ax bar
Sua saw his fader liand thar,
A gyrd rycht to the king he couth maik
And with the ax hym our-straik,
Bot he that had his sword on hycht
Roucht him sic rout in randoun rycht
That he the hede till the harnys claiff
And dede downe till the erd him draiff.
The tother broder that bar the sper
Saw his brodyr fallin ther
And with the sper as angry man
With a rais till the king he ran.
Bot the king that him dred sumthing
Waytyt the sper in the cummyng
And with a wysk the hed off strak,
And or the tother had toyme to tak
His swerd the king sic swak him gaiff
That he the hede till the harnys claiff,
he ruschyt down off blud all reid.
And quhen the king saw thai war all ded
All thre lyand he wipit his brand,
With that his boy come fast rynnand
And said, 'Our Lord mot lovyt be
That grantyt you mycht and powste
To fell the felny and the prid
Off thir thre in sua litill tid.'

248

The king said, 'Sa our Lord me se
Thai had bene worthi men all thre

Had thai nocht bene full off tresoun,
Bot that maid thar confusioun.'

BOOK VI

The king is went till his logyng
And off this deid sone come tithing
Till Schyr Ingrame the Umfravill
That thocht his sutelte and gyle
Haid al failyeit in that place.
Tharfor anoyit sua he was
That he agayne to Lothyane
Till Schyr Amer his gate has tane
And till him tauld all hale the cas,
That tharoff all forwonderyt was
How ony man sa sodanly
Mycht do so gret chevalry
As did the king that him allane
Vengeance off thre traytouris has tane,
And said, 'Certis, I may weill se
That it is all certante
That ure helpys hardy men[1]
As be this deid we may ken.
War he nocht outrageous hardy
He had nocht unabasytly[2]
Sa smertly sene his avantage.
I drede that his gret vassalag
And his travaill may bring till end
That at men quhile full litill wend.'
Sik speking maid he off the king
That ay foroutyn sojournyng
Travaillit in Carrik her and thar.
His men fra him sa scalit war
To purches thar necessite[3]
And als the countre for to se
That thai left nocht with him sexty.
And quhen the Gallowais wyst suthli[4]

That he wes with sa few mengye
Thai maid a preve assemble
Off wele twa hunder men and ma,
And slewth-hundis[5] with thaim gan ta,
For thai thocht him for to suppris
And giff he fled on ony wys
To folow him with the hundis sua
That he suld nocht eschaip thaim fra.
Thai schup thaim in ane evynnyng[6]
To suppris sodanly the king
And tillhim held thai straucht thar way,
Bot he, that had his wachis ay
On ilk sid, off thar cummyng
Lang or thai come had wyttering
And how fele that thai mycht be,
Tharfor he thocht with his menye
To withdraw him out off the place,
For the nycht weill fallyn was
And for the nycht he thocht that thai
Suld nocht haiff sycht to hald the way
That he war passyt with his menye.
And as he thocht rycht sua did he
And went him down till a morras
Our awatter that rynnand was,
And in the bog he fand a place
Weill strait that weill twa bow-draucht was
Fra the watter thai passit haid.
He said, 'Her may ye mak abaid
And rest you all a quhile and ly,
I will ga wach all prevely.
Giff Ik her oucht off thar cummyng[7]
And giff I may her onything

249

Isall ger warn you sa that we
Sall ay at our avantage be.'
The king now takys his gate to ga
And with him tuk he sergandis[8] twa
And Schyr Gilbert de le Hay left he
Thar for to rest with his menye.
To the watter he come in hy
And lysnyt full ententily
Giff he herd oucht off thar cummyng
Bot yeit then mocht he her na thing.
Endlang the watter then yeid he
On ather syd a gret quantite
And saw the brayis hey standand,
The watter holl throu slik rynnand
And fand na furd that men mycht pas[9]
Bot quhar himselvyn passit was,
And sua strait wes the up-cumming[10]
That twa men mycht nocht samyn thring
Na on na maner pres thaim sua
That thai togidder mycht land ta.
His twa men bad he than in hy
Ga to thair feris to rest and ly[11]
For he wald wach thar com to se.
'Schyr,' said thai, 'Quha sall with you be?'
'God,' he said, 'forouten ma
Pas on, for I will it be sua.'
Thai did as he thame biddin had
And he thar all allane abaid,
And quhen he a lang quhile had bene
      thar
He herknyt and herd as it war
A hundis questyng on fer[12]
That ay come till him ner and ner.
He stud still for till herkyn mar
And ay the langer he wes thar
He herd it ner and ner cummand,[13]
Bot he thocht he thar still wald stand
Tyll that he herd mar takynnyng.

Than for ane hundis questyng
He wald nocht wakyn his menye,
Tharfor he wald abid and se
Quhat folk thai war and quhethir thai
Held towart him the rycht way
Or passyt ane other way fer by.
The moyne wes schynand clerly,
And sua stude he herknand
Till that he saw cum at his hand
The hale rout intill full gret hy.
Then he umbethocht him hastily
Giff he held towart his menye
That or he mycht reparyt be
Thai suld be passit the furd ilkan,
And then behuffyt him ches ane
Off thir twa, other to fley or dey.
Bot his hart that wes stout and hey
Consaillyt hym allane to bid
And kepe thaim at the furd syde
And defend weill the upcummyng
Sen he wes warnyst of armyng
That thar arowys thurth nocht dreid,
And gyff he war off gret manheid
He mycht stunay thaim everilkane
Sen thai ne mycht cum bot ane and ane,
And did rycht as hys hart hym bad.
Strang utrageous curage he had
Quhen he sa stoutly him allane
For litill strenth off erd has tane
To fecht with twa hunder and ma.
Tharwith he to the furd gan ga,
And thai apon the tother party
That saw him stand thar anyrly
Thringand intill the water rad
For off him litill dout thai had
And raid till him in full gret hy.
He smate the fyrst sua vygorusly
With his sper that rycht scharp schar

Till he doun till the erd him bar.[14]
The lave come then intill a randoun,
Bot his hors that wes born doun
Combryt thaim the upgang to ta,
And quhen the king saw it wes sua
He stekyt the hors[15] and he gan flyng
And syne fell at the upcummyng.
The layff with that come with a schout,
And he that stalwart wes and stout
Met thaim rycht stoutly at the bra
And sa gud payment gan thaim ma
That fyvesum in the furd he slew.
The lave then sumdell thaim withdrew
That dred his strakys wondre sar
For he in na thing thaim forbar.
Then said ane, 'Certis we ar to blame.
Quhat sall we say quhen we cum ham
Quhen a man fechtis agane us all.
Quha wyst ever men sa foully fall
As us gyff that we thusgat leve.'
With that all haile a schoute thai geve
And cryit, 'On him, he may nocht last.'
With that thai pressyt him sa fast
That had he nocht the better bene
He had bene dede withoutyn wen,
Bot he sa gret defence gan mak
That quhar he hyt evyn a strak
Thar mycht nathing agane-stand.
In litill space he left liand
Sa fele that the upcummyng wes then
Dyttyt with slayn hors and men[16]
Sua that his fayis for that stopping
Mycht nocht cum to the upcummyng.
A! Der God, quha had then bene by
And sene howe he sa hardyly
Adressyt hym agane thaim all
I wate weile that thai suld him call
The best that levyt in his day,

And giff I the suth sall say
I herd never in na tym gane
Ane stynt sa mony him allane.
Suth is, quhen till Ethiocles
Fra his brother Polnices
Wes send Thedeus in message
To ask haly the heritage
Off Thebes till hald for a yer,
For thai twynnys off a byrth wer,
Thai strave, for ather king wald be.
Bot the barnage off thar cuntre
Gert thaim assent on this maner,
That the tane suld be king a yer,[17]
And then the tother and his mengye
Suld nocht be fundyn in the countre
Quhill the fyrst brother regnand wer,[18]
Syne suld the tother renge a yer
And then the fyrst suld leve the land
Quhill that the tother war regnand
Thus ay a yer suld regne the tane,
The tother a yer fra that war gane.
To ask haldyn off this assent
Wes Thedeus to Thebes sent,
And sua spake for Polnices
That off Thebes Ethiocles
Bad his constabill with him ta
Men armyt weill and forouth ga
To mete Thedeus in the way
And slay him but langer delay.
The constable his way is gane
And nyne and fourty with him tane
Sua that he with thaim maid fyfty.
Intill the evynnyng prevely
Thai set enbuschement in the way[19]
Quhar Thedeus behovyt away
Betuix ane hey crag and the se,
And he that off thar mavyte
Wyst na thing his way has tane

251

And towart Grece[20] agane is gane.
And as he raid into the nycht
Sa saw he with the monys lycht[21]
Schynyng off scheldys gret plente,
And had wondre quhat it mycht be.
With that all hale thai gaiff a cry
And he that hard sa suddanly
Sic noyis sumdele affrayit was,
Bot in schort time he till him tais
His spyritis full hardely,
For his gentill hart and worthy
Assuryt hym into that nede.
Then with te spuris he strak the sted
And ruschyt in amang thaim all.
The fyrst he met he gert him fall,
And syne his sword he swapyt out
And roucht about him mony rout
And slew sexsum swill sone and ma.
Then undre him his hors thai sla
And he fell, bot he smertly ras
And strykand rowm about him mas
And slew off thaim a quantite
Bot woundyt wondre sar wes he.
With that a litill rod he fand
Up towart the crag strekand.
Thidder went he in full gret hy
Defendand him full douchtely
Till in the crag he clam sumdell
And fand a place enclosyt weill
Quhar nane bot ane mycht him assail,
Thar stud he and gaiff thaim bataill
And thai assaylyt everilkane
And oft fell quhen that he slew ane
As he doun to the erd wald dryve
He wald ber doun weill four or fyve.[22]
Thar stud he and defendyt sua
Till he had slayne thaim halff and ma.
A gret stane then by him saw he

That throu the gret anciente
Wes lowsyt redy for to fall,
And quhen he saw thaim cummand all
He tumblyt doun on thaim the stane,
And aucht men[23] thar with it has slayn
And sua stonayit the remanand
That thai war weile ner recreand.
Then wald he presone hald no mar
Bot on thaim ran with swerd all bar
And hewyt and slew with all his mayn
Till he has nyne and fourty slayne.
The constabill syne gan he ta
And gert him swer that he suld ga
Till King Ethiocles and tell
The aventur that thaim befell.
Thedeus bar him douchtely
That him allane ourcome fyfty.
Ye that this redys, cheys yhe
Quhether that mar suld prysit be
The king, that with avisement
Undertuk sic hardyment
As for to stynt him ane but fer
The folk that twa hunder wer,
Or Thedeus, that suddanly
For thai had raysyt on him the cry
Throu hardyment that he had tane
Wane fyfty men allhim allane.
Thai did thar deid bath on the nycht
And faucht bath with the mone-lycht,
Bot the king discomfyt ma
And Thedeus then ma gan sla.
Now demys quhether mar loving
Suld Thedeus haiff or the king?
On this maner that Ik haiff tauld
The king that stout wes and bauld
Wes fechtand on the furd syd
Giffand and takand rowtis rid
Till he sic martyrdom thar has maid[24]

That he the ford all stoppyt haid[25]
That nane of thaim mycht till him rid.
Thaim thocht than foly for to byd
And halely the flycht gan ta
And went hamewartis quhar thai come fra,
For the kingis men with the cry
Walknyt full effrayitly
And com to sek thar lord the king.
The Galloway men hard thar cummyng
And fled and durst abid no mar.
The kingis men that dredand war
For thar lord full spedyly
Come to the furd and sone in hy
Thai fand the king syttand allane[26],
That off his bassynet has tane[27]
Till avent him for he wes hate.[28]
Than speryt thai at him off his state
And he tauld thaim all hale the case
And how that God him helpyt sua
That he eschapyt hale thaim fra.
Than lukyt thai how fele war ded,
And thai fand lyand in that sted
Fourtene that war slayne with his hand.
Than lovyt thai God fast all-weildand
That thai thar lord fand hale and fer,
And said thaim byrd on na maner
Drede thar fayis sen thar chyftane
Wes off sic hart and off sic mayn[29]
That he for thaim had undretan
With sua fele for to fecht him ane.
Syk wordis spak thai of the king,
And for his hey undretaking
Farlyit and yarnyt hym for to se
That with hym ay wes wont to be.
A! Quhat worschip is prisit thing,
For it mays men till haiff loving
Gyff it be folowit ythenly,
For pryce off worschip nocht-forthi

Is hard to wyn, for gret travaill
Oft to defend and oft assaill
And to be in thar dedis wys
Gerris men off worschip wyn the price,
And may na man haiff worthyhed
Bot he haiff wyt to ster his deid
And se quhat ys to leve or ta.
Worschip extremyteys has twa,
Fule-hardyment the formast is
And the tother is cowartys,
And thai ar bath for to forsak.
Fule-hardyment all will undertak,
Als weill thingis to leve as ta,
Bot cowardys dois na thing sua
But uttrely forsakis all,
Bot that war derer for to fal
Na war faute of discretioun.
Forthi has worschip sic renoun,
That it is mene betuix tha twa
And takys that is till underta[30]
And levys that is to leve, for it
Has sa gret warnysing of wyt
That it all perellis weile gan se
And all avantagis that may be.
I wald till hardyment heyld haly
With-thi away war the foly
For hardyment with foly is vice
Bot hardyment that mellyt is
With wyt is worschip ay perde,
For but wyt worschip may nocht be.
This nobile king that we off red
Mellyt all tyme with wit manheid,
That may men by this melle se.
His wyt schawyt him the strait entre
Off the furd and the uschyng alsua
That as him thocht war hard to ta
Apon a man that war worthy,
Tharfor his hardyment hastily

Thocht it mycht be weill undretan
Sen at anys mycht assail bot ane.
Thus hardyment governyt with wyt[31]
That he all tyme wald samyn knyt
Gert him off worschip haiff the price
And oft ourcum his ennymyis.
The king in Carrik dwellyt ay still,
Hys men assemblyt fast him till
That in the land war travailland
Quhen thai off this deid herd tithand
For thai thar ure wald with him ta
Gyff that he eft war assaylyt sua.
Bot yeit than James of Douglas
In Douglas daile[32] travailland was
Or ellysweill ner-hand tharby
In hydillys sumdeill prevely,
For he wald se his governyng
That had the castell in keping,
And gert mak mony juperty[33]
To se quhether he wald ische blythly.
And quhen he persavyt that he
Wald blthly ische with his menye,
He maid a gadring prevely
Of thaim that war on his party,
That war sa fele that thai durst fycht
With Thyrwall and all the mycht
Of thaim that in the castell war.
He schupe him in the nycht to far
To Sandylandis, and ner tharby
He him enbuschyt prevely
And send a few a trane to ma,
That sone in the mornyng gan ta
Catell that wes the castell by
And syne withdrew thaim hastily
Towart thaim that enbuschit war.
Than Thyrwall foroutyn mar
Gert arme his men foroutyn baid
And ischyt with all the men he haid

And folowyt fast efter the ky[34].
He wes armyt at poynt clenly
Outane his hede wes bar.[35]
Than with the men that with him war
The catell folowit he gud speid
Rycht as a man that had na dreid
Till that he gat off thaim a sycht.
Than prekyt thai with all thar mycht
Folowand thaim out off aray,
And thai sped thaim fleand quhill thai
Fer by thar buschement war past,
And Thyrwall ay chassyt fast.
And than thai that enbuschyt war
Ischyt till him bath les and mar
And rayssyt sudanly the cry,
And thai that saw sa sudandly
That folk come egyrly prekand
Rycht betwix thaim and thar warand,
Thai war into full gret effray
And for thai war out off array[36]
Sum off thaim fled and sum abad,
And the Douglas that thar with him had
A gret mengye full egrely
Assaylyt and scalyt thaim hastyly
And in schort tyme ourraid thaim sua
That weile nane eschapyyt thaim fra.
Thyrwall that wes thar capitane
Wes thar in the bargane slane
And off his men the mast party,
The lave fled full effraytly.
Douglas his menye fast gan chas,
And the flearis thar wayis tays
Till the castell in full gret hy.
The formast entryt spedyly
Bot the chaseris sped thaim sa fast
That thai ourtuk sum of the last
And thaim foroutyn mercy gan sla.
And quhen thai off the castell sua

Saw thaim sla off thar men thaim by
Thai sparyt the yattis hastily[37]
And in hy to the wallis rane.
James off Douglas his menye than
Sesyt weile hastily in hand
That thai about the castell fand
To thair resett, syne went thar way.
Thus ischyt Thyrwall that day.
Quhen Thyrwall on this maner
Had ischit as I tell you her,
James off Douglas and his men
Buskit thaim all samyn then
And went thar way towart the king
In gret hy, for thai herd tything
That off Valence Schyr Amery
With full gret chevalry
Bath off Scottis and Inglis men
With gret felny war rerdy then
Assemblyt for to sek the king,
That wes that tyme with his gadring
In Cumnok[38] quhair it straitast was.
Thidder went James of Douglas
And wes rycht welcum to the king
And quhen he had tauld that tithing,
How that Schyr Amer wes cummand
For till hunt him out off the land
With hund and horne rycht as he war
A woulff, a theyff, or theyffis fer,
Than said the king, 'It may weill fall
Thocht he cum and his power all
We sall abid in this countre,
And gyff he cummys we sall him se.'
The king spake apon this maner,
And of Valence Schyr Amer
Assemblyt a gret cumpany
Off noble men and off worthy
Off Ingland and of Lowthiane,[39]
And he has alsua with him tane

Jhone off Lorn and all his mycht
That had off worthi men and wycht
With him aucht hunder men and ma
A sleuth-hund had he thar alsua
Sa gud that wald chang for na thing,
And sum men sayis yeit that the king
As a strecour him noryst had[40]
And sa mekill off him he maid
That hys awyn handis wald him feid.
He folowyt him quharever he yeid
Sa that the hund him lovit sua
That he wald part na wys him fra.
Bot how that Jhon of Lorn him had
Ik herd never mencioun be mad,
Bot men sayis it wes certane thing
That he had him in his sesyng
And throu him thocht the king to ta,
For he wyst he him luffyt sua
That fra that he mycht anys fele
The kingis sent he wyst rycht weill
That he wald chaung it for na thing.
This Jhon off Lorne hattyt the king
For Jhon Cumyn his emys sak[41]
Mycht he him other sla or tak
He wald nocht prys his liff a stra
Sa that he vengeance of him mycht ta.
The wardane than Schyr Amery
With this Jhon in cumpany
And other off gud renoun alsua,
Thomas Randell was ane off tha,
Come intill Cumnok to sek the king
That wes weill war off that cummyng
And wes up in the strenthis then
And with him weill four hunder men.
His broder that tym with him was[42]
And alsua James off Douglas.
Schyr Amery rowte he saw
That held the plane ay and the law[43]

255

And in hale battaill alwayis raid.[44]
The king that na supposyn had
That thai wer may then he saw thar
Till thaim and nother ellisquhar
Had ey and wrocht unwittily,
For Jhon off Lorn full sutelly
Behind thocht to supprys the king.
Tharfor with all his gadring
About ane hill he held the way
And held him into covert ay
Till he sa ner come to the king
Or he persavyt his cummyng
That he wes cummyn on him weill ner.
The tother ost[45] and Schyr Amer
Pressyt apon the tother party.
The king wes in gret juperty
That wes on ather sid umbeset
With fayis that to sla him thret,
And the leyst party off the twa
Was starkar than he and ma.
And quhen he saw thaim pres him to
He thocht in hy quhat was to do
And said, 'Lordis we haiff na mycht
As at this tyme to stand and fycht,
Tharfor departis us in thre,
All sall nocht sa assailyt be,
And in thre partis hald our way.'
Syne till his preve folk gan he say
Betwix thaim into prevete
In quhat sted thar repayr suld be.
With that thar gate all ar thai gane
And in thre partis thar way has tane.
Jhon of Lorne come to the place
Fra quhar the king departyt was
And in his trace the hund he set[46]
That then foroutyn langer let
Held even the way efter the king
Rycht as he had off him knawing,

And left the tother partys twa
As he na kep to thaim wald ta.
And quhen the king saw his cummyng
Efter hys route intill a ling
He thocht thai knew that it wes he,
Tharfor he bad till his menye
Yeit then in thre depart thaim sone,
And thai did sua foroutyn hone
And held thar way in thre partys.
The hund did thar sa gret maistrys
That held ay foroutyn changing
Eftre the rowt quhar wes the king.
And quhen the king had sene thaim sua
All in a rowt efter him ga
The way and folow nocht his men
He had a gret persaving then
That thai knew him, forthi in hy
He bad his men rycht hastily
Scaile and ilkan hald his way
All himselff, and sua did thai.
Ilk man a syndry gate is gane[47]
And the king with him has tane
His foster broder foroutyn ma
And samyn held thar gate thai twa.
The hund folowyt alwayis the king
And changyt for na departing
Bot ay folowit the kingis trace
But waveryng as he passyt was
And quhen Jhon of Lorne saw
The hund sa hard eftre him draw
And folow strak after thai twa
He knew the king wes ane of tha,
And bad fyve off his cumpany
That war rycht wycht men and hardy
And als off fute spediast war[48]
Off all that in thair rowt war
Ryn eftre him and him ourta
And lat him na wys pas thaim fra,

And fra thai had herd the bydding
Thai held thar way efter the king
And folowyt him sa spedely
That thai him weill sone gan ourhy.
The king that saw thaim cummand ner
Wes anoyit on gret maner,
For he thocht giff thai war worthi
Thai mycht hi, travaile and tary
And hald him swagate tariand
Till the remanand com at hand,
Bot had he dred bot anerly
Thai fyve I trow all sekyrly
He suld have had na mekill dred.
And till his falow as he yeid
He said, 'Thir fyve ar fast cummand
Thai ar weill ner now at our hand,
Sa is thar ony help at the
For we sall sone assailyt be.'
'Ya, schyr,' he said, 'all that I may.'
'Thou sayis weill,' said the king. 'Perfay
I see thaim cummand till us ner.
I will na forthyr bot rycht her
I will byd quhill Ic am in aynd
And se quhat force that thai can faynd.'
The king than stud full sturdely
And the fyvesum in full gret hy
Come with gret schor and manassing[49].
Then thre off thaim went to the king,
And till his man the tother twa
With swerd in hand gan stoutly ga.
The king met thaim that till him socht
And to the fyrst sic rowt he roucht
That er and chek downe in the hals
He scharnand off the schuldir als,[50]
He ruschyt down all disyly.
The twa that saw sa sudanly
Thar falow fall effrayit war
And stert a litill ovyrmar.[51]

The king with that blenkit him by
And saw the twasome sturdely
Agane his man gret melle ma.
With that he left his awin twa
And till thaim that faucht with his man
A loup rycht lychtly maid he than
And smate the hed off the tane,
To mete his awne syne is he gane.
Thai come on him full sturdely,
He met the fyrst sa egrely
That with the swerd that scharply schar
The arme fra the body he bar.
Quhat strakys thai gaiff I can nocht tell,
Bot to the king sa fayr befell
That thocht he travaill had and payne
He off his fa-men four has slayn,
His foster broder tharefter sone
The fyft out of dawys has done.[52]
And quhen the king saw that all fyve
War on that wys broucht out off lyve
Till hys falow than gan he say,
'Thou has helpyt weile perfay.'
'It likys you to say sua,' said he,[53]
'Bot the gret part to you tuk ye
That slew four off the fyve you ane.'
The king said, 'As the glew is gane
Better than thou I mycht it do
For Ik had mar layser tharto,
For the twa falowys that delt with the
Quhen thai saw me assailyt with thre
Off me rycht nakyn dout thai had[54]
For thai wend I sa strayrly war stad,[55]
And forthi that thai dred me noucht
Noy thaim fer out the mar I moucht.'
With that the king lokyt him by
And saw off Lorn the company
Weill ner with thar sleuth-hund
    cummand.

Than till a wod that wes ner-hand
He went with his falow in hy.

God sayff thaim for his gret mercy.

BOOK VII

The king towart the wod is gane
Wery forswayt and will of wane[1]
Intill the wod sone entryt he
And held doun towart a vale
Quhar throu the woid a watter ran.
Thidder in gret hy wend he than
And begouth for to rest him thar
And said he mycht no forthirmar.
His man said, 'Schyr, it may nocht be.
Abyd ye her ye sall son se
Fyve hunder yarnand you to sla,
And thai ar fele aganys us twa.
And sen we may nocht dele with mycht
Help us all that we may with slycht.'
The king said, 'Sen that thou will sua,
Ga furth, and I sall with the ga.
Bot Ik haiff herd oftymys say
That quha endlang a watter ay[2]
Wald waid a bow-draucht[3] he suld ger
Bathe the slouth-hund and his leder
Tyne the slouth men gert him ta.
Prove we giff it will now do sa,
For war yone devillis hund away
I roucht nocht off the lave perfay.'[4]
As he dyvisyt thai haiff doyn[5]
And entryt in the watter sone
And held down endlang thar way,
And syne to the land yeid thai
And held thar way as thai did er.
And Jhone off Lorn with gret affer
Come with hys rout rycht to the place
Quhar that his fyve men slane was.

He menyt thaim quhen he thaim saw
And said eftre a litill thraw
That he suld veng thar bloude,[6]
Bot otherwayis the gamyn youde.[7]
Thar wald he mak na mar dwelling
Bot furth in hy folowit the king.
Rycht to the burn thai passyt war,
Bot the sleuth-hund maid styntyn thar
And waveryt lang tyme to and fra
That he na certane gate couth ga,
Till at the last that Jhon of Lorne
Persavyt the hund the slouth had lorn
And said, 'We haiff tynt this travaill.
To pas forthyr may nocht availe
For the void is bath braid and wid
And he is weill fer be this tid,
Tharfor is gud we turn agayn
And waist no mar travaill in vayne.'
With that relyit he his mengye
And his way to the ost tuk he.
Thus eschapyt the nobill king,
Bot sum men sayis this eschaping
Apon ane other maner fell[8]
Than throu the wading, for thai tell
That the king a gud archer had,
And quhen he saw his lord sua stad
That he wes left sa anerly
He ran on sid alwayis him by
Till he into the woude wes gane.
Than said he till him selff allane
That he arest rycht thar wald ma
To luk giff he the hund mycht sla,

For giff the hund mycht lest in lyve
He wyst rycht weile that thai wald dryve
The kingis trace till thai him ta,
Than wyst he weile thai wald him sla.
And for bhe wald his lord succur
He put his liff in aventur,
And stud intill a busk lurkand[9]
Till that the hund come at his hand
And with ane arow sone him slew
And throu the woud syne him withdrew.
Bot quhether this eschaping fell
As I tauld fyrst or I now tell,
I wate weill without lesing
That at the burn eschapyt the king.
The king has furth his wayis tane,
And Jhon of Lorne agayne is gane
To Schyr Aymer that fra the chace
With his men repayryt was
That sped lytill in thar chassyng
Thoucht at thai maid gret folowing
Full egrely thai wan bot small,
Thar fayis ner eschapyt all.
Men sayis Schyr Thomas Randell than
Chassand the kingis baner wan,[10]
Quharthrou in Ingland with the king[11]
He had rycht gret price and loving.[12]
Quhen the chasseris relyit war
And Jhon of Lorne had met thaim thar
He tauld Schyr Aymer all the cas,
How that the king eschapyt was
And how that he his fyve men slew
And syne to the wode him drew.
Quhen Schyr Aymer herd this, in hy
He sanyt him for the ferly
And said, 'He is gretly to prys,
For I knaw nane that liffand is
That at myscheyff gan help him sua.
I trow he suld be hard to sla

And he war bodyn evynly.'[13]
On this wis spak Schyr Aymery,
And the gud king held furth his way
Betwix him and his man quhill thai
Passyt out throu the forest war.
Syne in the more thai entryt ar
That wes bathe hey and lang and braid,
And or thai halff it passyt had
Thai saw on syd the men cummand
Lik to lycht men and waverand,[14]
Swerdis thai had and axiys als
And ane off thaim apon his hals[15]
A mekill boundyn wether bar.[16]
Thai met the king and halist him thar,
And the king thaim thar hailsing yauld
And askyt thaim quhether thai wauld.[17]
Thai said Robert the Bruys thai socht,
For mete with him giff that thai moucht
Thar dwelling with him wauld thai ma.
The king said, 'Giff that ye will sua,
Haldys furth your way with me
And I sall ger you sone him se.'
Thai persavyt be his speking
That he wes the selvyn Robert king,[18]
And chaungyt contenance and late
And held nocht in the fyrst state,
For thai war fayis to the king
And thocht to cum into Sculking
And dwell with him quhill that thai saw
Thar poynt, and bryng him than off daw.
Thai grantyt till his spek forthi,
Bot the king that wes witty[19]
Persavyt weill be thar having
that thai luffyt him nathing
And said, 'Falowis, ye mon all thre,
Forthir aquent till that we be,
All be yourselvyn forrouth ga,
And on the samyn wys we twa

Sall folow behind weill ner.'
Quod thai, 'Schyr, it is na myster
To trow in us ony ill.'
'Nane do I,' said he, 'bot I will
That yhe ga forrourth thus quhill we
Better with othyr knawin be.'
'We grant,' thai said, 'sen ye will sua.'
And furth apon thar gate gan ga.
Thus yeid thai till the nycht wes ner,
And than the formast cummyn wer
Till a waist husbandis hous[20], and thar
Thai slew the wethir that thai bar
And slew fyr for to rost thar mete,
And askyt the king giff he wald ete
And rest him till the mete war dycht.[21]
The king that hungry was, Ik hycht,
Assentyt till thar spek in hy,
Bot he said he wald anerly
Betwix him and his fallow be
At a fyr, and thai all thre
In the end off the hous suld ma
Ane other fyr, and thai did sua.
Thai drew thaim in the hous end
And halff the wethir till him send.
And thai rostyt in hy thar mete
And fell rycht freschly for till ete,[22]
For the king weill lang fastyt had
And had rycht mekill travaill mad,
Tharfor he eyt full egrely
And quhen he had etyn hastily
He had to slep sa mekill will
That he mocht set na let thartill,
For quhen the vanys fillyt ar[23]
Men worthys hevy evermar
And to slepe drawys hevynes.
The king that all fortravaillyt wes
Saw that him worthyt slep nedwayis.
Till his foser-broder he sayis,

'May I traist in the me to waik
Till Ik a litill sleping tak.'
'Ya, schyr,' he said, 'till I may dre.'
The king then wynkyt a litill wey,
And slepyt nocht full encrely
Bot gliffnyt up oft sodanly,[24]
For he had dreid of thai thre men
That at the tother fyr war then.
That thai his fais war he wyst,
Tharfor he slepyt as foule on twyst.[25]
The king slepyt bot a litill than
Quhen sic slep fell on his man
That he mycht nocht hald up his ey,
Bot fell in slep and rowtyt hey.
Now is the king in gret perile
For slep he sua a litill quhile
He sall be ded fotoutyn dreid,
For the thre tratouris tuk gud heid
that he on slep wes and his man.
In full gret hy thai rais up than
And drew thar swerdis hastily
And went towart the king in hy
Quhen that thai saw him sleip sua,
And slepand thocht thai wald him sla.
Till him thai yeid a full gret pas,
Bot in that tym throu Goddis grace
The king up blenkit hastily
And saw his man slepand him by
And saw cummand the tother thre.
Deliverly on fut gat he
And drew his swerd out and thaim mete,
And as he yude his fute he set
Apon his man weill hevily.
He waknyt and rais disily,
For the slep maistryt hym sway
That or he gat up ane off thai
That com for to sla the king
Gaiff hym a strak in his rysing

Sua that he mycht help him no mar.
The king sa straitly stad wes thar
That he wes never yeit sa stad,
Ne war the armyng that he had
He had bene dede foroutyn wer.
Bot nocht-forthi on sic maner
He helpyt him in that bargane
That thai thre tratouris he has slan
Throu Goddis grace and his manheid.
Hys fostyr brother thar wes dede,
Then wes he wondre will of wayn
Quhen he saw him left allane.
His foster broder meny he
And waryit all the tother thre,
And syne his way tuk him allane
And rycht towart his tryst is gane.
The king went furth way and angri
Menand his man full tenderly
And held his way all him allane,
And rycht towart the hous is gan
Quhar he set tryst to meit his men.
It wes weill inwyth nycht be then,
He come sone in the hous and fand
The houswyff on the benk sittand
That askit him quhat he was
And quhen he come and quethir he gais.
'A travailland man, dame,' said he,
'That travaillys throu the contre.'
Scho said, 'All that travailland er
For ane his sak ar welcum her.'
The king said, 'Gud dame, quhat is he
That gerris you haiff sik specialte[26]
To men that travaillis?' 'Schyr, perfay,'
Quod the gud-wyff, 'I sall you say,
The King Robert the Bruys is he,
That is rycht lord off this countre.
His fayis now haldis him in thrang,
Bot I think to se or ocht lang[27]

Him lord and king our all the land
That na fayis sall him withstand.'
'Dame, luffis thou him sa weil,' said he.
'Ya, schyr,' said scho, 'sa God me se.'
'Dame,' said he, 'hym her the by,
For Ik am he, I say the soithly[28],
Yha certis, dame.' 'And quhar ar gane
Your men quhen ye ar thus allane?'
'At this tyme, dame, Ik haiff no ma.'
Scho said, 'It may na wys be swa.
Ik haiff twa sonnys wycht and hardy,
Thai sall becum your men in hy.'
As scho divisyt thai haiff done,
His sworn men become thai sone.
The wyff syn gert him syt and ete,
Bot he has schort quhile at the mete
Syttyn quhen he hard gret stamping
About the hous, then but letting
Thai stert up the hous for to defende,
Bot sone eftre the king has kend
James off Douglas. Than wes he blyth
And bad oppyn the durris swyth[29]
And thai come in all that thar war.
Schyr Edward the Bruce wes thar,
And James alsua off Douglas
That wes eschapyt fra the chace
And with the kingis brother met,
Syn to the tryst that thaim wes set
Thai sped thaim with thar cumpany
That wer ane hunder and weile fyfty.[30]
And quhen that thai haiff sene the king
Thai war joyfull of thar meting
And askyt how that he eschapyt was,
And he thaim tauld all hale the cas.
How the fyve men him pressyt fast,
And how he throu the water past,
And how he met the thevis thre
And how he slepand slane suld be

261

Quhen he waknyt throu Goddis grace
And how his foster brodyr was
Slayne he tauld thaim all haly.
Than lovyt thai God commounly
That tthar lord wes eschapyt sua,
Than spak thai wordis to and fra
Till at the last the king gan say
'Fortoun us travaillyt fast today
That scalyt us sa sodanly.
Our fayis tonycht sall ly traistly[31]
For thai trow we so scalit ar[32]
And fled to-waverand her and thar
That we sall nocht thir dayis thre
All togiddir assemblit be.
Tharfor this nycht thai sall trastly
But wachys tak thar ese and ly.
Quharfor quha knew thar herbery
And wald cum on thaim sodanly
With few mengye mycht thaim scaith
And eschape foroutyn waith.'
'Perfay,' quod James of Douglas,
'As I come hyddyrwart per cas
I come sa ner thar herbery
That I can bring you quhar thai ly,
And wald ye speid you yeit or day
It may sua happin that we may
Do thaim a gretar scaith weile sone
Than thai us all day has done,
For thai ly scalyt as thaim lest.'
Than thocht thaim all it wes the best
To sped thaim to thaim hastily,
And thai did sua in full gret hy
And come on thaim in the dawing
Rycht as the day begouth to spryng.
Sa fell it that a cumpany
Had in a toun tane thar herbery
Weile fra the ost a myle or mar,
Men said that thai twa hunder war.

Thar assemblyt the nobill king,
And sone eftre thar assembling
Thai that slepand assaylyt war
Rycht hidwysly gan cry and rar,
And other sum that herd the cry
Ras sa rycht effrayitly
That sum of thaim nakit war
Fleand to warand her and thar,
and sum his armys with him drew,
And thai foroutyn mercy thaim slew
And sa evyll vengeance can ta
That the twa partis of thaim and ma
War slayn rycht in that ilk sted,
Till thar oist the remanand fled.
The oyst that hard the noyis and cry
And saw thar men sua wrechytly
Sum nakit fleand her and thar,
Sum all hale, sum woundyt sar,
Into full gret effray thai rais
And ilk man till his baner gays
Sua that tthe oyst wes all on ster.
The king and thai that with him wer
Quhen on ster the oyst saw sua
Towart thar warand gan thai ga,
And thar in savete com thai
And quhen Schyr Aymer herd say
How that the king thar men had slayn
And how that thai turnyt war agayn
He said, 'Now may we clerly se
That nobill hart quharever it be
It is hard till ourcum throu maystri,
For quhar ane hart is rycht worthy
Agayne stoutnes it is ay stoute,
Na as I trow thar may na doute
Ger it all-out dis cumfyt be
Quhill body levand is and fre,
As be this melle may be sene.
We wend Robert the Bruce had bene

Sua discomfyt that be gud skill
He suld nother haiff haid hart ne will
Swilk juperty till undreta[33]
For he put was at undre sua
That he wes left all him allane
And all his folk war fra him gayn,
And he sagat fortravaillyt
To put thaim off that him assaylit
That he suld haiff yarnyt resting
This nycht atour all other thing.
Bot his hart fillyt is off bounte
Sua that it vencusyt may nocht be.'
On this wys spak Schyr Aymery,
And quhen thai off his cumpany
Saw how thai travaillit had in vayn
And how the king thar men had slayn
And that his wes gane all fre,
Thaim thocht it wes a nycete
For to mak thar langer dwelling
Sen thai mycht nocht anoy the king,
And said that to Schyr Amery,
That umbethocht him hastily
That he to Carlele[34] wald ga
And a quhill tharin sojourn ma
And haff his spyis on the king
To knaw alwayis his contenyng,
And quhen that he his poynt mycht se
He thocht that with a gret menye
He suld schute apon him sudanly.
Tharfor with all his cumpany
Till Ingland he the way has tane,
And ilk man till his hous is gane.
In hy till Carlele went is he
And tharin thinkys for till be
Till he his poynt saw off the king,
That then with all his gadring
Wes in Carryk quhar umbestount[35]
He wald went with his men til hunt[36]

Sa happynyt that on a day
He went till hunt for till assay
Quhat gamyn was in that countre,
And sua hapnyt that day that he
By a woud-syd to sett is gane
With his twa hundys him allane,
Bot his swerd ay with him bar.
He had bot schort quhile syttyn thar
Quhen he saw fra the woud cummand
Thre men with bowys in thar hand
That towart him come spedely,
And he that persayvyt in hy
Be thar affer and thar having
That thai luffyt him nakyn thing,
He rais and his leysche till him drew he
And leyte hys hundis gang all fre.
God help the king now for his mycht,
For bot he now be wys and wycht
He sall be set in mekill pres,
For thai thre men foroutyn les
War his fayis all utrely,
And wachyt him sa bysyly
To se quhen thai vengeance mycht tak
Off the king for Jhon Comyn his sak
That thai thocht than thai layser had.
And sen he hym allane wes stad
In hy thai thocht thai suld him sla,
And gyff that thai mycht chevys sua
Fra that thai the king had slayn
That thai mycht wyn the woud agayn,
His men thaim thocht thai suld nocht
   dred.
In hy towart the king thai yeid
and bent thar bowys quhen thai war ner,
And he that dred on gret maner
thar arowys, for he nakyt was,
In hy a speking to thaim mais
And said, 'You aucht to schame perde[37]

Sen Ik am ane and ye ar thre
For to schute at me apon fer.
Bot had ye hardyment to cum ner
And with your swerdis till assay,
Wyn me apon sic wys giff ye may,
Ye sall wele oute mar prisyt be.'
'Perfay,' quod ane than off the thre
'Sall na man say we dred the sua
That we with arowys sall the sla.'
With that thar bowys away thai kest
And come on fast but langer frest.
The king thaim met full hardyly
And smate the fyrst sa vygorusly
that he fell dede doun on the gren.
And quhen the kingis hund has sene
Thai men assailye his maister sua
He lap till ane and gan him ta
Rycht be the nek full sturdyly.
Till top our tale he gert him ly,[38]
And the king that his swerd out had
Saw he sa fayr succour him maid.
Or he that fallyn wes mycht rys
He him assayllyt on sic wys
That he the bak strak evyn in twa.
The thrid that saw his falowis sua
Foroutyn recoveryng be slayne
Tok to the wod his way agane,
Bot the king folowit spedyly,
And als the hund that wes him by
Wquhen he the man saw fle him fra
Schot till him sone and gan him ta
Rycht be the nek and till him dreuch
And the king that wes ner yneucht
In his ryssing sik rowt him gaff
That stane-dede to the erd he draff.
The kingis men that wer than ner
Quhen that thai saw on sic maner
The king assailyt sa sodanly

Thai sped towart him in hy
And askyt how that cas befell,
And he all haly gan thaim tell
How thai assaillyt him all thre
'Perfay,' quod thai, 'we may wele se
That it is hard till undretak
Sic melling with you to mak[39]
That sua smertly has slayn tthir thre
Foroutyn hurt.' 'Perfay,' said he,
'I slew bot ane forouten ma
God and my hund has slayn the twa.
Thar tresoun combryt thaim perfay
For rycht wycht men all thre war thai.'
Quhen that the king throu Goddis grace
On this maner eschapyt was
He blew his horn and then in hy
His gud men till him gan rely,
then hamwartis[40] buskyt he to far
For that day wald he hunt no mar.
In Glentruell[41] all a quhile he lay,
And went weyle oft to hunt and play
For to purches thaim venesoun,
For than der war in sesoun.
In all that tyme Schyr Aymer
With nobill men in cumpany
Lay in Carlele hys poynt to se,
And quhen he hard the certante
That in Glentrewle wes the king
And went till hunt and till playing,[42]
He thocht with hys chevalry
To cum apon him sodanly
And fra Carlele on nychtys ryd
And in covert on dayis bid,
And swagate with sic tranonting[43]
He thocht he suld suppris the king.
He assemblyt a gret mengne
Off folk off full gud renomme
Bath off Scottis and Inglis-men.

Thar way all samyn held thai then
And raid on nycht sa prevely
Till thai come in a wod ner by
Glentruele, quhar logyt wes the king
That wyst rycht nocht off thar cummyng.
Into gret perile now is he,
For bot God throu his gret powste
Save him he sall be slayne or tane,
For thai war sex quhar he wes ane.
Quhen Schyr Amery, as Ik haiff tauld
With his men that war stout and bauld
Wes cummyn sa ner the king that thai
War bot a myle fra him away
He tuk avisement with his menm
On quhat maner thai suld do then.
For he said thaim that the king was
Logyt into sa strayt a place
That horsmen mycht nocht him assaile
And giff futemen gaiff him bataile
He suld be hard to wyn giff he
Off thar cummyng may wytteryt be.[44]
'Tharfor I rede all prevely
We send a woman him to spy
That pouerly arrayit be.
Scho may ask mete per cherite
And se thar convyn halily[45]
And apon quhat maner thai ly,[46]
The quhilis we and our menye
Cumand out-throu the wode may be
On fute all armyt as we ar.
May we do sua that we cum thar
On thaim or thai wyt our cummyng
We sall fynd in thaim na sturting.'
This consaill thocht thaim wes to best,
Then send thai furth but langer frest
The woman that suld be thar spy,
And scho hyr way gan hald in hy
Rycht to the logis quhar the king

That had na drede of supprising
Yheid unarmyt mery and blyth.
The woman has he sene alswyth,
He saw hyr uncouth and forthi
He beheld hyr mar encrely,
And be hyr ccontenance him thocht
That for gud cummyn was scho nocht.[47]
Then gert he men in hy hyr ta,
And scho that dred men suld hyr sla
Tauld how that Schyr Amery
With the Cliffurd in cumpany
With the flour off Northummyrland[48]
War cummand on thaim at thar hand.
Quhen that the king herd that tithing
He armyt him but mar dwelling,
Sa did thai all that ever wes thar,
Syne in a sop assemblyt ar,
I trow thai war thre hunder ner.
And quhen thai all assemblit wer
The king his baner gert display
And set his men in gud aray,
Bot thai had standyn bot a thraw
Rycht at thar hand quhen that thai saw
Thar fayis throu the wod cummand
Armyt on fute with sper in hand
That sped thaim full enforcely.
The noyis begouth sone and the cry,
For the gud king that formast was
Stoutly towart his fayis gays,[49]
And hynt out off a mannys hand
That ner besyd him wes gangand
A bow and a braid arow als,
And hyt the formast in the hals
Till thropill and wesand yeid in twa
And doun till the erd gan ga.
The laiff with that maid a stopping,
Than but mar bad the nobill king
Hynt fra his baneour his banar[50]

And said, 'Apon thaim, for thai ar
Discumfyt[51] all.' With that word
He swappyt swiftly out his sword
And on thaim ran sa hardely
That all thai off his cumpany
Tuk hardyment off his gud deid,
For sum that fryst thar wayis yeid
Agayne come to the fycht in hy
And met thair fayis vigorusly
That all the formast ruschyt war,
And quhen thai that war hendermar
Saw that the formast left the sted
Thai tornyt sone the bak and fled
And out off the wod thaim withdrew.
The king a few men off thaim slew
For thai rycht sone thar gat gan ga.
It discomfortyt thaim all sua
That the king with his mengne was
All armyt to defend that place
that thai wend throu thar tranonting
Till haiff wonnyn foroutyn fechtin
That thai effrayit war sodanly,
And he thaim soucht sa angyrly
That thai in full gret hy agane

Out off the wod rane to the plane
For thaim faillyt off thar entent.
Thai war that tyme sa foully schent
That fyften hunder men and ma
With a few mengne war reboytyt sua[52]
That thai withdrew thaim schamfully.
Tharfor amang thaim sodanly
Thar rais debate and gret distance,
Ilkan wytt other off thar myschance.
Cliffurd and Waus maid a melle[53]
Quhar Cliffurd raucht him a cole
And athir syne drew till partys,
Bot Schyr Aymer that wes wys
Departyt thaim with mekill payn,
And went till Ingland hame again.
He wyst fra stryff ras thaim amang
He suld thaim nocht hals samyn lang
Foroutyn debate or melle,
Tharfor till Ingland turnyt he
Eith mar schame then he went of ton,
Quhen sa mony off sic renone
Saw sa few men bid thaim battaill
Quhair thai ne war hardy till assaile.

BOOK VIII

The king fra Schyr Aymer wes gane
Gadryt his menye everilkan
And left bath woddis and montanys
And held hys way strak till the planys
For he wald fayne that end war maid
Off that that he begunnyn had,
And he wyst weill he mycht nocht bring
It to gud end but travalling.
To Kyle went he fryst and that land
He maid all till him obeysand,

The men maist force come till his pes.
Syne efterwart or he wald ses
Of Conyngayme[1] the maist party
He gert held till his senyoury.
In Bothweill[2] then Schyr Aymer was
That in hys hart gret angre has
For thai off Cunyngame and Kile
That war obeysand till him quhile
Left Inglismennys fewte.
Tharoff fayne vengyt wald he be,

266

And send Philip the Mowbray
With a thousand as Ik herd say
Off men that war in his leding
To Kile for to werray the king.
Bot James of Douglas that all tid
Had spyis out on ilka sid
Wyst off thar cummyng and that thai
Wald hald doune Makyrnokis way[3].
He tuk with him all prevely
Thaim that war off his cumpany
That war fourty withoutyn ma,
Syne till a strait place gan he ga
That is in Makyrnokis way,
The Edirford it hat perfay,
It lyis betwix marrais twa
Quhar that na hors on lyve may ga.
On the south halff quhar James was
Is ane upgang, a narow pas,
And on the north halff is the way
Sa ill as it apperis today.
Douglas with thaim he with him had
Enbuschyt him and thaim abaid,
He mycht weile fer se thar cummyng
Bot thai mycht se of hym na thing.
Thai baid in buschement all the nycht,
they stayed in their ambuscade
And quhen the sone was schynand brycht
Thai saw in bataillyng cum arayit
The vaward with baner displayit,
And syne sone the remanand
Thai saw weile ner behind cummand.
Then held thai thaim still and preve
Till the formast off that mengye
War entryt in the ford thaim by,
Then schot thai on thaim with a cry
And with wapnys that scharply schar
Sum in the ford thai bakwart bar,
And sum with arowis barblyt braid

Sa gret martyrdome on thaim has maid
That thai gan draw to voyd the place,
Bot byhynd thaim sa stoppyt was
The way that thai fast mycht nocht fle,
And that gert mony off thaim de,
For thai on na wys mycht away
Bot as thai come bot giff that thai
Wald throu thar fayis hald the gat,
Bot that way thocht thaim all to hat.
Thar fayis met thaim sa sturdely
And contenyt the fycht sa hardily
That thai sa dredand war that thai
That fyrst mycht fle fyrst fled away,
And quhen the rerward saw thaim sua
Discumfyt and thar wayis ga
Thai fled on fer and held thar way.
Bot Schyr Philip the Mowbray
That with the formast ridand was
That entryt wes in the place,
Quhen that he saw how he wes stad
Throu the gret worschip that he had
With spuris he strak the steid off pryce[4]
And magre all his ennymys
Throu the thikkest off thaim he raid,
And but challance eschapyt had
Ne war ane hynt him by the brand,
Bot he the gud steid that wald nocht
    stand
Lansyt furth deliverly.
Bot the tother sa stalwartly
Held that the belt braist off the brand
And swerd and belt left in hys hand,
And he but swerd his wayis raid
Weill otouth thaim and thair abaid,
And beheld how that his menye fled
And how his fayis clengyt the steid[5]
That war betwix him and his men.
Tharfor furth the wayis tuk he then

To Kylmarnok and Kilwynnyne[6]
And till Ardrossane[7] eftre syne,
Syne throu the Largis[8] him allane
Till Ennirkyp[9] the way has tane
Rycht to the castell that wes then
Stuffyt all with Inglismen
That him resaiffyt in daynte,
And fra thai wyst howgat that he
Sa fer had rydin him allane
Throu thaim that war his fayis ilkan
Thai prisyt him full gretumly
And lovyt fast his chevalry.
Schyr Philip thus eschapyt was,
And Douglas yet wes in the place
Quhar he sexty has slayne and ma,
The layff fouly thar gat gan ga
And fled to Bothwell hame agayne
Quhar Schyr Aymer wes na thing fayn
Quhen he herd tell on that maner
That his mengne discumfyt wer.
Bot quhen to King Robert wes tauld
How that the Douglas that wes bauld
Vencussyt sa fele with fewe menye
Rycht joyfull in his hart wes he,
And all his menye confortyt war
For thaim thocht weille bath les and mar
That thai suld less thar fayis dreid
Sen thar purpos sa with thaim yeid.
The king lay in Galliston[10]
That is evyn rycht anent Loudoun
And till his pes tuk the cuntre.
Quhen Schyr Aymer and his menye
Hard how he ryotyt the land
And how that nane durst him withstand
He wes intill his hart angry,
And with ane off his cumpany
He send him word and said giff he
Durst him into the planys se

He suld the tend day of May
Cum under Loudoun hill away,
And giff that he wald meyt him thar
He said his worschip suld be mar,
And mar be turnyt in nobillay,
To wyn him in the playne away
With hard dintis in evyn fechtyng
Then to do fer mar with skulking.
The king that hard his messynger
Had dispyt apon gret maner
That Schyr Aymer spak sa heyly,
Tharfor he answeryt irusly
And to the messynger said he,
'Say to thi lord giff that I be
In lyfe he sall me se that day
Weyle ner giff he dar hald the way
That he has said, for sekyrly
Be Loudoun hill mete him sall I.'
The messinger but mare abaid
Till his maistre the wayis raid
And his answer him tauld alswith
Quharof he wes bath glaid and blyth,
For he thocht throu his mekill mycht
Gyff the king durst cum to fycht
That throu the gret chevalry
That suld be in his cumpany
He suld sua ourcum the king
That thar suld be na recovering.
And the king on the tother party
That was all wis and averty
Raid for to se and cheis the place,
And saw the hey gat liand was
Apon a fayr feild evyn and dry,
Bot apon athir sid tharby
Wes a gret mos mekill and braid[11]
That fra the way wes quhar men raid
A bow-draucht weile on ather sid,
And that place thocht him all to wyd

268

Till abyd men that horsyt war.
Tharfor thre dykys our-thwort he schar[12]
Fra baith the mossis to the way
That war sa fer fra other that thai
War ytwyn a bow-draucht or mar.
So holl and hey the dykys war
That men mycht nocht but mekill pane
Pas thaim thocht nane war thaim agan,
Bot sloppys[13] in the way left he
Sa large and off sic quantite
That fyve hunder mycht samyn rid
In at the sloppis sid be sid.
Thar thocht he bataile for to bid
And bargane thaim, for he na drede
Had that thai suld on sid assaile
Na yeit behind giff thaim battaile,
And befor thocht him weill that he
Suld fra thar mycht defendyt be.
Thre dep dykys he gert thar ma,
For gyff he mycht nocht weill ourta
To mete thaim at the fyrst, that he
Suld havve the tother on his pouste,
Be than the thrid gyff it war sua
That thai had passyt the tother twa.
On this wys him ordanys he,
And syne assemblit his mengne
That war sex hunder fechtand men,
But rangale that wes with him then
That war als fele as thai or ma.
With all that mengne gan he ga
The evyn or that the bataill suld be
Till litill Loudoun quhar that he
Wald abid to se thar cummyng,
Syne with the men of his leding
He thocht to sped him sua that he
Suld at the dyk befor thaim be.
Schyr Aymer on the tother party
Gadryt sua gret chevalry

That he mycht be thre thousand ner
Armyt and dycht on gud maner,[14]
Than as man off gret noblay
He held towart his trist his way
Quhen the set day cummyn was.
He sped him fast towart the place
That he nemmyt for to fycht,
The sone wes ryssyn schynand brycht
thyat schawyt on the scheldis brade
In twa eschelis[15] ordanyt he had
The folk that he had in leding.
The king weile sone in the mornyng
Saw fyrst cummand thar fyrst eschele
Arrayit sarraly and weile,
And at thar bak sumdeill ner-hand
He saw the tother folowand,
Thar bassynettis burnyst all brycht
Agayne the son glemand off lycht,
Thar speris pennonys and thar scheldis
Off lycht enlumynyt all the feldis,
Thar best and browdyn brycht baneris
And hors hewyt on ser maneris
And cot-armouris off ser colour
And hawbrekis that war quhyt[16] as flour
Maid thaim gleterand as thai war lyk
Till angelys hey off hevynnys ryk.[17]
The king said, 'Lordis now ye se
How yon men throu thar gret poweste
Wald, and thai mycht fulfill thar will,
Sla us, and makys sembland thartill,
And sen we knaw thar felny
Ga we mete thaim sa hardily
That the stoutest of thar mengye
Off our meting abaysit be,
For gyff the formast egrely
Be met ye sall se sodanly
The henmaist sall abaysit be.
And thoucht that thai be ma than we

That suld abays us litill thing,
For quhen we cum to the fechting
Thar may mete us no ma than we.
Tharfor lordingis, ilkan suld be
Off us worthi off gret valour
For to maynteyme her our honour.
Thynkis quhat glaidschip us abidis
Gyff that we may aqs weile betidis
Haff victour off our fayis her,
For thar is nane than fer na ner
In all thys land that us thar doute.'
Then said thai all that stud about,
'Schyr gyff God will we sall sa do
That na reprov sall fall tharto.'
'Now ga we furth than,' said the king,
'Quhar He that maid off nocht all thing
Lede us and saiff us for his mycht
And help us for till hald our rycht.'
With that thai held thar way in hy
Weill sex hunder in cumpany
Stalwart and stout, worthi and wycht
Bot thai war all to few Ik hycht
Agayne sa fele to stand in stour
Ne war thar utrageous valour
Now gais the nobill king his way
Rycht stoutly and in gud aray,
And to the formast dyk is gane
And in the slop the feld has tane.
The cariage and the povyrall[18]
That war nocht worth in the bataill
Behynd him levyt he all still
Syttand all samyn on the hyll.
Schyr Aymer the king has sene
With his men that war cant and kene
Come to the playne doune fra the hill
As him thocht in full gud will
For to defend or to assaile
Gyff ony wald him bid bataill.

Tharfor his men confortit he
And bad thaim wycht and worthi be,
For gyff that thai mycht wyne the king
And haiff victour off his fechting
Thai suld rycht weile rewardyt be
And ek gretly thar renomme.
With that thai war weill ner the king
And he left his amonesting
And gert trump to the assemble,
And the formest off his mengne
Enbrasyt with the scheldis braid
And rycht sarraly togydder raid
With heid stoupand and speris straucht
Rycht to the king thar wayis raucht,
That met thaim with sa gret vigour
That the best and off maist valour
War laid at erd at thar meting
Quhar men mycht her sic a breking
Off speris that to-fruschyt war
And the woundyt sa cry and rar
That it anoyus wes to her
For thai that fyrst assemblyt wer
Fwyngyt and faucht full sturdely.
The noyis begouth then and the cry.
A! mychty God quha thar had bene
And had the kingis worschip sene
And his brodyr that waine him by
That stonayit thaim sa hardely
That thair gud deid and thair bounte
Gaiff gret confort to thar mengye,
And how Douglas sa manlily
Confortyt thaim that war him by,
He suld weile say that thai had will
To wyn honour and cum thar-till.
The kingis men sa worthi war
That with speris that scharply schar
Thai stekit men and stedis baith
Till rede blud ran off woundis raith.

The hors that woundyt war gan fling
And ruschyt thar folk in thar flynging
Sua that thai that the formast war
War skalyt in soppys her and thar.
The king that saw thaim ruschyt sua
And saw thaim reland to and fra
Ran apon thaim sa egrely
And dang on thaim sa hardely
That fele gart off his fayis fall.
The feild wes ner coveryt all
Bath with the slane hors and with men,
For the gud king thar folowit then
With fyve hunder that wapnys bar
That wald thar fayis na thing spar.
Thai dang on thaim sa hardely
That in schort tyme men mycht se ly
At erd ane hunder and wele mar.
The remanand sa fleyit war
That thai begouth thaim to withdraw,
And quhen thai off the rerward saw
Thar vaward be sa discumfyt
Thai fled foroutyn mar respyt
And quhen Schyr Aymer has sene
His men fleand haly beden
Wyt ye weile him wes full way
Bot he moucht nocht ammonys sway
That ony for him walde torne agane,
He turnyt his bridill and to-ga,
For the gud king thaim presit sua
That sum war dede and sum war tane
And the laiff thar gat ar gane
The folk fled apon this maner
Forout arest and Schir Aymer
Agane to Boithweill is gane
Menand the scaith that he has tane
Sa schamfull that he vencusit wais
That till Ingland in hy he gais
Rycht to the king and schamfully

He gaff up thar his wardanry,
Na nevyr syne for nakyn thing
Bot giff he come rycht with the king
Come he to werray Scotland,
Sa hevyly he tuk on hand
That the king into set battaill
With a quhone lik to poverall
Vencusyt him with a gret menye
That war renonyt off gret bounte.
Sic anoy had Schyr Amery,
And King Robert that wes hardy
Abaid rycht still into the place
Till that his men had left the chace,
Syne with presonaris that thai had tane
Thai ar towart thar innys gane
Fast lovand God off thar weilfar.
He mycht haiff sene that had bene thar
A folk that mery wes and glaid
For thar victour, and als thai haid
A lord that sa swete wes and deboner
Sa curtais and off sa fayr effer
Sa blyth and als weill bourdand
And in bataill sa styth to stand
Sua wys and rycht sua avise
That thai had gret cause blyth to be.
Sua war thai blyth withoutyn dout,
For fele that wynnyt thaim about
Fra thai the king saw help him sua
Till him thar homage gan thai ma.
Than woux his power mar and mar,
And he thoucht weile that he wald far
Oute-our the Mounth with his menye
To luk quha that his frend wald be.
Into Schyr Alexander Fraser
He traistyt for thai cosyngis wer
And his broder Symon, thai twa.
He had mystre weile of ma
For he had fayis mony ane.

Schir Jhon Cumyn erle off
   Bouchquhane[19]
And Schyr Jhon the Mowbray[20] syne
And gus Schyr David[21] off Brechyne
With all the folk off thar leding
War fayis to the noble king,
And for he wyst thai war his fayis
His viage thidderwart he tais,
For he wald se quhatkyn ending
Thai wald set on thar manassing.
The king buskyt and maid him yar
Northwartis with his folk to far,
His brodyr gan he with him ta
And Schyr Gilbert de le Hay alsua,
The erle off Levenax als wes thar
That with the king was our-all-quhar,
Schyr Robert Boyd and other ma.
The king gan furth his wayis ta,
And left James off Douglas
With all the folk that with him was
Behind him for to luk giff he
Mycht recover his countre.
He left into full gret perill,
Bot eftre in a litill quhile
Throu his gret worschip sa he wrocht
That to the kingis pes he brocht
The forest of Selcrik[22] all hale,
And alsua did he Douglasdale
And Jedworthis[23] forest alsua.
And quha-sa weile on hand couth ta
To tell his worschippis ane and ane
He suld fynd off thaim mony ane,
For in his tyme as men said me
Thretten tymys vencusyt wes he
And had victouris sevin and fyfty.
Hym semyt nocht lang ydill to ly,
Be his travaill he had na will,
Me think men suld him love with skill.

This James quhen the king wes gane
All prevely his men has tane
And went to Douglas daile agane,
And maid all prevely a trane
Till thaim that in the castell war.
A buschement slely maid he thar,
And off his men fourtene or ma
He gert as thai war sekkis ta[24]
Fyllyt with gres[25], and syne thaim lay
Apon thar hors and hald thar way
Rycht as thai wald to Lanark far
Outouth quhar thai enbuschyt war.
And quhen thai off the castell saw
Sa fele ladys gang on raw
Off that sycht thai war wonder fayn
And tald it to thar capitane
That hate Schyr Jhone of Webetoun.[26]
He wes baith yong stoute and felloun
Joly alsua and valageous,
And for that he wes amorous
He wald isch fer the blythlyar.
He gert his men tak all thar ger
And isch to get thaim vittaille,
For thar vittaile gan fast thaim faile.
Thai ischyt all abandounly
And prykkyt furth sa wilfully
To wyn the ladys that thai saw pas
Quhill that Douglas with his was
All betwix thaim and the castell.
The laid-men that persavyt weill,
Thai kest thar ladys doun in hy,
And thar gownys deliverly
That heylyt thaim thai kest away,
And in gret hy thar hors hint thai
And stert apon thaim sturdely
And met thar fayis with a cry
That had gret wonder quhen thai saw
Thaim that war er lurkand sa law

Cum apon thaim sa hardely.
Thai woux abaysit sodanly
And at the castell wald haiff bene,
Quhen thai on other halff has sene
Douglas brak his enbuschement
That agayne thaim rycht stoutly went.
Thai wyst nocht quhat to do na say,
Thar fayis on athir sid saw thai
That strak on thaim foroutyn sparing,
And thai mycht help thaim selvyn na thing
Bot fled to warrand quhar thai mocht,
And thai sa angryly thaim socht
That off thaim all eschapyt nane.
Schyr Jhoun Webetoun thar wes slane,
And quhen he dede wes as ye her
Thai fand intill his coffeir
A lettyr that him send a lady
That he luffyt per drouery,[27]
The letter spak on this maner
That said quhen he had yemyt a yer
In wer as a gud bachiller
And governit weill in all maner
The aventuris castell off Douglas
That to kepe sa peralus was

Than mycht he weile ask a lady
Hyr amouris and hyr drouery,
The lettyr spak on this maner.
And quhen thai slayne on this wyse wer
Douglas rycht to the castell raid
And thar sa gret debate he maid
That in the castell entryt he,
I wate nocht all the certante
Quhethyr it was throu strenth or slycht,
Bot he wrocht sua with mekill mycht
That the constabill and all the laiff
That war tharin, bath man and knav
He tuk and gaiff thaim dispending
And sent thaim hamr but mar greving
To the Cliffurd in thar countre.
And syne sa besily wrocht he
That he tumblyt doun all the wall
And destroyit the housis all,
Syne till the Forest held his way
Quhar he had mony ane hard assay
And mony fayr poynt off wer befell.
Quha couth thaim all rehers or tell
He suld say that his name suld be
Lestand into full gret renoune.

BOOK IX

Now leve we intill the Forest
Douglas that sall bot litill rest
Till the countre deliveryt be
Off Inglis folk and thar powste,
And turne we till the noble king
That with the folk off his leding
Towart the Month has tane his wai
Rycht stoutly and intill gud array,
Quhar Alysander Frayser him met
And als his broder Symonet

With all the folk thai with thaim had.
The king gud contenance thaim made
That wes rycht blyth off thar cummyne.
Thai tauld the king off the convyne
Off Jhon Cumyn erle of Bouchane
That till help him had with him tane
Schyr Jhon Mowbray and other ma,
Schyr David off Brechyn alsua,
With all the folk off thar leding,
'And yarnys mar na ony thing

273

Vengeance off you, schyr king, to tak
For Schyr Jhone the Cumyn his sak
That quhylum in Drumfres wes slayn.'
The king said, 'Sa our Lord me sayn,
Ik had gret caus him for to sla,
And sen that thai on hand will ta
Becaus off him to werray me
I sall thole a quhile and se
On quhat wys that thai pruve thar mycht,
And giff it fall that thai will fycht
Giff thai assaile we sall defend,
Syne fall eftre quhat God will send.'
Eftre this spek the king in hy
Held straucht his way till Enrowry[1],
And thar him tuk sik a seknes
That put him to full hard distress.
He forbar bath drynk and mete,
His men na medicyne couth get
That ever mycht to the king availe,
His force gan him halyly faile
That he mycht nother rid na ga.
Then wyt ye that his men war wa,
For nane wes in that cumpany
That wald haiff bene halff sa sary
For till haiff sene his broder ded
Lyand befor him in that steid
As thai war for his seknes,
For all thar confort in him wes.
Bot gud Schyr Edward the worthy
His broder that wes sa hardy
And wys and wycht set mekill payn
To comfort thaim with all his mayn,
And quhen the lordis that thar war
Saw that the ill ay mar and mar
Travaillyt the king, thaim thocht in hy
It war nocht spedfull thar to ly,
For thar all playne wes the countre
And thai war bot a few menye

To ly but strenth into the playne.
Forthi till that thar capitane
War coveryt off his mekill ill
Thai thocht to wend sum strenthis till.
For folk foroutyn capitane
Bot thai the better be apayn
Sall nocht be all sa gud in deid
As thai a lord had thaim to leid
That dar put him in aventur
But abaysing to tak the ure
That God will send, for quhen that he
Off sic will is and sic bounte
That he dar put him till assay
His folk sall tak ensample ay
Off his gud deid and his bounte,
And ane off thaim sall be worth thre
Off thaim that wikkyt chifftane hais,
His wrechytnes sa in thaim gais
That thai thar manlynes sall tyn
throu wrechitnes of his convyn.
For quhen the lord that thaim suld leid
May do nocht bot as he that war ded
Or fra his folk haldis his way
Fleand, trow ye nocht than that thai
Sall vencusyt in thar hartis be.
Yis sall thai, as I trow per de,
Bot giff thar hartis be sa hey
That thai na will for thar worschip flei,
And thaoct sum be of sic bounte
Quhen thai the lord and his menye
Seys fley, yeit sall thai fley apayn
For all men fleis the deid rycht fayne.
Se quhat he dois that sua foully
Fleys thus for his cowardy,
Bath him and his vencusys he
And gerris his fayis aboune be.
Bot he that throu his gret noblay
Till perallis him abandounys ay

To recomfort his menye
Gerris thame be off sa gret bounte
That mony tyme unlikly thing
Tha bring rycht weill to gud ending.
Sa did this king that Ik off reid,
And for his utrageous manheid
Confortyt his on sic maner
That nane had radnes quhar he wer.
Thai wald nocht fecht till that he wes
Liand intill his seknes,
Tharfor in litter thai him lay
And till the Slevauch[2] hald thar way
And thocht thar in that strenth to ly
Till passyt war his malady.
Bot fra the erle of Buchane
Wyst that thai war thidder gane
And wyst that sa sek wes the king
That men doutyt off his covering,
He sent eftre his men in hy
And assemblyt a gret cumpany,
For all his awine men war thar
And all his frendis with him war,
That wes Schir Jhonne the Mowbray
And his brodyr as Ik hard say
And Schyr David off Brechynge
With fele folk in thar ledyng.
And quhen thai all assemblit war
In hy thai tuk thar way to far
To the Slevauch with all thar men
For till assaile the king that then
Wes liand intill his seknes.
This wes eftyr the Martymes[3]
Quhen snaw had helyt all the land.
To the Slevauch thai come ner-hand
Arayit on thar best maner
And thane the kingis men that wer
War off thar come thaim apparaylyt
To defend giff thai thaim assaylyt

And nocht-forthi thar fayis war
Ay twa for ane that thai war thar.
The erlys men ner cummand war
Trumpand and makand mekill far
And maid knychtis quhen thai war ner,
And thai that in the woddis sid wer
Stud in aray rycht sarraly
And thocht to byd thar hardyly
The cummyng off thar ennymys,
Bot thai wald apon nakyn wys
Ische till assaile thaim in fechting
Till coveryt war the nobill king,
Bot and othir wald thaim assailye
Thai wald defend vailye que vailye.[4]
And quhen the erlis cumpany
Saw that thai wrocht sa wisely
That thai thar strenth schupe to defend,
Thar archeris furth to thaim thai send
To bykkyr thaim and men off mayn,
And thai send archeris thaim agayne
That bykkyrryt thaim sa sturdely[5]
Till thai off the erlis party
Intill thar bataill dryvyn war.
Thre dayis on this wys lay thai thar
And bykkyryt thaim everilk day
Bot thar bowmen the war had ay.
And quhen the kingis cumpany
Saw thar fayis befor thaim ly
That ilk day wox ma and ma,
And thai war quhone and stad war sua
That thai had na thing for till eyt
Bot giff thai travaillit it to get,
Tharfor thai tuk consale into hy
That thar wald thai na langer ly
Bot hald thar way quhar thai mycht get
To thaim and tharis vittaillis and mete.
In a littar the king thai lay
And redyit thaim and held thar way

That all thar fayis mycht thaim se,
Ilk man buskyt him in his degre
To fycht giff thai assaillyt war.
In myddis thaim the king thai bar
And yeid about him sarraly
And nocht full gretly thaim gan hy.
The erle and thai that with him war
Saw that thai buskit thaim to far,
And saw how with sa litill effray
Thai held furth with the king thar way
Redy to fycht quha wald assaile.
Thar hartis begouth all to faile
And in pes lete thaim pas thar way
And till thar housis hame went thai.
The erle his way tuk to Bouchane,
And Schyr Edward the Bruce is gane
Rycht to Strabolghy[6] with the king
And sua lang thar maid sojorning
Till he begouth to covyr and ga,
And syne thar wayis gan thai ta
Till Innerroury straucht agane
For thai wald ly into the plane,
The wynter sesone, for vittaile
Intill the plane mycht thaim nocht faile.
The erle wyst that thai war thar
And gaderyt a mengne her and thar.
Brechyne and Mowbray and thar men
All till the erle assemblyt then
And war a full gret cumpany
Off men arayit jolyly.
Till Auld Meldrum thai yeid the way
And thar with thar men logit thai
Befoir Yhule evyn a nycht but mar,
A thousand trow I weile thai war.
Thai logyt thaim all thar that nycht
And on the morn quhen day wes lycht
The lord off Brechyn Schyr Davy
Is went towart Innerroury

To luk gyff he on ony wys
Mycht do skaith till his ennymys,
And till the end off Innerroury
Come ridand sa sodanly
That off the kingis men he slew
A part, and other sum thaim withdrew
And fled thar way towart the king
That with the maist off his gadryng
On the yond half Doun wes than lyand.
And quhen men tauld him tithand
How Schyr Davy had slayn his men
His hors in hy he askyt then
And bad his men all mak thaim yar
Into gret hy, for he wald far
To bargane with his ennymys.
With that he buskyt for to rys
That wes nocht all weill coveryt then.
Then said sum off his preve men,
'Quhat think ye thusgat to far
To fycht and nocht yeit coveryt ar.'
'Yhis,' said the king, 'withoutyn wer,
Thar bost has maid me haile and fer,
For suld na medicyne sa sone
Haiff coveryt me as thai haiff done.
Tharfor, sa God himself me se,
I sall othir haiff thaim or thai me.'
And quhen his men has hard the king
Set him sa hale for the fechting,
Off his coveryng all blyth thai war
And maid thaim for the battaill yar.
The nobill king and his mengye
That mycht weile ner sevin hunder be
Towart Auld Meldrum tuk the way
Wuhar the erle and his menye lay.
The discurrouris[7] saw thaim cummand
With baneris to the wynd wavand
And yeid to thar lord in hy
That gert arme hys men hastely

And thaim arayit for battaile,
Behind thaim set thai thar merdale[8]
And maid gud sembland for to fycht.
The king come on with mekill mycht
And thai abaid makand gret fayr
Till thai ner at assembling wayr,
Bot quhen thai saw the nobill king
Cum stoutly on foroutyn fenyeing
A litill on bridill thai thaim withdrew,
And the king that rycht weill knew
That thai war all discumfyt ner
Pressyt on thaim with his baner
And thai withdrew mar and mar.
And quhen the small folk thai had thar
Saw thar lordis withdraw them sua
Thai turnyt the bak all and to-ga
And fled all scalyt her and thar.
The lordis that yeyt togydder war
Saw that thar small folk war fleand
And saw the king stoutly cummand,
Thai war ilkane abaysit swa
That thai the bak gave and to-ga,
A litill stound samyn held thai
And syne ilk man has tane his way.
Fell never men sa foule myschance
Eftre sa sturdy contenance
For quhen the kingis cumpany
Saw that thai fled sa foulyly
Thai chasyt thaim with all thair mayn
And sum thai tuk and sum has slayn.
The remanand war fleand ay,
Quha had gud hors gat best away.
Till Ingland fled the erle of Bouchquhane
Shyr Jhon Mowbray is with him gane
And war resett with the king,
Bot thai had bath bot schort lesting
For thai deyt sone eftre syne.
And Schyr David off Brechyne

Fled till Brechyne his awine castell
And warnyst it bath fayr and weill,
Bot the erle of Atholl, Davy,
His sone that wes in Kildromy
Come syne and him assegyt thar,
And he that wald hald were ne mar
Na bargane with the nobile king
Come syne his man with gud treting
Now ga we to the king agayne
That off his victory wes rycht fayn,
And gert his men bryn all Bowchane
Fra end till end and sparyt nane,
And heryit thaim on sic maner
That eftre weile fyfty yer
Men menyt the herschip off Bouchane.[9]
The king than till his pes has tane
The north cuntreys that humbly
Obeysyt till his senyoury[10]
Sua that benorth the Month war nane
Then thai his men war everilkan,
His lordschip wox ay mar and mar.
Towart Angus syne gan he far
And thocht sone to mak all fre
That wes on the north halff the Scottis se.[11]
The castell off Forfayr[12] wes then
Stuffyt all with Inglismen,
Bot Philip the Forestar of Platane
Has off his freyndis with him tane
And with leddrys all prevely[13]
Till the castell he gan him hy
And clam up our the wall off stane
And swagate has the castell tane
Throu faute off wach with litill pane,
And syne all that he fand has slayne
Syne yauld the castell to the king
That maid him rycht gud rewarding,
And syne gert brek doun the wall
And fordyd well and castell all.

277

Quhen that the castell off Forfar
And all the towris tumblyt war
Down till the erd as Ik haiff tauld
The king that wycht wes wys and bauld
That thocht that he wald mak all fre
Apon the north halff the Scottis se
Till Perth is went with all his rout
And umbeset the toun about
And till it a sege has set.
Bot quhill it mycht haiff men and met
It mycht nocht but gret payne be tane
For all the wall wes then of stane
And wycht towris and hey-standand,
And that tyme war tharin dwelland
Muschet and als Olyfard,[14]
Thai twa the toun had all in ward
And off Straitherne als the erle wes thar,[15]
Bot his sone and off his men war
Without intill the kingis rowt.
Thar wes oft bekering styth and stout
And men slayne apon ilk party,
Bot the gud king that all wytty
Wes in his dedis everilkane
Saw the wallis sa styth off stane
And saw defens that thai gan ma
And how the toun wes hard to ta
With opyn sawt strenth or mycht.
Tharfor he thocht to wyrk with slycht,
And in all tyme that he thar lay
He spyit and slely gert assay
Quhar at the dyk schaldest was,[16]
Till at the last he fand a place
That men mycht till thar schuldris wad.[17]
And quhen he that place fundyn had
He gert his men busk ilkane
Quhen sex woukis off the sege war gane,
And tursyt thar harnes halyly
And left the sege all opynly

And furth with all his folk gan fayr
As he wald do tharto no mayr.
And thai tha war within the toun
Quhen thai to fayr sa saw him boun
Thai schoutit him and skornyn mad,
And he furth on his wayis rad
As he ne had will agayne to turn
Na besyd thaim mak sojourn.
Bot in aucht dayis nocht-forthi
He gert mak leddrys prevely
That mycht suffice till his enent,
And in a myrk nycht syne is went
Toward the toun with his menye
Bath hors and knafis all left he
Fer fra the toun, and syne has tane
Thair ledderis and on fut ar gane
Towart the toun all prevely.
Thai hard na wachys spek na cry[18]
For thai war within may-fall
As men that dred nocht slepand all.
Thai haid na dreid then off the king
For thai off him herd na thing
All thai thre dayis befor or mar,
Thairfor sekyr and traist thai war.
And quhen the king thaim hard nocht ster
He was blyth on gret maner,
And his ledder in hand gan ta
Ensample till his men to ma,
Schot in the dik and with his sper
Taistyt till he it our-woud,
Bot till his throt the watyr stud.
That tyme wes in his cumpany
Aknycht off France wycht and hardy,
And quhen he in the watyr sua
Saw the king pas and with him ta
His ledder unabasytly,
He saynyt him for the ferly
And said, 'A, lord, quhat sall we say

278

Off our lordis off Fraunce that thai
With gud morsellis fayrcis thar pawnce
And will bot ete and drink and dawnce
Quhen sic a knycht and sa worthy
As this throu his chevalry
Into sic perell has him set
To win a wrechyt hamillet.'[19]
With that word to the dik he ran
And our efter the king he wan,
And quhen the kingis menye saw
Thar lord out-our intill a thraw
Thai passyt the dik and but mar let
Thar leddrys to the wall thai set
And to clymb up fast pressyt thai,
Bot the gud king as I herd say
Was the secund man tuk the wall
And bad thar till his mengye all
War cummyn up in full gret hy.
Yeit than rais nother noyis na cry,
Bot sone efter thai noyis maid
That off thaim fyrst persaving had
Swa that the cry rais throu the toun,
Bot he that with his men wes boun
Till assaill to thte toun is went
And the maist off his menye sent
All scalyt throu the toun, bot he
Held with himselvyn a gret mengne
Sa that he moucht be ay purvayit
To defend giff he war assayit.
Bot thai that he send throu the toun
Put to sa gret confusioun
Thar fayis that in beddis war
Or scalyt fleand her and thar
That or the sone rais thai had tane
Thar fayis or discumfyt ilkane.
The wardanys bath tharin war tane,
And Malice off Straithern is gane
Till his fadyr the Erle Malice

And with strenth tuk him and his,
Syne for his sak the noble king
Gave him his in governyng.
The lave that ran out-throu the toun
Sesyt to thaim into gret fusoun
Men and armyng and marchandis
And other gud on syndry wys,
Quhill thai that er war pour and bar
Off that gud rych and mychty war,
Bot thar wes few slayne for the king,
That thaim had gevyn in commanding
On gret payne that thai suld slay nane
That but gret bargane mycht be tane.
That thai war kynd to the countre
He wyst and off thaim had pite.
On this maner the toun wes tane
And syne towris everilkane
And wallis gert he tumble down.
He levyt nocht about that town
Towr standand na stane na wall
That ne haly gert stroy thaim all,
And presonerys that thar tuk he
He send quhar thai mycht haldyn be,
And till his pes tuk all the land.
Wes nane that durst him than withstand
Apon northhalff the Scottis se,
All obeysyt till his majeste
Outane the lord of Lorn and thai
Off Arghile[20] that wald with him ga.
He held him ay agayne the king
And hatyt him atour all thing,
Bot yete or all the gamyn ga
I trow weill that the king sall ta
Vengeance off his gret cruelte,
And that him sar repent sall he
That he the king contraryit ay,
May-fall quhen he it mend na may.
The kingis broder, quhen the toun

Wes takyn thus and dongyn doun,
Schyr Edward that wes sa worthy
Tuk with him a gret cumpany
And tuk his gayt till Galloway,
For with his men he wald assay
Giff he mycht recover that land
And wyn it fra Inglismennys hand.
This Schyr Edward forsuth Ik hycht
Wes off his hand a noble knycht
And in blythnes suete and joly,
Bot he wes outrageous hardy
And of sa hey undretaking
That he haid never yeit abaysyng
Off multitud off men, forthi
He discumfyt commounly
Mony with quhone, tharfor had he
Out-over his peris renomme.
And quha wald rehers all the deid
Off his hey worschip and manheid
Men mycht a mekill romanys mak,
And nocht-forthi I think to tak
On hand off him to say sum thing
Bot nocht tende part his travalyn.
This gud knycht that I spek off her
With all the folk that with him wer
Weill sone to Galloway cummyn is,
All that he fand he makyt his
And ryotyt gretly the land.
Bot than in Galloway war wonnand
Schyr Ingrahame the Umfravill that wes
Renommyt off sa hey prowes
that he off worschippassyt the rowt,
Tharfor he gert ay ber about
Apon a sper a rede bonet
Into takyn that he wes set
Into the hycht off chevalry,
And off Saynct Jhon als Schyr Aymry.
Thir twa the land had in stering,

And quhen thai hard off the cummyng
Off Schyr Edward that sa playnly
Oure-raid the land, thare in gret hy
Thai assemblyt all thar mengne,
I trow tuelf hunder thai mycht be.
Bot he with fewar folk thaim met
Besyd Cre[21] and sa hard thaim set
With hard battaill and stalwart fycht
That he thaim all put to the flycht
And slew twa hunder wrill and ma,
And the chyftanys in hy gan ta
Thar way to Buttill[22] for to be
Thar resavyt to sawfte,
And Schyr Edward thaim chasit fast,
Bot till the castell at the last
Gat Schyr Ingrahame and Schyr Amery,
Bot the best off thar cumpany
Left ded behind thaim in the place.
And quhen Schyr Edward saw the chace
Wes falyt he gert seys the pray
And sua gret cattell had away
That it war wonder for to se.
Out of Buttill thai saw how he
Gert his men dryve with him thar pray
Bot na let tharin mycht thai.
Throu his chevalrous chevalry
Galloway wes stonayit gretumly
And he dowtyt for his bounte.
Sum off the men off the countre
Cum till his pes and maid him aith.
Bot Schyr Amery that had the skaith
Off the bargane I tauld off er,
Raid till Ingland till purches ther
Off armyt men gret cumpany
To veng him off the velany
That Schyr Edward that noble knycht
Him did by Cre into the fycht.
Off gud men he assemblit thar

Weill fyften hunder men and mar
That war rycht of gud renowne.
His way with all that folk tuk he,
And in the land all prevely
Entryt with tha chevalry
Thynkand Schyr Edward to suppris
Giff that he moucht on ony wis
For he thocht he wald him assaile
Or that he left in playn bataill.
Now may ye her off gret ferly
And off rycht hey chevalry,
For Schyr Edward into the land
Wes with his mengne rycht ner-hand,
And in the mornyng rycht arly
Herd the countre men mak cry
And had wyttryng off thar cummyng.
Than buskyt he him but delaying
And lapp on hors deliverly,
He had than in toute fyfty
All apon gud hors armyt weill,
His small folk gert he ilk-deill
Withdraw thaim till a strait thar-by,
And he raid furth with his fyfty.
A knycht that then was in his rowt
Worthi and wycht stalwart and stout
Curtais and fayr and off gud fame
Schyr Alane off Catkert[23] be name
Tauld me this taile as I sall tell.
Gret myst into the mornyng fell
Sa thai mycht nocht se thaim by
For myst a bow-draucht fullely.
Sa hapnyt that thai fand the trais
Quhar at the rowt furth passyt wais
Off thair fayis that forouth raid.
Schyr Edward that gret yarnyn had
All tymys to do chevalry
With all his rout in full gret hy
Folowyt the trais quhar gane war thai,

And befor mydmorne off the day
The myst wox cler all sodanly
And than he and his cumpany
War nocht a bowdracht fra the rout.
than schot thai on thaim with a schout,
For gyff thai fled thai wyst that thai
Suld nocht weill feyrd part get away,
Tharfor in aventur to dey
He wald him put or he wald fle.
And quhen the Inglis cumpany
Saw on thaim cum sa sodanly
Sik folk foroutyn abaysyng
Thai war stonayt for effrayng,
And the tother but mar abaid
Swa hardely amang thaim raid
That fele off thaim till erd thai bar.
Stonayit sa gretly than thai war
Throu the force off that fyrst assay
That thai war intill gret effray,
And wend be fer thai had bene ma
For that thai war assailit sua.
Quhen thai had thyrlyt thaim hastily
Than Schyr Edwardis cumpany
Set stoutly in the heid agayne,
And at that cours borne doune and slayn
War off thar fayis a gret party
That thai effrayit war sa gretly
That thai war scalyt gretly then.
And quhen Schyr Edward and his men
Saw thaim intill sa evill aray
The thrid tyme on thaim prekyt thai,
And thai that saw thaim sa stouly
Come on dred thaim sa gretumly
That all thar rowt bath les and mar
Fled prekand scalyt her and thar.
Wes nane amang thaim sa hardy
To bid, bot all comonaly
Fled to warand, and he gan chas

That wilfull to distroy thaim was
And sum he tuk and sum war slayn,
Bot Schyr Amery with mekill payn
Eschapyt and his gat in gayn.
His men discumfyt war ilkane,
Sum tane, sum slayne, sum gat away,
It wes a rycht fayr poynt perfay.
Lo! how hardyment tane sa sudandly
And drevyn to the end scharply
May ger oftsys unlikly thingis
Cum to rycht fayr and gud endingis
As it fell into this cas her.
For hardyment withoutyn wer
Wan fyften hunder with fyfty
Quhar ay for ane thar wes thretty,
And twa men ar a mannys her,
Bot ure thaim led on swilk maner
That thai discumfyt war ilkane.
Schyr Amery hame his gat is gane
Rycht blyth that he swa gat away,
I trow he sall nocht mony day
Haiff will to werray that countre,
With-thi Schyr Edward tharin be.
And he dwelt furth into the land
Thaim that rebell war werrayand,
And in a yer sa werrayit he
That he wane quyt that countre
Till his broderys pes the king.
Bot that wes nocht but hard fechting,
For in that tyme thar him befell
Mony fayr poynt as Ik herd tell
The quhilk that ar nocht writyn her,
Bot I wate weile that in that yer
Thretten castellis[24] with strenth he wan
And ourcome mony a mody man.
Quha-sa off him the south will reid,
Had he had mesure in his deid
I trow that worthyar then he

Mycht nocht in his tym fundyn be
Outakyn his broder anerly,
To quham into chevalry
Lyk wes nane in his day,
For he led him with mesur ay,
And with wyt his chevalry
He governyt sa worthily
That he oft full unlikly thing
Broucht rycht weill to gud ending.
In all this tyme James off Douglas
In the Forest travaland was,
And it throu hardiment and slycht
Occupyit all magre the mycht
Off his fell fayis, the-quhether thai
Set him full oft in full hard assay,
Bot oft throu wyt and throu bounte
His purpos to gud end brocht he.
Intill that tyme him fell throu cas
On ane nycht as he travaland was
And thocht till haiff tane resting
In ane hous on the watyr off Lyne[25]
And as he come with his mengne
Ner-hand the hous sua lysnyt he
And herd thair sawis ilke deill,
And be that he persavyt weill
That thai war strang men that thar
That nycht tharin herbryd war.
And as he thocht it fell per cas,
For off Bonkle the lord thar was
Alexander Stewart hat he
With other twa off gret bounte,
Thomas Randell off gret renowne
And Adam alsua off Gordoune,
That thar come with gret cumpany
And thocht into the Forest to ly
And occupy it throu thar mycht,
And with travaill and stalwart fycht
Chace Douglas out of that countre.

Bot otherwayis then yeid the gle
For quhen James had wittering
That strang men had taken herbryng
In the place that he schup him to ly
He to the hous went hastily
And umbeset it all about.
Quhen thai within hard swilk a rout
About the hous thai rais in hy
And tuk thar ger rycht hastily
And schot furth fra thai harnasyt war.
Thar fayis thaim met with wapnys bar
And assaylit rycht hardely
And thai defendyt douchtely
With all thar mycht, till at the last
Thar fayis pressyt thaim sa fast
That thar folk failyt thaim ilkane.
Thomas Randell thar wes tane
And Alexander Stewart alsua
Woundyt in a place or twa.
Adam of Gordoun fra the fycht
Quhat throu his strenth and his mycht
Eschapyt and ser off thar men,
Bot thai that war arestyt then
War off thar taking wondre wa,
Bot neidlingis behovit it be sua.
That nycht the gud lord off Douglas
Maid to Schyr Alysander that was
His emys sone rycht glaidsome cher,
Sua did he als withoutyn wer

Till Thomas Randell for that he
Wes to the king in ner degre
Off blud, for his sistre him bar,
And on the morne foroutyn mar
Towart the noble king he raid
And with him bath thai twa he haid.
The king off his present wes blyth
And thankyt him weill fele syth,
And till his nevo gan he say,
'Thou has ane quhill renyid thi fay,
Bot thou reconsalit now mon be.'
Then till the king answerit he
And said, 'Ye chasty me, bot ye
Aucht bettre chastyt for to be,
For sene ye werrayit the king
Off Ingland, in playne fechtyng
Ye suld pres to derenyhe rycht
And nocht with cowardy na with slycht.'
The king said, 'Yeit may-fall it may
Cum or oucht lang to sic assay.
Bot sen thou spekys sa rudly
It is gret skyll men chasty
Thai proud wordis till that thou knaw
The rycht and bow it as thou aw.'
The king foroutyn mar delaying
Send him to be in ferme keping
Quhar that he allane suld be,
Nocht all apon his powste fre.

BOOK X

Quhen Thomas Randell on this wis
Wes takyn as Ik her devys
And send to dwell in gud keping
For spek that he spak to the king,
The gud king that thocht on the scaith

The dispyt and felny bath
That Jhon off Lorne had till him doyn
His ost assemblyt he then sone
And towart Lorn he tuk the way
With his men intill gud aray.

Bot Jhone off Lorn off his cummyng
Lang or he come had wittering,
And men on ilk sid gadryt he
I trow twa thousand thai mycht be
And send thaim for to stop the way
Quhar the gud king behovyt away,
And that wes in an evill plas
That sa strayt and sa narow was
That twasum samyn mycht nocht rid
In sum place off the hillis sid.
The nethyr halff was peralous
For schor crag hey and hydwous
Raucht to the se doun fra the pas,
On athyr halff the montane was
Sua combrous hey and stay
That it was hard to pas that way.
I trow nocht that in all Bretane
Ane heyar hill may fundyn be.
Thar Jhone off Lorne gert his menye
Enbuschyt be abovyn the way,
For giff the king held thar away
He thocht he suld sone vencussyt be,
And himselff held him apon the se
Weill ner the pais with his galayis.
Bot the king that in all assayis
Wes fundyn wys and avise
Persavyt rycht weill thar sutelte,
And that he neid that gait suld ga.
His men departyt he in twa
And till the gud lord off Douglas
Quham in herbryd all worschip was
He taucht the archerys everilkane
And this gud lord with him has tane
Schyr Alysander Fraser the wycht,
And Wylyam Wysman a gud knycht
And with thaim syne Schyr Andrew Gray.
Thir with thar mengne held thar way
And clamb the hill deliverly

And or thai off the tother party
Persavyt thaim thai had ilkane
The hycht abovyne thar fayis tane.
The king and his men held thar way,
And quhen intill the pas war thai
Entryt the folk of Lorne in hy
Apon the king raysyt the cry
And schot and tumblit on him stanys
Rycht gret and hevy for the nanys,
Bot thai scaith nocht gretly the king
For he had thar in his leding
Men that lycht and deliver war
And lycht armouris had on thaim thar
Sua that thai stoutly clamb the hill
And lettyt thar fayis to fulfill
The maist part of thar felny.
And als apon the tother party
Come James of Douglas and his rout
And schot apon thaim with a schout
And woundyt thaim with arowis fast,
And with thar swerdis at the last
Thai ruschyt amang thaim hardely,
For thai of Lorn full manlely
Gret and apert defens gan ma.
Bot quhen thai saw that thai war sua
Assaylit apon twa partys
And saw weill that thar ennemys
Had all the fayrer off the fycht
In full gret hy thai tuk the flycht,
And thai a felloun chas gan ma
And slew all that thai mycht ourta,
And thai that mycht eschap but delay
Rycht till ane water held thar way
That ran doun be the hillis syd.
It was sa styth and depe and wid
That men in na place mycht it pas
Bot at ane btyg that beneuth thaim was.
To that brig held thai straucht the way

284

And to brek it fast gan assay,
Bot thai that chassyt quhen thai thaim saw
Mak arest, but dred or aw
Thai ruschyt apon thaim hardely
And discumfyt thaim uterly,
And held the brig haile quhill the king
With all the folk off his leding
Passyt the brig all at thar ese.
To Jhone off Lorne it suld displese
I trow, quhen he his men mycht se
Oute off his schippis fra the se
Be slayne and chassyt in the hill,
That he mycht set na help thartill,
For it angrys als gretumly
To gud hartis that ar worthi
To se thar fayis fulfill thar will
As to thaim selff to thoke the ill.
At sic myscheiff war thai of Lorn,
'For fele the lyvys thar has lorne
And other sum war fled thar way.
The king in hy gert sese the pray
Off all the land, quhar men mycht se
Sa gret habundance come of fe¹
That it war wonder to behauld.
The king that stout wes stark and bauld
Till Dunstaffynch² rycht sturdily
A sege set and besily
Assaylit the castell it to get,
And in schort tym he has thaim set
In swilk thrang that tharin war than
That magre tharis he it wan,
And ane gud wardane tharin set
And betaucht hym bath men and met
Sua that he lang tyme thar mycht be
Magre thaim all off that countre.
Schyr Alerandir off Arghile that saw
The king dystroy up clene and law
His land send treyteris to the king

And cum his man but mar duelling,
And he resavit him till his pes,
Bot Jhone off Lorne his sone yeit wes
Rebell as he wes wont to be
And fled with schippis on the se,
Bot thai that left apon the land
War to the king all obeysand.
And he thar hostage all has tane
And towart Perth agayne is gane
To play him thar into the playne.
Yeit Lothyane was him agayne,
And at Lythkow wes than a pele³
Mekill and stark and stuffyt wele
With Inglismen, and wes reset
To thaim that with armuris or met
Fra Edynburgh wald to Strevelyn ga
And fra Strevelyng agane alsua,
And till the countre did gret ill.
Now may ye her giff that ye will
Entrmellys and juperdyis
That men assayit mony wys
Castellis and peyllis for to ta,
And this Lithquhow wes ane off tha
And I sall tell you how it wes tane.
In the contre thar wonnyt ane
That husband wes, and with his fe
Oftsys hay to the peile led he,
Wilyame Bunnok to name he hicht
That stalwart man wes into ficht.
He saw sa hard the contre staid
That he gret noy and pite had⁴
Throw the gret force that it was then
Governyt and led with Inglismen,
That travalyt men out-our mesure.
He wes a stout carle and a sture
And off himselff dour and hardy,
And had freyndis wonnand him by
And schawyt ti sum his prevete,

285

And apon his convyne gat he
Men that mycht ane enbuschement ma
Quhill that he with his wayne suld ga
To lede thaim hay into the pele
Bot his wayne suld be stuffyt wele,
For aucht men in the body
Off his wayn suld sit prevely
And with hay helyt be about,
And himselff that wes dour and stout
Suld be the wayne gang ydilly,
And ane yuman wycht and hardy
Befor suld dryve the wayne and ber
Ane hachat that war scharp to scher
Under his belt, and quhen the yat[5]
War apynnyt[6] and thai war tharat
And he hard him cry sturdely,
'Call all, call all,' than hastyly
He suld stryk with the ax in twa
the soyme, and than in hy suld tha
That war within the wayne cum out
And mak debate quhill that thar rout
That suld nerby enbushyt be
Cum for to manteyme the melle
This wes intill the hervyst tyd
Quhen feldis that ar fayr and wid
Chargyt with corne all fully war,
For syndry cornys that thai bar
Wox ryp to wyn to mannys fud,
And the treys all chargyt stud
With ser frutis on syndry wys.
In this swete tyme that I devys
Thai off the pele had wonnyn hay
And with this Bunnok spokyn had thai
To lede thar hay, for he wes ner,
And he assentyt but daunger
And said that he in the mornyng
Weile sone a fothyr he suld bring
Fayrer and gretar and weile mor

Than he brocht ony that yer befor,
And held thaim cunnand sekyrly.
For that nycht warnyt he prevely
Thaim that in the wayne suld ga
And that in the buschement suld be alsua,
And thai sa graithly sped thaim thar
That or day thai enbuschyt war
Weile ner the pele quhar thai mycht her
The cry als sone as ony wer,
And held thaim sua still but stering
That nane off thaim had persaving.
And this Bunnok fast gan him payne
To dres his menye in his wayne
And all a quhile befor the day
He had thaim helyt weile with ha
And maid him to yok his fe
Till men the son schynand mycht se,
And sum that war within the pele
War ischyt on thar awne unsele
To wyn thar hervyst ner tharby.
Than Bunnok with the cumpany
That in his wayne closyt he had
Went on his way but mar abaid
And callit his wayne towart the pele,
And the portar that saw him wele
Cum ner the yet, it opnyt sone,
And then Bunnok foroutyn hone
Gert call the wayne deliverly,
And quhen it wes set evynly[7]
Betwix the chekis of the yat[8]
Sua that men mycht it spar na gat
He cryit hey, 'Call all, call all,'
And he than lete the gad-wand fall
And hewyt in twa the soyme in hy.
Bonnok with that deliverly
Roucht till the portar sic a rout
That blud and harnys bath come out,
And thai that war within the wayne

286

Lap out belyff and sone has slayne
Men off the castell that war by
Than in ane quhile begouth the cry,
And thai that ner enbuschyt war
Lap out and come with swerdis bar
And tuk the casell all but payn
And has thaim that war tharin was slayn,
And thai that war went furth beforn
Quhen thai the castell saw forlorn
Thai fled to warand to and fra,
And sum till Edinburgh gan ga
And sum till Strevilline ar other gane
And sum inyill the gat war slayne.
Bonnok on this wis with his wayne
The pele tuk and the men has slane,
Syne taucht in till the king in hy
That him rewardyt worthely
And gert dryve it doun to the ground,
And syne our all the land gan found
Settand in pes all the countre
That at his obeysance wald be.
And quhen a litill time wes went
Eftre Thomas Randell he sent
And sa weile with him tretit he
That he his man hecht for to be,
And the king his ire him forgave
And for to hey his state him gave
Murreff and erle tharoff him maid,
And other syndry landis braid
He gave him intill heritage.
He knew his worthi vasselage
And his gret wyt and his avys
His traist hart and his lele service,
Tharfor in him affyit he
And ryche maid him off land and fe,
As it wes certis rycht worthi.
For and men spek off him trewly
He wes sua curageous ane knycht

Sa wys, sa worthy and sa wycht
And off sa soverane gret bounte
That mekill off him may spokyn be,
And for I think off him to rede
And to schaw part off his gud dede
I will discryve now his fassoun
And part off his condicioun.
He wes off mesurabill statur
And weile porturat at mesur
With braid vesage plesand and fayr,
Curtais at poynt and debonayr
And off rycht sekyr contenyng.
Lawte he lovyt atour all thing,
Falset tresoun and felony
He stude agayne ay encrely,
He heyit honour ay and larges
And ay mentemyt rychtwysnes.[9]
In cumpany solacious
He was and tharwith amorous,
And gud knychtis he luffyt ay,
And giff I the suth sall say
He wes fulfilly off bounte
As off vertuys all maid was he.
I will commend him her no mar
Bot ye sall her weile forthyrmar
That he for his dedis worthy
Suld weile be prisyt soverandly.
Quhen the king thus was with him sauch
And gret lordschyppis had him betaucht
He wox sa wyse and sa avyse
That his land fyrst weill stablyst he
And syne he sped him to the wer
Till help his eyme in his myster
And with the consent off the king
Bot with a symple aparaling
Till Edinburgh he went in hy
With gud men intill cumpany,
And set a sege to the castell

That than was warnyst wonder weill
With men and vyttalis at all rycht
Sua that it dred na mannys mycht.
Bot this gud erle nocht-forthi
The sege tuk full apertly
And pressyt the folk that tharin was
Sua that nocht ane the yet durst pas.
Thai may abid tharin and ete
Thair vittaill quhill thai oucht mai get
Bot I trow thai sall lettyt be
To purchas mar in the contre.
That tyme Edward off Ingland king[10]
Had gevyn that castell in keping
Till Schyr Perys Lombert a Gascoun,[11]
And quhen thai of his warnysoun[12]
Saw the sege set thar sa stythly
Thai mystrowit him off tratoury
For that he spokyn had with the king,
And for that ilk mystrowing
Thai tuk him and put in presoun,
And off thar awine nacioun
Thai maid ane constable thaim to lede
Bath wys and war and wycht off deid,
And he set wyt and strenth and slycht
To kep the castell at his mycht.
Bot now off thaim I will be still,
And spek a litill quhill I will
Off the douchty lord off Douglas
At that tyme in the Forest was
Quhar he mony a juperty
And fayr poyntis off chevalry
Servyt als weill be nycht as day
Till thaim that in the castellis lay
Of Roxburch and Jedwort, bot I[13]
Will let fele off thaim pas forby
For I can noucht rehers thaim all,
And thoucht I couth, weill trow ye sall
That I mycht nocht suffice tharto,

Thar suld mekill be ado,
Bot thai that I wate utterly
Eftre my wyt rehers will I.
This tyme that the gud erle Thomas
Assegyt as the lettre sayis
Edinburgh, James off Douglas
Set all his wit for to purchas
How Roxburch throu sutelte
Or ony craft mycht wonnyn be,
Till he gert Syme off the Leidhous[14]
A crafty man and a curious
Off hempyn rapis leddris ma[15]
With treyn steppis bundyn sua
That brek wald nocht on nakyn wis.
A cruk thai maid at thair divis
Off irne that wes styth and squar
That fra it in a kyrneill war
And the ledder tharfra straitly
Strekit, it suld stand sekyrly.
This gud lord off Douglas alsone
As this divisit wes and dome
Gaderyt gud men in prevete
Thre scor I trow thai mycht be,
And on the fasteryngis evyn rycht
In the begynnyng off the nycht
To the castell thai tuk thar way.
With blak frogis[16] all helyt thai
The armouris that thai on thaim had.
Thai come nerby thar but abad
And send haly thar hors thaim fra,
And thai on raunge in ane route gan ga
On handis and fete quhen thai war ner
Rycht as thai ky or oxin wer
That war wont to be bondyn left tharout.
It wes rycht myrk withoutyn dout,
The-quhether ane on the wall that lay
Besid him till his fere gan say,
'This man thinkis to mak gud cher,'

And nemmyt ane husband tharby ner,
'That has left all his oxyn out.'
The tother said, 'It is na dout
He sall mak mery tonycht thocht thai
Be with the Douglas led away.'
Thai wend the Douglas and his men
Had bene oxin, for thai yeid then
On handis and fete ay ane and ane.
The Douglas rycht gud tent has tane
Till thar spek, bot all sone thai
Held carpand inwart thar way.
Douglas men tharoff war blyth
And to the wall thai sped thaim swith,
And sone has up thar ledder set
That maid ane clap quhen the cruchet
Wes fixit fast in the kyrneill.
That herd ane off the wachis weill
And buskyt thidderwart but baid,
Bot Ledehous that the ledder maid
Sped him to clymb fyrst to the wall,
Bot or he wes up gottyn all
He at that ward had in keping
Met him rycht at the up-cummyng,
And for he thocht to ding him doun
He maid na noys na cry na soun
Bot schot till him deliverly.
And he that wes in juperty
To de a launce he till him maid
And gat him be the nek but baid
And stekyt him upwart with a knyff
Quhill in his hand he left the lyff.
And quhen he ded sua saw him ly
Up on the wall he went in hy
And doun the body kest thaim till
And said, 'All gangis as we will,
Spede you upwart deliverly.'
And thai did sua in full gret hy.
Bot or thai wan up thar come ane

And saw Ledhous stand him allane
And knew he wes nocht off thar men.
In hy he ruschyt till him then
And him assailit sturdely,
Bot he slew him deliverly
For he wes armyt and wes wycht,
The tother nakyt wes, Ik hicht
And had nocht for to stynt the strak.
Sic melle tharup gan he mak
Quhill Douglas and his mengne all
War cummyn up apon the wall,
Than in the tour thai went in hy.
The folk wes that tyme halily
Intill the hall at thar daunsing
Syngyng and other wayis playing,
And apon Fasteryngis[17] evyn this
As custume is to mak joy and blys
Till folk that ar into pouste.
Sua trowyt thai that tyme to be,
Bot or thai wyst rycht in the hall
Douglas and his rout cummyn war all
And cryit on hycht, 'Douglas! Douglas!'
And thai that ma war than he was
Hard 'Douglas!' criyt hidwysly,
Thai war abaysit for the cry
And schup rycht na defens to ma,
And thai but pite gan thaim sla
Till thay had gottyn the overhand.
The tother fled to sek warand
That out off mesure ded gane dreid.
The wardane saw how that it yeid
That callyt wes Gilmyn de Fynys[18],
In the gret toure he gottyn is
And other off his cumpany
And sparryt the entre hastily.
The lave that levyt war without
War tane or slayne, this is na dout,
Bot giff that ony lap the wall.

The Douglas that nycht held the hall
Allthocht his fayis tharoff war wa,
His men was gangand to and fra
Throu-out the castell all that nycht
Till on the morn that day wes lycht.
The wardane that was in the tour
That wes a man off gret valour
Gilmyn the Fynys, quhen he saw
The castell tynt be clene and law
He set his mycht for to defend
The tour, bot thai without him send
Arowys in sa gret quantite
That anoyit tharoff wes he,
Bot till the tother day nocht-forthi
He held the tour full sturdely,
And than at ane assalt he was
Woundyt sa felly in the face
That he wes dredand off his lyff.
Tharfor he tretit than beliff
And yauld the tour on sic maner
That he and all that with him wer
Suld saufly pas in Ingland.
Douglas held thaim gud conand
And convoid thaim to thar countre,
Bot thar full schort tyme levyt he
For throu the wound intill the face
He deyt sone and beryit was.[19]
Douglas the castell sesyt all
That thane wes closyt with stalwart wall,
And send this Leidhous till the king
That maid him full gud rewarding
And hys brother in full gret hy
Schyr Edward that wes sa douchty
He send thidder to tumbill it doun
Bath tour and castell and doungeoun.
And he come with gret cumpany
And gert travaile sa besyly
That tour and wall rycht to the ground

War tumblit in a litill stound,
And dwelt thar quhill all Tevidale[20]
Come to the kingis pes all haile
Outane Jedwort and other that ner
The Inglismennys boundis wer.
Quhen Roxburgh wonnyn was on this wis
The Erle Thomas that hey empris
Set ay on soverane he bounte
At Edynburgh with his mengne
Wes lyand at a-sege as I
Tauld you befor all opynly.
Bot fra he hard how Roxburgh was
Tane with a trayne, all his purchas
And wyt and besines Ik hycht
He set for to purches sum slycht
How he mycht halp him throu body
Mellyt with hey chevalry
To wyn the wall off the castell
Throu sumkyn slycht, for he wyst weill
That na strenth mycht it playnly get
Quhill thai within had men and met.
Tharfor prevely speryt he
Giff ony man mycht fundyn be
That couth fynd ony juperty
To clymb the wallis prevely
And he suld have his warysoun,
For it wes his entencioun
To put him till all aventur
Or that a sege on him mysfur.
Than wes thar ane Wilyame Francus
Wycht and apert wys and curyus
That intill hys youtheid had bene
In the castell. Quhen he has sene
The erle sua enkerly him set
Sum sutelte or wile to get
Quharthrou the castell have mycht he
He come till him in prevete
And said, 'Me think ye wald blythly

That men fand you sum jeperty
How ye mycht our the wallis wyn,
And certis giff ye will begyn
For till assay on sic a wys
Ik undertak for my service
To ken you to clymb to the wall,
And I sall formast be off all,
Quhar with a schort ledder may we,
I trow off tuelf fute it may be,
Clymb to the wall up all quytly,
And gyff that ye will wyt how I
Wate this I sall you blythly say.
Quhen I wes young this hendre day
My fader wes kepar of yone hous,
And I wes sumdeill valegeous[21]
And lovyt a wench her in the toun,
And for i but suspicioun
Mycht repayr till hyr prevely
Off rapys a leddre to me mad I
And tharwith our the wall I slaid.
A strait roid that I sperit had
Intill the crage syne doun I went
And oftsys come till myn entent,
And quhen it ner drew to the day
Ik held agayne that ilk way
And ay come in but persaving.
Ik usyt lang that travaling
Sua that I kan that roid ga rycht
Thoucht men se nevyr sa myrk the nycht.
And giff ye think ye will assay
To pas up efter me that way
Up to the wall I sall you bring,
Giff God us savys fra persaving
Off thaim that wachys on the wall.
And giff that us sua fayr may fall
that we our ledder up may set,
Giff a man on the wall may get
He sall defend and it be ned

Quhill the remanand up thaim sped.'
The erle wes blyth off his carping
And hycht him fayr rewarding
And undretuk that gat to ga
And bad him sone his ledder ma
And hald him preve quhill thai mycht
Set for thar purpos on a nycht.
Sone efter was the ledder made,
And than the erle but mar abaid
Purvayt him a nycht prevely
With thretty men wycht and hardy,
And in a myrk nycht held thar way
That put thaim till full hard assay
And to gret perell sekyrly.
I trow mycht thai haiff sene clerly
That gat had nocht bene undretane
Thoucht thai to let thaim had nocht ane,
For the crag wes hey and hidwous
And the clymbing rycht peralous,
For hapnyt ony to slyd and fall
He suld sone be to-fruschyt all.
The nycht wes myrk as Ik hard say,
And to the fute sone cummyn ar thai
Off the crag that wes hey and schor,
Than Wilyame Fransoys thaim befor
Clamb in crykes forouth ay
And at the bak him folowyt thai.
With mekill payne quhile to quhile fra
Thai clamb into thai crykys sua
Quhile halff the crag thai clumbyn had
And thar a place thai fand sa brad
That thai mycht syt on anerly,
And thai war ayndles and wery[22]
And thar abaid thar aynd to ta,
And rycht as thai war syttand sua
Rycht aboune thaim up apon the wall
The chak-wachys[23] assemblyt all.
Now help thaim God that all thing mai

For in full gret perell ar thai!
For mycht thai se thaim thar suld nane
Eschape out off that place unslane,
To dede with stanys thai suld thaim ding
That thai mycht halp thaimselvyn na
    thing.
Bot wonder myrk wes the nycht
Sua that thai off thaim had na sicht,
And nocht-forthi yete wes thar ane
Off thaim that swappyt doun a stane
And said, 'Away, I se you weile,'
The-quhether he saw thaim nocht a dele.
Out-our thar hedis flaw the stane
And thai sat still lurkand ilkane.
The wachys quhen thai herd nocht ster
Fra that ward samyn all passit er
And carpand held fer by thar way.
The erle Thomas alsone and thai
That on the crag thar sat him by
Towart the wall clamb hastily
And thidder come with mekill mayn
And nocht but gret perell and payn.
For fra thine up wes grevouser
To clymb up ne beneth be fer.
Bot quhatkyn payne sua ever thai had
Rycht to the wall thai come but bad
That had weile ner twelf fute of hycht,
And forout persaving or sycht
Thai set thar ledder to the wall,
And syne Fransoys befor thaim all
Clamb up and syne Schyr Androw Gray,
And syne the erle himselff perfay
Was the thrid that the wall can ta.
Qhuhen thai thar-doune thar lord sua
Saw clumbyne up apon the wall
As woud men thai clamb eftre all,
Bot or all up clumbene war thai
Thai that war wachys till assay

Hard steryng and preve speking
And alsua fraying off armyng
And on thaim schot full sturdely,
And thai met thaim rycht hardely
And slew off thaim dispitously.
Than throu the castell rais the cry,
'Tresoun! Tresoun!' thai cryit fast.
Than sum of thaim war sua agast
That thai fled and lap our the wall,
Bot to sa swyth thai fled nocht all,
For the constabill that wes hardy
All armyt schot furth to the cry
And with him fele hardy and stout.
Yeyt wes the erle with his rout
Fechtand with thaim apon the wall
Bot sone he discumfit thaim all.
Be that his men war cummyn ilkan
Up to the wall and he has tane
His way doun to the castell sone.
In gret perell he has him doyn
For thai war fer ma men tharin
And thai had bene of gud covyn
Than he, bot thai effrayit war,
And nocht-forthi with wapnys bar
The constabill and his cumpany
Met him and his rycht hardely.
Thar mycht men se gret bargane ris,
For with wapnys of mony wis
Thai dang on other at thar mycht
Quhill swerdis that war fayr and brycht
War till the hiltis all bludy.
Then hydwysly begouth the cry
For thai that fellyt or stekyt war
Hidwysly gan cry and rar.
The gud erle and his cumpany
Faucht in that fycht sa sturdely
That all thar fayis ruschyt war.
The constable wes slane rycht thar,

And fra he fell the ramanand
Fled quhar thai best mycht to warand,
Thai durst nocht bid to ma debate.
The erle wes handlyt thar sa hat
That had it nocht hapnyt throu cas
That the constable thar slane then was
He had bene in gret perell thar,
Bot quhen thai fled thar wes no mar,
Bot ilk man to sauff his lyff
Fled furth his dayis for to dryve,
And sum slaid doune out-our the wall.
The erle has tane the castell all
For then wes nane durst him withstand.
I hard nevyr quhar in nakin land
Wes castell tane sa hardely
Outakyn Tyre[24] all anerly,
Quhen Alexandir the conquerour[25]
That conqueryt Babylonys tour
Lap fra a berfrois[26] on the wall
Quhar he amang his fayis all
Defendyt him full douchtely
Quhill his noble chevalry
With leddris our the wall yeid
That nother left for deid no dreid,
For thai wyst weill that the king
Wes in the toune thar wes na thing
Intill that tym that stynt thaim moucht,
For all the perell thai set at nocht.
Thai clamb the wall and Ariste
Come fyrst to the gud king quhar he
Defendyt him with all his mycht
That then sa hard wes set Ik hycht
That he wes fellit on a kne,
He till his bak had set a tre
For dred thai suld behind assaile. ‧
Ariste[27] then to the bataile
Sped him in all hy sturdely
And dang on thaim sa douchtely

That the king weile reskewit was,
For his men into syndri plas
Clamb our the wall and soucht the king
And him reskewit with hard fechting
And wane the toun deliverly.
Outane this taking anerly
I herd nevyr in na tym gane
Quhar castell wes sa stoutly tane.
And off this taking that I mene
Sanct Margaret the gud haly quene
Wyst in hyr tyme throu reveling
Off him that knawis and wate all thing,[28]
Tharfor in sted of prophecy
Scho left a taknyng rycht joly,
That is that intill hyr chapele
Scho gert weile portray a castell,
A ledder up to the wall standand
And a man up thar-apon climband,
And wrat outht him as auld men sais
In Frankis, 'Gardys vous de Francais.'
And for this word scho gert writ sua
Men wend the Frankis-men suld it ta,
Bot for Fraunsois hattyn wes he
That sua clamb up in prevete
Scho wrat that as in prophecy,
And it fell efterwart sothly
Rycht as scho said, for tane it was
And Fraunsoys led thaimup that pas.
On this wis Edinburgh wes tane
And thai that war tharin ilkane
Other tane or slane or lap the wall.
Thar gudis haiff thai sesyt all
And souch the hous everilkane.[29]
Schyr Peris Lubaut that wes tane,
As I said er, befor thai fand
In boyis and hard festnyng sittand.
Thai brocht him till the erle in hy
And he gert lous him hastily,

Then he become the kingis man.
Thai send word to the king rycht than
And tauld how the castell wes tane,
And he in hy is thidder gane
With mony ane in cumpany
And gert myne doun all halily
Bath tour and wall rycht to the grond,
And syne our all the land gan fond
Sesand the countre till his pes.
Off this deid that sa worthy wes
The erle wes prisyt gretumly,
The king that saw him sa worthi
Wes blyth and joyfull our the lave
And to manteyme his stat him gave
Rentis and landis fayr inewch,
And he to sa gret worschip dreuch
That all spak off his gret bounte.
Hys fayis gretly stonayit he
For he fled never for force off fycht.
Quhat sall I mar say off his mycht?
His gret manheid and his bounte
Gerris him yeit renownyt be.
In this tyme that thir jupertys
Off thir castellis that I devis
War eschevyt sa hardely,
Schyr Edward the Bruce the hardy
Had all Galloway and Nydysdale[30]
Wonnyn till his liking all haile
And doungyn doun the castellis all
Rycht in the dyk bath tour and wall.

He hard then say and new it weill
That into Ruglyne[31] wes a pele,
Thidder he went with his menye
And wonnyn it in schort tyme has he,
Syne to Dunde[32] he tuk the way
That then wes haldyne as Ic herd say
Agayne the king, tharfor in hy
He set a sege tharto stoutly
And lay thar quhill it yoldyn was.
To Strevillyne[33] syne the way he tais
Quhar gud Schyr Philip the Mowbray
That wes sa douchty at assay
Wes wardane and had in keping
That castell of the Inglis king.
Thartill a sege thai set stythly,
Thai bykyrrit oftsys sturdely
Bot gret chevalry done wes nane.
Schyr Edward fra the sege wes tane
A weile lang tyme about it lay,
Fra the Lentryne that is to say
Quhill forouth the Sanct Jhonys mes.
The Inglis folk that tharin wes
Begouth to failye vitaill be than.[34]
Than Schyr Philip that douchti man
Tretyt quhill thai consentit war
That gyff at mydsomer the neyst yer
To cum it war nocht with bataile
Reskewyt, then that foroutyn faile
He suld the castell yauld quytly,
That connand band thai sickerly.

BOOK XI

And quhen this connand thus wes mad[1]
Schir Philip intill Ingland raid
And tauld the king all haile his tale,
How he a tuelf moneth all hale

Had as it writyn wes in thar taile
To reskew Strevillyne with bataill.
And quhen he hard Schyr Philip say
That Scottismen had set a day

To fecht and that sic space he had
To purvay him he wes rycht glaid,
And said it wes gret sukudry
That set thaim apon sic foly,
For he thocht to be or that day
Sa purvayit and in sic aray
That thar suld nane strenth him withstand,
And quhen the lordis off Ingland
Herd that this day wes set planly
Thai jugyt all to gret foly,
And thoucht to haiff all thar liking
Giff men abaid thaim in fechting,
Bot oft faillys the fulis thocht
And yeit wys mennys ay cummys nocht
To sic end as thai wene allwayis.
A litill stane oft, as men sayis,
May ger weltyr a mekill wayn,[2]
Na mannys mycht may stand agayn
The grace off God that all thing steris,
He wate quhat till all thing afferis
And disponys at his liking
Efter his ordynance all thing.
Quhen Schyr Edward, as I you say,
Had gevyn sa outrageous a day[3]
To yeld or reskew Strevillyne,
Rycht to the king he went him syne
And tauld quhat tretys he had mad
And quhat day he thaim gevyn had.
The king said quhen he hard the day,
'That wes unwisly doyn, perfay.
Ik herd never quhar sa lang warnyng
Wes gevyn to sa mychty a king
As is the king off Ingland,
For he has now intill hand
Ingland, Ireland and Walis alsua
And Aquitayngne[4] yeit with all tha,
And off Scotland yeit a party
Dwellis under his senyoury,

And off tresour sa stuffyt is he
That he may wageouris[5] haiff plente,
And we are quhoyne agayne sa fele.
God may rycht weill oure werdys dele,
Bot we ar set in juperty
To tyne or wyn then hastely.'
Schyr Edward said, 'Sa God me rede,
Thocht he and all that he may led
Cum, wes sall fecht, all war thai ma.'
Quhen the king hard his broder sua
Spek to the bataile sa hardyly
He prisyt him in hys hart gretumly
And said, 'Broder, sen sua is gane
That this thing thus is undretane
Schap we us tharfor manlely,
And all that luffis us tenderly
And the fredome off this countre
Purvay thaim at that time to be
Boune with all mycht that ever thai may,
Sua giff that our fayis assay
To reskew Strevillyne throu bataill
That we off purpos ger thaim faill.'
To this thai all assentyt ar
And bad thar men all mak thaim yar
For to be boun agayne that day
On the best wis that ever thai may.
Than all that worthi war to fycht
Off Scotland set all hale thar mycht
To purvay thaim agane that day,
Wapynnys and armouris purvayit thai
And all that afferis to fechting.
And in Ingland the mychty king
Purvayit him in sa gret aray
That certis hard I never say
That Inglismen mar aparaile
Maid than did than for bataill,[6]
For quhen the tyme wes cummyn ner
He assemblit all his power,

And but his awne chevalry
That wes sa gret it wes ferly
He had of mony ser countre
With him gud men of gret bounte.
Of Fraunce worthi chevalry
He had intill his cumpany,
The erle off Henaud[7] als wes thar
And with him men that worthi war,
Off Gascoyne and off Almany[8]
And off the duche of Bretayngny
He had wycht men and weill farand
Armyt clenly bath fute and hand,
Off Ingland to the chevalry
He had gaderyt sa clenly
That nane left that mycht wapynnys weld
Or mycht war to fecht in feild,
All Walis als with him had he
And off Irland a gret mengne,
Off Pouty Aquitane and Bayoun[9]
He had mony off gret renoune,
And off Scotland he had yeit then
A gret menye of worthy men.
Quhen all thir sammyn assemblit war
He had of fechtaris with him thar
Ane hunder thousand men and ma
And fourty thousand war of tha
Armyt on hors bath heid and hand,
And of thai yeit war thre thousand
With helyt hors in plate and mailye
To mak the front off the batailye,
And fyfty thousand off archeris
He had foroutyn hobeleris,
And men of fute and small rangale
That yemyt harnays and vittaile
He had sa fele it wes ferly.
Off cartis als thar yeid thaim by
Sa fele that, but all thai that bar
Harnays and als that chargyt war

With pailyounys and veschall with-all[10]
And aparaile of chambyr and hall
And wyne and wax schot and vittaile
Aucht scor wes chargyt with pulaile.[11]
Thai war sa fele quhar that thai raid
And thar bataillis war sa braid
And sua gret roume held thar chare
That men that mekill ost mycht se
Ourtak the landis largely.
Men mycht se than that had bene by
Mony a worthi man and wycht
And mony ane armur gayly dycht
And mony a sturdy sterand stede
Arayit intill ryche wede,
Mony helmys and haberjounys[12]
Scheldis and speris and penounys,[13]
And sa mony a cumbly knycht
That it semyt that into fycht
Thai suld vencus the warld all haile.
Quhy suld I mak to lang my taile?
To Berwik[14] ar thai cummyn ilkane
And sum tharin has innys tane
And sum logyt without the town ys
In tentis and in pailyounys.
And quhen the king his ost has sene
So gret and sa gud men and clene
So gret and sa gud men and clene
He wes rycht joyfull in his thocht
And weile supposyt that thar wes nocht
In warld a king mycht him withstand,
Him thocht all wonnyn till his hand,
And largly amang his men
The land of Scotland delt he then,
Off other mennys thing larg wes he.
And thai that war off his menye
Manausyt the Scottismen hely
With gret wordis, bot nocht-forthi
Or thai cum all to thar entent

296

Howis in haile claith sall be rent.
The king throu consaile of his men
His folk delt in bataillis ten,[15]
In ilkane war weile ten thousand
That lete thai stalwartly suld stand
In the bataile and stythly fycht
And leve nocht for thar fayis mycht.
He set ledaris till ilk bataile
That knawin war of gud governaile,
And till renownyt erlis twa
Off Glosyster and Herfurd war tha[16]
He gaf the vaward in leding
With mony men at thar bidding
Ordanyt into full gud aray.
Thai war sa chevalrous that thai
Trowyt giff thai come to fycht
Thar suld na strenth withstand thar mycht.
And the king quhen his mengne wer
Divisit intill bataillis ser
His awyne bataill ordanyt he
And quha suld at his bridill be,
Schyr Gilis Argente[17] he set
Apon a half his reyngye to get,
And off Valence Schyr Amery
On other half that wes worthy,
For in thar soverane bounte
Out-our the lave affyit he.
Quhen the king apon this kyn wys
Had ordanyt as Ik her divis
His bataillis and his stering
He rais arly in a mornyng
And fra Berwik he tuk the way.
Bath hillis and valis hely thai
As the bataillis that war braid
Departyt our the feldis raid.
The sone wes brycht and schynand cler
And armouris that burnysyt wer
Sua blomyt with the sonnys beme

That all the land wes in a leme,
Baneris rycht fayrly flawmand
And penselys to the wynd wavand
Sua fele thar wer of ser quentis
That it war gret slycht for to divise,
And suld I tell all thar affer
Thar contenance and thar maner
Thoucht I couth I suld combryt be.
The king with all that gret menye
Till Edinbyrgh he raid him rycht,
Thai war all-out to fele to fycht
With few folk of a symple land,
Bot quhar God helpys quhat ma with-
    stand.
The king Robert quhen he hard say
That Inglismen in sic aray
And into sua gret quantite
Come in his land, in hy gert he
His men be somound generaly,
And thai come all full wilfully
To the Torwod quhar that the king
Had ordanyt to mak thar meting.
Schir Edward the Bruce the worthi
Come with a full gret cumpany
Off gud men armyt weill at rycht
Hardy and forsy for to fycht,
Walter Stewart off Scotland syne
That than wes bot a berdles hyne[18]
Come with a rout of noble men,
That men mycht be contynence ken.
The gud lord off Douglas alsua
Brocht with him men Ik underta
That weile war usit in fechting,
Thai sall the les haiff abaysimg
Giff thaim betid in thrang to be,
Avantage thai sall tittar se
For to stonay thar fayis mycht
Than men that usis nocht to fycht.

The erle off Murreff[9] with his men
Arayit weile come alsua then
Into gud covyne for to fycht
And gret will for to manteym thar mycht
Outakyn other mony barounys
And knychtis that of gret renowne is
Come with thar men full stalwartly.
Quhen thai war assemblyt halely
Off fechtand men I trow thai war
Thretty thousand and sumdele mar,
Foroutyn cariage and pettaill
That yemyt harnayis and vittaill.
Our all the ost than yeid the king
And beheld to thar contenyng
And saw thaim of full fayr affer.
Off hardy contenance thai wer,
Be liklynes the mast cowart
Semyt full weill to do his part.
The king has sene all thar having
That knew him weile into sic thing,
And saw thaim all commounaly
Off sic contenance and sa hardy
Forout effray or abaysing.
In his hart had he gret liking
And thoucht that men of sa gret will
Giff thai wald set thar will thartill
Suld be full hard to wyn perfay.
Ay as he met thaim in the way
He welcummyt thaim with glaidsum far
Spekand gud wordis her and thar,
And thai that thar lord sa mekly
Saw welcum thaim and sa hamly
Joyfull thai war, and thocht that thai
Aucht weill to put thaim till assay
Off hard fechting or stalwart stur
For to maynteyme hys honur.
The worthi king quhen he has sene
Hys ost assemblit all bedene

And saw thaim wilfull to fulfill
His liking with gud hart and will
And to maynteyme weill thar franchis
He wes rejosyt mony wys
And callyt all his consaile preve
And said thaim, 'Lordis, now ye se
That Inglismen with mekill mycht
Has all disponyt thaim for the fycht
For thai yone castell wald reskew.
Tharfor is gud we ordane now
How we may let thaim of thar purpos
And sua to thaim the wayis clos
That thai pas nocht but gret letting.
We haiff her with us at bidding
Weile thretty thousand men and ma,
Mak we four bataillis of tha
And ordane us on sic maner
And quhen our fayis cummys ner
We to the New Park hald our way,
For thar behovys thaim nede away
Bot giff that thai will beneuth us ga
And our the merrais pass, and sua
We sall be at avantage thar.
And me think that rycht spedfull war
To gang on fute to this fechting
Armyt bot in litill armyng,
For schup we us on hors to fycht
Sen our fayis ar mar off mycht
And bettyr horsyt than ar we
We suld into gret perell be,
And gyff we fecht on fute perfay
At a vantage we sall be ay,
For in the park amang the treys
The horsmen alwayis cummerit beis,
And the sykis alssua that ar thar-doun
Sall put thaim to confusioune.'
All thai consentyt till that saw
And than intill a litill thraw

Thar four bataillis ordanyt thai,
And till the Erle Thomas perfay
Thai gaiff the vaward in leding
For in his noble governyng
And in his hey chevalry
Thai assoueryt rycht soveranly,
And for to maynteyme his baner
Lordis that off gret worschip wer
Wer assygnyt with thar mengne
Intill his bataill for to be.
The tother bataill wes gevyn to led
Till him that douchty wes of deid
And prisyt off hey chevalry,
Thar wes Schyr Edward the worthy,
I trow he sall maynteyme it sua
That howsaever the gamyn ga
His fayis to plenye sall mater haf.
And syne the thrid bataill thai gaff
Till Walter Stewart for to leid
And to Douglas douchty of deid
Thai war cosyngis in ner degre
Tharfor till him betaucht wes he
For he wes young, bot nocht-forthi
I trow he sall sa manlily
Do his devour and wirk sa weill
That him sall nede ne mar yemseill.
The ferd bataile the noble king
Tuk till his awne governyng,
And had intill his cumpany
The men of Carrik halely
And off Arghile and of Kentyr
And off the Ilis quharof wes syr
Angus of Ile, and but all tha
He off the plane land had alsua
Off armyt men a mekill rout,
His bataill stalwart wes and stout.
He said the rerward he wald ma
And evyn forrouth him suld ga

The vaward, and on ather hand
The tother bataillis suld be gangand
Besid on sid a litill space,
And the king that behind thaim was
Suld se quhar thar war mast myster
And releve thar with his baner.
The king thus that wes wycht and wys
And rych avise at divis
Ordanyt his men for the fechting
In gud aray in alkyn thing.
And on the morn on Setterday
The king hard his discourouris say
That inglismen with mekill mycht
Had lyin at Edinburgh all nycht.
Tharfor withoutyn mar delay
He till the New Park held his way
With all that in his leding war
And in the Park thaim herberyt thar,
And in a plane feld be the way
Quhar he thoucht ned behovyd away
The Inglismen, gif that thai wald
Throu the Park to the castell hald
He gert men mony pottis ma
Off a fute-breid round, and al tha
War dep up till a mannys kne,
Sa thyk that thai mycht liknyt be
Till a wax cayme that beis mais.
All that nycht travailland he wais
Sua that or day he has maid
Thai pottis, and thaim helit haid
With stykkis and with gres all grene
Sua that thai moucht nocht weil be sen.
On Sonday than in the mornyng
Weile sone after the sone rising
Thai hard thar mes commounaly
And mony thaim schraiff full devotly
That thocht to dey in that melle
Or than to mak thar contre fre.

299

To God for thar rycht prayit thai,
Thar dynit nane of thaim that day
Bot for the vigil off Sanct Jhane
Thai fastyt water and breid ilkan.
The king quhen that the mes wes don
Went furth to se the pottis[20] sone
And at his liking saw thaim mad,
On ather sid rycht weill braid
It wes pittyt as Ik haif tauld.
Giff that thar fayis on hors wald hald
Furth in that way I trow thai sall
Nocht weill eschaip foroutyn fall.
Throu-out the ost thar gert he cry
That all suld arme thaim hastily
And busk thaim on thar best maner,
And quhen thai assemblyt wer
He gert aray thaim for the fycht,
And syne gert cry our-all on hycht
That quha-sa-ever he war that fand
Hys hart nocht sekyr for to stand
To wyn all or dey with honur
For to maynteyme that stalwart stour
That he betyme suld hald his way,
And suld duell with him bot thai
That wald stand with him to the end
And tak the ure that God wald send.
Than all answerd with a cry
And with a voce said generaly
That nane for dout off deid suld faile
Quhill discumfyt war the gret bataile.
Quhen the gud king has hard his men
Sa hardely answer him then
Sayand that nother dede na dreid
Till sic discomfort suld thaim leid
That thai suld eschew the fechting
In hart he had gret rejosing,
For him thocht men off sic covyn
Sa gud and hardy and sa fyne

Suld weile in bataill hald thar rycht
Agayne men off full mekill mycht.
Syne all the smale folk and pitall
He send with harnays and with vitaill
Intill the Park weill fer him fra
And fra the bataillis gert thaim ga
And als he bad thai went thar way,
Twenty thousand weile ner war thai.
Thai held thar way till a vale,
The king left with a clene mengne
The-quhethir thai war thretty thousand
That I trow sall stalwartly stand
And do thar devour as thai aw.[21]
Thai stud than rangyt all on a raw
Redy for to gyff hard bataill
Giff ony folk wald thaim assaile.
The king gert thaim all buskit be
For he wyst in certante
That his fayis all nycht lay
At the Fawkyrk[22], and syne that thai
Held towart him the way all straucht
With mony men of mekill maucht.
Tharfor till his nevo bad he
The erle off Murreff with his menye
Besid the kyrk to kepe the way[23]
That na man pas that gat away
For to debate the castell,
And he said himself suld weill
Kepe the entre with his bataill
Giff that ony wald assale,
And syne his broder Schyr Edward
And young Walter alsua Steward
And the lord off Douglas alsua
With thar mengne gud tent suld ta
Quhilk off thaim had of help myster
And help with thaim that with him wer
The king send than James off Douglas
And Schyr Robert the Keyth[24] that was

Marschell off the ost of fe
The Inglismennys come to se,
And thai lap on and furth thai raid
Weile horsyt men with thaim thai haid,
And sone the gret ost haf thai sene
Quhar scheildis schynand war sa schene
And bassynetis burnyst brycht
That gave agayne the sone gret lycht.
Thai saw sa fele browdyne baneris[25]
Standaris and pennounys and speris,
And sa fele knychtis apon stedis
All flawmand in thar wedis,[26]
And sa fele bataillis and sa braid
That tuk sa gret roume as thai raid
That the maist ost and the stoutest
Off Crystyndome[27] and the grettest
Suld be abaysit for to se
Thair fayis into sic quantite
And sua arayit for to fycht.
Quhen thar discourrouris has had sycht
Off thar fayis as I you say
Towart the king thai tuk thair way,
And tauld him intill prevete
The multitud and the beaute
Off thair fayis that come sa braid
And off the gret mycht that thai haid.
Than the king bad thaim thai suld ma
Na contenance that it war sua
Bot lat thaim into commoune say
That thai cum intill evyll aray
To confort his on that wys,
For oftsys throu a word may rys
Discomford and tynsaill with-all,
And throu a word als weill may fall
Comford may rys and hardyment
May ger men do thar entent.
On the samyn wys it did her,
Thar comford and thar hardy cher

Comford thaim sa gretumly
Off thar ost that the leyst hardy
Be contenance wald formast be
For to begyne the gret melle.
Apon this wis the noble king
Gaff all his men recomforting
Throu hardy contenance of cher
That he maid on sa gud maner.
Thaim thocht that na myscheiff mycht be
Sa gret with-thi thai him mycht se
Befor thaim sua tha thaim suld greve,
That ne his worschip suld thaim releve,
His worschip confort thaim sua
And contenince that he gan ma
That the mast coward wes hardy.
On other half full sturdely
The Inglismen in sic aray
As ye haf herd me forouth say
Comed with thar bataillis approchand
The baneris to the wynd wavand,
And quhen thai cummyn war sa ner
That bot twa myle betwix thaim wer
Thai chesyt a joly company[28]
Off men that wicht war and hardy
On fayr courseris[29] armyt at rycht,
Four banrentis[30] off mekill mycht
War capitanys of that route,
The Syr the Clyffurd that wes stout
Wes off thaim all soverane leidar,
Aucht hunder armyt I trow thai war.
Thai war all young men and joly
Yarnand to do chevalry,
Off best of all the ost war thai
Off contenance and off aray.
Thai war the fayrest cumpany
That men mycht find of sa mony,
To the castell thai thocht to far
For giff that thai weill mycht cum thar

Thai thocht it suld reskewit be.
Forth on thar way held this menye
And towart Strevillyne held thar way,
The New Park all eschewit thai
For thai wist weill the king wes thar
And newth the New Park gan thai far
Weill newth the kyrk intill a rout.
The Erle Thomas that wes sa stout
Quhen he saw thaim sa ta the plane
In gret hy went he thaim agane
With fyve hunder foroutyn ma
Anoyit in his hart and wa
That thai sa fer wer passit by,
For the king haid said him rudly
That a rose of his chaplete
Was fallyn, for quhar he wes set
To kep the way thai men war passit
And tharfor he hastyt him sa fast
That cummyn in schort tyme wes he
To the plane feld with his menye,
For he thocht that he suld amend
That he trespassit had or than end.
And quhen the Inglismen him saw
Cum on foroutyn dyn or aw
And tak sa hardely the plane
In hy thai sped thaim him agane
And strak with spuris the stedis stith
That bar thaim evyn hard and swith.
And quhen the erle saw that menye
Cum sa stoutly, till his said he
'Be nocht abaysit for thar schor,
Bot settis speris you befor
And bak to bak set all your rout[31]
And all the speris poyntis out,
Suagate us best defend may we
Enveronyt with thaim gif we be.'[32]
And as he bad thaim thai haif done,
And the tother come on alsone.

Befor thaim all come prikand
A knycht hardy off hart and hand
And a wele gret lord at hame
Schyr Gilyame Danecourt[33] wes his nam
And prikyt on thaim hardely
And thai met him sturdely
That he and hors wes borne doune
And slayne rycht thar forout ransoun,
With Inglismen gretly wes he
Menyt that day and his bounte.
The lave come on rycht sturdely
Bot nane off thaim sa hardely
Ruschyt amang thaim as did he,
Bot with fer mar maturyte
Thai assemblyt all in a rout
And enveround thaim all about
Assailyeand thaim on ilka sid.
And thai with speris woundis wyd
Gaff till the hors that come thaim ner,
And thai that ridand on thaim wer[34]
That doune war borne losyt the lyvis,[35]
And other speris dartis and knyffis
And wapynnys on ser maner
Kast amang thaim that fechtand wer
That thaim defendyt sa wittily
That thar fayis had gret ferly,
For sum wald schout out of thar rout
And off thaim that assaylyt about
Stekyt stedis and bar doun men.
The Inglismen sa rudly then
Kest amang thaim swerdis and mas
That ymyd thaim a monteyle was
Off wapynnys that war warpyt thar.
The erle and his thus fechtand war
At gret myscheiff as I you say,
For quhonnar be full far war thai
Than thar fayis and all about
War inveround, quhar mony rout

War roucht full dispitously
Thar fayis demenyt thaim full starkly,
On ather half thai war sa stad
For the rycht gret heyt that thai had
For fechtyn and for sonnys het
That all thar flesche of swate wes wete,
And sic a stew rais out off thaim then
Off aneding bath of hors and men
And off powdyr that sic myrknes[36]
Intill the ayr abovyne thaim wes[37]
That it wes wondre for to se.
Thai war in gret perplexite
Bot with gret travaill nocht-forthi
Thai thaim defendyt manlily
And set bath will and strenth and mycht
To rusch thar fayis in that fycht
That thaim demanyt than angyrly.
Bot gyff God help thaim hastily
Thai sall thar fill have of fechting.
Bot quhen the noble renownyt king
With other lordis that war him by
Saw how the erle abandounly
Tuk the plane feld, James off Douglas
Come to the king rycht quhar he was

And said, 'A! Schyr, Sanct Mary!
The erle off Murref opynly
Tays the plane feld with his mengne,
He is in perell bot he be
Sone helpyt for his fayis ar ma
Than he and horsyt weill alsua,
And with your leve I will me speid
To help him for he has ned,
All umbeveround with his fayis is he.'
The king said, 'Sa our Lord me se,
A fute till him thou sall nocht ga,
Giff he weile dois lat him weile ta.
Quhatever him happyn, to wyn or los,
I will nocht for him brek purpos.'
'Certis,' said James, 'I may na wis
Se that his fayis him suppris
Quhen that I may set help thartill,
With your leve sekyrly I will
Help him or dey into the payn.'
'Do than and speid the sone agayn,'
The king said, and he held his way.
Gyff he may cum in tyme perfay
I trow he sall him help sa weill
That off his fayis sall it feill.

BOOK XII

Now Douglas furth his wayis tais,
And in that selff tyme fell throw cais
That the king off Ingland quhen he
Was cummyn with his gret menye
Ner to the place, as I said ar,
Quhar Scottismen arayit war,
He gert arest all his bataill
And other alsua to tak consaill
Quhether thai wald herbry thaim that
    nycht

Or than but mar ga to the fycht.
The vaward that wist na thing
Off this arest na his dwelling
Raid to the Park all straucht thar way
Foroutyn stinting in gud aray,
And quhen the king wist that thai wer
In hale bataill cummand sa ner
His bataill gert he weill aray.
He raid apon a litill palfray
Laucht and joly arayand

His bataill with ane ax in hand,
And on his bassynet he bar
Ane hat off quyrbolle[1] ay-quhar,
And thar-upon into taknyng
Ane hey croune that he wes king.
And quhen Glosyster and Herfurd wer
With thar bataill approchand ner
Befor thaim all thar come ridand
With helm on heid and sper in hand
Schyr Henry the Boune[2] the worthi,
That was a wycht knycht and a hardy
And to the erle off Herfurd cusyne,
Armyt in armys gud and fyne
Come on a sted a bow-schote ner
Befor all other that thar wer,
And knew the king for that he saw
Him sua rang his men on raw
And by the croune that wes set
Alsua apon his bassynet,
And towart him he went in hy.
And quhen the king sua apertly
Saw him cum forouth all his feris
In hy till him the hors he steris.
And quhen Schyr Henry saw the king
Cum on foroutyn abaysing
Till him he raid in full gret hy,
He thocht that he suld weill lychtly[3]
Wyn him and haf him at his will
Sen he him horsyt saw sa ill.[4]
Sprent thai samyn intill a ling,
Schyr Hanry myssit the noble king
And he that in his sterapys stud
With the ax that wes hard and gud
With sua gret mayne raucht him a dynt
That nother hat na helm mycht stynt
The hevy dusche that he him gave
That ner the heid till the harnys clave.
The hand-ax schaft fruschit in twa,

And he doune to the erd gan ga
All flatlynys for him faillyt mycht.
This wes the fryst strak off the fycht
That wes perfornyst douchtely,
And quhen the kingis men sa stoutly
Saw him rycht at the fyrst meting
Foroutyn dout or abaysing
Have slayne a knycht sua at a strak
Sic hardyment tharat gan thai tak
That thai come on rycht hardely.
Quhen Inglismen saw thaim sa stoutly
Cum on tthai had gret abaysing
And specially for that the king
Sa smartly that gud knycht has slayne
That thai withdrew thaim everilkane
And durst nocht ane abid to fycht
Sa dred thai for the kingis mycht.
And quhen the kingis men thaim saw
Sua in hale bataill thaim withdraw
A gret schout till thaim gan thai mak
And thai in hy tuk all the bak,
And thai that folowit thaim has slane
Sum off thaim that thai haf ourtane
Bot thai war few forsuth to say
Thar hors fete had ner all away.
Bot how-sa quhoyne deyt thar
Rebutyt fouilly thai war
And raid thar gait with weill mar schame
Be full fer than thai come fra hame.
Quhen that the king reparyt was
That gert his men all leve the chas
The lordis off his cumpany
Blamyt him as thai durst gretumly
That he him put in aventur
To mete sa styth a knycht and sture
In sic poynt as he than wes sene,
For thai said weill it mycht haiff bene
Cause off thar tynsaill everilkan.[5]

The king answer has maid thaim nane
Bot menyt hys handax schaft that sua
Was with the strak brokyn in twa.
The Erle Thomas wes yete fechtand
With fayis apon athyr hand
And slew off thaim a quantite,
Bot wery war his men and he
The-quhether with wapynnys sturdely
Thai thaim defendyt manlely
Quhill that the Douglas come ner
That sped him on gret maner,
And Inglismen that war fechtand
Quhen thai the Douglas saw ner-hand
Thai wandyst and maid ane opynnyng.
James off Douglas be thar relying
Knew that thai war discumfyt ner,
Than bad thaim that with him wer
Stand still and pres na forthyrmar.
'For thai that yonder fechtand ar,'
He said, 'ar off sa gret bounte
That thar fayis weill sone sall be
Discumfyt throu thar awne mycht
Thocht na man help thaim for to fycht,
And cum we now to the fechting
Quhen thai ar at discumfiting
Men suld say we thaim fruschit had,
And sua suld thai that caus has mad
With gret travaill and hard fechting
Los a part of thar loving,
And it war syn to les thar prys
That off sa soverane bounte is.
And he throu plane and hard fechting
Has her eschevyt unlikly thing
He sall haff that he wonnyn has.'
The erle with that that fechtand was
Quhen he hys fayis saw brawland sua[6]
And hy apon thaim gan he ga,
And pressyt thame sa wonder fast

With hard strakys quhill at the last
Thai fled that dust abid ne mar.
Bath hors and men slane left thai thar
And held thar way in full gret hy
Nocht all togydder bot syndryly
And thai that war ourtane war slayn,
The lave went till thar ost agayne
Off thar tynsall sary and wa.
The erle that had him helpyn sua
And his als that wer wery
Hynt off thar bassynettis in hy
Till avent thaim for thai war wate,
Thai war all helyt into swate.
Thai semyt men forsuth Ik hycht
That had fandyt thar force in fycht
And sua did thai full douchtely.
Thai fand off all thar cumpany
That thar wes bot a yuman slayne
And lovyt God and wes full fayne
And blyth that thai eschapyt sua.
Towart the king than gan thai ga
And till him weill sone cummyn ar.
He wyttyt at thaim of thar far
And glaidsome cher to thaim mad
For thai sa weile thaim borne had.
Than pressyt into gret daynte
The erle off Murreff for to se,
For his hey worschip and gret valour
All yarnyt to do him honour,
Sa fast thai ran to se him thar
That ner all samyn assemblit ar.
And quhen the gud king gan thaim se
Befor thaim sua assemblit be
Blyth and glaid that thar fayis wer
Rabutyt apon sic maner
A litill quhill he held him still,
Syne on this wys he said his will.
'Lordingis, we aucht to love and luff

Allmychty God that syttis abuff
That sendis us sa fayr begynnyng.
It is a gret discomforting
Till our fayis that on this wis
Sa sone has bene rabutyt twis,
For quhen thai off thar ost sall her
And knaw suthly on quhat maner
Thar vaward that wes sa stout,
And syne yone othyr joly rout
That I trow off the best men war
That thay mycht get amang thaim thar,
War rebutyt sa sodanly,
I trow and knawis it all clerly
That mony ane hart sall waverand be
That semyt er off gret bounte,
And fra the hart be discumfyt
The body is nocht worth a myt,
Tharfor I trow that gud ending
Sall folow till our begynnyng.
The-quhether I say nocht this you till
For that ye suld folow my will
To fycht, bot in you all sall be,
For gyff you thinkis spedfull that we[7]
Fecht we sall, and giff ye will
We leve, your liking to fulfill.
I sall consent on alkyn wis
To do rycht as ye will dyvys,
tharfor sayis off your will planly.'
And with a voce than gan thai cry,
'Gud king, foroutyn mar delay
Tomorne alsone as ye se day[8]
Ordane you hale for the bataill,
For doute[9] off dede we sall nocht faill
Na na payn sall refusyt be
Quhill we haiff maid our countre fre.'
Quhen the king had hard sa manlily
Thai spak to fechting and sa hardely
In hart gret gladschip can he ta

And said, 'Lordingis, sen ye will sua
Schaip we us tharfor in the mornyng
Sua that we be the sone-rysing
Haff herd mes and buskyt weill[10]
Ilk man intill his awn eschell[11]
Without the palyounys arayit
In bataillis with baneris displayit,
And luk ye na wis brek aray.
And, as ye luf me, I you pray
That ilk man for his awne honour
Purvay him a gud baneour,
And quhen it cummys to the fycht
Ilk man set hart will and mycht
To stynt our fayis mekill prid.
On hors thai will arayit rid
And cum on you in full gret hy,
Mete thaim with speris hardely
And think than on the mekill ill
That thai and tharis has done us till,
And ar in will yeit for to do
Giff thai haf mycht to cum tharto.
And certis me think weill that ye
Forout abasing aucht to be
Worthy and of gret vasselagis
For we haff thre gret avantagis
The fyrst is that we haf the rycht
And for the rycht ay God will fycht.
The tother is that thai cummyn ar
For lyppynyng off thar gret powar
To sek us in our awne land,
And has brocht her rycht till our hand
Ryches into sa gret quantite
That the pourest of you sall be
Bath rych and mychty tharwithall
Giff that we wyne, as weill may fall.
The thrid is that we for our lyvis
And for our childer and for our wyvis
And for our fredome and for our land

Ar strenyeit in bataill for to stand,
And thai for thar mycht anerly
And for thai lat of us heychtly
And for thai wald distroy us all
Mais thaim to fycht, bot yeit may fall
That thai sall rew thar barganyng.
And certis I warne you off a thing
That happyn thaim, as God forbed,
Till fynd fantis intill our deid
That thai wyn us opynly
Thai sall off us haf na mercy,
And sen we knaw thar felone will
Me think it suld accord to skill
To set stoutnes agayne felony
And mak sa-gat a juperty.
Quharfor I you requer and pray
That with all your mycht that ye may
That ye pres you at the begynnyng
But cowardys or abaysing
To mete thaim at sall fyrst assemble
Sa stoutly that the henmaist[12] trymble,
And menys of your gret manheid
Your worschip and your douchti deid
And off the joy that we abid
Giff that us fall, as weill may tid,
Hap to vencus this gret bataill.
In your handys without faile
Ye ber honour price and riches
Fredome welth and blythnes
Giff you contene you manlely,
And the contrar all halily
Sall fall giff ye lat cowardys
And wykytnes your hertis suppris.
Ye mycht have lyvyt into threldome,
Bot for ye yarnyt till have fredome
Ye ar assemblyt her with me,
Tharfor is nedfull that ye be
Worthy and wycht but abaysing.

And I warne you weill off a thing,
That mar myscheff may fall us nane
Than in thar handys to be tane,
For thai suld sla us, I wate weill
Rycht as thai did my brothyr Nele.
Bot quhen I mene off your stoutnes
And off the mony gret prowes
That ye haff doyne sa worthely
I traist and trowis sekyrly
To haff plane victour in this fycht,
For thoucht our fayis haf mekill mycht
Thai have the wrang, and succudry
And covatys of senyoury
Amovys thaim foroutyn mor.
Na us thar dreid thaim bot befor
For strenth off this place as ye se
Sall let us enveronyt to be.
And I pray you als specially
Bath mar and les commonaly
That nane of you for gredynes
Haff ey to tak of thar riches
Ne presonaris for to ta[13]
Quhill ye se thaim contraryit sa[14]
That the feld anerly youris be,
And than at your liking may ye
Tak all the riches that thar is.
Giff ye will wyrk apon this wis
Ye sall haff victour sekyrly.
I wate nocht quhat mar say sall I
Bot all wate ye quhat honour is,
Contene you than on sic a wis
That your honour ay savyt be.
And Ik hycht her in leaute
Gyff ony deys in this bataille
His ayr but ward releff or taile
On the fyrst day his land sall weld
All be he never sa young off eild.
Now makys you redy for to fycht,

307

God help us that is maist of mycht.
I rede armyt all nycht that we be
Purvayit in bataill sua that we
To mete our fayis ay be boune.'
Than answeryt thai all with a soune,
'As ye dyvys all sall be done.'
Than till tha innys went thai sone
And ordanyt thaim for the fechting
Syne assemblyt in the evynnyng,
And suagat all the nycht bad thai
Till on the morn that it wes day.
Quhen the Cliffurd, as I said ar,
And all his rout rebutyt war
And thar gret vaward alsua
War distrenyeit the bak to ta
And thai had tauld thar rebuting –
Thai off the vaward how the king
Slew at a strak sa apertly
A knycht that wycht wes and hardy,
And how all haile the kingis bataill
Schup thaim rycht stoutly till assaill
And Schyr Edward the Bruce alsua
Quhen thai all haill the bak gan ta
And how thai lesyt of thar men,
And Cliffurd had tauld alsua then
How Thomas Randell tuk the plane
With a few folk and how wes slane
Schyr Gilyame Danecourt the worthi,
And how the erle faucht manly
That as ane hyrchoune all his rout
Gert set out speris all about
And how that thai war put agayne
And part off thar gud men slayne –
The Inglismen sic abasing
Tuk and sic drede of that tithing
That in fyve hunder placis and ma
Men mycht se samyn routand ga
Sayand, 'Our lordis for thar mycht

Will allgate fecht agane the rycht,
Bot quha-sa werrayis wranguysly
Thai fend God all to gretumly
And thaim may happyn to mysfall,
And swa may tid that her we sall.'
And quhen thar lordys had persaving
Off discomfort and rownnyng
That thai held samyn twa and twa,
Throu-out the ost sone gert thai ga
Heraldis to mak a crye
That nane discomfort suld be,
For in punye is oft hapnyne
Quhile for to wyn and quhile to tyne,
And that into the gret bataill
That apon na maner may faill
Bot giff the Scottis fley thar way
Sall all amendyt be perfay.
Tharfor thai monest thaim to be
Off gret worschip and off bounte
And stoutly in the bataill stand
And tak amendis at thar hand.
Thai may weill monys as thai will
And thai may hecht als to fulfill
With stalwart hart thar bidding all
Bot nocht-forthi I trow thai sall
Intill thar hartis dredand be.
The king with his consaill preve
Has tane to rede that he wald nocht
Fecht or the morne bot he war socht,
Tharfor thai herberyd thaim that nycht
Doune in the Kers[15], and gert all dycht
And maid redy thar aparaill
Agayne the morne for the bataill,
And for in the Kers pulis war
Housis thai brak and thak[16] bar
To mak briggis quhar thaim mycht pas,
And sum sayis that yeit the folk that was
In the castell quhen nycht gan fall

For that thai knew the myscheiff all
Thai went full ner all that thai war
And duris and wyndowys[17] with thaim bar,
Swa that thai had befor the day
Briggyt the pulis swa that thai
War passyt our everilkane,
And the hard feld on hors has tane
All reddy for till gif batale
Arayit intill thar apparaill.
The Scottismen quhen it wes day
Thar mes devotly gert thai say
Syne tuk a sop and maid thaim yar,
And quhen thai all assemblyt war
And in thar bataillis all purvayit
With thar braid baneris all displayit
Thai maid knychtis, as it afferis
To men that usys thai mysteris.
The king maid Walter Stewart knycht
And James off Douglas that wes wycht,
And other als of gret bounte
He maid ilkane in thar degre.
Quhen this wes doyne that I you say
Thai went all furth in gud aray
And tuk the plane full apertly,
Mony gud man wicht and hardy
That war fulfillyt of gret bounte
Intill thai routis men mycht se.
The Inglismen on other party
That as angelis schane brychtly
War nocht arayit on sic maner
For all thar bataillis samyn wer
In a schilthrum, but quhether it was
Throu the gret straitnes of the place
That thai war in to bid fechting
Or that it was for abaysing
I wate nocht, bot in a schiltrum
It semyt thai war all and sum,
Outane the avaward anerly

That rycht with a gret cumpany
Be thaimselvyn arayit war.
Quha had bene by mycht have sene thar
That folk ourtak a mekill feild
On breid quhar mony a schynand scheld
And mony a burnyst brycht armur
And mony man off gret valour
And mony a brycht baner and schene
Mycht in that gret schiltrum be sene.
And quhen the king of Ingland
Swa the Scottis saw tak on hand
Takand the hard feyld sa opynly
And apon fute he had ferly
And said, 'Quhat, will yone Scottis fycht?'
'Ya sekyrly, schir,' said a knycht,
Schyr Ingrahame the Umfravill hat he,
And said, 'Forsuth now, schyr, I se
It is the mast ferlyfull sycht
That evyre I saw quhen for to fycht
The Scottismen has tane on hald
Agayne the mycht of Ingland
In plane hard feld to giff bataile.
Bot and ye will trow my consaill
Ye sall discomfy thaim lychtly.
Withdrawys you hyne sodandly
With bataillis and with penounys
Quhill that we pas our palyounys,
And ye sall se alsone that thai
Magre thar lordys sall brek aray
And scaile thaim our harnays to ta.
And quhen we se thaim scalit sua
Prik we than on thaim hardely
And we sall haf thaim wele lychtly
For than sall nane be knyt to fycht
That may withstand your mekill mycht.'
I will nocht,' said the king, 'perfay
Do sa, for thar sall na man say
That I sall eschew the bataill

Na withdraw me for sic rangaile.'[18]
Quhen this wes said that er said I
The Scottismen commounaly
Knelyt all doune to God to pray
And a schort prayer thar maid thai
To God to help thaim in that fycht,
And quhen the Inglis king had sycht
Off thaim kneland he said in hy,
'Yone folk knelis to ask mercy.'
Schyr Ingrahame said, 'Ye say suth now,
Thai ask mercy bot nane at you,
For thar trespas to God thai cry.
I tell you a thing sekyrly,
That yone men will all wyn or de,
For doute of dede thai sall nocht fle.'
'Now be it sa,' than said the king,
And than but langer delaying
Thai gert trump till the assemble.
On ather sid men mycht than se
Mony a wycht man and worthi
Redy to do chevalry.
Thus war thai boune on ather sid,
And Inglismen with mekill prid
That war intill thar avaward
To the bataill that Schyr Edward
Governyt and led held straucht thar way
The hors with spuris hardnyt thai
And prikyt apon thaim sturdely,
And thai met thaim rycht hardely
Sua that at thar assemble thar
Sic a fruschyng of speris war
That fer away men mycht it her.
At that meting foroutyn wer
War stedis stekyt mony ane
And mony gude man borne doune and
    slayne,
And mony ane hardyment douchtely
Was thar eschevyt, for hardely

Thai dang on other with wapnys ser.
Sum of the hors that stekyt wer
Ruschyt and relyt tycht rudlye,
Bot the remanand nocht-forthi
That mycht cum to the assembling
For that led maid na stinting
Bot assemblyt full hardely,
And thai met thaim full sturdely
With speris that wer scharp to scher
And axys that weile groundyn wer
Quhar-with was roucht mony a rout.
The fechting wes thar sa fell and stout
That mony a worthi man and wicht
Throu fors wes fellyt in that fycht
That had na mycht to rys agane.
The Scottismen fast gan thaim payn
Thar fayis mekill mycht to rus,
I trow thai sall na payn refuse
Na perell quhill thar fayis be
Set in weill hard perplexite.
And quhen the erle of Murref swa
Thar vaward saw sa stoutly ga
The way to Schyr Edward all straucht
That met thaim with full mekill maucht,
He held hys way with his baner
To the gret rout quhar samyn wer
The nyne bataillis that war sa braid,
That sa fele baneris with thaim haid
And of men sa gret quantite
That it war wonder for to se.
The gud erle thidder tuk the way
With his battaill in gud aray
And assemblit sa hardily
That men mycht her that had bene by
A gret frusch of the speris that brast,
For thar fayis assemblyt fast
That on stedis with mekill prid
Come prikand as thai wald our-rid

The erle and all his cumpany,
Bot thai met thaim sa sturdely
That mony of thaim till erd thai bar,
For mony a sted was stekyt thar
And mony gud man fellyt under fet
That had na hap to rys up yete.
Thar mycht men se a hard bataill
And sum defend and sum assaile
And mony a reale romble rid
Be roucht thar apon ather sid
Quhill throu the byrnys bryst the blud
That till erd doune stremand yhude.
The erle of Murreff and his men
Sa stoutly thaim contenyt then
That thai wan place ay mar and mar
On thar fayis the-quhether thai war
Ay ten far ane or may perfay,
Sua that it semyt weill that thai
War tynt amang sa gret menye
As thai war plungyt in the se.

And quhen the Inglismen has sene
The erle and all his men bedene
Faucht sa stoutly but effraying
Rycht as thai had nane abasing
Thaim pressyt thai with all thar mycht
And thai with speris and swerdis brycht
And axis that rycht scharply schar
Ymyddis the vesag met thaim thar[19]
Thar mycht men se a stalwart stour
And mony men of gret valour
With speris mas and knyffis
And other wapynnys wyssyll thar lyvis[20]
Sua that mony fell doune all dede,
The greys woux with the blud all reid
The erle that wycht wes and worthi
And his men faucht sa manlyly
That quha-sa had sene thaim that day
I trow forsuth that thai suld say
That thai suld do thar devor wele[21]
Swa that thar fayis suld it fele.

BOOK XIII

Quhen thir twa fyrst bataillis wer
Assemblyt as I said you er,
The Stewart Walter that than was
And the gud lord als off Douglas
In a bataill, quhen that thai saw
The erle foroutyn dred or aw
Assembill with his cumpany
On all that folk sa sturdely
For till help him thai held thar way
And thar bataill in gud aray,
And assemblyt sa hardely
Besid the erle a litill by
That thar fayis feld thar cummyn wele,

For with wapynnys stalwart of stele
Thai dang apon with all thar mycht.
Thar fayis resavyt weile Ik hycht
With swerdis speris and with mase,
The bataill thar sa feloune was
And sua rycht gret spilling of blud
That on the erd the flousis stud.
The Scottismen sa weill thaim bar
And sua gret slauchter maid thai thar
And fra sa fele the lyvis revyt
That all the feld bludy wes levyt.
That tyme thar thre bataillis wer
All syd be sid fechtand weill ner,

311

Thar mycht men her mony dynt
And wapynnys apon armuris stynt,
And se tumble knychtis and stedis
And mony rich and reale wedis[1]
Defoullyt foully under fete,
Sum held on loft sum tynt the suet.
A lang quhill thus fechtand thai war
That men na noyis mycht her thar,
Men hard nocht bot granys and dintis[2]
That slew fyr as men slayis on flyntis,
Thai faucht ilk ane sa egerly
That thai maid nother moyis na cry
Bot dang on other at thar mycht
With wapnys that war burnyst brycht.
The arowys als sua thyk thar flaw
That thai mycht say wele that thaim saw
That thai a hidwys schour gan ma,
For quhar thai fell Ik undreta
Thai left efter thaim taknyng
That sall ned as I trow leching.
The Inglis archeris schot sa fast
That mycht thar schot haff ony last
It had bene hard to Scottismen
Bot King Robert that wele gan ken
That thar archeris war peralous
And thar schot rycht hard and grevous
Ordanyt forouth the assemble
Hys marschell with a gret menye,
Fyve hunder armyt into stele
That on lycht[3] hors war horsyt welle,
For to pryk amang the archeris
And sua assaile thaim with thar speris
That thai na layser haiff to schut.
This marschell that Ik off mute
That Schyr Robert of Keyth was cauld
As Ik befor her has you tauld
Quhen he saw the bataillis sua
Assembill and togidder ga

And saw the archeris schoyt stoutly,
With all thaim off his cumpany
In hy apon thaim gan he rid
And ourtuk thaim at a sid,
And ruschyt amang thaim sa rudly
Stekand thaim sa dispitously
And in sic fusoun berand doun
And slayand thaim foroutyn ransoun
That thai thaim scalyt everilkane,
And fra that tyme furth thar wes nane
That assemblyt schot to ma.
Quhen Scottis archeris saw that thai sua
War rebutyt thai woux hardy
And with all thar mycht schot egrely
Amang the horsmen that thar raid
And woundis wid to thaim thai maid
And slew of thaim a full gret dele.
Thai bar thaim hardely and wele
For, fra thar fayis archeris war
Scalyt as I said till you ar
That ma na thai war be gret thing
Sua that thai dred nocht thar schoting
Thai woux sa hardy that thaim thocht
Thai suld set all thar fayis at nocht.
The merschell and his cumpany
Wes yeit, as till you er said I,
Amang the archeris quhar thai maid
With speris roume quhar that thai raid
And slew all that thai mycht ourta,
And thai wele lychtly mycht do sua
For thai had nocht a strak to stynt
Na for to hald agayne a dynt,
And agayne armyt men to fycht
May nakyt[4] men have litill mycht.
Thai scalyt thaim on sic maner
That sum to thar gret bataill wer
Withdrawyn thaim in full gret hy
And sum war fled all utrely,

312

Bot the folk that behind thaim was,
That for thar awne folk had na space
Yheyt to cum to the assembling
In agayn smertly gan thai ding
The archeris that thai met fleand
That then war maid sa recreand
That thar hartis war tyny clenly,
I trow thai sall nocht scaith gretly
The Scottismen with schot that day.
And the gud King Robert that ay
Wes fillyt off full gret bounte
Saw how that his bataillis thre
Sa hardely assemblyt thar
And sa weill in the fycht thaim bar
And sua fast on thair fayis gan ding
That him thocht nane had abaysing
And how the archeris war scalyt then,
He was all blyth and till his men
He said, 'Lordingis, now luk that ye
Worthy and off gud covyn be
At thys assemble and hardy,
And assembill sa sturdely
That na thing may befor you stand.
Our men ar sa freschly fechtand
That thai thar fayis has contrayit sua
That be thai pressyt, Ik underta,
A litill fastyr, ye sall se
That thai discumfyt sone sall be.'
Quhen this wes said thai held thar way
And on ane feld assemblyt thai
Sa stoutly that at thar cummyng
Thar fayis war ruschyt a gret thing.
Thar mycht men se men felly fycht
And men that worthi war and wycht
Do mony worthi vasselage,
Thai faucht as thai war in a rage,
For quhen the Scottis ynkirly
Saw thar fayis sa sturdely

Stand into bataill thaim agayn
With all thar mycht and all thar mayn
Thai layid on as men out of wit
And quhar thai with full strak mycht hyt
Thar mycht na armur stynt thar strak.
Thai to-fruschyt that thai mycht ourtak
And with axis sic duschys gave
That thai helmys and hedis clave,
And thar fayis rycht hardely
Met thaim and dang on thaim douchtely
With wapmys that war styth of stele.
Thar wes the bataill strikyn wele.
Sa gret dyn tthar wes of dyntis
As wapnys apon armur styntis,
And off speris sa gret bresting
And sic thrang and sic thrysting,
Sic gyrnyng granyng and sa gret
A noyis as thai gan other beit
And ensenyeys on ilka sid
Gevand and takand woundis wid,
That it wes hydwys for to her.
All four thar bataillis with that wer
Fechtand in a frount halyly.
A! mycht God! how douchtely
Schyr Edward the Bruce and his men
Amang thar fayis contenyt thaim then
Fechtand in sa gud covyn
Sa hardy worthy and sa fyne
That thar vaward ruschyt was
And maugre tharis left the place,
And till thar gret rout to warand
Thai went that tane had apon hand
Sa gret anoy that thai war effrayit
For Scottis that thaim hard assayit
That than war in a schiltrum all.
Quha hapnyt into that fycht to fall
I trow agane he suld nocht rys.
Thar mycht men se on mony wys

Hardimentis eschevyt douchtely,
And mony that wycht war and hardy
Sone liand undre fete all dede
Quhar all the feld off blud wes red,
Armys and quyntys that thai bar
With blud war sa defoulyt thar
That thai mycht nocht descroyit be.
A! mychty God! quha than mycht se
That Stewart Walter and his rout
And the gud Douglas that wes sa stout
Fechtand into that stalwart stour,
He suld say that till all honour
Thai war worthi that in that fycht
Sa fast pressyt thar fayis mycht
That thaim ruschyt quhar thai yeid.
Thar men mycht se mony a steid
Fleand on stray that lord had nane.
A! Lord! quha then gud tent had tane
Till the gud erle of Murreff
And his that sua gret routis geff
And faucht sa fast in that battaill
Tholand sic paynys and travail[5]
That thai and tharis maid sic debat
That quhar thai come thai maid thaim gat.
Than mycht men her ensenyeis cry
And Scottismen cry hardely,
'On thaim, on thaim, on thaim, thai faile.'
With that sa hard thai gan assaile
And slew all that thai mycht ourta,
And the Scottis archeris alsua
Schot amang thaim sa deliverly
Engrevand thaim sa gretumly
That quhat for thaim that with thaim
   faucht
That sua gret routis to thaim raucht
And pressyt thaim full egrely
And quhat for arowis that felly
Mony gret woundis gan thaim ma

And slew fast off thar hors alsua,
That thai wandyst a litill wei.
Thai dred sa gretly then to dey
That thar covyn wes wer and wer,
For thaim that fechtand with thaim wer
Set hardyment and strenth and will
And hart and corage als thar-till
And all thar mayne and all thar mycht
To put thaim fully to flycht.
In this tyme that I tell off her
At that bataill on this maner
Wes strykyn quhar on ather party
Thai war fechtand enforcely,
Yomen and swanys and pitaill
That in the Park to yeme vittaill
War left, quhen thai wist but lesing
That thar lordis with fell fechting
On thar fayis assemblyt wer,
Ane off thaimselvyn that war thar
Capitane off thaim all thai maid,
And schetis that war sumdele brad
Thai festnyt in steid of baneris
Apon lang treys and speris,
And said that thai wald se the fycht
And help thar lordis at thar mycht.
Quhen her-till all assentyt wer
In a rout thai assemblit er
Fyften thousand thai war or ma,
And than in gret hy gan thai ga
With thar baneris all in a rout
As thai had men bene styth and stout.
thai come with all that assemble
Rycht quhill thai mycht the bataill se,
Than all at anys thai gave a cry,
'Sla! sla! apon thaim hastily!'
And thar-withall cumand war thai,
Bot thai war wele fer yete away.
And Inglismen that ruschyt war

Throuch fors of fycht as I said ar
Quhen thai saw cummand with sic a cry
Towart thaim sic a cumpany
That thaim thocht wele als mony war
As that wes fechtand with thaim thar
And thai befor had nocht thaim sene,
Than wit ye weill withoutyn wene
Thai war abaysit sa gretumly
That the best and the mast hardy
That war intill thar ost that day
Wald with thar mensk haf bene away.
The King Robert be thar relyng
Saw thai war ner at discomfiting
And his ensenye gan hely cry,
Than with thaim off his cumpany
His fayis he pressyt sa fast that thai
War intill sa gret effray
That thai left place ay mar and mar,
For the Scottismen that thar war
Quhen thai saw thaim eschew the fycht
Dang on thaim with all thar mycht
That thai scalyt thaim in troplys ser
And till discomfitur war ner
And sum off thaim fled all planly,
Bot thai that wycht war and hardy
That schame lettyt to ta the flycht
At gret myscheiff mantemyt the fycht
And stythly in the stour gan stand.
And quhen the king of Ingland
Saw his men fley in syndry place,
And saw his fayis rout that was
Worthyn sa wycht and sa hardy
That all his folk war halyly
Sa stonayit[6] that thai had na mycht
To stynt thar fayis in the fycht,
He was abaysyt sa gretumly
That he and his cumpany
Fyve hunder armyt all at rycht

Intill a frusch all tok the flycht
And to the castell held thar way,
And yeit haiff Ik hard som men say
That off Valence Schir Aymer
Quhen he the feld saw vencusyt ner
Be the reyngye led away the king
Agayne his will fra the fechting.
And quhen Schyr Gylis the Argente
Saw the king thus and his menye
Schap thaim to fley sa spedyly,
He come rycht to the king in hy
And said, 'Schyr, sen it is sua
That ye thusgat your gat will ga
Havys gud day for agayne will I,
Yeit fled I never sekyrly
And I cheys her to bid and dey
Than for to lyve schamly and fley.'
His bridill but mar abad
He turnyt and agayne he rade
And on Edward the Bruys rout
That wes sa sturdy and sa stout
As drede off nakyn thing had he
He prikyt, cryand, 'the Argente,'
And thai with speris sua him met
And sua fele speris on him set
That he and hors war chargyt sua
That bathe till the erd gan ga
And in that place thar slane wes he.
Off hys deid wes rycht gret pite,
He wes the thrid best knycht perfay
That men wyst lyvand in his day,
He did mony a fayr journe.
On Saryzynys thre derenyeys faucht he[7]
And intill ilk derenye off tha[8]
He vencussyt Saryzynnys twa.[9]
His gret worschip tuk thar ending.[10]
And fra Schyr Aymer with the king
Was fled wes nane that durst abid

Bot fled scalyt on ilka sid,
And thar fayis thaim pressyt fast.
Thai war to say suth sua agast
And fled sa fast rycht effrayitly
That off thaim a full gret party
Fled to the water of Forth and thar
The mast part off thaim drownyt war,
And Bannokburne betwix the brays
Off men and hors sua stekyt wais
That apon drownyt hors and men
Men mycht pas dry out-our it then.
And laddis swanys and rangaill
Quhen thai saw vencussyt the bataill
Ran amang thaim and sua gan sla
As folk that na defens mycht ma
That war pitte for to se.
Ik herd never quhar in na contre
Folk at sa gret myscheiff war stad,
On ane sid thai thar fayis bad
That slew thaim doun foroutyn mercy,
And thai had on the tother party
Bannokburne that sua cumbyrsum was
For slyk and depnes for to pas
That thar mycht nane out-our it rid,
Thaim worthit maugre tharis abid
Sua that sum slayne sum drownyt war,
Mycht nane eschap that ever come thar
The-quhether mony gat away
That ellisquhair fled as I sall say.
The king with thaim he with him had
In a rout till the castell rad
And wald haiff bene tharin, for thai
Wyst nocht quhat gat to get away,
Bot Philip the Mowbra said him till,
'The castell, Schyr, is at your will,
But cum ye in it ye sall se
That ye sall sone assegyt be
And thar sall nane of Ingland

To mak you rescours tak on hand
And but rescours may na castell
Be haldyn lang, ye wate this wele.
Tharfor confort you and rely
Your men about you rycht starkly
And haldis about the Park your way
Knyt als sadly as ye may,[11]
For I trow that nane sall haff mycht
That chassys with sa fele to fycht.'
And his consaill thai haiff doyne
And beneuth the castell went thai sone
Rycht be the Rond Table away,
And syne the Park enveround thai
And towart Lythkow held in hy.
Bot I trow thai sall hastily
Be conveyit with sic folk that thai
I trow mycht suffre wele away,
For Schyr James lord off Douglas
Come to the king and askyt the chace
And he gaff him it but abaid,
Bot all to few of hors he haid,
He haid nocht in his rout sexty
The-quhether he sped him hastely
The way eftyr the king to ta.
Now lat him on his wayis ga
And eftre this we sall weill tell
Quhat him intill the chace befell.
Quhen the gret battaill on this wis
Was discumfyt as Ik devys
Quhar thretty thousand wele war ded
Or drownyt in that ilk sted,
And sum war intill handis tane
And other sum thar gate war gane.
The erle of Herfurd fra the melle
Departyt with a gret mengne
And straucht to Bothwell tok the wai
That than in the Inglismennys fay
Was, and haldyn as place of wer,

Schyr Walter Gilbertson wes ther
Capitane and it had in ward.
The erle of Herfurd thidderward
Held and wes tane in our the wall
And fyfty of his men withall,
And set in housis sindryly
Sua that thai had thar na mastry.
The lave went towart Ingland
Bot off that rout I tak on hand
The thre partis war slane or tane,
The lave with gret payn hame ar gan.
Schyr Maurice alsua the Berclay
Fra the gret bataill held hys way
With a gret rout off Walis-men,
Quharever thai yeid men mycht thaim ken
For thai wele ner all nakyt war[12]
Or lynnyn clathys had but mar.
Thai held thar way in full gret hy
Bot mony off thar cumpany
Or thai till Ingland come war tane
And mony als off thaim war slayne.
Thair fled als other wayis ser,
Bot to the castell that wes ner
Off Strevillyne fled sic a mengye
That it war wonder for to se,
For the craggis all helyt war
About the castell her and thar
Off thaim that for strenth of that sted
Thidderwart to warand fled,
And for thai war sa fele that thar
Fled under the castell war
The King Robert that wes wytty
Held his gud men ner him by
For dred that ris agayne suld thai.
This was the caus forsuth to say
Quharthrouch the king of Ingland
Eschapyt hame intill his land
Quhen that the feld sa clene wes maid

Off Inglismen that nane abaid
The Scottismen sone tuk in hand
Off tharis all that ever thai fand,
As silver gold clathis and armyng
With veschall and all other thing
That ever thai mycht lay on thare hand.
So gret a riches thair thai fand
That mony man mychty wes maid
Off the riches that thai thar haid.
Quhen this wes doyne that her say I
The king send a gret cumpany
Up to the crag thaim till assaile
That war fled fra the gret battaill,
And thai thaim yauld foroutyn debate,
And in hand has tane thaim fute-hate
Syne to the king thai went thar way.
Thai dispendyt haly that day
In spulyeing and riches takyng
Fra end was maid off the fechting
And quhen thai nakyt spulyeit war
That war slane in the bataill thar
It wes forsuth a gret ferly
To se samyn sa fele dede ly.
Twa hundyr payr off spuris reid
War tane of knychtis that war deid,
The erle of Glosyster ded wes thar
That men callyt Schyr Gilbert of Clar,
And Gylis de Argente alsua
And Payn Typtot and other ma
That thar namys nocht tell can I.
And apon Scottismennys party
Thar wes slane worthi knychtis twa,
Wilyame the Vepoynt wes ane of tha
And Schyr Walter of Ross ane other
That Schyr Edward the kingis brother
Luffyt and had in sic daynte
That as himselff him luffyt he.
And quhen he wyst that he wes ded

He wes sa wa and will of reide
That he said makand ivill cher
That him war lever that journay wer
Undone than he sua ded had bene.
Outakyn him men has nocht sene
Quhar he for ony man maid menyng,
And the caus wes of his luffing
That he his sister paramouris
Luffyt, and held all at rebouris
His awyne wyff dame Ysabell.
And tharfor sa gret distance fell
Betwix him and the erle Davi
Off Athole, brother to this lady
That he apon Saynct Jhonys nycht,
Quhen bath the kingis war boun to fycht,
In Cammyskynnell the kingis vittaill
He tuk and sadly gert assaile
Schyr Wilyam off Herth and him slew
And with him men ma then ynew.
Tharfor syne intil Ingland
He wes bannyst and all his land
Wes sesyt as forfaut to the king
That did tharoff syne his liking.
Quhen the feld as I tauld you ar
Was dispulyeit and left all bar
The king and all his cumpany
Blyth and joyfull glaid and mery
Off the grace that thaim fallin was
Towart thar innys thar wayis tays
To rest thaim, for thai wery war.
Bot for the erle Gilbert of Clar[13]
That slane wes in the bataill-place
The king sumdele anoyit was
For till him wele ner sib wes he,
Than till a kirk he gert him be
Brocht and walkyt all that nycht.
But on the morn quhen day wes lycht
The king rais as his willis was.

Than ane Inglis knycht throu cas
Hapnyt that he yeid waverand
Swa that na man laid on him hand,
In a busk he hyd hys armyng
And waytyt quhill he saw the king
In the morne cum furth arly
Till him than is he went in hy,
Schyr Marmeduk the Tweingue[14] he
    hycht.
He raykyt till the king all rycht
And halyst him apon his kne.
'Welcum, Schyr Marmeduk,' said he,
To quhat man art thou presoner?'
'To nane,' he said, 'bot to you her
I yeld me at your will to be.'
'And I ressave the, schyr,' said he.
Than gert he tret him curtasly,
He dwelt lang in his cumpany,
And syne till Ingland him send he
Arayit weile but ransoun fre
And geff him gret gyftis tharto.
A worthi man that sua wald do
Mycht mak him gretly for to prise.
Quhen Marmeduk apon this wis
Was yoldyn, as Ik to you say,
Than come Schyr Philip the Mowbra
And to the king yauld the castell,
His cunnand has he haldyn well,
And with him tretyt sua the king
That he belevyt of his dwelling[15]
And held him lely his fay
Quhill the last end off his lyf-day.
Now will we of the lord off Douglas
Tell how that he folowit the chas.
He had to quhone in his cumpany
Bot he sped him in full gret hy,
And as he throuch the Torwod fur
Sa met he ridand on the mur

Schyr Laurence off Abyrnethy[16]
That with four scor in cumpany
Come for till help the Inglismen
For he was Inglisman yet then,
Bot quhen he hard how that it wes
He left the Inglis-mennys pes
And to the lord Douglas rycht thar
For to be lele and trew he swar.
And than thai bath folowit the chas,
And or the king off Ingland was
Passyt Lythkow thai come sa ner
With all the folk that with thaim wer
That weill amang thaim schout thai
   mycht,
Bot thai thocht thaim to few to fycht
With the gret rout that thai had thar
For fyve hunder armyt thai war.
Togidder sarraly raid thai
And held thaim apon bridill ay,
Thai wat governyt wittily
For it semyt ay thai war redy
For to defend thaim at thar mycht
Giff thai assailyt war in fycht.
And the lord Douglas and his men,
How that he wald nocht schaip him then
For to fecht with thaim all planly,
He convoyit thaim sa narowly
That of the henmaist ay tuk he,
Mycht nane behin his falowis be
A pennystane cast[17] na he in hy
Was dede, or tane deliverly
That nane rescours wald till him ma
All-thocht he luvyt him never sua.
On this maner convoyit he
Quhill that the king and his menye
To Wenchburg[18] all cummyn ar.
Than lychtyt all that thai war
To bayt thar hors that wer wery,

And Douglas and his cumpany
Baytyt alsua besid thaim ner.
Thai war sa fele withoutyn wer
And in armys sa clenly dycht
And sua arayit for to fycht,
And he sa quhoyne and but supleyng
That he wald nocht in plane fechting
Assaile thaim, bot ay raid thaim by
Waytand hys poynt ay ythandly.
A litill quhill thai baytyt thar
And syne lap on and furth thai far
And he was alwayis by thaim ner,
He leyt thaim nocht haff sic layser
As anys water for to ma,
And giff ony stad war sa
That he behind left ony space
Sesyt alsone in hand he was.
Thai convoyit thaim on sic a wis
Quhill that the king and his rout is
Cummyn to the castell of Dunbar
Quhar he and sum of his menye war
Resavyt rycht weill, for yete than
The Erle Patrik was Inglisman,
That gert with mete and drynk alsua
Refresche thaim weill, and syne gert ta
A bate and send the king by se
To Baumburgh[19] in his awne contre.
Thar hors thar left thai all on stray
Bot sesyt I trow weill sone war thai.
The lave that levyt thar-without
Addressyt thaim intill a rout
And till Berwik held straucht thar way
In route, bot, and we suth say,
Stad thai war full narowly
Or thai come thar, bot nocht-forthi
Thai come to Berwik weill and thar
Into the toune ressavyt war,
Ellys at gret myscheff had thai bene.

And quhen the lord off Douglas has sene
That he had losyt all hys payne
Towart the king he went agane.
The king eschapyt on this wis.
Lo! quhat fading in fortoun is
That will apon a man quhill smyle
And prik on him syne a nothyr quhill,
In na tym stable can scho stand.
This mychty king off Ingland
Scho had set on hyr quheill on hycht
Quham with sa ferlyfull a mycht
Off men off armys and archeris
And off futemen and hobeleris
He come ridand out off his land
As I befor has borne on hand,
And in a nycht syne and a day
Scho set him in sa hard assay
That he with few men in a bate
Wes fayne for till hald hame his gate.
Bot off this ilk quhelys[20] turning
King Robert suld mak na murnyng
For on his syd the quheyle on hycht
Rais quhen the tother doun gan lycht,
For twa contraris yhe may wit wele
Set agane othir on a quhele
Quhen ane is hye the tothir is law,
And gif it fall that fortoune thraw
The quheill about, it that on hicht
Was ere it most doune lycht,
And it that undre lawch was ar
Mon lepe on loft in the contrar.
Sa fure it off thir kingis twa,
Quhen the King Robert stad was sua
That in gret myscheiff wes he
The tother was in his majeste,
And quhen the King Edwardis mycht
Wes lawyt King Robert wes on hycht,
And now sic fortoun fell him till

That he wes hey and at his will.
At Strevillyne wes he yeyt liand,
And the gret lordis that he fand
Dede in the feld he gert bery
In haly place honorabilly,
And the lave syne that dede war thar
Into gret pyttis erdyt war thar
The castell and the towris syne
Rycht till the ground gert he myn,
And syne to Bothwell send he
Schyr Edward with a gret menye
For thar wes thine send him word
That the rich erle off Herford
And other mychty als wer ther.
Sua tretyt he with Schyr Walter
That erle and castell and the lave
In Schyr Edwardis hand he gave,
And till the king the erle send he
That gert him rycht weill yemyt be
Quhill at the last thai tretyt sua
That he till Ingland hame suld ga
Foroutyn paying of raunsoune fre,
And that for him suld changyt be
Bischap Robert that blynd was mad
And the queyne that thai takyn had
In presoune as befor said I
And hyr douchter Dame Marjory.
The erle was changyt for thir thre,
And quhen thai cummyn war hame all fre
The king his douchter that was far[21]
And wes als aperand ayr[22]
With Walter Stewart gan he wed
And thai wele sone gat of thar bed
A knav child throu our Lordis grace,
That eftre his gud eldfader was
Callyt Robert and syne wes king,
And had the land in governyng
Eftyr his worthy eyme Davy

That regnyt twa yer and fourty.
And in the tyme of the compiling
Off this buk this Robert wes king,
And off hys kynrik passit was
Fyve yer, and wes the yer of grace
A thousand thre hunder sevynty
And fyve, and off his eld sexty,
And that wes efter that the gud king
Robert wes broucht till his ending
Sex and fourty winter but mar.
God grant that thai that cummyn ar
Off his ofspring manteyme the land
And hald the folk weill to warand
And manteyme rycht and leawte
Alls wele as in his tyme did he
King Robert now wes wele at hycht
For ilk day than grew his mycht,
His men woux rich and his contre
Haboundyt weill of corne and fe
And off alkyn other ryches,
Myrth and solace and blythnes
War in the land commonaly
For ilk man blyth war and joly.
The king eftre the gret journe

Throu rede off his consaill preve
In ser townys gert cry on hycht
That quha-sa clemyt till haf rycht
To hald in Scotland land or fe,
That in thai twelf moneth suld he
Cum and clam yt and tharfor do
To the king that pertenyt tharto,
And giff thai come nocht in that yer
Than suld thai wit withoutyn wer
That hard thareftre nane suld be.
The king that wes of gret bounte
And besines, quhen this wes done
Ane ost gert summound eftre sone
And went thaim intill Ingland
And our-raid all Northummyrland,
And brynt housis and tuk tharpray
And syne went hame agane thar way.
I lat it schortly pas forby
For thar wes done na chevalry
Provyt that is to spek of her.
The king went oft on this maner
In Ingland for to rich his men
That in riches haboundyt then.

BOOK XIV

The erle off Carrik Schyr Edward,
That stoutar wes than a libard
And had na will to be in pes,
Thocht that Scotland to litill wes
Till his brother and him alsua,
Tharfor to purpos gan he ta
That he off Irland wald be king.
Tharfor he send and had tretyng
With the Irschery off Irland,
That in thar leawte tuk on hand

Off all Irland to mak him king
With-thi that he with hard fechting
Mycht ourcum the Inglismen
That in the land war wonnand then,
And thai suld help with all thar mycht.
And he that hard thaim mak sic hycht
Intill his hart had gret liking
And with the consent of the king
Gadryt him men off gret bounte
And at Ayr syne schippyt he

321

Intill the neyst moneth of Mai,
Till Irland held he straucht his wai.
He had thar in his cumpany
The Erle Thomas that wes worthi
And gud Schyr Philip the Mowbray
That sekyr wes in hard assay,
Schyr Jhone the Soullis[1] ane gud knycht
And Schyr Jhone Stewart[2] that wes wycht
The Ramsay als of Ouchterhous[3]
That wes wycht and chevalrous
And Schyr Fergus off Ardrossane[4]
And other knychtis mony ane.
In Wolringis Fyrth aryvyt thai[5]
Sauffly but bargan or assay[6]
And send thar schippis hame ilkan.
A gret thing have thai undretane
That with sa quhoyne as thai war thar
That war sex thousand men but mar
Schup to werray all Irland,
Quhar thai sall se mony thousand
Cum armyt on thaim for to fycht,
But thocht thai quhone war thai war wicht,
And forout drede or effray
In twa bataillis tuk thar way
Towart Cragfergus[7] it to se.
Bot the lordis of that countre
Mandveill, Besat and Logane[8]
Thar men assemblyt everilkane,
The Savagis[9] wes alsua thar,
And quhen thai assemblit war
That war wele ner twenty thousand.
Quhen thai wyst that intill thar land
Sic a menye aryvyt war
With all the folk that thai had thar
Thai went towart thaim in gret hi,
And fra Schyr Edward wist suthly
That ner till him cummand war thai
His men he gert thaim wele aray,

The avaward had the Erle Thomas
And the rerward Schyr Edward was.
Thar fayis approchyt to the fechting
And thai met thaim but abaysing.
Thar mycht men se a gret melle,
For Erle Thomas and his menye
Dang on thar fayis sa douchtely
That in schort tym men mycht se ly
Ane hunder that all blody war,
For hobynys[10] that war stekyt thar
Relyt and flang and gret rowme mad
And kest thaim that apon thaim rad,
And Schyr Edwardis cumpany
Assemblyt syne sa hardely
That thai thar fayis ruschyt all.
Quha hapnyt in that fycht to fall
It wes perell off his rysing.
The Scottismen in that fechting
Sua apertly and wele thaim bar
That thar fayis sua ruschyt war
That thai haly the flycht has tane.
In that bataill wes tane or slane
All hale the flur off Ulsyster.
The Erle off Murreff gret price had ther,
For his worthi chevalry
Comfort all his cumpany.
This wes a full fayr begynnyng,
For newlingis[11] at thar aryving
In plane bataill thai discomfyt thar
Thar fayis that four ay for ane war,
Syne to Cragfergus ar thai gane
And in the toune has innys tane.
The castell weill wes stuffyt then
Off new with vittaill and with men,
Thartill thai set a sege in hy.
Mony eschewe full apertly
Wes maid quhill thar the sege lay
Quhill trewys at the last tuk thai,

Quhen that the folk off Hulsyster[12]
Till his pes haly cummyn wer,
For Schyr Edward wald tak on hand
To rid furth forthyr in the land.
Off the kingis[13] off that countre
Thar come till him and maide fewte
Weill ten or twelf as Ik hard say,
Bot thai held him schort quhile thar fay,
For twa off thaim, ane Makgullane
And ane other hat Makartane,
Withset a pase intill his way
Quhar him behovyt ned away[14]
With twa thousand off men with speris
And als mony of thar archeris,
And all the catell of the land
War drawyn thidder to warand.
Men callys that plase Innermallane,
In all Irland straytar is nane.
For Schyr Edward that kepyt thai,
Thai thoucht he suld nocht thar away,
Bot he his viage sone has tane
And straught towart the pas is gane.
The erle off Murreff Schyr Thomas
That put him fyrst ay till assayis
Lychtyt on fute with his menye
And apertly the pase tuk he.
Thir Ersch kingis that I spak off ar
With all the folk that with thame war
Met him rycht sturdely, bot he
Assaylyt sua with his menye
That maugre tharis thai wan the pas.
Slayne off thar fayis fele thar was,
Throu-out the wod thaim chasyt thai
And sesyt in sic fusoune the pray
That all the folk off thar ost war
Refreschyt weill ane wouk or mar.
At Kilsagart[15] Schyr Edward lay,
And wele sone he has hard say

That at Dundalk wes assemble
Made off the lordis off that countre.
In ost thai war assemblyt thar,
Thar wes fyrst Schyr Richard of Clar[16]
That in all Irland lufftenande[17]
Was off the king off Ingland
The erle of Desmond[18] wes thar
And the erle alsua of Kildar,[19]
The Breman and the Wardoune[20]
That war lordis of gret renoune,
The Butler alsua thar was
And Schyr Morys le fys Thomas,[21]
Thai with thar men ar cummyn thar,
A rycht gret ost forsuth thai war.
And quhen Schyr Edward wyst suthly
That thar wes swilk chevalry
His ost in hy he gert aray
And thidderwartis tuk the way
And ner the toune tuk his herbery,
Bot for he wyst all witterly
That in the toune war mony men
His bataillis he arayit then,
And stud arayt in bataill
To kep thaim gif thai wald assaile,
And quhen that Schyr Rychard of Clar
And other lordis that thar war
Wyst that the Scottis men sa ner
With thar bataillis cummyn wer,
Thai tuk to consaile thar that nycht
For it wes layt thai wald nocht fycht
Bot on the morne in the mornyng
Weile sone aftre the sone-rysing
Thai suld isch furth all that thar war,
Tharfor that nycht thai did no mar
Bot herbryit thaim on athyr party.
That nycht the Scottis cumpany
War wachyt rycht weill all at rycht,
And on the morn quhen day wes lycht

In twa bataillis thai thaim arayit,
Thai stud with baneris all displayit
For the bataill all redy boun.
And thai that war within the toun
Quhen sone wes rysyn schenand cler
Send furth of thaim that within wer
Fyfty to se the contenyng
Off Scottismen and thar cummyng,
And thai raid furth and saw thaim sone,
Syne come agayne withoutyn hone.
And quhen thai samyn lychtyt war
thai tauld thar lordis that wer thar
That Scottismen semyt to be
Worthi and off gret bounte,
'Bot thai ar nocht withoutyn wer
Half-dell a dyner till us her.'
The lordys had off this tithing
Gret joy and gret reconforting
And gert men throu the cite cry
That all suld arm thaim hastily.
Quhen thai war armyt and purvayit
And for the fycht all hale arayit
Thai went thaim furth in gud aray,
Sone with thar fayis assemblyt thai
That kepyt thaim rycht hardely.
The stour begouth thar cruelly
For athyr part set all thar mycht
To rusche thar fayis in the fycht
And with all mycht on other dang.
The stalwart stour lestyt wele lang
That men mycht nocht persave na se
Qyha maist at thar above suld be,
For fra sone eftre the sone-rissing
Quhill eftre mydmorne the fechting
Lestyt intill swilk a dout.
Bot than Schyr Edward that wes stout
With all thaim of his cumpany
Schot apon thaim sa sturdely

That thai mycht thole no mar the fycht,
All in a frusche thai tuk the flycht
And thai folowyt full egrely,
Into the toun all commonaly
Thai entryt bath intermelle.
Thar men mycht felloune slauchter se,
For the rycht noble erle Thomas
That with his rout folowyt the chas
Maid swilk a slauchter in the toun
And sua felloune occisioun
That the rewys[22] all bludy war
Off slayne men that war lyand thar,
The lordis war gottyn all away.
And quhen the toun as I you say
Wes throu gret force of fechting tane
And all thar fayis fled or slayne
Thai herbryit thaim all in the toun
Quhar off vitaill wes sic fusoun[23]
And sua gret haboundance of wyne
That the gud erle had doutyne
That off thar men suld drunkyn be
And mak in drunkynnes sum melle.
Tharfor he maid of wyne levere[24]
Till ilk man that he payit suld be,
And thai had all yneuch perfay.
That nycht rycht weill at ese war thai
And rycht blyth of the gret honour
That thaim befell for thar valour.
Eftyr this fycht thai sojornyt thar
Into Dundalk thre dayis but mar,
Syne tuk thai southwartis thar way.
The Erle Thomas wes forouth ay
And as thai raid throu the countre
Thai mycht apon the hillis se
Sua mony men it wes ferly,
And quhen the erle wald sturdely
Dres him to thaim with his baner
Thai wald fle all that evir thai wer

Sua that in fycht nocht ane abad.
And thai southwart thar wayis raid
Quhill till a gret forest come thai,
Kylrose it hat as Ik hard say,
And thai tuk all thar herbery thar.
In all this tyme Rychard of Clar
That wes the kingis luftenand
Off the barnagis of Irland
A gret ost he assemblyt had,
Thai war fyve bataillis gret and braid
That soucht Schir Edward and his men,
Weill ner him war thai cummyn then.
He gat sone wittring that thai wer
Cummand on him and war sa ner.
His men he dressyt thaim agayn
And gert thaim stoutly ta the playn
And syne the erle thar come to se
And Schyr Philip the Mowbray send he,
And Schyr Jhone Stewart went alsua.
Furth to discover thar way thai ta,
Thai saw the ost sone cum at hand
Thai war to ges fyfty thousand,
Hame till Schyr Edward raid thai then
And said weill thai war mony men.
He said agayne, 'The ma thai be
The mar honour all-out haff we
Giff that we ber us manlyly.
We ar set her in juperty
To wyn honour or for to dey,
We ar to fer fra hame to fley
Tharfor lat ilk man worthi be.
Yone ar gadryngis of this countre
And thai sall fley I trow lychly
And men assaile thaim manlyly.'
All said than that thai weile suld do,
With that approchand ner thaim to
The bataillis come redy to fycht,
And thai met thaim with mekill mycht

That war ten thousand worthi men.
The Scottismen all on fute war then,
And thai on stedys trappyt weile
Sum helyt all in irne and stele,
Bot Scottismen at thar meting
With speris persyt thar armyng
And stekyt hors and men doun bar.
A feloun fechting wes than thar,
I can nocht tell thar strakys all
Na quha in fycht gert other fall
Bot in schort tyme Ik underta
Thai of Irland war contraryit sua
That thai durst than abyd no mar
Bot fled scalyt all that thai war,
And levyt in the bataill sted
Weill mony off thar gud men dede,
Off wapnys, armyng and of ded men
The feld was haly strowyt then.
That gret ost rudly ruschyt was
Bot Schyr Edward let na man chas
Bot with presonaris that thai had tane
Thai till the woud agayne ar gane
Quhar that thar harnys levyt war.
That nycht thai maid thar men gud cher
And lovyt God fast off his grace.
This gud knycht that sa worthi was
Till Judas Machabeus[25] mycht
Be lyknyt weill that into fycht
Forsuk na multitud off men
Quhill he had ane aganys ten.
Thus as I said Rychard of Clar
And his gret ost rebutyt war,
Bot he about him nocht-forthi
Wes gaderand men ay ythenly
For he thocht yete to covyr his cast.
It angyrryt him rycht ferly fast
That twys intill batell wes he
Discomfyt with a few mengne.

And Scottismen that to the forest
War ridyn for to mak thar rest
All thai twa nychtis thar thai lay
And maid thaim myrth solace and play.
Towart Ydymsy syne thai raid,
Ane Yrsche king that aith had maid
To Schyr Edward of fewte,
For forouth that him prayit he
To se his land and na vittaill
Na nocht that mycht thaim help suld
    faile.
Schyr Edward trowit in his hycht
And with his rout raid thidder rycht
A gret ryver he gert him pas
And in a rycht fayr place that was
Lauch by a bourne[26] he gert thaim ta
Thar herbery, and said he wald ga
To ger men vittaill to thaim bring,
He held hys way but mar dwelling.
For he betrais thaim wes his thocht,
In sic a place he has them broucht
Quharof twa journais wele and mar
All the cattell withdrawyn war,
Swa that thai in that land mycht get
Na thing that worth war for til ete,
With hungyr he thocht thaim to feblis[27]
Syne bring on thaim thar ennemys.
This fals traytouris men had maid
A litill outh quhar he herbryit had
Schyr Edward and the Scottismen
The ischow off a louch to den[28]
And leyt it out into the nycht.
The water than with a swilk a mycht
On Schyr Edwardis men com doun
That thai in perell war to droun
For or thai wist on flot war thai.
With mekill payn thai gat away
And held thar lyff as God gaff grace,

Bot off thar harnayis tynt thar was.
He maid thaim na gud fest perfay
And nocht-forthi yneuch had thai,
For thoucht thaim faillyt of the mete
I warn you wele thai war wele wet
In gret distres thar war thai stad
For gret defaut off mete thai hade,
And thai betwix reveris twa
War set and mycht pas nane off tha,
The Bane[29] that is ane arme of the se
That with hors may nocht passyt be
Wes betwix thaim and Hulsyster.
Thai had bene in gret perell ther
Ne war a scowmar of the se,
Thomas of Downe hattyn wes he,
Hard that the ost sa straytly than
Wes stad, and salyt up the Ban
Quhill he come wele ner quhar thai lay,
Thai knew him weil and blyth war thai,
Than with four schippys that he had tane
He set our the Ban ilkane.
And quhen thai come in biggit land
Vittaill and mete yneuch thai fand
And in a wod thaim herberyt thai,
Nane of the land wist quhar thai lay,
Thai esyt thaim and maid gud cher.
Intill that tym besid thaim ner
With a gret ost Schyr Richard of Clar
And othyr gret of Irland war
Herberyt in a forest syde,
And ilk day thai gert men rid
To bring vittaill on ser manerys
To thaim fra the toun off Coigneris[30]
That wele ten gret myle wes thaim fra.
Ilk day as thai wald cum and ga
Thai come the Scottis ost sa ner
That bot twa myle betwix thaim wer,
And quhen the Erle Thomas persaving

Had off thar cummyng and thar ganging
He gat him a gud cumpany,
Thre hunder on hors wycht and hardy,
Thar wes Schyr Philip the Mowbray
And Schyr Jhone Stewart als perfay
And Schyr Alan Stewart alsua
Schyr Robert Boid and other ma.
Thai raid to mete the vittaleris
That with thar vittaill fra Coigneris
Come haldand to thar ost the way.
Sua sudanly on thaim schot thai
That thai war sua abaysyt all
That thai leyt all thar wapnys fall
And mercy petously gan cry,
And thai tuk thaim in thar mercy
And has thaim up sa clenly tane
That off thaim all eschapyt nane.
The erle of thaim gat wittering
That off thar ost in the evynnyng
Wald cum out at the woddis sid
And agaynys thar vittail rid.
He thocht than on ane juperty,
And gert his menye halily
Dycht thaim in the presoneris aray,
Thair pennounys als with thaim tuk thai,
And quhill the nycht wes ner thai bad
And syne towart the ost thai raid.
Sum of thar mekill ost has sene
Thar come and wend thai had bene
Thar vittalouris, tharfor thai raid
Agaynys thaim scalyt, for thai haid
Na dred that thai thar fayis war
And thaim hungryt alsua weill sar,
Tharfor thai come abandounly.
And quhen thai ner war in gret hi
The erle and all that with him war
Ruschyt on thaim with wapnys bar
And thar ensenyeis hey gan cry.

Than thai that saw sua sodanly
Thar fayis dyng on thaim war sa rad
That thai na hart to help thaim had
Bot to the ost thar way gan ta,
And thai chassyt and sua fele gan sla
That all the feldys strowyt war,
Ma than a thousand ded war thar.
Rycht till thar ost thai gan thaim chas
And syne agane thar wayis tais.
On this wis wes that vittaill tane
And of the Irche-men mony slane.
The erle syne with his cumpany
Presoneris and vittalis halily
Thai broucht till Schyr Edward alswith
And he wes of thar cummyn blyth.
That nycht thai maid thaim mery cher
For rycht all at thar eys thai wer,
Thai war ay walkyt sekyrly.
And thar fayis on the tother party
Quhen thai hard how thar men war slane
And how thar vittalis als wes tane
Thai tuk to consaill that thai wald
Thair wayis towart Coigneris hald
And herbery in the cite ta,
And than in gret hy thai haf don sua
And raid be nycht to the cite,
Thai fand thar of vittalis gret plente
And maid thaim rycht mery cher
For all traist in the toun thai wer.
Apon the morne thai send to spy
Quhar Scottismen had tane herbery,
Bot thai war withall als tane
And brocht rycht till the ost ilkane.
The erle of Murreff rycht mekly
Speryt at ane of thar cumpany
Quhar thar ost wes and quhat thai thocht
To do, and said him gif he moucht
Fynd that till him the suth said he

He suld gang hame but ransoun fre.
He said, 'Forsuth I sall you say,
Thai think to-morn, quhen it is day,
To sek you with all thar menye
Giff thai may get wit quhar ye be.
Thai haff gert throu the countre cry
Off payne of lyve full felounly
That all the men of this countre
Tonycht into the cyte be,
And trewly thai sall be sa fele
That ye sall na wis with thaim dele.'
'De pardew,' said he, 'weill may be.'
To Schyr Edward with that yeid he
And tauld him utrely this tale.
Than haf thai tane for consale hale
That thai wald rid to the cite
That ilk nycht sua that thai mycht be
Betwix the toune with all thar rout
And thaim that war to cum with-out.
Als thai devisyt thai haf done,
Befor the toune thai come alsone
And bot halfindall a myle of way
Fra the cite arest tuk thai.
And quhen the day wes dawyn lycht
Fyfty on hobynys that war wycht
Come till a litill hill that was
Bot fra the toun a litill space
And saw Schyr Edwardis herbery,
And off the sycht had gret ferly
That sua quhone durst on ony wis
Undretak sa hey enprys
As for to cum sa hardely
Apon all the chevalry
Off Irland for to bid battaill.
And sua it wes withoutyn faill,
For agane thaim war gadryt thar
With the wardane Richard of Clar
The Butler and erlis twa,

Off Desmound and Kildar war tha,
Bryman, Werdoune and fis Waryne[31]
And Schyr Paschall the Florentine[32]
That wes a knycht of Lumbardy
And wes full of chevalry.
The Maundveillis war thar alsua
Besatis Loganys and other ma
Savages als, and yeit wes ane
Hat Schyr Nycholl of Kylkenane[33],
And with thir lordis sa fele wes then
That for ane of the Scottismen
I trow that thai war fyve or ma.
Quhen thir discourouris seyne had sua
The Scottis ost thai went in hy
And tauld thair lordis opynly
How thai to thaim war cummyn ner
To sek thaim fer wes na myster.
And quhen the erle Thomas had sene
That thai men at the hill had bene
He tuk with him a gud menye
On hors, ane hunder thai mycht be,
And till the hill thai tuk thar way.
In a slak thaim enbuschyt thai
And in schort tyme fra the cite
Thai saw cum ridand a mengne
For to discur to the hill.
Then war thai blyth and held thaim still
Quhill thai war cummyn to thaim ner,
Than in a frusche all that thai wer
Thai schot apon thaim hardely,
And thai that saw sa sudandly
That folk cum on abaysit war.
And nocht-forthi sum of thaim thar
Abad stoutly to ma debate,
And other sum ar fled thar gate,
And into wele schort tym war thai
That maid arest contraryit sua
That thai fled halyly thar gat,

And thai thaim chassyt rycht to the yat
And a gret part off thaim has slayn,

And syne went till thar ost agayn.

BOOK XV

Quhen thai within has sene sua slayn
Thar men and chassyt hame agayn
Thai war all wa, and in gret hy
'Till armys!' hely gan thai cry.
Than armyt thaim all that thai war
And for the bataill maid thaim yar
Thai ischyt out all wele arayit
Into the bataill baner displayit
Bowne on thar best wis till assaile
Thar fayis into fell bataill.
And quhen Schyr Philip the Mowbra
Saw thaim ische in sa gud aray
Till Schyr Edward the Bruys went he
And said, 'Schyr, it is gud that we
Schap for sum slycht that may availe
To help us into this bataill.
Our men ar quhoyne, bot thai haf will
To do mar than thai may fulfill,
Tharfor I rede our carriage[1]
Foroutyn ony man or page
Be thaimselvyn arayit be
And thai sall seyme fer ma than we,
Set we befor thaim our baneris,
Yone folk that cummys out of Coigneris
Quhen thai our baneris thar may se
Sall trow traistly that thar ar we
And thidder in gret hy sall thai rid.
Cum we than on thaim at a sid
And we sall be at avantag,
For fra thai in our cariag
Be entryt thai sall combryt be,
And than with all our mycht may we

Lay on and do all that we may.'
All as he ordanyt done haf thai,
And thai that come out of Coigneris
Addressyt thaim to the baneris
And smate with spuris the hors in hy
And ruschit thaim sudandly.
The barell-ferraris that war thar
Cumbryt thaim fast that ridand war,
And than the erle with his bataill
Come on and sadly gan assaill,
And Schyr Edward a litill by
Assemblit sua rycht hardely
That mony a fey fell undre fete,
The feld wox sone of blud all wete.
With sa gret felny thar thai faucht
And sic routis till other raucht
With stok with stane and with retrete[2]
As ather part gan other bet
That it wes hidwys for to se.
Thai mantemyt that gret melle
Sa knychtlik[3] apon ather sid
Giffand and takand routis rid
That pryme wes passyt or men mycht se
Quha mast at thar abov mycht be,
Bot sone eftre that prime wes past
The Scottismen dang on sa fast
And schot on thaim at abandoun
As ilk man war a campioun
That all thar fayis tuk the flycht,
Wes nane of thaim that wes sa wicht
That evyr durst abid his fer
Bot ilk man fled thar wayis ser.

To the toun fled the mast party,
And Erle Thomas sa egrely
And his route chassyt with swerdis bar
That amang thame mellyt war
That all togidder come in the toun.
Than wes the slaughter sa felloune
That all the ruys ran of blud,
Thaim that thai gat to ded all yhud
Sua that than thar weill ner wer dede
Als fele as in the bataill-stede.
The fys Warine wes takyn thar,
Bot sua rad wes Richard of Clar
That he fled to the south countre,
All that moneth I trow that he
Sall haf na gud will for to fycht.
Schyr Jhone Stewart a noble knycht
Wes woundyt throu the body thar
With a sper that scharply schar,
Bot to Monpeller[4] went he syne
And lay thar lang intill helyne
And at the last helyt wes he.[5]
Schyr Edward than with his menye
Tuk in the toun thar herbery,
That nycht thai blyth war and joly
For the victour that thai had thar.
And on the morn foroutyn mar
Schyr Edward gert men gang and se
All the vittaill of that cite,
And thai fand sic foysoun tharin
Off corne and flour and wax and wyn
That thai had of it gret ferly,
And Schyr Edward gert halily
Intill Cragfergus it caryit be,
Syne thidder went his men and he
And held the sege full stalwartly
Quhill Palme Sonday wes passit by.
Than quhill the Twysday in Pays wouk[6]
On ather half thai trewys[7] touk

Sua that thai mycht that haly tid
In pennance[8] and in prayer bid.
Bot apon the Pasche[9] evyn richt
To the castell into the nycht
Fra Devillyne[10] schippis come fyften
Chargyt with armyt men bedene,
Four thousand trow I weill thai war,
In the castell thai entryt ar.
The Maundveill auld Schyr Thomas
Capitane of that menye was.
Intill the castell prively
Thai entryt for thai had gert spy
That mony of Schyr Edwardis men
War scalyt in the contre then,
Tharfor thai thocht in the mornyng
Till isch but langer delaying
And to suppris thaim suddanly,
For thai thocht thai suld traistly
For the trewys that takyn war,
Bot I trow falset evermar
Sall have unfayr and evill ending.
Schyr Edward wist of this nathing
For off tresoun had he na thoucht,
Bot for the trew he levyt nocht[11]
To set wachis to the castell,
Ilk nycht he gert men walk it wele
And Nele Flemyng[12] wachit that nycht
With sexty men worthi and wycht.
And als sone as the day wes cler
Thai that within the castell wer
Had armyt thaim and maid thaim boun
And sone thar brig avalit down
And ischit intill gret plente,
And quhen Nele Flemyng gan thaim se
He send ane to the king in hy
And said to thaim that war him by,
'Now sall men se, Ik undretak,
Quha dar dey for his lordis sak.

Now ber you weill, for sekyrly
With all this mengne fecht will I,
Intill bargane thim hald sall we
Quhill that our maister armyt be.'
With that word assemblyt thai,
Thai war to few all-out perfay
With sic a gret rout for to fycht,
Bot nocht-forthi with all thar mycht
Thai dang on thaim sa hardely
That all thar fayis had gret ferly
That thai war all of swilk manheid
As thai na drede had of thar dede.
Bot thar fayis sa gane assaile
That na worschip thar mycht availe,
Than thai war slayne up everilkane
Sa clene that thar eschapyt nane
And the man that went to the king
For to warne him of thar isching
Warnyt him in full gret hy.
Schyr Edward wes commonaly
Callyt the king of Irland.
And quhen he hard sic thing on hand
In full gret hast he gat his ger,
Twelff wycht men in his chawmer wer
That armyt thaim in full gret hy,
Syne with his baner hardily
The myddis of the toun he tays.
Weill ner cummand war his fayis
That had delt all thar men in thre,
The Maundvell with a gret menye
Rycht throu the toun the way held doun,
The lave on athyr sid the toun
Held to mete thaim that fleand war,
Thai thoucht that all that thai fand thar
Suld dey but ransoune everilkane.
Bot uthyr-wayis the gle is gane,
For Schyr Edward with his baner
And his twelff I tauld you of er

On all that route sua hardely
Assemblyt that it wes ferly,
For Gib Harpar[13] befor him yeid
That wes the douchteast in deid
That than wes livand off his state,
And with ane ax maid him sic gat
That he the fyrst fellyt to ground,
And off thre in a litill stound
The Maundveill be his armyng[14]
He knew and roucht him sic a swyng
That he till erd yeid hastily.
Schyr Edward that wes ner him by
Reversyt him and with a knyff
Rycht in that place him reft the liff.
With that off Ardrossane Fergus
That wes a knycht rycht curageous
Assemblyt with sexty and ma,
Thai pressyt than thar fayis sua
That thai that saw thar lord slayne
Tynt hart and wald haf bene again,
And ay as Scottismen mycht be
Armyt thai come to the melle
And dang apon thar fayis sua
That thai all the bak gan ta,
And thai thaim chassyt to the yat,
Thar wes hard fycht and gret debat.
Thar slew Schyr Edward with his hand
A knycht that of all Irland
Was callit best and of maist bounte,
To surname Maundveill had he,
His awne name I can nocht say,
Bot his folk to sa hard assay
War set as thai of the doungeoun
Durst opyn na yhat na brig lat doun.
And Schyr Edwarde, Ik tak on hand,
Soucht thaim that fled thar to warand
Sa felly that of all perfay
That ischyt apon him that day

331

Thar eschapyt never ane
That thai ne war other tane or slayn,
For to the fycht Maknakill then
Come with twa hundreth spermen
And thai slew all thai mycht to-wyn.
This ilk Maknakill with a gyn
Wan off thar schippis four or fyve
And haly reft the men thar lif.
Quhen end wes maid of this fechting
Yeit then wes lyffand Nele Fleming.
Schyr Edward went him for to se,
About him slayne lay his menye
All in a lump on athyr hand
And he redy to dey throwand.
Schyr Edward had of him pite
And him full gretly menyt he
And regratyt his gret manheid
And his worschip and douchty deid,
Sic mayn he maid men had gret ferly
For he wes nocht custummabilly
Wont for to meyne men ony thing
Na wald nocht her men mak menyng.
He stud tharby till he wes ded
And syne had him till haly sted
And him with worschip gert he be
Erdyt with gret solemnite.
On this wis ischit Maundvill,
Bot sekyrly falset and gyle
Sall allwayis haif ane ivill ending
As weill is sene be this isching,
In tyme of trewys ischit thai
And in sic tyme as on Pasche day
Quhen God rais for to sauf mankin
Fra wem of auld Adamys syne,[15]
Tharfor sa gret myschaunce thaim fell
That ilkane as ye hard me tell
War slayne up or takyn thar.
And thai that in the castell war

War set intill sic fray that hour
For thai couth se quhar na succour
Suld cum to releyff, and thai
Tretyt and till a schort day
The castell till him yauld fre
To sauff thaim lyff and lym, and he
Held thaim full weill his cunnand.
The castell tuk he in his hand
And vyttalyt weill and has set
A gud wardane it for to get,
And a quhill tharin restyt he.
Off him no mar now spek will we
Bot to King Robert will we gang
That we haff left unspokyn of lang.
Quhen he had convoyit to the se
His brodyr Edward and his menye
With schippes he maid him yar
Intill the Ilis for till fare
Walter Steward with him tuk he
His mawch and with him gret menyhe
And other men off gret noblay.
To Tarbart thai held thar way
In galayis ordanyt for thar far,
Bot thaim worthyt draw thar schippis thar,
And a myle wes betwix the seys
Bot that wes lownyt all with treis.
The king his schippis thar gert draw,
And for the wynd couth stoutly blaw
Apon thar bak as thai wald ga
He gert men rapys and mastis ta
And set thaim in the schippis hey
And sayllis to the toppis tey
And gert men gang tharby drawand,
The wyind thaim helpyt that wes blawand
Sua that in a litill space
Thar flote all our-drawin was.
And quhen thai that in the Ilis war
Hard how the gud king had thar

Gert his schippis with saillis ga
Out-our betwix the Tarbartis twa
Thai war abaysit sa uterly
For thai wyst throu auld prophecy
That he that suld ger schippis sua
Betwix thai seis with saillis ga
Suld wyne the Ilis sua till hand
That nane with strenth suld him with-
   stand.
Tharfor thai come all to the king,
Wes nane withstud his bidding
Outakyn Jhone off Lorne allane,
Bot weill sone eftre wes he tane
And present rycht to the king,
And thai that war of his leding
That till the king had brokyn fay
War all dede and distroyit away.
This Jhone of Lorne the king has tane
And send him furth to Dunbertane[16]
A quhill in presoun thar to be,
Syne to Louchlevyn[17] send wes he
Quhar he wes quhill in festnyng,
I trow he maid tharin ending.
The king quhen all the Ilis war
Brocht till his liking les and mar,
All that sesoun thar dwellyt he
At huntyng gamyn and at gle.
Quhill the king apon this maner
Dauntyt the Ilis as I tell her
The gud Schyr James off Douglas
Intill the Forest dwelland was
Defendand worthely the land.
That tyme in Berwik wes dwelland
Edmound de Cailow a Gascoun[18]
That wes a knycht of gret renoune
And intill Gascoune his contre
Lord off gret senyoury wes he.
He had Berwik in keping

And maid a prive gadering
And gat him a gret cumpany
Of wycht men armyt jolily,
And the nethyr end of Tevidale
He prayit doun till him all hale
And of the Mers[19] a gret party,
Syne towart Berwik went in hy.
Schyr Adam of Gordoun that than
Wes becummyn Scottisman
Saw thaim dryf sua away thar fe
And wend thai had bene quhone for he
Saw bot the fleand scaill perfay
And thaim that sesyt in the pray.
Than till Schyr James of Douglas
Into gret hye the way he tais
And tauld how Inglismen thair pray
Had tane and syne went thar way
Toward Berwik with all thar fee,
And said thai quheyn war and gif he
Wald sped him he suld weill lichtly
Wyn thaim and reskew all the ky.
Schyr James rycht soyne gaf his assent
Till follow thame and furth is went
Bot with the men that he had thair
And met hym by the gat but mair.
Thai followit thame in full gret hy
And com weill neir thame hastely
For or thai mycht thame fully se
Thai come weill ner with thair menye,
And than bath the forreouris and the scaill
Intill a childrome[20] knyt all haill
And wes a rycht fair cumpany.
Befor thame gert thai driff the ky
With knavis and swanys that na mycht
Had for to stand in feld and fycht,
The lave behynd thaim maid a stale.
The Douglas saw thar lump all hale
And saw thaim of sa gud covyn

333

And saw thai war sa mony syne
That thai for ane of his war twa.
'Lordingis,' he said, 'sen it is sua
That we haf chassyt of sic maner
That we now cummyn ar sa ner
That we may nocht eschew the fycht,
Bot gif we fouly ta the flycht,
Lat ilkane on his lemman mene[21]
And how he mony tyme has bene
On gret thrang and weill cummyn away.
Think we to do rycht sua today,
And tak we of this furd her-by
Our avantage for in gret hy
Thai sall cum on us for to fycht.
Set we than will and strenth and mycht
For to mete thaim rycht hardely.'
And with that word full hastily
He displayit his baner
For his fayis war cummand ner
That quhen thai saw he wes sa quhoyne[22]
Thocht thai suld with thaim sone haf
    done
And assemblit full hardely.
Thar men mycht se men fecht felly
And a rycht cruell melle mak
And mony strakys giff and tak.
The Douglas thar weill hard wes stad,
Bot the gret hardyment that he hade
Comfort hys men on sic a wys
That na man thocht on cowardys
Bot faucht sa fast with all thar mayn
That thai fele of thar fayis has slayn,
And thoucht thai be weill fer war ma
Than thai, yeit ure demanyt thaim sua[23]
That Edmound de Cailow wes ded
Rycht in that ilk fechtyn-stede,
And all the lave fra he wes done
War planly discomfyt sone,

And thai that chassyt sum has slayn
And turnyt the prayis all agayn.
The hardast fycht forsuth this wes
That ever the gud lord off Douglas
Wes in as off sa few mengne,
For nocht had bene his gret bounte
That slew thar chyftane in that fycht
His men had all to dede bene dycht.
He had intill custoume alway
Quhenever he come till hard assay
To preys him the chiftane to sla,
And her fell hap that he did sua,
That gert him haff victour fele sys.
Quhen Schyr Edmound apon this wis
Wes dede the gud lord off Douglas
To the Forest his wayis tays.
His fayis gretly gan him dred,
The word sprang weile fer of his deid
Sua that in Ingland ner tharby
Men spak of it commonaly.
Schir Robert Nevile that tid[24]
Wonnyt at Berwik ner besid
The march quhar the lord Douglas
In the forest repayrand was
And had at him gret invy,
For he saw him sa manlyly
Mak ay his boundis mar and mar.
He hard the folk that with him war
Spek off the lord Douglas mycht
And how he forsye wes in fycht
And how him fell oft fayr fortoun.
He wrethyt tharat all-soun
And said, 'Quhat wene ye, is thar nane
That ever is worth bot he allane.
Ye set him as he wer but per,
Bot Ik avow befor you her
Giff ever he cum intill this land
He sall fynd me ner at his hand,

And gif Ik ever his baner
May se displayit apon wer
I sall assembill on him but dout
All-thocht yhe hald him never sa stout.'
Of this avow sone bodword was
Brocht to Schyr James of Douglas
That said, 'Gif he will hald his hycht
I sall do sa he sall haiff sycht
Off me an my cumpany
Yeyt or oucht lang wele ner him by.'
Hys retenew than gaderyt he
That war gud men of gret bounte,
And till the march in gud aray
Apon a nycht he tuk the way
Sua that into the mornyng arly
He wes with all his cumpany
Befor Berwik and thar he maid
Men to display his baner brad,
And of his menye sum sent he
For to bryn townys twa or thre,
And bad thaim sone agayne thaim sped
Sua that on hand giff thar come ned
Thai mycht be for the fycht redy.
The Nevill that wyst witterly
That Douglas cummyn wes sa ner
And saw all braid stand his baner,
Than with the folk that with him war
And he had a gret menye thar
For all the gud off that countre
Intill that tyme with him had he
Sua that he thar with him had then
Wele may then war the Scottismen,
He held his way up till a hill
And said, 'Lordingis, it war my will
To mak end off the gret deray
That Douglas mayis us ilk day,
Bot me think it spedfull that we
Abid quhill his men scalit be

Throu the countre to tak thar pray,
Than fersly schout on thaim we may
And we sall haf thaim at our will.'
Than all thai gaf assent thar-till
And on the hill abaid howand.
The men fast gaderyt of the land
And drew till him in full gret hy.
The Douglas then that wes worthi
Thoucht it wes foly mar to bid,
Towart the hill than gan he rid,
And quhen the Nevill saw that thai
Wald nocht pas furth to the forray
Bot pressyt to thaim with thar mycht
He wyst weill than that thai wald fycht
And till his mengye gan he say,
'Lordingis, now hald we furth our way,
Her is the flour of the countre
And may then thai alsua ar we,
Assembill we then hardely,
For Douglas with yone yhumanry
Sall haf na mycht till us perfay.'
Then in a frusch assemblyt thai,
Than mycht men her the speris brast
And ilkane ding on other fast,
And blude bryst out at woundis wid.
Thai faucht fast apon athyr sid
For athyr party gan thaim payn
To put thar fayis on bak agayn.
The lordis off Nevill and Douglas
Quhen at the fechting fellast was
Met togidder rycht in the preys,
Betwix thaim than gret bargane wes.
Thai faucht felly with all thar maucht,
Gret routis ather othyr raucht,
Bot Douglas starkar wes Ik hycht
And mar usyt alsua to fycht,
And he set hart and will alsua
For to deliver him of his fa

Quhill at the last with mekill mayn
Off fors the Nevill has he slayn,
Then his ensenye hey gan cry
And the lave sa hardely
He ruschyt with his menye
That intill schort tym men mycht se
Thar fayis tak thaim to the flycht
And thai thaim chassyt with all thar mycht
Schir Rauff Nevill in the chas
And the baron of Hiltoun[25] was
Takyn and other of mekill mycht.
Thar wes fele slayne into that fycht
That worthi in thar tym had bene.
And quhen the feld wes clengit clen
Sua that thar fayis everilkane
War slayne or chassyt awai or tan
Than gert he forray all the land
And sesyt all that ever thai fand
And brynt townys in thar way,
Syne hale and fer cummyn ar thai.
The prayis amang his menye
Eftre thar meritis delt he
And held na thing till his behuff.
Sic dedis aucht to ger men luff
Thar lord, and sua thai did perfay.
He tretyt thaim sa wisly ay
And with sa mekill luff alsua
And sic avansement wald ma

Off thar deid that the mast cowart
He maid stoutar then a libart,
With cherysing thusgat maid he
His men wycht and of gret bounte.
Quhen Nevill thus was brocht to ground
And of Cailow auld Schyr Edmound,
The drede of the lord of Douglas
And his renoune sa scalit was
Throu-out the marchis of Ingland
That all that war tharin wonnand
Dred him as the fell devill of hell,
And yeit haf Ik hard otfsys tell
That he sa gretly dred wes than
That quhen wivfys wald childer ban[26]
Thai wald rycht with ane angry face
Betech thaim to the blak Douglas.
Throu his gret worschip and bounte
Sua with his fayis dred wes he
That thaim growyt to her his name.
He may at ese now dwell at hame
A quhill for I trow he sall nocht
With fayis all a quhile be socht.
Now lat him in the Forest be,
Off him spek now no mar will we,
Bot off Schyr Edward the worthi
That with all his chevalry
Wes at Cragfergus yeit liand
To spek mar we will tak on hand

BOOK XVI

Quhen Schyr Edward, as Ik said ar,
Had discomfyt Richard of Clar
And of Irland all the barnage[1]
Thris throu his worthi vasselag
And syne with all his men of mayn
Till Cragfergus wes cummyn agayn,

The gud erle of Murreff Thomas
Tuk leyff in Scotland for to pas,
And he him levyt with a gruching,
And syne him chargyt to the king
To pray him specialli that he
Cum intill Irland him to se,

336

For war thai bath into that land
Thai suld fynd nane suld thaim withstand.
The erle furth thane his way has tane
And till his schipping is he gayn
And sayllyt weill out-our the se.
Intill Scotland sone aryvit he,
Syne till the king he went in hy,
And he resavyt him glaidsumly
And speryt of his brodyr fayr
And of journayis that thai had thar,
And he him tauld all but lesing.
Quhen the king left had the spering
His charge to the gud king tauld he,
And he said he wald blythly se
Hys brother and se the affer
Off that cuntre and off thar wer.
A gret mengye then gaderyt he,
And twa lordys of gret bounte
The tane the Stewart Walter was
The tother James off Douglas
Wardanys in his absence maid he
For to maynteyme wele the countre,
Syne to the se he tuk the way
And at Lochriane[2] in Galloway
He schippyt with all his menye,
To Cragfergus sone cummyn is he.
Schyr Edward of his come wes blyth
And went doun to mete him swyth
And welcummyt him with glaidsome cher,
Sa did he all that with him wer
And specially the erle Thomas
Off Murreff that his nevo[3] was,
Syne till the castell went thai yar
And maid thaim mekill fest and far.
Thai sojournyt that dayis thre
And that in myrth and jolyte.
King Robert apon this kyn wis[4]
Intill Irland aryvit is,

And quhen in Cragfergus had he
With his men sojournyt dayis thre
Thai tuk to consaill that thai wald
With thar folk thar wayis hald
Throu all Irland fra end till other.
Schyr Edward than the kingis brother
Befor in the avaward raid,
The king himselff the rerward maid[5]
That had intill his cumpany
The erle Thomas that wes worthi.
Thar wayis southwart haff thai tane
And sone ar passyt Inderwillane[6].
This wes in the moneth of May
Quhen byrdis syngis in ilk spray
Melland thar notis with seymly soune
For softnes of the swet sesoun,
And levys off the branchys spredis
And blomys brycht besid tham bredis
And feldis ar strowyt with flouris
Well saverand of ser colouris
And all thing worthis blyth and gay,
Quhen that this gud king tuk his way
To rid southwart as I said ar.
The wardane than Richard of Clar
Wyst the king wes aryvyt sua
And wyst that he schup him to ta
His way towart the south contre,
And of all Irland assemblit he
Bath burges[7] and chevalry
And hobilleris and yhumanry[8]
Quhill he had ner fourty thousand.
Bot he wald nocht yet tak on hand
With all his fayis in feld to fycht
Bot he umbethocht him of ane slycht,
That he with all his gret menye
Wald in a wod enbuschit be
All prively besid the way
Quhar that thar fayis suld away,

337

And lat the avaward pas fer by
And syne assembill hardely
On the rerward with all thar men.
Thai did as thai divisyt then,
In ane wod thai enbuschit wer,
The Scottis ost raid by thaim ner
Bot thai na schawing of thaim maid.
Schyr Edward weill fer forouth rad
With thaim that war of his menye,
To the rerward na tent tuk he,[9]
And Schyr Richard of Clar in hy
Quhen Schyr Edward wes passyt by
Send lycht yomen that weill couth schout
To bykkyr the rerward apon fute.
Then twa of thaim that send furth war
At the wod sid thaim bykkerit thar
And schot amang the Scottismen.
The king that had thar with him then
Weill fyve thousand wicht and worthi
Saw thai twa sa abandounly
Schut amang thaim and cum sa ner.
He wist rycht weill withoutyn wer
That thai rycht ner suppowall had,[10]
Tharfor a bidding has he mad
That na man sall be sa hardy
To prik at thaim, bot sarraly
Rid redy ay into bataill
To defend gif men wald assail,
'For we sall sone, Ik undreta,'
He said, 'haf for to do with ma.'
Bot Schyr Colyne Cambell, that ner
Was by quhar thai twa yhumen wer
Schoutand amang thaim hardily,
Prykyt on thaim in full gret hy
And sone the tane has our-tane
And with the sper him sone has slane,
The tother turnyt and schot agayne
And at the schot his hors has slane.

With that the king come hastily
And intill his malancoly
With a trounsoun[11] intill hys new
To Schyr Colyne sic dusche he geve
That he dynnyt on his arsoun,
Than bad he smertly tit him doun.
Bot other lordis that war him by
Ameyssyt the king into party,[12]
And he said, 'Breking of bidding[13]
Mycht caus all our discumfiting.
Weyne ye yone ribaldis durst assaill
Us sa ner intill our bataill
Bot giff thai had suppowaill ner.
I wate rycht weill withoutyn wer
That we sall haf to do in hy,
Tharfor luk ilk man be redy.'
With that weill neir thretty or ma
Off bowmen come and bykyrit sua
That thai hurt off the kingis men.
The king has gert his archeris then
Schoute for to put thai men agayn.
With that thai entryt in a playn
And saw arayit agayn thaim stand
In four bataillis fourty thousand.
The king said, 'Now, lordingis, lat se
Quha worthy in this fycht sall be,
On thaim foroutyn mar abaid.
Sa stoutly than on thaim thai raid
And assemblyt sa hardely
That off thar fayis a gret party
War laid at erd at thar meting.
Thar wes off speris sic bristing
As ather apon other raid
That it a wele gret frusch has maid,
Hors come thar fruschand heid for heid
Sua that fele on the ground felle deid.
Mony a wycht and worthi man
As ather apon other ran

338

War duschyt dede[14] doun to the ground,
The red blud out off mony a wound
Ruschyt in sa gret foysoun than
That off the blud the stremys ran.
And thai that wraith war and angry
Dang on other sa hardily
With wapnys that war brycht and bar
That mony a gud man deyit thar,
For thai that hardy war and wycht
And frontlynys with thar fayis gan fycht
Pressyt thaim formast for to be.
Thar mycht men cruell bargane se
And hard bataill. Ik tak on hand
In all the wer off Irland
Sa hard a fechting wes nocht sene,
The-quhether of gret victours nynteyne[15]
Schyr Edward has withoutyn wer,
And into les than in thre yer,
And in syndry bataillis of tha
Vencussyt thretty thousand and ma
With trappyt hors rycht to the fete,
Bot in all tymys he wes yete
Ay ane for fyve quhen lest wes he.
Bot the king into this melle
Had alwayis aucht of his fa-men
For ane, bot he sua bar him then
That his gud deid and his bounte
Confortyt sua all his menye
That the mast coward hardy wes,
For quhar he saw the thikkest pres
Sa hardely on thaim he raid
That thar about him roume he maid,
And Erle Thomas the worthi
Wes in all tyme ner him by
And faucht as he war in a rage,
Sua that for thar gret vasselage
Thar men sic gret hardyment gan tak
That thai na perell wald forsak

Bot thaim abandound sa stoutly
And dang apon thaim sa hardely
That all thar fayis affrayit war.
And thai that saw weill be thar far
That thai eschewyt sumdele the fycht
Than dang thai on with all thar mycht
And pressit thame dyngand so fast
That thai the bak gaf at the last,
And thai that saw thaim tak the flicht
Pressit thame than with all thare mycht
And in thar fleyng fele gan sla.
The kingis men has chassyt sua
That thai war scalyt everilkane.
Rychard off Clar the way has tane
To Devillyne into full gret hy
With other lordys that fled him by
And warnysyt bath castellis and townys
That war in thar possessiounys.
Thai war sa felly fleyit thar
That I trow Schyr Richard off Clar
Sall haiff na will to faynd his mycht
In bataill na in fors to fycht
Quhill King Robert and his menye
Is dwelland in that cuntre.
Thai stuffyt strenthis on this wis,
And the king that wes to pris
Saw in the feld rycht mony slane,
And ane of thaim that thar wes tane
That wes arayit jolyly
He saw greyt wonder tenderly,[16]
And askyt him quhy he maid sic cher.
He said him, 'Schyr, withoutyn wer
It is na wonder thocht I gret.
I se fele her lossyt the suet,
The flour of all north Irland
That hardyast war of thar hand
And mast doutyt in hard assay.'
The king said, 'Thou dois wrang perfay,

Thou has mar caus myrthis to ma[17]
For thou the dede eschapyt sua.'[18]
Richard off Clar on this maner
And all his folk discomfyt wer
With few folk, as I to you tauld,
And quhen Edward the Bruys the bauld
Wyst at the king had fochtyn sua
With sa fele folk, and he tharfra,
Mycht na man se a waer man.
Bot the gud king said till him than
That it wes his awne foly
For he raid sua unwittely
Sa far befor, and na vaward
Maid to thaim of the rerward,
For he said quha on wer wald rid
In a vaward he suld na tid
Pas fra his rerward fer of sycht
For gret perell sua fall thar mycht.
Off this fycht will we spek no mar,
Bot the king and all that thar war
Raid furthwartis in bettyr aray
And nerar togidder than er did thai.
Throu all the land playnly thai raid,
Thai fand nane that thaim obstakill maid.
Thai raid evyn forouth Drochindra[19]
And forouth Devillyne[20] syne alsua
And to giff battaill nane thai fand,
Syne went thai southwart in the land
And rycht till Lynrike[21] held thar way
That is the southmaist toun perfay
That in Irland may fundyn be.
Thar lay thai dayis twa or thre
And buskyt syne agayn to far,
And quhen that thai all redy war
The king has hard a woman cry,
He askyt quhat that wes in hy.
'It is the laynder[22], schyr,' said ane,
'That hyr child-ill rycht now has tane[23]

And mon leve now behind us her,[24]
Tharfor scho makys yone ivill cher.'[25]
The king said, 'Certis, it war pite
That scho in that poynt left suld be,
For certis I trow thar is no man
That he ne will rew a woman than.'[26]
His ost all thar arestyt he[27]
And gert a tent sone stentit be[28]
And gert hyr gang in hastily,
And other wemen to be hyr by.
Quhill scho wes deliver he bad
And syne furth on his wayis raid,
And how scho furth suld caryit be
Or ever he furth fur ordanyt he.
This wes a full gret curtasy
That swilk a king and sa mychty
Gert his men dwell on this maner
Bot for a pouer lauender.
Agayne northwart thai tuk thar way
Throu all Irland than perfay,
Throu all Connach[29] rycht to Devillyne,
And throu all Myth and Irell[30] syne
And Monester and Lenester,[31]
And syne haly throu Ulsister,
To Cragfergus foroutyn bataill,
For thar wes nane durst thaim assaill.
The kingis off Irchery
Come to Schyr Edward halily
And thar manredyn gan him ma
Bot giff that it war ane or twa.
Till Cragfergus thai come again,
In all that way wes nane bargain
Bot giff that ony poynye wer
That is nocht for to spek of her.
The Irsche kingis than everilkane
Hame till thar awne repayr ar gane,
And undretuk in allkyn thing
For till obey to the bidding

Off Schyr Edward that thar king callit thay.
He wes now weill set in gud way
To conquer the land halyly,
For he had apon his party
The Irschery and Ulsyster,
And he wes sa furth on his wer
That he wes passyt throu Irland
Fra end till uthyr throu strenth of hand.
Couth he haf governyt him throu skill
And folowyt nocht to fast his will
Bot with mesur haf led his dede
It wes weill lik withoutyn drede
That he mycht haiff conqueryt weill
The land of Irland ilkadele,
Bot his outrageous sucquedry
And will that wes mar than hardy
Off purpose lettyt him perfay,
As Ik herefter sall you say,
Now leve we her the noble king
All at his ese and his liking,
And spek we of the lord off Douglas
That left to kep the marches was.
He gert set wrychtis that war sleye
And in the halche of Lintaile
He gert thaim mak a fayr maner,
And quhen the housis biggit wer
He gert purvay him rycht weill thar
For he thoucht to mak ane infa
And to mak gud cher till his men.
In Rychmound wes wonnand then
Ane erle that men callit Schyr Thomas,
He had invy at the Douglas
And said gif that he his baner
Mycht se displayit apon wer
That sone assemble on it suld he.
He hard how the Douglas thocht to be
At Lyntailey[32] and fest to ma,
And he had wittering weill alsua

That the king and a gret menye
War passyt than of the countre
And the erle of Murref Thomas,
Tharfor he thocht the countre was
Febill of men for to withstand
Men that thame soucht with stalwart
    hand,
And of the marchis than had he
The governaile and the pouste.
He gaderyt folk about him then
Quhill he wes ner ten thousand men,
And wod-axys gert with him tak
For he thocht he his men wald mak
To hew Jedwort Forrest sa clene[33]
That na tre suld tharin be sene.
Thai held thaim forthwart on thar way,
Bot the gud lord Douglas that ay
Had spyis out on ilka sid
Had gud wittering that thai wald rid
And cum apon him suddanly.
Than gaderyt he rycht hastily
Thaim that he moucht of his menye,
I trow that than with him had he
Fyfty that worthy war and wicht
At all poynt armyt weill and dycht,
And off archeris a gret menye
Assemblyt als with him had he.
A place thar was thar in the way
Quhar he thocht weill thai suld away
That had wod apon athyr sid,
The entre wes weill large and wid
And as a scheild it narowit ay
Quhill at intill a place the way
Wes nocht a pennystane cast of breid.[34]
The lord of Douglas thidder yeid
Quhen he wyst thai war ner cummand,
And a-lauch on the ta hand
All his archeris enbuschit he

341

And bad thaim hald thaim all preve
Quhill that thai hard him rays the cry,
And than suld schut hardely
Amang thar fayis and sow thaim sar
Quhill that he throu thaim passyt war,
And syne with him furth hald suld thai.
Than byrkis on athyr sid the way
That young and thik war growand ner
He knyt togidder on sic maner
That men moucht nocht weill throu thaim
    rid.
Quhen this wes done he gan abid
Apon the tother half the way,
And Richmound in gud aray
Come ridand in the fyrst escheill.
The lord Douglas has sene him weill
And gert his men all hald thaim still
Quhill at thar hand thai come thaim till
And entryt in the narow way,
Than with a schout on thaim schot thai
And criyt on hycht, 'Douglas! Douglas!'
The Richmound than that worthi was
Quhen he has hard sua rais the cry
And Douglas baner saw planly
He dressyt thidderwart in hy
And thai come on sa hardily
That thai throu thaim maid thaim the way,
All that thai met till erd bar thai.
The Richmound borne doun thar was,
On him arestyt the Douglas[35]
And him reversyt and with a knyff[36]
Rycht in that place reft him the lyff.
Ane hat apon his helm he bar
And that tuk with him Douglas thar
In taknyng, for it furryt was,
And syne in hy thar wayis tays
Quhill in the wod thai entryt war.
The archeris weill has borne thaim thar

For weill and hardily schot thai.
The Inglis rout in gret affray
War set, for Douglas suddanly
With all thaim of his cumpany
Or ever thai wyst wes in thar rout
And thyrlyt thaim weill ner throchout,
And had almast all doyn his deid
Or thai to help thaim couth tak heid.
And quhen thai saw thar lord slayn
Thai tuk him up and turnyt agayn
To draw thaim fra the schot away,
Than in a plane assemblit thai
And for thar lord that thar wes dede
Thai schup thaim in that ilk sted
For to tak herbery all that nycht.
And than the Douglas that wes wicht
Gat wytteryng ane clerk Elys[37]
With weill thre hunder ennymys
All straucht to Lintaile war gayn
And herbery for thar ost had tane.
Than thidder is he went in hy
With all thaim of his cumpany
And fand clerk Elys at the mete
And his round about him set,
And thai come on thaim stoutly thar
And with swerdis that scharply schar
Thai servyt thaim full egrely.
Slayn war thai full grevously
That wele ner eschapyt nane,
Thai servyt thaim on sa gret wane
With scherand swerdis and with knyffis
That weile ner all left the lyvys.
Thai had a felloun efter mes,
That sourchargis to chargand wes.
Thai that eschapyt thar throu cas
Rycht till the ost the wayis tais
And tauld how that thar men war slayn
Sa clene that ner eschapyt nane.

342

And quhen thai of thar ost had herd
How that the Douglas with thaim ferd
That had thar herbryouris slane
And ruschyt all thaim self agayn
And slew thar lord in-myd thar rout,
Thar wes nane of thaim all sa stout
That mar will than had till assaile
The Douglas, tharfor to consaill
Thai yeid and to purpose has tane
To wend hamwart, and hamwart ar gan
And sped thaim sua apon thar way
That in Ingland sone cummyn ar thai.
The forest left thai standand still,
To hew it than thai had na will
Specially quhill the Douglas
Sua ner-hand by thar nychtbur was.
And he that saw thaim torne agayn
Persavyt weill thar lord wes slayn
And be the hat that he had tane
He wist alsua weill, for ane
That takyn wes said him suthly
That Rychmound commounly
Wes wount that furryt hat to wer.
Than Douglas blythar wes than er
For he wist weill that Rychmound
His felloun fa wes brocht to the ground.
Schyr James off Douglas on this wis
Throu his worschip and his empris
Defendyt worthely the land.
This poynt of wer, I tak on hand,
Wes undretane full apertly
And eschevyt rycht hardely,
For he stonayit foroutyn wer
That folk that well ten thousand wer
With fyfty armyt men but ma.
I can als tell you other twa
Poyntis that wele eschevit wer
With fyfty men, and but wer

Thai war done sua rycht hardely
That thai war prisit soveranly
Atour all othir poyntis of wer
That in that tym eschevit wer
This wes the fyrst that sua stoutly
Wes brocht till end wele with fifty
Into Galloway the tother fell
Quhen as ye forouth herd me tell
Schyr Edward the Bruys with fifty
Vencussyt of Sanct Jhon Schyr Amery
And fyften hunder men be tale.
The thrid fell intill Esdaill[38]
Quhen that Schyr Jhone the Soullis was
The governour of all that place,
That to Schyr Androw Hardclay[39]
With fifty men withset the way
That had thar in his cumpany
Thre hunder horsyt jolyly.
This Schyr Jhone intill playn melle
Throu soverane hardiment and bounte
Vencussyt thaim sturdely ilkan
And Schyr Andrew in hand has tane,
I will nocht rehers the maner
For quha-sa likis thai may her
Young wemen quhen thai will play
Syng it amang thaim ilk day.
Thir war the worthi poyntis thre
That I trow evermar sall be
Prissyt quhile men may on thaim mene.
It is well worth foroutyn wene
That thar namys for evermar,
That in thar tym sua worthi war
That men till her yeit has daynte,
For thar worschip and thar bounte
Be lestand ay furth in loving,
Quhar He that is of hevynnys king
Bring thaim he up till hevynnys blis
Quhar allwayis lestand loving is.

In this tym that the Richmound
Was on this maner brocht to ground
Men off the cost off Ingland
That dwelt on Humbre or nerhand[40]
Gaderyt thaim a gret mengne
And went in schippes to the se,
And towart Scotland went in hy
And in the Fyrth[41] come hastely.
Thai wend till haiff all thar liking
For thai wist weile that the king
Wes then fer out of the countre,
With him mony of gret bounte,
Tharfor into the Fyrth come thai
And endlang it up held thai
Quhill thai besid Ennerkething[42]
On west half towart Dunferlyng[43]
Tuk land and fast begouth to ryve.
The erle of Fyff and the schyrreff[44]
Saw to thar cost schippis approchand
Thai gaderyt to defend thar land
And a-forgayn the schippis ay
As thai saillyt thai held thar way
And thocht to let thaim land to tak.
And quhen the schipmen saw thaim mak
Swilk contenance in sic aray
Thai said amang thaim all that thai
Wald nocht let for thaim land to ta,
Than to the land thai sped thaim sua
That thai come thar in full gret hy
And aryvyt full hardely.
The Scottismen saw thar cummyng
And had of thaim sic abasing
That thai all samyn raid thaim fra
And the land letles lete thaim ta.
Thai durst nocht fecht with thaim, forthi
Thai withdrew thaim all halily
The-quhethyr thai war fyve hunder ner.
Quhen thai away thus ridand wer

And na defens begouth to schape,
Off Dunkeldyn the gud byschap[45]
That men callyt Wilyam the Sanctecler[46]
Come with a rout in gud maner.
I trow on hors thai war sexty,
Himselff was armyt jolyly
And raid apon a stalwart sted,
A chemer for till hele his wed
Apon his armour had he then
And armyt weill als war his men.
The erle and the schyrreff met he
Awaywart with thar gret menye,
And askyt thaim weill sone quhat hy
Maid thaim to turne sa hastily.
Thai said thar fayis with stalwart hand
Had in sic foysoun takyn the land
That thai thocht thaim all out to fele
And thaim to few with thaim to dele.
Quhen the bischap hard it wes sua
He said, 'The king aucht weill to ma
Off you, that takys sa wele on hand
In his absence to wer his land.
Certis giff he gert serff you weill
The gilt spuris rycht be the hele
He suld in hy ger hew you fra,
Rycht wald with cowartis men did sua.
Quha luffis his lord or his cuntre
Turne smertly now agayne with me.'
With that he kest of his chemer
And hynt in hand a stalwart sper
And raid towart his fayis in hy,
All turnyt with him halyly
For he had thaim reprovyt sua
That off thaim all nane fled him fra.
He raid befor thaim sturdely
And thai him folowyt sarraly
Quhill that thai come ner approchand
To thar fayis that had tane land,

344

And sum war knyt in gud aray
And sum war went to the foray.
The gud bischap quhen he thaim saw
He said, 'Lordingis, but drede or aw
Pryk we apon thaim hardely
And we sall haf thaim wele lychtly.
Se thai us cum but abaysing
Sua that we mak her na stinting
Thai sall weill sone discumfyt be.
Now dois weill, for men sall se
Quha luffis the kingis mensk today.'[47]
Than all togidder in gud aray
Thai prekyt apon thaim sturdely,
The byschap that wes rycht hardy
And mekill and stark raid forouth ay.
Than in a frusche assemblit thai,
And thai that at the fryst meting
Feld off the speris sa sar sowing
Wandyst and wald haiff bene away,
Towart thar schippis in hy held thai,
And thai thaim chassyt fellounly
And slew thaim sua dispitously
That all the feldis strowyt war
Off Inglismen that slane war thar,
And thai yeyt that held unslayne
Pressyt to the se agayne,
And Scottismen that chassyt sua
Slew all that ever thai mycht ourta.
Bot thai that fled yeit nocht-forthi
Sua to thar schippis gan thaim hy,
And in sum barge sua fele gan ga
And thar fayis hastyt thaim sua
That thai our-tumblyt and the men
That war tharin war drownyt then.
Thar did ane Inglisman perfay
A weill gret strenth as Ik hard say,
For quhen he chassyt wes till his bat
A Scottisman that him handlyt hat

He hynt than be the armys twa,
And, war him wele or war him wa,
He evyn apon his bak him slang
And with him to the bat gan gang
And kest him in all mawgre his,
This wes a wele gret strenth i-wis.
The Inglismen that wan away
To thar schippis in hy went thai
And saylyt hame angry and wa
That thai had bene rebutyt sua.
Quhen that the schipmen on this wis
War discumfyt as I devys
The byschap that sa weill him bar
That he all hartyt that thar war
Was yeyt into the fechtyn-sted
Quhar that fyve hunder ner war ded
Foroutyn thaim that drownyt war,
And quhen the feld was spulyeit bar
Thai went all hame to thar repar.
To the byschap is fallyn fayr
That throu his price and his bounte[48]
Wes eschevyt swilk a journe.
The king tharfor ay fra that day
Him luffyt and prisyt and honoryt ay
And held him in suylk daynte
That his awne bischop him callit he.
Thus thai defendyt the countre
Apon bath halffis the Scottis se[49]
Quhill that the king wes out off land
That than as Ik haf borne on hand
Throu all Irland his cours had maid
And agane to Cragfergus raid.
And quhen his broder as he war king[50]
Had all the Irschery at bidding
And haly Ulsistre alsua
He buskyt hame his way to ta.
Off his men that war mast hardy
And prisyt mast of chevalry

With his broder gret part left he,
And syne is went him to the se.
Quhen thar levys on ather party
Wes tane he went to schip him in hy,
The Erle Thomas with him he had,

Thai raissyt sayllis but abaid
And in land off Galloway
Forout perell aryvyt thai.

BOOK XVII

The lordis off the land war fayne
Quhen thai wist he wes cummyn agan
And till him went in full gret hy,
And he ressavit thaim hamlyly
And maid thaim fest and glaidsum cher,
And thai sa wonderly blyth wer
Off his come that na man mycht say,
Gret fest and fayr till him maid thai.
Quharever he raid all the countre
Gaderyt in daynte him to se,
Gret glaidschip than wes in the land.
All than wes wonnyn till his hand,
Fra the Red Swyre to Orknay
Wes nocht off Scotland fra his fay
Outakyn Berwik it allane.[1]
That tym tharin wonnyt ane
That capitane wes of the toun,
All Scottismen in suspicioun
He had and tretyt thaim tycht ill.
He had ay to thaim hevy will
And held thaim fast at undre ay,
Quhill that it fell apon a day
That a burges Syme of Spalding[2]
Thocht that it wes rycht angry thing
Suagate ay to rebutyt be.
Tharfor intill his hart thocht he
That he wald slely mak covyne
With the marchall, quhays cosyne
He had weddyt till him wiff,

And as he thocht he did belyff.
Lettrys till him he send in hy
With a traist man all prively,
And set him tym to cum a nycht
With leddrys and with gud men wicht
Till the kow yet all prively,
And bad him hald his trist trewly
And he suld mete thaim at the wall,
For his walk thar that nycht suld fall.[3]
Quhen the marchell the lettre saw
He umbethocht him than a thraw,
For he wist be himselvyn he
Mycht nocht off mycht no power be
For till escheyff sa gret a thing,
And giff he tuk till his helping
Ane, other suld wrethit be.
Tharfor rycht to the king yeid he
And schawyt him betwix thaim twa
The letter and the charge alsua.
Quhen that the king hard that this trane
Spokyn wes intill certayne
That him thocht tharin na fantis
He said him, 'Certis thou wrocht as wis
That has discoveryt the fyrst to me,
For giff thou had discoveryt the
To my nevo the Erle Thomas
Thou suld disples the lord Douglas,
And him alsua in the contrer,
Bot I sall wyrk on sic maner

That thou at thine entent sall be
And haff of nane of thaim mawgre.
Thou sall tak kep weill to the day,
And with thaim that thou purches may
At evyn thou sall enbuschit be
In Duns Park[4], bot be preve,
And I sall ger the Erle Thomas
And the lord alsua of Douglas
Ather with a soume of men
Be thar to do as thou sall ken.'
The marchell but mar delay
Tuk leve and held furth on his way
And held his spek preve and still
Quhill the day that wes set him till.
Than of the bast of Lothiane
He with hym till his tryst has tane
For schyrreff tharoff than wes he.
To Duns Park with his menye
He come at evyn prively,
And syne with a gud cumpany
Sone eftyr come the Erle Thomas
That wes met with the lord Douglas.
A rycht fayr cumpany thai war
Quhen thai war met togidder thar,
And quhen the marchell the covyn
To bath the lordis lyne be lyne
Had tauld, thai went furth on thar way.
Fer fra the toun thar hors left thai,
To mak it schort sua wrocht thai then
That but seyng off ony men
Outane Sym of Spaldyn allane
That gert that deid be undertane
Thai set thar leddrys to the wall,
And but persaving come up all
And held thaim in a nuk preve
Quhill that the nycht suld passit be,
And ordanyt that the maist party
Off thar men suld gang sarraly

With thar lordis and hald a stale,
And the remanand suld all hale
Skaill throu the toun and tak or sla
The men that thai mycht ourta.
Bot sone this ordynance brak thai,
For alsone as it dawyt day
The twa partis off thar men and ma
All scalyt throu the toun gan ga.
Sa gredy war thai to the gud
That thai ran rycht as thai war woud
And sesyt housis and slew men,
And thai that saw thar fayis then
Cum apon thaim sa suddanly
Throu-out the toun thai raissyt the cry
And schot togidder her and thar,
As ay as thai assemblyt war
Thai wald abid and mak debate.
Had thai bene warnyt wele I wate
Thai suld haiff sauld thar dedis der
For thai war gud men and thai wer
Fer ma than thai were that thaim socht,
Bot thai war scalyt that thai mocht
On na maner assemblyt be.
Thar war gret melleys twa or thre,
Bot Scottismen sa weile thaim bar
That thar fayis ay ruschyt war
And contraryit at the last war sua
That thai haly the bak gan ta,
Sum gat the castell bot nocht all
And sum ar slydyn our the wall
And sum war intill handis tane
And sum war intill bargane slane.
On this wis thaim contenyt thai
Quhill it wes ner none of the day,
Than thai that in the castell war
And other that fled to thaim thar
That war a rycht gret cumpany
Quhen thai the baneris saw simply

347

Standand and stuffyt with a quhone
Thar yattis haff thai opnyt sone
And ischit on thaim hardely.
Than the Erle Thomas that wes worthi
And the gud lord als off Douglas
With the few folk that with thaim was
Met thaim stoutly with wapnys ser.
Thar mycht men se that had bene ner
Men abandoune thaim hardely.
The Inglismen faucht cruelly[5]
And with all mychtis gan thaim payn
To rusche the Scottis men agayn.
I trow thai had done sua perfay
For thai war fewar fer than thai
Giff it na had bene a new-mad knycht
That till his name Schyr Wilyam[6] hycht,
Off Keyth and off Gallistoun
He hycht throu difference of sournoune,
That bar him sa rycht weill that day
And put him till sua hard assay
And sic dyntis about him dang
That quhar he saw the thikkest thrang
He pressyt with sa mekill mycht
And sua enforslye gan fycht
That he maid till his mengne way,
And thai that ner war by him ay
Dang on thar fayis sua hardely
That thai haff tane the bak in hy
And till the castell held the way,
And at gret myscheiff entryt thai
For thai war pressyt thar sa fast
That thai fele lesyt of the last.
Bot thai that entryt nocht-forthi
Sparyt thar yattis hastily
And in hy to the wallis ran
For thai war nocht all sekyr than.
The toun wes takyn on this wis
Throu gret worschip and hey empris,

And all the gud that thai thar fand
Wes sesyt smertly intill hand.
Vittaill they fand in gret foysoun
And all that fell to stuff off toun
That kepyt thai fra destroying,
And syn has word send to the king,
And he wes off that tything blyth
And sped him thidderwart swith
And as he throu the cuntre raid
Men gaderyt till him quhill he haid
A mekill rout of worthi men,
And the folk that war wonnand then
Intill the Mers and Tevidaill
And in the Forest als all hale
And the est end off Lothiane
Befor that the king come ar gane
To Berwik with sa stalwart hand
That nane that wes that tyme wonnand
On yond half Tweid durst weil apper.[7]
And thai that in the castell wer
Quhen thai thar fayis in sic plente
Saw forouth thaim assemblyt be
And had na hop of reskewing
Thai war abaysit in gret thing,
Bot thai the castell nocht-forthi
Held thai fyve dayis sturdely
Syne yauld it on the sext day,
And till thar countre syne went thai.
Thus wes the castell and the toun
Till Scottis mennys possessioun
Brocht, and sone eftre he king
Come ridand with his gadering
To Berwik, and in the castell
He wes herbrid bath fayr and weill
And all his lordis him by,
The remanand commonaly
Till herbry till the toun ar gane.
The king has then to consaill tan

That he wald nocht brek doun the wall
Bot castell and the toun witthall
Stuff weill with men and with vittaill
And alkyn other apparaill
That mycht availe or ellis myster
To hald castell or toun off wer,
And Walter Stewart of Scotland
That than wes young and avenand
And sone-in-laucht wes to the king
Haid sa gret will and sic yarnyng
Ner-hand the marchis for to be
That Berwik to yemsell tuk he,
And resavit of the king the toun
And the castell and the dongeoun.
The king gert men of gret noblay
Ryd intill Ingland for to pray
That brocht out gret plente of fe,
And sum contreis trewyt he
For vittaill, that in gret foysoun
He gert bring smertly to the toun
Sua that bath castell and toun war
Well stuffyt for a yer and mar.
The gud Stewart off Scotland then
Sent for his frendis and his men
Quhill he had with him, but archeris
And but burdouris and awblasteris,
Fyve hunder men wycht and worthi
That bar armys of awncestry.
Jhone Crab a Flemyng[8] als had he
That wes of sa gret sutelte
Till ordane and mak apparaill
For to defend and till assaill
Castell of wer or than cite
That nane sleyar mycht fundyn be.
He gert engynys and cranys ma
And purvayit Grec fyr[9] alsua,
Spryngaldis[10] and schot on ser maneris
That to defend castellis afferis

He purvayit intill full gret wane,
Bot gynnys for crakys had he nane
For in Scotland yeit than but wene
The us of thaim had nocht bene sene.
Quhen the toun apon this wis
Was stuffyt as Ik her divis
The nobill king his way has tane
And riddyn towart Lowthiane,
And Walter Stewart[11] that wes stout
Be-left at Berwik with his rout
And ordanyt fast for apparaill
To defend giff men wald assail.
Quhen to the king of Ingland
Was tauld how that with stalwart hand
Berwik wes tane and stuffyt syn
With men and vittaill and armyn
 He wes anoyit gretumly
And gert assermbill all halely
His consaill, and has tane to reid
That he hys ost will thidder leid
And with all mycht that he mycht get
To the toune ane assege set,
And gert dyk thaim sa stalwartly
That quhill thaim likyt thar to ly
Thai suld fer out the traister be.
And gif the men of the contre
With strenth of men wald thaim assaill
At thar dykis into bataill
Thai suld avantage have gretly,
Thocht all Scottis for gret foly
War till assaill into fechting
At hys dykis sa stark a thing.
Quhen this consaill on this maner
Wes tane he gert bath fer and ner
Hys ost haly assemblyt be,
Ane gret folk than with him had he.
Off Longcastell the Erle Thomas[12]
That syne wes sanct as men sayis

In his cumpany wes thar
And all the erllys that als war
In Ingland worthi for to fycht,
And baronys als of mekill mycht
With him to that assege had he,
And gert his schippis by the se
Bring schot and other apparaill
And gret warnysone of vittaill.
To Berwik with all his menye
With his bataillis arayit come he,
And till gret lordis ilkane sindry
Ordanyt a feld for thar herbry.
Than men mycht sone se pailyounys
Be stentyt of syndry fassounys
That thai a toune all sone maid thar
Mar than bath toun and castell war.
On other half syne on the se
The schippis come in sic plente
With vittaill armyng and with men
That all the havyn wes stoppyt then.
And quhen thai that war in the toun
Saw thar fayis in sic foysoun
Be land and se cum sturdely,
Thai as wycht men and rycht worthi
Schup thaim to defend thar steid
That thai in aventur of deid
Suld put thaim or than rusch agane
Thar fayis, for thar capitane
Tretyt thaim sa luflely,
And thar-with-all the mast party
Off thaim that armyt with him wer
War of his blud and sib him ner,
Or ellis war his elye.
Off sic confort men mycht thaim se
And of sa rycht far contenyng
As nane of thaim had abaysing.
On dayis armyt weill war thai
And on the nycht wele walkyt ay,

Weill sex dayis sua thai abaid
That na full gret bargane haid.
Intill this tyme that I tell her
That thai withoutyn bargayne wer
The Inglismen sa clossyt had
Thar ost with dykis that thai maid
That thai war strenthit gretumly.
Syne with all handis besely
Thai schup thaim with thair apparaill
Thaim of the toun for till assaill,
And of our ladys evyn Mary
That bar the byrth that all gan by
That men callis hyr nativite
Sone in the mornyng men mycht se
The Inglis ost arme thaim in hy
And display baneris sturdely,
And assembill to thar baneris
With instrumentis of ser maneris
As scaffoldis leddris and covering
Pikkys, howis and with staff-slyng.
Till ilk lord and his bataill
Wes ordanyt quhar he suld assaill.
And thai within, quhen that thai saw
That mengne raung thaim sua on raw
Till thar wardis thai went in hy
That war stuffyt rycht stalwartly
With stanys and schot and other thing
That nedyt to thar defending,
And into sic maner abaid
Thair fayis that till assail thaim maid.
Quhen thai without war all redy
Thai trumpyt till asalt in hy,
And ilk man with his apparaill
Quhar he suld be went till assaill,
Till ilk kyrnell that war thar
Archeris to schut assignyt war,
And quhen on this wys thai war boun
Thai went in hy towart the toun

And fillyt the dykis hastily,
Syne to the wall rycht hardely
Thai went with leddris that thai haid.
Bot thai sa gret defend has maid
That war abovyne apon the wall
That oft leddris and men with-all
Thai gert fall flatlingis to the ground,
That men mycht se in a litill stound
Men assailand hardely
Dressand up leddris douchtely
And sum on leddris pressand war.
Bot thai that on the wall war thar
Till all perellis gan abandoun
Thaim till thar fayis war dongyn doun.
At gret myscheff defendyt thai
Thar toun, for, giff we suth sall say,
The wallis of the toun than wer
Sa law that a man with a sper
Mycht stryk ane other up in the face,
And the schot alsa thik thar was
That it war wondre for to se.
Walter Stewart with a menye
Raid ay about for to se quhar
That for to help mast myster war,
And quhar men presit mast he maid
Succour till his that myster haid.
The mekill folk that wes without
Haid enveronyt the toun about
Sua that na part of it wes fre.
Thar mycht men the assailiaris se
Abandoun thaim rycht hardely,
And the defendouris douchtely
With all thar mychtis gan thaim payn
To put thar fayis with force agayn.
On this wis thaim contenyt thai
Quhill none wes passit off the day,
Than thai that in the schippis wer
Ordanyt a schip with full gret fer

To cum with all hyr apparaill
Rycht to the wall for till assaill.
Till myd-mast up thar bat thai drew
With armyt men tharin inew,
A brig thai had for to lat fall
Rycht fra the bat apon the wall,
With bargis by hir gan thai row
And pressyt thaim rycht fast to tow
Hyr by the brighous to the wall,
On that entent thai set thaim all.
Thai brocht hyr quhill scho come well ner,
Than mycht men se on seir maner
Sum men defend and sum assaill
Full besyly with gret travaill.
Within sa stoutly thai thaim bar
That the schipmen sa handlyt war
That thai the schip on na maner
Mycht ger to cum the wall sa ner
That thar fall-brig mycht neych thartill
For oucht thai mycht gud or ill,
Quhill that scho ebbyt on the grund,
Than mycht men in a litill stound
Se thaim be fer of wer covyn
Than thai war er that war hyr in.
And quhen the se wes ebbyt sua
That men all dry mycht till hyr ga,
Out off the toun ischit in hy
Till hyr a weill gret cumpany
And fyr till hyr has keyndlyt son.
Into schort tyme sua haif thai done
That thai in fyr has gert hyr bryn
And sum war slayn that war hyr in
And sum fled and away ar gane.
Ane engynour thar haif thai tane
That wes sleast of that myster
That men wist ony fer or ner,
Intill the toun syne entryt thai.
It fell thaim happily perfay

That thai gat in sa hastily
For thar come a gret cumpany
In full gret hy up by the se
Quhen thai the schip saw brynnand be,
Bot or thai come, the tother war past
The yat and barryt it rycht fast.
That folk assaylyt fast that day,
And thai within defendyt ay
On sic a wis that thai that war
With gret enforce assailland thar
Mycht do thar will on na maner.
And quhen that evynsang tym wes ner
The folk without that war wery
And sum woundyt full cruelly
Saw thaim within defend thaim sua,
And saw it wes nocht eyth to ta
The toun quhill sic defens wes mad,
And thai that intill stering had
The ost saw that thar schip war brynt
And of thaim that tharin wes tynt,
And thar folk woundyt and wery,
Thai gert blaw the retreit in hy.
Fra the schipmen rebotyt war
Thai lete the tother assaill no mar,
For throu the schip thai wend ilkan
That thai the toun wele suld haf tane.
Men sayis that ma schippis than sua
Pressyt that tym the toun to ta,
Bot for that thar wes brynt bot ane
And the engynour tharin wes tane
Her-befor mencioun maid I
Bot off a schip allanerly.
Quhen that thai blawyn had the retret
Thar folk that tholyt had paynys gret
Withdrew thaim haly fra the wall,
The assalt have thai left all.
And thai within that wery war
And mony of thaim woundyt sar

War blyth and glaid quhen that thai saw
Thar fayis on that wis thaim withdraw,
And fra thai wyst suthly that thai
Held to thar pailyounys thar way
Set gud wachys to thar wall,
Syne till thar innys went thai all
And essyt thaim that wery war,
And other that had woundis sar
Had gud lechys forsuth Ik hycht
That helpyt thaim as thai best mycht.
On athyr sid wery war thai,
That nycht thai did no mar perfay.
Fyve dayis eftyr thai war still
That nane till other did mekill ill.
Now leve we thir folk her lyand
All still as Ik have borne on hand
And turne the cours of our carping
To Schyr Robert the douchty king,
That assemblyt bath fer and ner
Ane ost quhen that he wist but wer
That the king sua of Ingland
Had assegyt with stalwart hand
Berwik quhar Walter Stewart was.
To purpose with his men he tais
That he wald nocht sua sone assaile
The king of Ingland with bataill
And at his dykis specially,
For that moucht weill turne to foly.
Tharfor he ordanyt lordis twa,
The erle off Murreff wes ane of tha
The tother wes the lord off Douglas
With fyften thousand men to pas
In Ingland for to bryn and sla
And sua gret ryote thar to ma
That thai that lay segeand the toun[13]
Quhen thai hard the destructioun
That thai suld intill Ingland ma,
Suld be sua dredand and sua wa

For thar childer and for thar wiffis
That thai suld drede to lese the lyvis,
And thar gudis alsua that thai
Suld dreid than suld be had away,
Thai suld leve thar sege in hy
And wend to reskew hastily
Thar gud thar frendis and thar land.
Tharfor, as Ik haf born on hand,
Thir lordis send he furth in hy
And thai thar way tuk hastily
And in Ingland gert bryn and sla,
And wrocht tharin sa mekill wa
As thai forrayit the countre
That it wes pite for to se
Till thaim that wald it ony gud,
For thai destroyit all as thai yhud.
Sua lang thai raid destroyand sua
As thai traversyt to and fra
That thai ar cummyn to Repoun[14]
And destroyit haly that toun,
At Borowbrig[15] syne thar herbry
Thai tuk and at Mytoun[16] tharby.
And quhen the men of that countre
Saw thar land sua destroyit be
Thai gaderyt into full gret hy
Archeris burges and yhumanry
Preystis clerkys monkis and freris[17]
Husbandis and men of all maneris
Quhill that thai samyn assemblit war
Wele twenty thousand men and mar,
Rycht gud armys inew thai had.[18]
The archebyschop of York thai mad
Thar capitane, and to consaill
Has tane that thai in plane bataill
Wald assaill the Scottismen[19]
That fewar than thai war then.[20]
Than he displayit his baner
And other byschappis that thar wer

Gert display thar baneris alsua,
All in a rout furth gan thai ga
Towart Mytoun the redy way.
And quhen the Scottismen hard say
Thai war to thaim cummand ner
Thai buskyt thaim on thar best maner
And delyt thaim in bataillis twa,[21]
Douglas the avaward gan ma,
The rerward maid Erle Thomas
For chyftane of the ost he was
And sua ordanyt in gud aray
Towart thar fayis thai held thar way.
Quhen athyr had on other sycht
Thai pressyt on bath half to the fycht.
The Inglismen come rycht sadly
With gud contenance and hardy
Rycht in a frusch with thar baner
Quhill thar fayis come sa ner
That thai thar visag mycht se,
Thre sper lenth[22] I trow weill mycht be
Betwix thaim, quhen sic abasing
Tuk thaim that but mar in a swyng
Thai gaff the bak all and to-ga.
Quhen the Scottismen had sene thaim
    sua
Effrayitly fle all thar way
In gret hy apon thaim schot thai
And slew and tuk a gret party,
The laiff fled full effrayitly
As thai best moucht to sek warand[23]
Thai chassyt sa ner at hand
That ner a thousand deyt thar.
Off thaim yet thre hunder war
Preystis that deyt in that chas,
Tharfor that bargane callit was
The chaptur of Mytone[24] for thar
Slayn sa mony prestis war.
Quhen this folk thus discomfyt was

353

And Scottismen had left the chas
Thai went thaim forthward in the land
Slayand sua and destroyand,
And thai that at the sege lay
Or it wes passyt the fyft day
Had maid thaim syndry apparal
To gang eftsonys till assaill.
Off gret gestis a sow thai maid
That stalwart heildyne aboun it had
With armyt men inew tharin
And instrumentis for to myne,[25]
Syndry scaffaldis thai maid withall
That war weill heyar than the wall,
And ordanyt als that be the se
The toun suld weill assaillyt be.
Thai within that saw thaim sua
Sua gret apparaill schap to ma
Throu Crabys consaill that wes sley
A crane thai haiff gert dres up hey
Rynnand on quheillis that thai mycht
    bring
It quhar that nede war of helping,
And pyk and ter als haiff thai tane
And lynt and herdis and brynstane
And dry treyis that weill wald brin
And mellyt ather other in,
And gret fagaldis[26] tharoff thai maid
Gyrdyt with irne bandis braid,
The fagaldis weill mycht mesuryt be
Till a gret townys quantite.
Thai fagaldis brynnand in a baill
With thar cran thocht thai till availl,
And gyff the sow come to the wall
To let it brynnand on hyr fall
And with stark chenyeis hald it thar
Quhill all war brynt up that thar war.
Engynys alsua for to cast
Thai ordanyt and maid redy fast

And set ilk man syne till his ward,
And Schyr Walter the gud Steward
With armyt men suld rid about
And se quhar that thar war mast dout
And succour thar with his menye.
And quhen thai in sic degre
Had maid thaim for defending,
On the Rud Evyn in the dawning[27]
The Inglis ost blew till assaill.
Than mycht men with ser apparaill
Se that gret ost cum sturdely,
The toun enveround thai in hy[28]
And assaillyt with sua gret will
For all thar mycht thai set thartill
That thaim pressyt fast on the toun.
Bot thai that gan thaim abandoun
To dede or than to woundis sar
Sa weill has thaim defendit thar
That leddrys to the ground thai slang,
And with stanys sa fast thai dang
Thar fayis that fele thar left liand
Sum dede sum hurt and sum swonand.
Bot thai that held on feyt in hy
Drew thaim away deliverly
And scounryt[29] nocht for that thing
Bot went stoutly till assailling,
And thai aboun defendyt ay
And set thaim to sa hard assay
Quhill that fele of thaim woundyt war,
And thai sa gret defens maid thar
That thai styntit thar fayis mycht.
Apon sic maner gan thai fycht
Quhill it wes ner none of the day,
Than thai without on gret aray
Pressyt thar sowe[30] towart the wall.
And thai within sone gert call
The engynour that takyn was,
And gret mannance till him mais

And swour that he suld dey bot he
Provyt on the sow sic sutelte
That he to-fruschyt hir ilk-dele,
And he that has persavyt wele
That the dede wes weill ner him till
Bot giff he mycht fulfill thar will
Thocht that he at his mycht wald do.
Bendyt in gret hy than wes scho
That till the sow wes evyn set,
In hy he gert draw the cleket[31]
And smertly swappyt out a stane.
Evyn our the sow the stane is gane
And behind it a litill wey
It fell, and than thai criyt hey
That war in hyr, 'Furth to the wall,
For dredles[32] it is ouris all.'
The gynour than deliverly[33]
Gert bend the gyn in full gret hy[34]
And the stane smertly swappyt out,
It flaw out quhetherand with a rout
And fell rycht evyn befor the sow.
Thar hartis than begouth to grow,
Bot yeyt than with thar mychtis all
Thai pressyt the sow towart the wall
And has hyr set tharto juntly.
The gynour than gert bend in hy
The gyne and wappyt out the stane
That evyn towart the lyft is gane[35]
And with gret wecht syne duschit down
Rycht be the wall in a randoun,
And hyt the sow in sic maner
That it that wes the mast summer[36]
And starkest for to stynt a strak
In sunder with that dusche it brak.
The men ran out in full gret hy,
And on the wallis thai gan cry
That thar sow wes feryt thar.
Jhone Crab that had his ger all yar

In his fagaldis has set the fyr
And our the wall syne gan thaim wyr
And brynt the sow till brundis bar.
With all thys fast assailyeand war
The folk without with felloun fycht,
And thai within with mekill mycht
Defendyt manlily thar steid
Into gret aventur off deid.
The schipmen with gret apparaill
Come with thar schippis till assail
With top-castell warnyst weill[37]
Off wicht men armyt into steill,[38]
Thar batis up apon thar mast
Drawyn weill hey and festnyt fast,
And pressyt with that gret atour
Towart the wall, bot the gynour
Hyt in the aspyne with a stane,
That the men that tharin war gane
Sum ded sum dosnyt come doun wyn-
land[39].
Fra thyne furth durst nane tak on hand
With schippis to preys thaim to the wall,
Bot the lave war assailyeand all
On ilk sid sa egrely
That certis it wes gret ferly
That that folk sic defens has maid
With the gret myscheiff that thai had,
For thar wallis sa law than wer
That a man rycht weill with a sper
Mycht stryk ane other up in the face
As her-befor said to you was,
And fele of thaim war woundit sar,
And the laiff sa fast travaillyt war
That nane had tyme rest for to ma,
Thar adversouys assaillyt sua.
Thai war within sa straitly stad
That thar wardane, that with him had
Ane hunder men in cumpany

Armyt that wicht war and hardy
And raid about for to se quhar
That his folk hardest presyt war
To releve thaim that had myster,
Come sindry tymys in placis ser
Quhar sum of the defendouris war
All dede and other woundyt sar,
Sua that he of his cumpany
Behuffyt for to leve thar party,
Sua that be he a cours had maid
About, of all the men he haid
Thar wes levyt with him bot ane
That he ne had left thaim everilkan
To releve quhar he saw myster.
And the folk that assailland wer[40]
At Mary yat[41] tohewyn haid
The barrais and a fyr had maid[42]
At the drawbrig and brynt it doun,[43]
And war thringand in gret foysoun
Rycht to the yat a fyr to ma.
Than thai within gert smertly ga
Ane to the wardane far to say
How thai war set in hard assay,
And quhen Schyr Walter Stewart herd
How men sa straitly with thaim ferd
He gert cum of the castell then
All that thar war off armyt men,
For thar that day assaillyt nane,
And with that rout in hy is gane
To Mary yat and to the wall
He send and saw the myscheff all,
And umbethocht him suddanly
Bot giff gret help war set in hy
Tharto, thai suld bryn up the yet
That fra the wall thai suld nocht let.
Tharfor apon gret hardyment
He suddanly set his entent,
And gert all wyd set up the yat

And the fyr that he fand tharat
With strenth of men he put away.
He set him to full hard assay,
For thai that war assailyeand thar
Pressyt on him with wapnys bar
And he defendyt with his mycht.
Thar mycht men se a felloun sycht
Off stabing, stocking and striking,
Thair maid thai sturdy defending
For with gret strenth of men the yat
Thai defendyt and stud tharat
Mawgre thar fayis, quhill the nycht
Gert thaim on bath half leve the fycht.
Thai off the ost quhen nycht gan fall
Fra the assalt withdrew thaim all.
Woundyt and wery and forbeft
With mad cher the assalt thai left
And till thar innys went in hy
And set thar wachis hastily,
The lave thaim esyt as thai mycht best
For thai had gret myster of rest.
That nycht thai spak commonaly
Off thaim within and had ferly
That thai sua stout defens had maid
Agayne the gret assalt thai haid.
And thai within on other party
Quhen thai thar fayis sa hastily
Saw withdraw thaim thai war all blyth,
And has ordanyt thar wachis swith
And syne ar till thar innys gane.
Thar wes bot full few of thaim slane
Bot fele war woundyt utterly,
The lave our mesur war wery.
It was ane hard assault perfay,
And certis I herd never say
Quhar quheyn mar defence had maid
That sua rycht hard assailling haid,
And off a thing that thar befell

356

Ik haff ferly that I sall tell,
That is that intill all that day
Quhen all thar mast assailyeit thai
And the schot thikkerst wes withall
Women with child and childer small[44]
In armfullis gaderyt up and bar[45]
Till thaim that on the wallis war[46]
Arrowes, and nocht ane slayne wes thar
Na yeit woundyt, and that wes mar
The myrakill of God almichty
And to noucht ellis it set can I.
On athyr syd that nycht thai war
All still, and on the morn but mar
Thar come tythandis out off Ingland
To thaim of the ost, that bar on hand
How that by Borowbrig at Mytoun
Thar men war slayn and dongyn doun,
And at the Scottismen throu the land
Raid yeit brynnand and destroyand.
And quhen the king had hard this tale
His consaile he assemblyt haile
To se quhether fayr war him till
To ly about the toun all still
And assailye quhill it wonnyn war,
Or than in Ingland for to fayr
And reskew his land and his men.
His consaill fast discordyt then,
For sotheroun men wald that he mad
Arest thar quhill he wonnyn haid
The toun and the castell alsua,
Bot northyn men wald na thing sua
That dred thar frendis for to tyn
And mast part of thar gudis syne
Throu Scottismennys cruelte,
Thai wald he lete the sege be
And raid for to reskew his land.
Off Longcastell I tak on hand
The Erle Thomas wes ane of tha

That consaillyt the king hame to ga,
And for that mar inclynyt he
To the folk of the south countre
Na to the northyn mennys will,
He tuk it to sa mekill ill
That he gert turs his ger in hy
And with his bataill halily[47]
That off the ost ner thrid part was
Till Ingland hame his way he tais.
But leve he hame has tane his gat,
Tharfor fell efter sic debat
Betwix him and the king that ay
Lastyt quhill Androw Harclay
That throu the king wes on him set
Tuk him rycht in Pomfret[48],
And on ane hill beside the toun
Strak off his hede but ransoun,
Tharfor syne hyngyt and drawyn[49] wes he
And with him a weill gret menye.
Men said syne efter this Thomas
That on this wis maid marter[50] was
Was saynct and myrakillis did,
Bot envy syne gert thaim be hid,
Bot quhether he haly wes or nane
At Pomfret thus was he slane.
And syne the king of Ingland
Quhen that he saw him tak on hand
To pas his way sa opynly,
Him thocht it wes perell to ly
Thar with the lave of his menye
Hys harnays tharfor tursit he
And intill Ingland hame gan he far.
The Scottismen that destroyand war
In Ingland sone hard tell tithing
Off this gret sege departing,
Tharfor thai tuk westwart the way
And till Carlele[51] hame went ar thai
With prayis and with presoneris

And other gudis on ser maneris.
The lordis to the king ar gain,
And the lave has thar wayis tain
Ilk man till his repayr agayne.
The king i-wys was wondre fayn
That thay war cummyn hale and fer,
And that thai sped on sic maner
That thai thar fayis discomfyt hade
And but tynsaill of men has maid
Rescours to thaim that in Berwik
War assegyt rycht till thar dyk.
And quhen the king had speryt tithand
How thai had farne in Ingland
And thai had tauld him all hale thar far
How Inglismen discumfyt war,
Rycht blyth intill his hart wes he
And maid them fest with gamyn and gle.
Berwik wes on this maner
Reskewyt and thai that tharin wer
Throu manheid and throu sutelte.
He wes worthi a prynce to be
That couth with wit sa hey a thing
But gret tynsaill bring till ending.
Till Berwik syne the way he tays
And quhen he hard thar how it ways
Defendyt rycht sua apertly,
He lovyt thaim that war thar gretly.
Walter Stewart his gret bounte

Out-our the laiff commendyt he
For the rycht gret defens he maid
At the yat quhar men brynt had
The brig as ye herd me dyvis,
And certis he wes weill to pris
That sa stoutly with plane fechting
At opyn yate maid defending.
Mycht he haff levyt quhill he had bene
Off perfyt eild, withoutyn wene
His renoun suld have strekyt fer,
Bot dede that walkis ay to mer
With all hyr mycht waik and worthy
Had at his worschip sic invi
That in the flour of his youtheid
So endyt all his douchti deid,
As I sall tell you forthermar.
Quhen the king had a quhill bene thar
He send for maysonys[52] fer and ner
That sleast war off that myster[53]
And gert weill ten fute hey the wall
About Berwykis toune our-all,
And syne towart Louthyane
With his menye his gat is gane.
And syne he gert ordane in hy
Bath armyt men and yhumenry
Intill Irland in hy to fayr
To help his brother that wes thar.

BOOK XVIII

Bot he that rest anoyit ay
And wald in travaill be alway,
A day forouth thar aryving
That war send till him fra the king,
He tuk his way southwart to far
Magre thaim all that with him war,

For he had nocht than in that land
Of all men I trow twa thousand,
Outane the kingis off Irchery
That in gret routis raid him by.
Towart Dundalk he tuk the way,
And quhen Richard of Clar hard say

That he come with sa few menye
All that he mycht assemblit he
Off all Irland off armyt men,
Sua that he had thar with him then
Off trappyt hors twenty thousand
But thai that war on fute gangand,
And held furth northward on his way.
And quhen Schyr Edward has hard say
That cummyn ner till him wes he
He send discouriouris him to se,
The Soullis and the Stewart war thai
And Schyr Philip the Mowbray,
And quhen thai sene had thar cummyng
Thai went agayne to tell tithing,
And said weill thai war mony men.
In hy Schyr Edward answerd then
And said that he suld fecht that day
Thoucht tribill and quatribill war thai.[1]
Schyr Jhone Stewart said, 'Sekyrly
I reid nocht ye fecht on sic hy,
Men sayis my brother is cummand
With fyften thousand men ner-hand,
And war thai knyt with you ye mycht
The traistlyer abid to fycht.'
Schyr Edward lukyt all angrely
And till the Soullis said in hy,
'Quhat sayis thou?' 'Schyr,' he said, 'Perfay
As my falow has said I say.'
And than to Schyr Philip said he.
'Schyr,' said he, 'sa our Lord me se
Me think na foly for to bid
Your men that spedis thaim to rid,
For we ar few, our fayis ar fele,
God may rycht weill our werdis dele,
Bot it war wondre that our mycht
Suld our-cum sa fele in fycht.'
Than with gret ire 'Allace,' said he,
I wend never till her that of the.[2]

Now help quha will for sekyrly
This day but mar baid fecht will I,
Sall na man say quhill I may drey
That strenth of men sall ger me fley.
God scheld that ony suld us blam
Gif we defend our noble nam.'
'Now be it swagat than,' quod thai,
'We sall tak that God will purvai.'
And quhen the kingis of Irchery
Herd say and wyst sekyrly
That thar king with sa quhone wald fycht
Agane folk of sa mekill mycht
Thai come till him in full gret hy
And consaillyt him full tenderly
For till abid his men, and thai
Suld hald thar fayis all that day
Doand, and on the morn alsua
With thar ronnyngis that thai suld ma.
Bot thar mycht na consail availe,
He wald algat hav bataile.
And quhen thai saw he wes sa thra
To fycht, thai said, 'Ye ma well ga
To fycht with yone gret cumpany,
Bot we acquyt us uterly
That nane of us will stand to fycht.
Assuris nocht tharfor in our mycht,
For our maner is of this land
To folow and fecht fleand
And nocht to stand in plane melle
Quhill the ta part discomfyt be.'
He said, 'Sen that your custum is
Ik ask at you no mar bot this,
That is that ye and your menye
Wald all togidder arayit be
And stand on fer but departing
And se our fycht and the ending.'
Thai said weill that thai suld do sua,
And syne towart thar men gan thai ga

That war weill twenty thousand ner.
Edward with thaim that with him wer
That war nocht fully twa thousand
Arayit thaim stalwartly to stand
Agayne fourty thousand and ma.
Schyr Edward that day wald nocht ta
His cot-armour, bot Gib Harper
That men held as withoutyn per[3]
Off his estate[4], had on that day
All hale Schyr Edwardis aray.
The fycht abad thai on this wis,
And in gret hy thar ennymys
Come till assemble all redy
And thai met thaim hardely.
Bot thai sa few war, south to say,
That ruschyt with thar fayis war thai,
And thai that pressyt mast to stand
War slane doun, and the remanand
Fled till the Irche to succour.
Schyr Edward that had sic valour
Wes dede and Jhone Stewart alsua
And Jhone the Soullis als with tha
And other als off thar cumpany.
Thai war vancussyt sa suddanly
That few intill the place war slane,
For the lave has thar wayis tane
Till the Irsche kingis that war thar
And in hale bataill howand wer.
Jhone Thomas-sone[5] that wes leder
Off thaim of Carrik that thar wer
Quhen he saw the discumfiting
Withdrew him till ane Irsch king
That off his aquentance had he,
And he resavit him in leawte.
And quhen Jhone cummyn wes to that king
He saw be led fra the fechting
Schyr Philyp the Mowbray the wicht

That had bene dosnyt into the fycht,
And with armys led wes he
With twa men apon a cause[6]
That wes betwix thaim and the toun
And strekyt lang in a randown.
Towart the toun thai held thar way,
And quhen in myd-cause war thai
Schyr Philip of his desynes
Ourcome, and persavit he wes
Tane and led suagat with twa.
The tane he swappyt sone him fra
And syne the tother in gret hy,
And drew the swerd deliverly
And till the fycht his wayis tays
Endlang the cause that than was
Fillyt intill gret foysoun
Off men that than went till the toun,
And he that met thaim agayn gan ma
Sic payment quhar he gan ga
That weile a hundre men gert he
Leve maugre tharis the cause.
As Jhone Thomas-sone said suthly
That saw his deid all halily
Towart the bataill evyn he yeid.
Jhone Thomas-sone that tuk gud heid
That thai war vencussyt all planly
Cryit on him in full gret hy
And said, 'Cum her for thar is nane
On lyve for thai ar dede ilkane.'
Than stud he still a quhill and saw
That thai war all doune of daw[7],
Syne went towart him saraly.
This Jhone wrocht syne sa wittely
That all that thidder fled than wer
Thocht that thai lossyt of thar ger
Come till Cragfergus hale and fer.
And thai that at the fechting wer
Socht Schyr Edward to get his heid

Amang the folk that thar wes dede
And fand Gib Harper in his ger,
And for sa gud hys armys wer
Thai strak hys hed of and syn it[8]
Thai have gert salt intill a kyt[9]
And sent it intill[10] Ingland
Till the King Edward in presand.[11]
Thai wend Schyr Edwardis it had bene,
Bot for the armyng that wes schene
Thai of the heid dissavyt wer[12]
All thocht Schyr Edward[13] deyt ther.
On this wis war thai noble men
For wilfulnes all lesyt then,
And that wes syne and gret pite
For had thar outrageous bounte
Bene led with wyt and with mesur,
Bot gif the mar mysaventur
Be fallyn thaim, it suld rycht hard thing
Be to lede thaim till outraying,
Bot gret outrageous surquedry[14]
Gert thaim all deir thar worschip by.
And thai that fled fra the melle
Sped thaim in hy towart the se
And to Cragfergus cummyn ar thai,
And thai that war into the way
To Schyr Edward send fra the king
Quhen thai hard the discumfiting
To Cragfergus thai went agayne.
And that wes nocht foroutyn payn,
For thai war mony tyme that day
Assailyeit with Irschery, bot thai
Ay held togidder sarraly
And defendyt sa wittely
That thai eschapyt oft throu mycht
And mony tyme alsua throu slycht,
For oft of tharis to thaim gaff thai
To lat thaim scaithles pas thar way,
And till Cragfergus come thai sua

That batis and schyppis gan thai ta
And saylyt till Scotland in hy
And thar aryvyt all saufly.
Quhen thai of Scotland had wittering
Off Schyr Edwardis vencussing
Thai menyt him full tenderly
Our all the land commounaly,
And thai that with him slayn war thar
Full tenderly als menyt war.
Edward the Bruys as I said her
Wes discumfyt on this maner
And quhen the feld wes clengit clene
Sua that na resistens wes sene
The wardane than Schyr Richard of Clar
And all the folk that with him war
Towart Dundalk has tane the way
Sua that rycht na debat maid thai
At that tym with the Irschery,
Bot to the toun thai held in hy,
And syne had send furth to the king
That had Ingland in governyng
Gib Harperis heid in a kyt.
Jhone Maupas till the king had it
And he ressavyt it in daynte,
Rycht blyth off that present wes he
For he wes glaid that he wes sua
Deliveryt off a felloun fa.
In hart tharoff he tuk sic prid
That he tuk purpos for to rid
With a gret ost in Scotland
For to veng him with stalwart hand
Off tray of travaill and of tene
That done tharin till him had bene,
And a rycht gret ost gaderit he
And gert his schippis be the se
Cum with gret foysoun of vittaill,
For at that tyme he wald him taile
To dystroy up sa clene the land

That nane suld leve tharin levand,
And with his folk in gret aray
Towart Scotland he tuk the way.
And quhen King Robert wist that he
Come on him with sic a mengne
He gaderyt his men bath fer and ner
Quhill sa fele till him cummyn wer,
And war als for to cum him to,
That him thocht he rycht weill suld do.
He gert withdraw all the catell
Off Lowthiane everilkdeill,
And till strenthis gert thaim be send
And ordanyt men thaim to defend,
And with his ost all still he lay
At Culros[15], for he wald assay
To gert hys fayis throu fasting
Be feblyst and throu lang walking,
And fra he feblist had thar mycht
Assembill than with thaim to fycht.
He thocht to wyrk apon this wis,
And Inglismen with gret maistrys
Come with thar ost in Lowthian
And sone till Edynburgh ar gan,
And thar abaid thai dayis thre.
Thar schippys that war on the se
Had the wynd contrar to thaim ay
Sua that apon na maner thai
Had power to the Fyrth to bring
Thar vittailis to releve the king,
And thai of the ost that faillyt met
Quhen thai saw that thai mycht nocht get
Thar vittaillis till thaim be the se
Thai send furth rycht a gret menye
For to forray all Lowthiane,
Bot cataill haf thai fundyn nane
Outakyn a bule that wes haltand[16]
That in Tranentis[17] corne thai fand.
That brocht thai till thar ost agayne,

And quhen the erle of Warayne
Saw that bule anerly cum swa
He askyt giff thai gat na ma,
And thai haff said all till him nay.
Than said he, 'Certis I dar say
This is the derrest best that I
Saw ever yeit, for sekyrly
It cost a thousand pound and mar.'
And quhen the king and thai that war
Off his consaill saw thai mycht get
Na cattell till thar ost till ete
That than of fasting had gret payn
Till Ingland turnyt thai agayn.
At Melros[18] schup thai for to ly
And send befor a cumpany
Thre hunder ner of armyt men.
Bot the lord Douglas that wes then
Besyd intill the Forest ner
Wyst of thar come and quhat thai wer,
And with thaim of his cumpany
Into Melros all prevely
He howyt in a buschement,
And a rycht sturdy frer he sent
Without the yate thar come to se,
And bad him hald him all preve
Quhill that he saw thaim cummand all
Rycht to the coynye thar of the wall,
And than cry hey, 'Douglas! Douglas!'
The frer than furth his wayis tais
That wes all stout derff and hardy,
Hys mekill hud helyt haly
The armur that he on him had,
Apon a stalwart hors he rad
And in his hand he had a sper,
And abaid apon that maner
Quhill that he saw thaim cummand ner,
And quhen the formest[19] passyt wer
The coynye[20] he criyt 'Douglas! Douglas!'

Than till thaim all a cours he mas
And bar ane doun deliverly,
And Douglas and his cumpany
Ischyt apon thaim with a schout,
And quhen thai saw sa gret a rout
Cum apon thaim sa suddanly
Thai war abaysyt gretumly
And gaf the bak but mar abaid.
The Scottis men amang thaim raid
And slew all that thai mycht our-ta,
A gret martyrdome thar gan thai ma,
And thai that eschapyt unslayne
Ar till thar gret ost went agayne
And tauld thaim quhatkyn welcummyng
Douglas thaim maid at thar meting
That convoyit thaim agayn rudly
And warnyt planly herbery.
The king of Ingland and his men
That saw thar herbriouris then
Cum rebutyt on that maner
Anoyit in thar hart thai wer,
And thocht that it war gret foly
Intill the wod to tak herbery,
Tharfor by Dryburgh[21] in the playn
Thai herbryit thaim and syne again
Ar went till Ingland thar way.
And quhen the King Robert hard say
That thai war turnyt hame agayn
And how thar herbriouris war slayn,
In hy his ost assemblit he
And went south our the Scottis se
And till Ingland his wayis tais.
Quhen his ost assemblyt ways
Auchty thousand he wes and ma
And aucht batallis he maid of tha,
In ilk bataill war ten thousand,
Syne went he furth till Ingland
And intill hale rout folowit sa fast

The Inglis king, quhill at the last
He come approchand to Biland[22]
Quhar at that tyme thar wes lyand
The king of Ingland with his men.
King Robert that had witteryng then
That he lay thar with mekill mycht
Tranountyt sua on him a nycht
That be the morn that it wes day
Cummyn in a plane feld war thai
Fra Biland bot a litill space,
Bot betwix thaim and it thar was
A craggy bra strekyt weill lang
And a gret peth up for to gang,
Other wayis mycht thai nocht away
To pas to Bilandis abbay
Bot gif thai passyt fer about.
And quhen the mekill Inglis rout
Hard that the King Robert wes sa ner,
The mast part of thaim that thar wer
Went to the peth and tuk the bra,
Thai thocht thar defens to ma,
Thar baneris thar thai gert display
And thar bataillis on braid aray,
And thocht weill to defend the pas.
Quhen the King Robert persavit was
That thai thocht thar thaim to defend
Efter his consaill has he send
And askyt quhat wes best to do.
The lord Douglas answeryt thar-to
And said, 'Schyr, I will underta
That in schort tyme I sall do sa
That I sall wyn yon pas planly,
Or than ger all yon cumpany
Cum doun to you her to this plane.'
The king said than till him agayn,
'Do than, quhar mychty God the speid.'
Than he furth on his wayis yeid,
And of the ost the mast hardy

Put thaim intill his cumpany
And held thar way towart the pas.
The gud erle of Murreff Thomas
Left his bataill and in gret hy
Bot with four men of his cumpany
Come till the lordis rout of Douglas
And or he entryt in the pas
Befor thaim all the pas tuk he
For he wald that men suld him se.
And quhen Schyr James off Douglas
Saw that he suagat cummyn was
He prisyt him tharoff gretly
And welcummyt him hamlyly,
And syne the pas thai samyn ta.
Quhen Inglis men saw thaim do sua
Thai lychtyt and agayn thaim yeid
Twa knychtis rycht douchty of deid,
Thomas Ouchtre[23] ane had to name
The tother Schyr Rauf of Cobhame[24]
Thai war bath full of gret bounte
And met thar fayis manlely,
Bot thai war pressyt rycht gretumly.
Thar mycht men se rycht weill assaile
And men defend with stout bataill
And arowes fley in gret foysoun
And thai that owe war tumbill doun
Stanys apon thaim fra the hycht,
Bot thai that set bath will and mycht
To wyn the peth thaim pressyt sua
That Schyr Rauff of Cobhame gan ta
The way up till hys hors in hy,
And left Schyr Thomas manlily
Defendand with gret mycht the pas
Quhill that he sua supprisit was
That he wes tane throu hard fechting.
And tharfor syne in his ending
He wes renownyt for best of hand
Off a knycht off all Ingland,

For this ilk Schyr Rauf of Cobhame
Intill all Ingland he had name
For the best knycht of all that land,
And for Schyr Thomas dwelt fechtand
Quhar Schyr Rauff as befor said we
Withdrew him, prisit our him was he.
Thus war thai fechtand in the pas,
And quhen the King Robert that was
Wys in his deid and averty
Saw his men sa rycht douchtely
The peth apon thar fayis ta
And saw his fayis defend thaim sa,
Than gert he all the Irschery[25]
That war intill his cumpany
Off Arghile and the Ilis[26] alsua
Speid thaim in gret hy to the bra,
And bad thaim leif the peth haly
And clym up in the craggis hy
And speid thaim fast the hycht to ta.
Than mycht men se thaim stoutly ga
And clymb all-gait up to the hycht
And leve nocht for thar fayios mycht,
Magre thar fayis thai bar thaim sua
That thai ar gottyn aboun the bra.
Than mycht men se thaim fecht felly
And rusch thar fayis sturdely,
And thai that till the pas war gane
Magre thar fayis the hycht has tane.
Than laid thai on with all thar mycht,
Thar mycht men se men felly fycht.
Thar wes a peralous bargane,
For a knycht Schyr Jhone the Bretane[27]
That lychtyt wes aboune the bra
And his men gret defens gan ma,
And Scottismen sua gan assaill
And gave thaim sa felloun bataill
That thai war set in sic affray
That thai that mycht fley fled away,

364

Schyr Jhone the Bretane thar wes tane
And rycht fele off his folk war slane.
Off Fraunce thar tane wes knychtis twa,[28]
The lord the Sule wes ane of tha,[29]
The tother wes the merschell Bretayn[30]
That wes a wele gret lord at hame,
The lave sum ded war and sum tane
And the remanand fled ilkane.
And quhen the king of Ingland
That yeit at Biland wes liand
Saw his men discumfyt planely
He tuk his way in full gret hy
And furthwart fled with all his mycht,
Scottismen chassyt fast, Ik hycht,
And in the chas has mony tane,
The king quitly away is gane
And the mast part of his menye.
Stewart Walter that gret bounte
Set ay on hey chevalry
With fyve hunder in cumpany
Till Yorkis[31] yettis the chas gan ma
And thar sum of thar men gan sla
And abade thar quhill ner the nycht
To se giff ony wald ische to fycht,
And quhen he saw nane wald cum out
He turnyt agane with all his rout
And till his ost he went in hy
That tane had than thar herbery
Intill the abbay off Biland
And Ryfuowis[32] that was by ner-hand.
Thai delt amang thaim that war ther
The king off Inglandis ger
That he had levyt in Biland,
All gert thai lep out our thar hand,
And maid thaim all glaid and mery.
And quhen the king had tane herbery
Thai brocht till him the prisoneris
All unarmyt as it afferis,

And quhen he saw Jhon of Bretangne
He had at him rycht gret engaigne,[33]
For he wes wont to spek hychtly
At hame and our dispitusly,
And bad have him away in hy
And luk he kepyt war straitly,
And said war it nocht that he war
Sic a catyve he suld by sar
Hys wordys that war sua angry,
And he humbly criyt him mercy.
Thai led him furth foroutyn mar
And kepyt him wele quhill thai war
Cummyn hame till thar awne countre,
Lang eftre syne ransonyt wes he
For twenty thousand pund to pay
As Ik haff hard syndry men say.
Quhen that the king this spek had maid
The Frankys knychtis men takyn had
War brocht rycht thar befor the king,
And he maid thaim fayr welcummyng
And said, 'I wate rycht weill that ye
For your gret worschip and bounte
Come for to se the fechting her.
For sen ye in the countre wer
Your strenth your worschyp[34] and your
    mycht
Wald nocht lat you eschew the fycht,[35]
And sen that caus you led thartill
And nother wreyth na ivill will
As frendis ye sall resavyt be,
Quhar all tyme welcum her be ye.'
Thai knelyt and thankyt him gretly,
And he gert tret thaim curtasly
And lang quhill with thaim had he
And did thaim honour and bounte,
And quhen thai yarnyt to thar land
To the king of Fraunce in presand
He send thaim quit but ransoun fre[36]

And gret gyftis to thaim gaff he.
His frendis thusgat curtasly
He couth ressave and hamely,
And his fayis stoutly stonay.
At Biland all that nycht he lay,
For thar victour all blyth thai war,
And on the morn foroutyn mar
Thai haff forthwart tane thar way.
Sa fer at that tyme travaillyt thai
Brynnand slayand and destroyand
Thar fayis with all thar mycht noyand
Quhill till the Wald cummyn war thai,
Syne northwart tuk hame thar way

And destroyit in thar repayr
The vale all planly off Beauewar.
And syne with presoneris and catell
Riches and mony fayr jowell
To Scotland tuk thai hame thar way
Bath blyth and glaid joyfull and gay,
And ilk man went to thar repayr
And lovyt God thaim fell sa fayr
That thai the king off Ingland
Throu worschip and throu strenth of
   hand
And throu thar lordis gret bounte
Discumfyt in his awne countre.

BOOK XIX

Than wes the land a quhile in pes,
Bot covatys, that can nocht ces
To set men apon felony
To ger thaim cum to senyoury,
Gert lordis off full gret renoune
Mak a fell conjuracioun[1]
Agayn Robert the douchty king,
Thai thocht till bring him till ending
And to bruk eftre his dede
The kynrik and to ryng in hys steid.[2]
The lord the Soullis, Schyr Wilyam,[3]
Off that purches had mast defame,
For principale tharoff was he
Off assent of that cruelte.
He had gottyn with him sindry,
Gilbert Maleherbe, Jhone of Logy[4]
Thir war knychtis that I tell her
And Richard Broun als a squyer,[5]
And gud Schyr Davy off Breichyn
Wes off this deid arettyt syne

As I sall tell you forthermar.
Bot thai ilkane discoveryt war
Throu a lady as I hard say
Or till thar purpos cum mycht thai,
For scho tauld all to the king
Thar purpose and thar ordanyng,
And how that he suld haf bene ded
And Soullis ryng intill his steid,
And tauld him werray taknyng
This purches wes suthfast thing.
And quhen the king wist it wes sua
Sa sutell purches gan he ma
That he gert tak thaim everilkan,
And quhar the lord Soullis was tane
Thre hunder and sexty had he
Off squyeris cled in his lyvere[6]
At that tyme in his cumpany
Outane knychtis that war joly.[7]
Into Berwik takyn wes he
That mycht all his mengne se

Sary and wa, bot suth to say
The king lete thaim all pas thar way
And held thaim at he takyn had.
The lord Soullis sone eftre maid
Plane granting of all that purchas.
A parlement set tharfor thar was
And brocht thidder this mengne war.
The lord the Soullis has grantyt thar
The deid into plane parleament,
Tharfor sone eftre he wes sent
Till his pennance to Dunbertane[8]
And deit thar in a tour off stane.[9]
Schyr Gilbert Maleherbe and Logy
And Richard Broune thir thre planly
War with a sys thar ourtane,
Tharfor thai drawyn war ilkane
And hangyt and hedyt tharto
As men had dempt thaim for to do.
And gud Schyr Davy off Breichyn
Thai gert chalance rycht straitly syne,[10]
And he grauntyt[11] that off that thing
Was wele maid till him discovering[12]
Bot he thartill gaf na consent,[13]
And for he helyt thar entent[14]
And discoveryt it nocht to the king
That he held of all his halding
And maid till him his fewte
Jugyt till hang and draw wes he.
And as thai drew him for to hing
The pepill ferly fast gan thring
Him and his myscheyff for to se
That to behald wes gret pite.
Schyr Ingrahame the Umfravill that than
Wes with the king as Scottisman,
Quhen he that gret myscheiff gan se
He said, 'Lordingis, quharto pres ye
To se at myscheiff sic a knycht
That wes sa worthi and sa wicht

That Ik haff sene ma pres to se
Him for his rycht soverane bounte
Than now doys for to se him her.'
And quhen thir wordis spokyn wer
With sary cher he held him still
Quhill men had done of him thar will,
And syne with the leve of the king
He brocht him menskly till erding.
And syne to the king said he,
'A thing I pray you graunt me,
That is that ye off all my land
That is intill Scotland liand
Wald giff me leve to do my will.'
The king that sone has said him till,
'I will wele graunt that it sua be,
Bot tell me quhat amovis the.'
He said agane, 'Schyr, graunt mercy
And I sall tell you planely,
Myne hart giffis me na mar to be
With you dwelland in this countre,
Tharfor bot that it nocht you greve
I pray you hartly of your leve.
For quhar sua rycht worthi a knycht
An sa chevalrous and sa wicht
And sa renownyt off worschip syne
As gud Schyr David off Brechyn
And sa fullfyllyt off all manheid
Was put to sa velanys a ded,
Myn hart forsuth may nocht gif me
To dwell for na thing that may be.'
The king said, 'Sen that thou will sua
Quhenever the likys thou may ga,
And thou sall haiff gud leve tharto
Thi liking off thi land to do.'
And he thankyt him gretumly
And off his land in full gret hy
As hym thocht best disponyt he,
Syne at the king of gret bounte

367

Befor all thaim that with him war
He tuk his leve for evermar,
And went in Ingland to the king[15]
That maid him rycht fayr welcummyng
And askyt him of the north tithing.
And he him tauld all but lesing
How thai knychtis destroyit war
And as I tauld till you ar,
And off the kingis curtassy
That levyt him debonarly
To do off his land his liking.
In that tyme wes send fra the king
Off Scotland messyngeris to trete
Off pes giff that thai mycht it get,
As thai befor oft-sys war send
How that thai coutht nocht bring till end.
For the gud king had in entent,
Sen God sa fayr grace had him lent
That he had wonnyn all his land
Throu strenth off armys till his hand,
That he pes in his tyme wald ma
And all landis stabill sua
That his ayr eftre him suld be
In pes, gif men held lawte.
Intill this tyme that Umfravill
As I bar you on hand er quhill
Come till the king of Ingland
The Scottis messingeris thar he fand
Of pes and rest to haiff tretis.
The king wist Schyr Ingrahame wes wis
And askyt consaile tharto
Quhat he wald rede him for to do,
For he said him thocht hard to ma
Pes with the King Robert his fa
Quhill that he off him vengit war.
Schyr Ingrahame maid till him answar
And said, 'He delt sa curtasly[16]
With me that on na wis suld I[17]

Giff consaill till his nethring.'[18]
'The behovis nedwayis,' said the king,
'To this thing her say thine avis.'
'Schyr,' said he, 'sen your willis is
That I say, wit ye sekyrly
For all your gret chevalry
To dele with him yhe haf na mycht.
His men all worthyn ar sa wicht
For lang usage of fechting
That has bene nuryst in swilk thing
That ilk yowman is sa wicht[19]
Off his that he is worth a knycht.[20]
Bot, and ye think your wer to bring
To your purpos and your liking,
Lang trewys with him tak ye.
Than sall the mast off his menye
That ar bot simple yumanry
Be dystrenyit commonaly[21]
To wyn thar mete with thar travaill,[22]
And sum of thaim nedis but faill
With pluch and harow for to get
And other ser crafftis thar mete,
Sua that thar armyng sall worth auld[23]
And sall be rottyn stroyit and sauld[24]
And fele that now of wer ar sley[25]
Intill the lang trew sall dey[26]
And other in thar sted sall rys
That sall conn litill of that mastrys.
And quhen thai disusyt er
Than may ye move on thaim your wer
And sall rycht well as I suppos
Bring your entent to gud purpos.'
Till this assentyt thai ilkane,
And eftre sone war trewis tane
Betwix the twa kingis that wer
Tailyeit to lest for thretten yer[27]
And on the marchis gert thaim cry.
The Scottismenn kepyt thaim lelely,

Bot the Inglismen apon the se
Distroyit throu gret inyquyte
Marchand schippis[28] that sailand war
Fra Scotland till Flaundris[29] with war,
And destroyit everilkane
And to thar oys the gud has tane.
The king send oft till ask redres,
Bot nocht off it redressyt wes
And he abaid all tyme askand,
The trew on his half gert he stand
Apon the marchis stabilly
And gert men kep thaim lelely.
In this tyme that trewis war
Lestend on marchis as I said ar
Schyr Walter Stewart that worthi was
At Bathgat[30] a gret seknes tas.
His ivill ay woux mar and mar
Quhill men persavit be his far
That him worthit nede to pay the det
That na man to pay may let,
Schryvyn[31] and als repentit weill
Quhen all wes doyn him ilkdeill
That Crystyn[32] man nedyt till have
As gud Crystyn the gast he gave.
Then men mycht her men gret and cry
And mony a knycht and mony a lady
Mak in apert rycht evill cher,
Sa did thai all that ever thai war,
All men him menyt commounly
For off his eild he wes worthy.
Quhen thai lang quhill thar dule had
    maid
The cors to Paslay[33] haiff thai haid,
And thar with gret solempnyte
And with gret dule erdyt wes he,
God for his mycht his saule bring
Quhar joy ay lestis but ending.
Efftre his dede as I said ar

The trewys that sua takyn war
For till haff lestyt thretten yer,
Quhen twa yer of thaim passyt wer
And ane halff as I trow allsua
The King Robert saw men wald nocht
    ma
Redres of schippys that war tane
And off the men als that war slane,
Bot contynowyt thar mavtye
Quhenever thai met thaim on the se.
He sent and acquit him planly
And gave the trewis up opynly,
And in the vengeance of this trespas
The gud erle of Murreff Thomas
And Donald erle of Mar[34] alsua
And James of Douglas with thai twa,
And James Stewart that ledar wes
Efter his gud brotheris disceis
Off all his bruderys men in wer,
He gert apon thar best maner
With mony men bowne thaim to ga
In Ingland for to bryn and sla,
And thai held furth till Ingland.
Thai war of gud men ten thousand,
Thai brynt and slew intill thar way,
Thar fayis fast destroyit thai
And suagat southwart gan thai far
To Wardaill[35] quhill thai cummyn war.
That tyme Edward off Carnaverane
The king wes ded and laid in stane,[36]
And Edward his sone that wes ying[37]
In Ingland crownyt wes to king
And surname off Wyndyssor[38].
He had in France bene thar-befor
With his moder Dame Ysabell,
And wes weddyt as Ik herd tell
With a young lady fayr of face
That the erlis douchter was

Off Hennaud[39], and off that cuntre
Brocht with him men of gret bounte,
Schyr Jhone the Hennaud[40] wes thar leder
That was wys and wycht in wer.
And that tyme that Scottismen wer
At Wardaile, as I said you er,
Intill York wes the new-maid king,
And herd tell of the destroying
That Scottismen maid in his countre.
A gret ost till him gaderyt he,
He wes wele ner fyfty thousand,
Than held he northwart in the land
In haill battaill with that mengne,
Auchtene yer auld that tyme wes he.
The Scottismen a day Cokdaile[41]
Fra end till end had heryit haile
And till Wardaile again thai raid.
Thar discourriouris that sycht has haid
Off cummyn of the Inglismen
To thar lordis thai tauld it then.
Than the lord Douglas in a ling
Raid furth to se thar cummyng
And saw that sevyn battaillis war thai
That cum ridand in gud aray,
Quhen he that folk behaldyn had
Towart his ost agayn he rad.
The erle speryt gif he had sene
That ost. 'Ya, schyr,' he said, 'but wene.'
'Quhat folk ar thai?' 'Schyr, mony men.'
The erle his ayth has sworn then,
'We sall fecht with thaim thocht thai war
Yeit ma eftsonys than thai ar.'
'Schyr, lovyt be God,' he said agayn,
'That we haiff sic a capitayn
That sua gret thing dar undreta,
Bot, be saynct Bryd, it beis nocht sua
Giff my consaill may trowyt be,
For fecht on na maner sall we

Bot it be at our avantage,
For methink it war na outrage
To fewar folk aganys ma
Avantage quhen thai ma to ta.'
As thai war on this wis spekand
Our ane hey rig thai saw ridand
Towart thaim evyn a battaill braid,
Baneris displayit inew thai haid,
And a nothyr come eftre ner
And rycht apon the samyn maner
Thai come quhill sevin battaillis braid
Out-our that hay rig passyt haid.
The Scottismen war than liand
On north halff Wer[42] towart Scotland.
The dale wes strekyt weill Ik hycht,
On athyr sid thar wes ane hycht
And till the water doune sumdeill stay.
The Scottismen in gud aray
On thar best wis buskyt ilkane
Stud in a strenth that thai had tane,
And that wes fra the water of Wer
A quartar of a myle weill ner,
Thar stud thai battaill till abid,
And Inglismen on athyr sid
Come ridand dounwart quhill thai wer
To Weris water cummyn als ner
As on other halff thar fayis war.
Than haf thai maid a rest rycht thar
And send out archerys a thousand
With hudis off and bowys in hand
And gert thaim drink weill of the wyn,
And bad thaim gang to bykker syne
The Scottis ost in abandoun
And ger thaim cum apon thaim doun,
For mycht thai ger thaim brek aray
To haiff thaim at thar will thocht thai.
Armyt men doune with thaim thai send
Thaim at the water to defend.

The lord Douglas has sene thar fer,
And men that rycht weill horsyt wer
And armyt a gret cumpany
Behind the bataillis prevely
He gert howe to bid thar cummyng,
And quhen he maid to thaim taknyng
Thai suld cum prekand fast and sla
With sperys that thai mycht ourta,
Donald off Mar thar chiftane was
And Archebald with hym of Douglas.[43]
The lord Douglas towart thaim raid,
A gowne on his armur he haid,
And traversyt all wayis up agayn
Thaim ner his bataillis for to trayn,
And thai that drunkyn had off the wyne
Come ay up lingand in a lyne
Quhill thai the battaill come sa ner
That arowis fell amang thaim ser.
Robert off Ogill[44] a gud squyer
Come prikand than on a courser
And on the archeris criyt agane,
'Ye wate nocht quha mays you that trayn,
That is the lord Douglas that will
Off his playis ken sum you till,'
And quhen thai herd spek of Douglas
The hardyest effrayit was
And agayn turnyt halely.
His takyn maid he than in hy,
And the folk that enbuschit war
Sa stoutly prekyt on thaim thar
That weile thre hunder haiff thai slane
And till the water hame agane
All the remanand gan thai chas.
Schyr Wilyam off Erskyn[45] that was
Newlyngis makyn knycht that day
Weill horsit intill gud aray
Chasyt with other that thar war
Sa fer furth that hys hors him bar

Amang the lump of Inglismen,
And with strang hand wes takyn then,
Bot off him wele sone chang wes maid
For other that men takyn haid.
Fra thir Inglis archeris wes slane
Thar folk raid till thar ost agane,
And rycht sua did the lord off Douglas.
And quhen that he reparyt was
Thai mycht amang thar fayis se
Thar pailyounys sone stentyt be,
And thai persavyt sone in hy
That thai that nycht wald tak herbery
And schup to do no mar that day,
Tharfor thaim alsua herbryit thay
And stent pailyounys in hy,
Tentis and lugis als tharby[46]
Thai gert mak and set all on raw.
Twa novelryis that day thai saw
That forouth in Scotland had bene nene,
Tymmeris for helmys war the tane
That thaim thoucht thane off gret bewte
And alsua wondyr for to se,
The tother crakys war off wer
That thai befor herd never er,
Off thir twa thingis thai had ferly.
That nycht thai walkyt stalwartly,
The mast part off thaim armyt lay
Quhill on the morn that it wes day.
The Inglismen thaim umbethocht
Apon quhat mener that thai moucht
Ger Scottis leve thar avantage,
For thaim thocht foly and outrage
To gang up till thaim till assaill
Thaim at thar strenth in plane battaill,
Tharfor of gud men a thousand
Armyt on hors bath fute and hand
Thai send behind thar fayis to be
Enbuschit intill a vale,

And schup thar bataillis as thai wald
Apon thaim till the fechtyn hald,
For thai thocht Scottismen sic will
Had that thai mycht nocht hald thaim
    still,
For thai knew thaim off sic curage
That tharthrouch strenth and avantage
Thai suld leve and mete them planly.
Than suld thar buschement halily
Behind brek on thaim at the bak,
Sa thocht thai wele thai suld thaim mak
For to repent thaim off thar play.
Thar enbuschment furth send haiff thai
That thaim enbuschit prevely,
And on the morn sum-dele arly
Intill this ost hey trumpyt thai
And gert thar braid bataillis aray,
And all arayit for to fycht
Thai held towart the water rycht.
Scottismen that saw thaim do swa
Boune on thar best wis gan thaim ma
And in bataill planly arayit
With baneris till the wynd displayit
Thai left thar strenth, and all planly
Come doune to mete thaim hardely
In als gud maner as thai moucht
Rycht as thar fayis befor had thocht.
Bot the lord Douglas that ay was war
And set out wachis her and thar
Gat wyt off thar enbuschement,
Than intill gret hy is he went
Befor the bataillis and stoutly
He bad ilk man turn him in hy
Rycht as he stud, and turnyt sua
Up till thar strenth he bad thaim ga
Sua that na let thar thai maid,
And thai did as he biddyn haid
Quhill till thar strenth thai come agayne,

Than turnyt thai thaim with mekill mayn
And stud redy to giff battaill
Giff thar fayis wald thaim assaill.
Quhen Inglismen had sene thaim sua
Towart thar strenth agayne up ga
Thai criyt hey, 'Thai fley thar way.'
Schyr Jhone Hennaud said, 'Perfay
Yone fleyng is rycht degyse,[47]
Thar armyt men behind I se
And thar baneris, sua that thaim thar
Bot turne thaim as thai standand ar
And be arayit for to fycht
Giff ony presyt thaim with mycht.
Thai haiff sene our enbuschement
And agane till thar strenth ar went.
Yone folk ar governyt wittily,
And he that ledis is worthi
For avise worschip and wysdome
To governe the empyr off Rome.'
Thus spak that worthi knycht that day,
And the enbuschement fra that thai
Saw that thai sua discoveryt war
Towart thar ost agane thai fair,
And the bataillis off Inglismen
Quhen thai saw thai had faillyt then
Off thar purpos to thar herbery
Thai went and logit thaim in hy.
On other halff rycht sua did thai,
Thai maid na mar debat that day.
Quhen thai that day ourdrevyn had
Fyris in gret foysoun thai maid
Alsone as the nycht fallyn was.
And than the gud lord off Douglas,
That had spyit a place tharby
Twa myile thin that quhar mar traistly
The Scottis ost mycht herbery ta
And defend thaim better alsua
Than ellys in ony place tharby,

372

It wes a park all halily
Wes envyround about with wall,
It wes ner full of treys all
Bot a gret plane intill it was,[48]
Thidder thocht the lord of Douglas
Be nychtyrtale[49] thar ost to bring.
Tharfor foroutyn mar dwelling
Thai bet thar fyris and maid thaim mar,
And syne all samyn furtht thai far
And till the park foroutyn tynseill
Thai come and herbryit thaim weill
Upon the water and als ner
Till it as thai beforouth wer.
And on the morn quhen it wes day
The Inglis ost myssyt away
The Scottismen and had ferly,
And gert discourriouris hastily
Pryk to se quhar thai war away,
And be thar fyris persavyt thai
That thai in the park of Werdale
Had gert herbry thar ost all hale.
Tharfor thar ost but mar abaid
Buskyt, and evyn anent thaim raid
And on athyr halff the water of Wer
Gert stent thar palyounys als ner
As thar befor stentyt war thai.
Aucht dayis on baith halff sua thai lay
That Inglismen durst nocht assaill
The Scottismen with plane battaill
For strenth of erd[50] that thai had thar.
Thar wes ilk day justyn of wer
And scrymyn[51] maid full apertly
And men tane on athyr party,
And thai that war tane on a day
On ane other changyt war thai,
Bot other dedis nane war done
That gretly is apon to mone,
Till it fell on the sevynd day

The lord Douglas had spyit a way
How that he mycht about thaim rid
And com on the ferrer sid.
And at evyn purvayit him he
And tuk with him a gud mengne
Fyve hunder on hors wicht and hardy,
And in the nycht all prevely
Forout noyis sa fer he raid
Quhill that he ner enveronyt had
Thar ost and on the ferrar sid
Towart thaim slely gan he rid.
And the men that with him war
He gert in hand have swerdis bar
And bad thaim hew rapis in twa[52]
That thai the palyounys mycht ma[53]
To fall on thaim that in thaim war,[54]
Than suld the lave that folowit thar
Stab doune with speris sturdely,
And quhen thai hard his horne in hy
To the water hald doune thar way.
Quhen this wes said that Ik her say
Towart thar fayis fast thai raid
That on that sid na wachis haid.
And as thai ner war approchand
Ane Inglisman that lay bekand
Him be a fyr said till his fer,
'I wat nocht quhat may tyd us her
Bot rycht a gret growyng me tais,
For I dred sar for the blak Douglas,'
And he that hard him said, 'Perfay
Thou sall haiff caus gif that I may.'
With that with all him cumpany
He ruschyt in on thaim hardely
And pailyounys doune he bar,
With sperys that scharply schar
Thai stekyt men dispitously.
The noys weill sone rais and cry,
And thai stabbyt stekyt and slew

And pailyounys doun yarne thai drew.
A felloune slauchter maid thai thar
For thai that liand nakit war
Had na power defens to ma
And thai but pite gan thaim sla.
Thai gert thaim weill wyt that foly
Wes ner thar fayis for to ly
Bot giff thai traistly wachit war.
The Scottismen war slayand thar
Thar fayis on this wis quhill the cry
Ras throu the ost commonaly
That lord and other war on ster,
And quhen the Douglas wyst thai wer
Armand thaim all commonaly
He blew his horn for to rely
His men and bad thaim hald thar way
Towart the water and sua did thai,
And he abaid henmast to se
That nane of hys suld levyt be.
And as he bade sua howand
Sua come thane ane with a club in hand
And sua gret a rout till him raucht
That had nocht bene his mekill maucht
And his rycht soverane manheid
Intill that place he had bene dede,
Bot he that na tyme wes effrayit
Thocht he weill oft wes hard assayit
Throu mekill strenth and gret manheid
Has brocht the tother to the ded.
His men that till the water doun
War ridyne intill a raundoun
Myssyt thar lord quhen thai come thar,
Than war thai dredand for him sar,
Ilkan at other speryt tithing
Bot yeit off him thai hard na thing.
Than gan thai consaill samyn ta
That thai to sek him up wald ga,
And as thai war in sic effray

A tutilling off his horne hard thai
And thai that has it knawyn swith
War of his cummyn wonder blyth
And speryt at him of his abaid.
And he tauld how a carle him maid
With a club sic felloun pay
That met him stoutly in the way
That had nocht fortoun helpit the mar
He had bene in gret perell thar.
Thusgat spekand thai held thar way
Quhill till thar ost cummyn ar thai
That on fute armyt thaim abaid
For till help giff thai myster haid,
And alsone as the lord Douglas
Met with the erle off Murreff was
The erle speryt at thaim tithing
How thai had farne in thar outing.
'Schyr,' said he, 'we haf drawyn blud.'
The erle that wes of mekill mude[55]
Said, 'And we all had thidder gayne
We haid discumfyt thaim ilkan.'
'That mycht haff fallyn weill,' said he,
'Bot sekyrly ynew war we
To put us in yone aventur,
For had thai maid discumfitur
On us that yonder passyt wer
It suld all stonay that ar her.'[56]
The erle said, 'Sen that it sua is
That we may nocht with jupertys
Our feloune fayis fors assaill
We sall do it in plane battaill.'
The lord Douglas said, 'Be saynct Brid[57]
It war gret foly at this tid
Till us with swilk ane ost to fycht
That growys ilk day off mycht
And has vittaill tharwith plente,
And in thar countre her ar we
Quhar thar may cum us na succourys,

374

Hard is to mak us her rescours
Na we ne may ferrar mete to get,
Swilk as we haiff her we mon et.
Do we with our fayis tharfor
That ar her liand us befor
As Ik herd tell this othyr yer
That a fox did with a fyscher[58].'
'How did the fox?' the erle gan say.
He said, 'A fyscher quhilum lay
Besid a ryver for to get
Hys nettis that he had thar set.
A litill loge tharby he maid,
And thar-within a bed he haid,
And a litill fyr alsua,
A dure thar wes foroutyn ma.
A nycht, his nettis for to se
He rase and thar wele lang dwelt he,
And quhen he had doyne his deid
Towart his loge agayn he yeid,
And with licht of the litill fyr
That in the loge wes brynnand schyr
Intill his luge a fox he saw
That fast on ane salmound gan gnaw.
Than till the dur he went in hy
And drew his swerd deliverly
And said, 'Reiffar thou mon her out.'[59]
The fox that wes in full gret dout
Lukyt about sum hole to se,
Bot nane eschew persave couth he
Bot quhar the man stud sturdely.
A lauchtane mantell than him by[60]
Liand apon the bed he saw,
And with his teth he gan it draw
Out-our the fyr, and quhen the man
Saw his mantill ly brinnand than
To red it ran he hastily.
The fox gat out than in gret hy
And held his way his warand till.

The man leyt him begilyt ill
That he his gud salmound had tynt
And alsua his mantill brynt,
And the fox scaithles gat away.
This ensample weill I may say
Be yone ost and us that ar her,
We ar the fox and thai the fyscher
That stekis forouth us the way.
Thai wene we may na-gat away
Bot rycht quhar thai ly, bot perde
All as thai think it sall nocht be,
For I haff gert se us a gait
Suppos that it be sumdele wate,
A page off ouris we sall nocht tyne.
Our fayis for this small tranountyn
Wenys weill we sall prid us sua
That we planely on hand sall ta
To giff thaim opynly battaill.
Bot at this tyme thar thocht sall faill,
For we to-morne her all the day
Sall mak als mery as we may,
And mak us boune agayn the nycht,
And than ger mak our fyris lycht
And blaw our hornys and mak far
As all the warld our awne war
Quhill that the nycht weill fallin be.
And than with all our harnays we
Sall tak our way hamwart in hy,
And we sall gyit be graithly
Quhill we be out off thar daunger
That lyis now enclossyt her.
Than sall we all be at our will
And thai sall lete thaim trumpyt ill
Fra thai wyt weill we be away.'
To this haly assentyt thai,
And maid thaim gud cher all that nycht
Quhill on the morn that day wes lycht.
Apon the morn all prevely

375

Thai tursit harnays and maid redy
Sua that or evyn all boun war thai,
And thar fayis that agane thaim lay
Gert haiff thar men that thar war ded
In cartis till ane haly sted.
All that day cariand thai war
With cartis men that slayn war thar,
That thai war fele mycht men well se
That in carying sa lang suld be.
The ostis baith all that day wer
In pes, and quhen the nycht wes ner
The Scottis folk that liand war
Intill the park maid fest and far
And blew hornys and fyris maid
And gert thaim mak brycht and braid,
Sua at that nycht thar fyris war mar
Than ony tym befor thai war.
And quhen the nycht wes fallin weill
With all the harnayis ilka-dele
All prevely thai raid thar way.
Sone in a mos entryt ar thai
That had wele twa myle lang of breid,
Out-our that mos on fute thai yeid
And in thar hand thar hors leid thai.
It wes rycht a noyus way
Bot flaikkis[61] in the wod thai maid
Of wandis and thame with thame had[62]
And sykis thairwith briggit thay,
And sua had weill thair hors away
On sic wyse that all that thair weir
Come weill out-our it hale and fer,
And tynt bot litill off thar ger
Bot giff it war ony summer
That in the mos wes left liand.
Quhen all as Ik haff born on hand
Out-our that mos that wes sa braid
War cummyn a gret glaidschip thai haid
And raid furth hamwart on thar way.

And on the morn quhen it wes day
The Inglismen saw the herbery
Quhar Scottismen war wont to ly
All void. Thai wondryt gretly then
And send furth syndry off thar men
To spy quhar thai war gayn away
Quhill at the last thar trais fand thai
That till the mekill mos thaim haid
That wes sua hidwous for to waid
That awntyr thaim tharto durst nane,
Bot till thar ost agayne ar gayn
And tauld how that thai passyt war
Quhar never man passit ar.
Quhen Inglismen hard it wes sua
In hy to consaill gan thai ta
That thai wald folow thaim no mar,
Thar ost rycht than thai scalit thar
And ilk man till his awn raid.
And King Robert that wittering haid
At his men in the park sua lay
And at quhat myscheiff thar war thai,
Ane ost assemblyt he in hy
And ten thousand men wicht and hardy
He has send furth with erllis twa
Off the Marche and Angus war tha[63]
The ost in Werdale to releve,
And giff thai mycht sa weill escheve
That samyn mycht be thai and thai
Thai thocht thar fayis till assay.
Sua fell that on the samyn day
That the mos, as ye hard me say,
Wes passyt, the discourrouris that thar
Ridand befor the ost war
Off athyr ost has gottyn sycht,
And thai that worthy war and wicht
At thar metyng justyt of wer,
Ensenyeys hey thai criyt ther.
And be thar cry persavyt thai

That thai war frendys and at a fay,
Than mycht men se thaim glaid and blyth
And tauld it to thar lordis swith.
The ostis bath met samyn syne,
Thar wes rycht hamly welcummyn
Maid amand thai gret lordis thar,
Off thar metyng joyfull thai war.
The erle Patrik[64] and his menye
Had vittaillis with thaim gret plente
And tharwith weill relevyt thai
Thar frendis, for the suth to say
Quhill thai in Wardale liand war

Thai had gret defaut off mete, bot thar
Thai war relevyt with gret plente.
Towart Scotland with gamyn and gle
Thai went and hame wele cummyn ar
    thai
And scalyt syne ilk man thar way.
The lordis ar went to the king
That has maid thaim fair welcumyng,
For off thar come rycht glaid wes he,
And that thai sic perplexite
Forout tynsaill eschapyt haid
All war thai blyth and mery maid.

BOOK XX

Sone eftre that the erle Thomas
Fra Wardaill thus reparyt was
The king assemblyt all his mycht
And left nane that wes worth to fycht,
A gret ost than assemblit he
And delt his ost in partis thre.
A part to Norame[1] went but let
And a stark assege has set
And held thaim in rycht at thar dyk,
The tother part till Anwyk[2]
Is went and thar a sege set thai,
And quhill that thir assegis lay
At thir castellis I spak off ar,
Apert eschewys oft maid thar war
And mony fayr chevalry
Eschevyt war full douchtely.
The king at thai castellis liand
Left his folk, as I bar on hand
And with the thrid ost held hys way
Fra park to park hym for to play
Huntand as all hys awn war,
And till thaim that war with him thar

The landis off Northummyrland
That neyst to Scotland war liand
In fe and heritage gave he,
And thai payit for the selys fe.
On this wys raid he destroyand
Quhill that the king of Ingland
Throu consaill of the Mortymar[3]
And his moder that that tym war[4]
Ledaris of him that than young wes
To King Robert to tret off pes
Send messyngeris, and sua sped thai
That thai assentyt on this way
Than a perpetuale pes to tak,
And thai a mariage suld mak
Off the King Robertis sone Davy[5]
That than bot fyve yer had scarsly
And off Dame Jhone[6] als off the Tour
That syne wes of full gret valour,
Systre scho wes to the ying king
That had Ingland in governyng,
That than of eild had sevyn yer.
And monymentis and lettrys ser

That thai of Ingland that tyme had
That oucht agayn Scotland maid
Intill that tretys up thai gaff,
And all the clame that thai mycht haff
Intill Scotland on ony maner,
And King Robert for scaithis ser
That he to thaim off Ingland
Had done off wer with stalwart hand
Full twenty thousand pund suld pay
Off silver into gud monay.
Quhen men thir thingis forspokyn had
And with selis and athis maid
Festnyng off frendschip and of pes
That never for na chaunc suld ces,
The mariage syne ordanyt thai
To be at Berwik and the day
Thai haff set quhen that this suld be,
Syne went ilk man till his countre.
Thus maid wes pes quhar wer wais ar
And thus the segis raissyt war.
The King Robert ordanyt to pay
The silver, and agane the day
He gert wele for the mangery[7]
Ordane quhen that his sone Davy
Suld weddyt be, and Erle Thomas
And the gud lord of Douglas
Intill his steid ordanyt he
Devisouris of that fest to be,
For a malice him tuk sa sar
That he on na wis mycht be thar.
His malice off enfundeying
Begouth, for throuch his cald lying
Quhen in his gret myscheiff wes he
Him fell that hard perplexite.
At Cardros[8] all that tyme he lay,
And quhen ner cummyn wes the day
That ordanyt for the weddyn was
The erle and the lord of Douglas

Come to Berwik with mekill far
And brocht young Davy with thaim thar,
And the queyn and the Mortymer
On other part cummyn wer
With gret affer and reawte,
The young lady of gret bewte
Thidder thai brocht with rich affer.
The weddyn haf thai makyt thar
With gret fest and solempnyte,
Thar mycht men myrth and glaidschip se
For rycht gret fest thai maid thar
And Inglismen and Scottis war
Togidder in joy and solace,
Na felloune betwix thaim was.
The fest a wele lang tym held thai,
And quhen thai buskyt to far away
The queyn has left hyr douchter thar
With gret riches and reale far,
I trow that lang quhile na lady
Wes gevyn till hous sa richely,
And the erle and the lord Douglas
Hyr in daynte ressavyt has
As it war worthi sekyrly
For scho wes syne the best lady
And the fayrest that men thurft se.
Eftre this gret solemnyte,
Quhen of bath half levys war tane
The queyn till Ingland hame is gane
And had with hyr Mortymar.
The erle and thai that levyt war
Quhen thai a quhill hyr convoyit had
Towart Berwik again thai raid,
And syne with all thar cumpany
Towart the king thai went in hy,
And had with thaim the young Davy
And Dame Jhone als that young lady.
The king maid thaim fair welcumyng
And efter but langer delaying

He has gert set a parleament
And thidder with mony men is went,
For he thocht he wald in his lyff
Croun his young sone and his wyff
And at that parleament sua did he.
With gret fayr and solemnyte
The King Davy wes crownyt thar,
And all the lordis that thar war
And als off the comynyte
Maid him manredyn and fewte.[9]
And forouth that thai crownyt war
The King Robert gert ordane thar,
Giff it fell that his sone Davy
Deyit but ayr male off his body
Gottyn, Robert Stewart[10] suld be
Kyng and bruk all the realte
That hys douchter bar Marjory,
And at this tailye suld lelely
Be haldyn all the lordis swar
And it with selys affermyt thar.
And gyff it hapnyt Robert the king
To pas to God quhill thai war ying,
The gud erle of Murreff, Thomas,
And the lord alsua off Douglas
Suld haiff thaim into governyng
Quhill thai had wyt to ster thar thing,
And than the lordschip suld thai ta.
Her-till thar athys gan thai ma
And all the lordis that thar war
To thir twa wardanys athis swar
Till obey thaim in lawte
Giff thaim hapnyt wardanys to be.
Quhen all this thing thus tretit wes
And affermyt with sekyrnes
The king to Cardros went in hy,
And thar him tuk sa felely
The seknes and him travailit sua
That he wyst him behovyt to ma

Off all this liff the commoun end
That is the dede quhen God will send,
Tharfor his lettrys sone send he
For the lordis off his countre
And thai come as thai biddyng had.
His testament than has he maid
Befor bath lordis and prelatis,
And to religioun of ser statis
For hele of his saule gaf he
Silver in gret quantite.
He ordanyt for his saule weill,[11]
And quhen this done wes ilkadele
He said, 'Lordingis, sua is it gayn
With me that thar is nocht bot ane,
That is the dede withoutyn drede
That ilk man mon thole off nede.
And I thank God that has me sent
Space in this lyve me to repent,
For throuch me and my werraying
Off blud has bene rycht gret spilling
Quhar mony sakles men war slayn,
Tharfor this seknes and this payn
I tak in thank for my trespas.
And myn hart fichyt sekyrly was
Quhen I wes in prosperite
Off my synnys to sauffyt be
To travaill apon Goddis fayis,[12]
And sen he now me till him tayis
Sua that the body may na wys
Fullfill that the hart gan devis
I wald the hart war thidder sent
Quharin consavyt wes that entent.
Tharfor I pray you everilkan
That ye amang you ches me ane
That be honest wis and wicht
And off his hand a noble knycht
On Goddis fayis my hart to ber
Quhen saule and cors disseveryt er,

For I wald it war worthily
Brocht thar, sen God will nocht that I
Haiff power thidderwart to ga.'
Than war thar hartis all sa wa
That nane mycht hald him fra greting.
He bad thaim leve thar sorowing
For it he said mycht not releve
And mycht thaim rycht gretly engreve,
And prayit thaim in hy to do
The thing that thai war chargit to.
Than went thai furth with drery mode,
Amang thaim thai thocht it gode
That the worthi lord of Douglas
Quham in bath wit and worschip was
Suld tak this travaill apon hand,
Heir-till thai war all accordand,
Syne till the king thai went in hy
And tald hym at thai thocht trewly
That the douchty lord Douglas
Best schapyn for that travaill was.[13]
And quhen the king hard that thai sua
Had ordanyt him his hart to ta
That he mast yarnyt suld it haff
He said, 'Sa God himself me saiff
Ik hald me rycht weill payit that yhe
Haff chosyn him, for his bounte
And his worschip set in my yarnyng
Ay sen I thocht to do this thing
That he it with him thar suld ber,
And sen ye all assentit er
It is the mar likand to me.
Lat se now quhat thar-till sayis he.'
And quhen the gud lord of Douglas
Wist that thing thus spokyn was
He come and knelit to the king
And on this wis maid him thanking.
'I thank you gretly lord,' said he,
'Off the mony larges and gret bounte

That yhe haff done me fel-sys
Sen fyrst I come to your service,
Bot our all thing I mak thanking
That ye sa dyng and worthy thing
As your hart that enlumynyt wes
Off all bounte and all prowes
Will that I in my yemsall tak.
For you, schyr, I will blythly mak
This travaill, gif God will me gif
Layser and space sua lang to lyff.'
The king him thankyt tendrely,
Than wes nane in that cumpany
That thai na wepyt for pite,
Thar cher anoyis wes to se.
Quhen the lord Douglas on this wis
Had undretane sa hey empris
As the guid kyngis hart to ber
On Goddis fayis apon wer
Prissyt for his empris wes he.
And the kingis infirmyte
Woux mar and mar quhill at the last
The dulfull dede approchit fast,
And quhen he had gert till him do
All that gud Crystyn man fell to
With verray repentance he gaf
The gast, that God till hevyn haiff
Amang his chossyn folk to be
In joy solace and angell gle.
And fra his folk wist he wes ded
The sorow rais fra steid to steid,
Thar mycht men se men ryve thar har[14]
And commounly knychtis gret full sar
And thar newffys oft samyn dryve
And as woud men thar clathis ryve,
Regratand his worthi bounte
His wyt his strenth his honeste
And our-all the gret cumpany
That he maid thaim oft curtasly.

'All our defens,' thai said, 'allace
And he that all our comford was
Our wit and all our governyng
Allace is brocht her till ending.
His worschip and his mekill mycht
Maid all that war with him sa wycht
That thai mycht never abaysit be
Quhill forouth thaim thai mycht him se.
Allace! what sall we do or say,
For on lyff quhill he lestyt ay
With all our nychtbouris dred war we,
And intill mony ser countre
Off our worschip sprang the renoun
And that wes all for his persoune.'
With swilk wordis thai maid thar mayn
And sekyrly wounder wes nane,
For better governour than he
Mycht in na countre fundyn be.
I hop that nane that is on lyve
The lamentacioun suld discryve
That that folk for thar lard maid.
And quhen thai lang thus sorowit had,
And he debowaillyt[15] wes clenly
And bawmyt[16] syne richly,
And the worthi lord of Douglas
His hart as it forspokyn was
Has ressavyt in gret daynte
With gret fayr and solemnyte,
Thai haiff had hym to Dunferlyne[17]
And him solemply erdyt syne
In a fayr tumb intill the quer.
Byschappys and prelatis that thar wer
Assoilyeit him quhen the service
Was done as thai couth best devis
And syne on the tother day
Sary and wa ar went thar way.
Quhen that the gud king beryit was
The erle of Mureff, Schyr Thomas,

Tuk all the land in governyng,
All obeyit till his bidding,
And the gud lord of Douglas syne
Gert mak a cas of silver fine[18]
Ennamylyt throu sutelte,[19]
Tharin the kingis hart did he
And ay about his hals it bar
And fast him bownyt for to far.
His testament divisyt he
And ordanyt how his land suld be
Governyt quhill his gayn-cummyng
Off frendis, and all other thing
That till him pertenyt ony wis
With sik forsych and sa wys
Or his furth-passing ordanyt he
That na thing mycht amendyt be.
And quhen that he his leve had tane
To schip to Berwik is he gane,
And with a noble cumpany
Off knychtis and off squyery
He put him thar to the se.
A lang way furthwart saylit he,
For betwix Cornwaill and Bretaynne[20]
He sayllyt, and left the Grunye of
    Spainye[21]
On northalff him, and held thar way
Quhill to Sabill[22] the Graunt com thai,
Bot gretly war his men and he
Travaillyt with tempestis of the se,
Bot thocht thai gretly travaillit war
Hale and fer ar thai cummyn thar.
Thai aryvyt at Gret Sabill
And eftre in a litill quhill
Thar hors to land thai drew ilkane
And in the toun has herbry tane,
He hym contenyt rychly
For he had a fayr cumpany
And gold ynewch for to dispend.

The King Alfons[23] him eftre send
And hym rycht weill ressavyt he
And perofferyt him in gret plente
Gold and tresour hors and armyng,
Bot he wald tak tharoff na thing
For he said he tuk that vaiage
To pas intill pilgramage
On Goddis fayis, that his travaill
Mycht till his saule hele availl,
And sen he wyst that he had wer
With Saryzynys he wald dwell thar
And serve him at hys mycht lely.
The king him thankyt curtasly
And betaucht him gud men that war
Weill knawyn of that landis wer
And the maner tharoff alsua,
Syne till his innys gan he ga
Quhen that the king him levit had.
A weill gret sojourne thar he mad,
Knychtis that come of fer countre
Come in gret hy him for to se
And honouryt him full gretumly,
And out-our all men fer soveranly
The Inglis knychtis that war thar
Honour and company him bar.
Amang thai strangeris was a knycht
That wes haldyn sa worthi and wicht
That for ane of the gud wes he
Prissyt off the Cristiante,
Sa fast till-hewyn was his face
That it our-all ner wemmyt was.
Or he the lord Douglas had sene
He wend his face had wemmyt bene[24]
Bot never a hurt tharin had he.
Quhen he unwemmyt gan it se
He said that he had gret ferly
That swilk a knycht and sa worthi
And prissyt of sa gret bounte

Mycht in the face unemmyt be,
And he answerd tharto makly
And said, 'Love God, all tym had I
Handis my hed for to wer.'
Quha wald tak kep to this answer
Suld se in it understanding
That, and he that maid that asking
Had handis to wer, hys face
That for faute of defence sa was
To-fruschyt intill placis ser
Suld have may-fall left hale and fer.
The gud knychtis that than war by
Pryssyt hys answer gretumly,
For it wes maid with mek speking
And had rycht hey understanding.
Apon this maner still thai lay
Quhill throu the countre thai hard say
That the hey king of Balmeryne[25]
With mony a mody Saryzine
Was entryt intill the land off Spaynye
All hale the countre to manye.
The king off Spaynye on other party
Gaderyt his ost deliverly
And delt hym intill bataillis thre,
And to the lord Douglas gaff he
The avaward to led and ster,
All hale the strangeris with him wer,
And the gret maister off Saynct Jak
The tother bataill gert he tak,
The rerward maid himselvyn thar.
Thusgat divisyt furth thai far
To mete thar fayis that in bataill
Arayit redy till assaill
Come agayn thaim full sturdely.
The Douglas that wes sa worthi
Quhen he to thaim of his leding
Had maid a fayr monesting[26]
To do weill and na deid to dred,

For hevynnys blys suld be thar mede
Gyff that thai deyt in Goddis service
Than as gud werrayouris and wis,
With thaim stoutly assemblit he.
Thar mycht men felloun fechtyn se,
For thai war all wicht and worthi
That war on the Cristyn party
And faucht sa fast with all thar mayne
That Saryzynys war mony slayne,
The-quhether with mony fele fachoun
Mony a Cristyn dang thai doun,
Bot at the last the lord Douglas
And the gret rout that with him was
Pressyt the Saryzynys sua
That thai haly the bak gan ta,
And thai chassyt with all thar mayn
And mony in the chas has slayn.
Sa fer chassyt the lord of Douglas
With few, that he passyt was
All the folk that war chassand then,
He had nocht with him our ten
Off all men that war with him thar.
Quhen he saw all reparyt war
Towart hys ost than turnyt he,
And quhen the Saryzynys gan se
That the chasseris turnyt agayn
Thai relyit with mekill mayn.
And as the gud lord of Douglas
As I said er, reparand was
Sa saw he rycht besid thaim ner
Quhar that Schyr Wilyam the Sanctecler[27]
With a gret rout enveround was.
He was anoyit and said, 'Allace!
Yone worthy knycht will sone be ded
Bot he haff help, and our manheid
Biddys us help him in gret hy
Sen that we ar sa ner him by,
And God wate weill our entent is

To lyve or de in hys service,
Hys will in all thing do sall we.
Sall na perell eschewyt be
Quhill he be put out of yone payn
Or than we all be with him slayn.'
With that with spuris spedely
Thai strak the hors and in gret hy
Amang the Saryzynys thai raid
And roume about thaim haf thai maid,
Thai dang on fast with all thar mycht
And fele off thaim to ded has dycht.
Grettar defens maid never sa quhone
Agayne sa fele as thai haf done,
Quhill thai mycht last thai gaf battaill
Bot mycht na worschip thar availl
That thai ilkan war slayn doun thar,
For Saryzynys sa mony war
That thai war twenty ner for ane.
The gud lord Douglas thar was slane
And Schyr Wilyam the Sanct Cler alsua
And other worthy knychtis twa,
Schyr Robert Logane hat the tane
And the tother Schyr Walter Logane,
Quhar our Lord for his mekill mycht
Thar saulis haff till his hevynnys hycht.
The gud lord Douglas thus wes ded,
And Sarazynys in that sted
Abaid no mar bot held thar way,
Thai knychtis dede thar levyt thai.
Sum off the lord Douglas men
That thar lord ded has fundyn then
Yeid weill ner woud for dule and wa,
Lang quhill our him thai sorowit sua
And syne with gret dule hame him bar.
The kingis hart haiff thai fundyn thar
And that hame with thaim haf thai tane,
And ar towart thar innys gane
With gretyng and with ivill cher,

Thar sorow wes angry for till her.
And quhen of Keth gud Schyr Wilyam
That all that day had bene at hame,
For at sua gret malice wes he
That he come nocht to the journe
For his arme brokyn wes in twa,
Quhen he that folk sic dule saw ma
He askyt quhat it wes in hy
And thai him tauld all opynly
How that thar douchty lord wes slayn
With Sarazynys that releyt agayn,
And quhen he wyst that it was sua
Out-our all othyr him was wa
And maid sa wondyr yvill cher
That all wondryt that by him wer.
Bot to tell off thar sorowing
It noyis and helpis litill thing,
Men may weill wyt thoucht nane thaim
    tell
How angry for sorow and how fell
Is to tyne sic a lord as he
To thaim that war off his mengne,
For he wes swete and debonar
And weill couth trete hys frendis far,
And his fayis rycht fellounly
Stonay throu his chevalry
The-quhether off litill affer wes he.
Our all thing luffit he lawte,
At tresoun growyt he sa gretly
That na traytour mycht be him by
That he mycht wyt that he ne suld be
Weill punyst off his cruelte.
I trow the lele Fabricius
That fra Rome to werray Pyrrus
Wes send with a gret mengne
Luffyt tresoun na les than he,
The-quhether quhen Pirrus had
On him and on his mengne maid

Ane outrageous discumfitour
Quhar he eschapyt throu aventour
And mony off his men war slayne,
And he had gadryt ost agayne,
A gret maistre off medicyne
That had Pyrrus in governyne
Peroffferyt to Fabricius
In tresoun to sla Pyrrus,
For intill his neyst potioun
He suld giff him dedly pusoun.
Fabricius that wonder had
Off that peroffre that he him maid
Said, 'Certis, Rome is welle off mycht
Throu strenth off armys into fycht
To vencus thar fayis, thocht thai
Consent to treusoun be na way,
And for thou wald do sic trewsoun
Thou sall to et a warysoun
Ga to Pyrrus and lat him do
Quhatever him lyis on hart tharto.'
Than till Pyrrus he send in hy
This maistre and gert opynly
Fra end till end tell him this tale.
Quhen Pyrrus had it hard all hale
He said, 'Wes ever man that sua
For leawte bar him till his fa
As her Fabricius dois to me.
It is als ill to ger him be
Turnyt fra way of rychtwisnes
Or ellis consent to wikkitnes
As at midday to turne agayn
The sone that rynnys his cours playn.'
Thus said he off Fabricius,
That syne vencussyt this ilk Pyrrus
In plane bataill throu hard fechting.
His honest leawte gert me bring
In this ensample her, for he
Had soverane price off leawte,

And sua had the lord off Douglas
That honest lele and worthy was
That wes ded as befor said we,
All menyt him strang and preve.
Quhen his men lang had mad murnyn,
Thai debowalyt him and syne
Gert seth him sua that mycht be tane
The flesch all haly fra the bane
And the carioune thar in haly place
Erdyt with rycht gret worschip was.
The banys have tha with thaim tane
And syne ar to thar schippis gane
Quhen thai war levit off the king
That had dule for thar sorowing.
To se thai went, gud wind thai had,
Thar cours till Ingland haiff thai maid
And thar sauffly aryvyt thai,
Syne towart Scotland held thar way
And thar ar cummyn in full gret hy,
And the banys honorabilly
Intill the kyrk off Douglas war
Erdyt with dule[28] and mekill car.
Schyr Archebald his sone gert syn
Off alabast bath fair and fyne
Ordane a tumbe sa richly
As it behovyt to sua worthy.
Quhen that on this wis Schyr Wilyam
Off Keth had brocht his banys hame

And the gud kingis hart alsua,
And men had richly gert ma
With fayr effer his sepultur,
The erle off Murreff that had the cur
That tyme off Scotland halely
With gret worschyp has gert bery
The kingis hart at the abbay
Off Melros, quhar men prayis ay
That he and his have paradys.
Quhen this wes done that I devys
The gud erle governyt the land
And held the power weill to warand,
The lawe sa weill mantemyt he
And held in pes sua the countre
That it wes never or his day
Sa weill, as Ik hard auld men say.
Bot syne, allace! pusonyt wes he,
To se his dede wes gret pite.
Thir lordis deyt apon this wis.
He that hey Lord off all thing is
Up till his mekill blis thaim bring
And graunt his grace that thar ofspring
Leid weill the land, and ententyve
Be to folow in all thar lyve
Thar nobill eldrys gret bounte.
Quhar afauld God in trinyte
Bring us hey till his mekill blis
Quhar alwayis lestand liking is.

NOTES TO *THE BRUCE*

BOOK I

1 delightful
2 fable
3 truthful
4 reciting

5 To man's hearing are pleasant
6 that truly existed
7 good Sir James Douglas
8 the baronage

9 the Lord of Annandale
10 Robert Bruce, Earl of Carrick
11 Ought to succeed to the kingdom
12 Edward of England
13 scathe/damage
14 a sympathetic arbiter
15 Wales and also Ireland
16 such slavery
17 of high estate
18 should run on foot like the poor
19 lose life and limb
20 power
21 trusted in loyalty
22 lordship (of Scotland)
23 as a vassal
24 my predecessors
25 In 'free' kingship
26 Sir John Balliol, later John I
27 little while
28 subtlety and guile
29 for little or no reason
30 soon captured
31 degraded
32 so soon
33 Edward I
34 from Wick, near Orkney
35 to the mull of Galloway
36 Sheriffs and bailies
37 affairs
38 haughty and arrogant
39 wives and daughters raped without pity
40 angry
41 great harm
42 right or wrong they would have it
43 condemned [Scots] at will
44 condemned as criminals
45 good knights
46 their foes were their judges
47 slavery is worse than death
48 while in thrall his life may lead
49 it harms him, body and bones
50 But death troubles him only once
51 both poor and those of high estate
52 prison
53 without cause or reason
54 Sir William Douglas

55 Sir Robert Clifford
56 a great lord
57 wisely
58 no success
59 he knew not what to do or say
60 Paris
61 Robert Count of Artois
62 news from over the sea
63 that his father was dead
64 might regain his heritage
65 courteously
66 received
67 generous and friendly
68 And above all, loved loyalty
69 somewhat grey
70 had black hair as I heard say
71 in speech lisped somewhat
72 like Hector of Troy
73 and lisped as did he [Sir James]
74 with great pride
75 to Stirling with a great following
76 To hold an assembly
77 there went many barons
78 Bishop William de Lamberton
79 in charity
80 receive his homage
81 has always loyally served me
82 Gentlemen, who like to hear
83 the romance beginning here
84 against all their foes
85 strong and oppressive
86 Maccabees
87 Bible
88 before
89 Sir John Comyn
90 riding from Stirling
91 without cause
92 right makes the weak strong
93 indentures [contracts] and oaths
94 Africa, Arabia, Egypt and Syria
95 completely
96 he vanquished Lucius Iber
97 the barons of his domains
98 gathering
99 My seal is not always with me
100 I pledge my entire heritage

BOOK II

1 went swiftly to his inn
2 steeds [horses] two

3 Lochmaben
4 his brother Edward

5   escaped
6   mounted and rode to that place
7   took the life
8   to Edward I
9   with his barons
10 since yesterday
11 remained in his room
12 with only a clerk
13 with their retinues
14 the prophecy of Thomas of Ercildoune
15 disinherit me of my land
16 against
17 heard and had pity
18 off your own bat
19 and if the groom tries to stop
20 you – take the horse anyway
21 gave him silver to spend
22 felled him with a mighty blow
23 the Arickstone [local landmark]
24 waxed ever more and more
25 for he served loyally always
26 Sir Aymer de Valence
27 dragon [banner signifying no mercy]
28 Fife
29 walled all around
30 with great fortified towers
31 by 1,500 as I heard say
32 two earls
33 of Lennox and Atholl
34 I do not know their names
35 St John's town [Perth]
36 if you will trust me
37 issue forth to battle
38 out of their armour
39 Methven
40 Methven

41 you are each strong and worthy
42 they levelled their spears
43 their spears were broken
44 he shouted his battle-cry
45 they weaken fast
46 he rallied many a knight
47 Sir Thomas Randolph
48 knight
49 grabbed his [Robert's] reins
50 luck runs against us here
51 galloped away
52 Edward of Caernarvon
53 some they ransomed
54 he trusted none completely
55 other than his immediate followers
56 about 500
57 a bold baron
58 as outlaws
59 he dare not go to the plains
60 all the commoners deserted him
61 to enter the 'peace' of the English
62 none can rely on commoners
63 But he who can defend them
64 he lived in the hills
65 his retinue
66 Aberdeen
67 Neil Bruce and the queen
68 partners in their adversity
69 the army mustered quickly
70 and hoped to surprise him
71 Where they had little to eat
72 always working busily
73 to buy/acquire meat for the ladies
74 traps to catch pike and salmon
75 trout, eels and minnows

BOOK III

1   when he knew the king was near
2   was hurt at that time
3   he rallied those who were fleeing
4   likened him to Gadifer of Larys
5   Duke Betis
6   Gadres
7   two brothers were in that land
8   the sons of the door ward
9   a lochside and a brae [hill]
10 between the stirrup and his foot
11 fine for trespass

12 achieved such great chivalry
13 his sentries set
14 Carthage
15 voyage
16 and made them all knights
17 Julius Caesar
18 without failing
19 encouraged them to be cheerful
20 Kildrummy Castle
21 well provisioned
22 the ladies cried

23 sighed, wept and moaned
24 accepted hardships
25 Kintyre
26 Loch Lomond
27 the lochside
28 sunken boat
29 could swim very well
30 and carry a parcel on their backs
31 Fierabrace
32 Oliver
33 Aigremore
34 King Lavan
35 Lavan and all his fleet
36 searching woods and setting traps
37 most sombrely
38 sails and oars and other things

39 not in a position to fight
40 he had no succour nearby
41 removing our armour
42 the things that were floating there
43 they took and turned away
44 the loss is trifling
45 Angus Og
46 Dunaverty
47 he was afraid of betrayal
48 utterly
49 to go by sea to Rathlin
50 Brittany
51 between Morocco and Spain
52 they had a favourable wind
53 victuals for 300 men
54 knelt and made homage

BOOK IV

1   they spared none
2   of church or monastery
3   Marjory, daughter of Robert I
4   to the sanctuary of Tain
5   Caernarvon
6   false scum
7   Osbarn
8   glowing hot
9   burst into flames
10 stop
11 confirmed with assurances
12 Kildrummy Castle (or perhaps a tower or the gatehouse)
13 The king will fall in battle, and not be buried honourably, your Ferrand, Minerva my dear, will go to Paris with a great following of gentlemen
14 grinning

15 commands
16 are heavily burdened
17 by we who lie here idly
18 Arran
19 and squires and yeomanry
20 Brodick, Arran
21 a farmstead
22 mastery
23 galleys
24 When you come into your own
25 David and Jeremiah
26 Samuel, Joel and Isaiah
27 ability of astrology
28 wickedness
29 to evil given
30 Aristotle
31 Philistines
32 renown

BOOK V

1   his fleet and a few men
2   alone
3   such bounty to those folk
4   villainously
5   tearfully she told the king
6   Sir Walter de Lisle
7   bandits
8   bowed and took his leave
9   satisfactory
10 rich of goods and cattle

11 in hiding
12 mantle/cloak
13 secretly wearing armour
14 Saint Bride's Church
15 Easter palms
16 Except the cook and the doorman
17 dying
18 carried away
19 broke the tuns [barrels]
20 for meal

21 larder
22 rebuilt the castle
23 Thirwall family
24 his near relative
25 he was missing an eye

26 land worth £40 p.a.
27 willed
28 a bow and a bolt [a crossbow]
29 he released the bolt

BOOK VI

1 fortune helps brave men
2 fearlessly
3 fulfil their needs
4 the Galloway men realised
5 hunting dogs
6 took position one night
7 if I hear them coming
8 sergeants/soldiers
9 and found no pass
10 so narrow was the path
11 join their comrades to rest
12 a hound baying far away
13 he heard it coming nearer
14 threw him to the ground
15 he stabbed the horse
16 dotted with slain horses and men
17 one should be king for a year
18 while the first brother reigned
19 they set an ambush
20 Greece
21 the moon's light
22 would easily defeat four or five
23 and eight men
24 until he killed so many
25 that the ford was blocked up
26 sitting alone
27 took off his bacinet [helmet]
28 to cool him for he was hot

29 of such heart and strength
30 and does what needs doing
31 courage governed by sense
32 in Douglasdale
33 jeopardy
34 after the cattle
35 Except his head was bare
36 because they were disorganised
37 they quickly barred the gates
38 Cumnock, Ayrshire
39 of England and Lothian
40 had trained him for the hunt
41 for the sake of his uncle, John Comyn
42 his brother [Edward Bruce]
43 and the hill
44 rode ready for battle
45 the other force
46 set the hound to the chase
47 each took a different route
48 those most fleet of foot
49 with threats
50 he sheared off the shoulder
51 they hesitated
52 the fifth ran out of days
53 you are kind to say so
54 they were not concerned about me
55 they could see I was in trouble

BOOK VII

1 worn out and unsure what to do
2 who walks along a river bed
3 as far as a bow-shot
4 I would not care about the rest
5 they did that very thing
6 avenge their blood [deaths]
7 But things turned out otherwise
8 happened differently
9 hid in a bush
10 captured the king's standard
11 which endeared him to the king

12 English king [Edward I]
13 if armed [armoured] as well as us
14 unarmoured and undependable
15 his shoulders
16 carried a large sheep
17 what did they want?
18 he was the king in person
19 perceptive
20 a ruined farmhouse
21 The meat was done
22 ate ravenously

23 when replete
24 often glanced up
25 like a bird on a bough
26 generosity
27 before very long
28 the truth
29 opened the doors wide
30 at least 150
31 our foes will rest easy tonight
32 for they believe that we are scattered
33 to accept such danger
34 Carlisle
35 Carrick where he was accustomed
36 to hunt with his companions
37 ought to be ashamed
38 he knocked him head over heels

39 such a melee
40 homeward
41 Glentrool, Ayrshire
42 for hunting and recreation
43 and with such precautions
44 might be warned
45 and see their whole force
46 and disposition
47 she was up to no good
48 the best troops of Northumberland
49 goes toward his foes
50 taking his banner from its bearer
51 disorganised/beaten
52 were repulsed by just a few
53 started a fight

BOOK VIII

1 Cunningham
2 Bothwell
3 [near Fenwick Muir]
4 his costly horse
5 clung to the horse
6 Kilmarnock and Kilwinning
7 Ardrossan
8 Largs
9 Inverkip
10 Galston
11 a large broad marsh
12 he had three ditches dug
13 slips–passages
14 well armoured and armed

15 formations [echelons]
16 white [silver, i.e. steel armour]
17 the angels of heaven's kingdom
18 the transport and camp followers
19 earl of Buchan
20 Sir John Moubray
21 Sir David Brechin
22 Selkirk
23 Jedburgh
24 they took sacks and filled them
25 with [grass] hay
26 Sir John Webiton [Weston?]
27 that he loved greatly

BOOK IX

1 Inverurie
2 Slioch
3 Martinmas [2 November]
4 whatever occurred
5 attacked them fiercely
6 Strathbogie
7 the sentries
8 their troops
9 destruction of Buchan
10 accept his lordship
11 north of the River Forth
12 Forfar
13 stealthily, with ladders

14 Mohaut and Olifard
15 the earl of Strathearn
16 the ditch was shallowest
17 wade up to their shoulders
18 heard no sentries speak
19 a wretched hamlet
20 Argyll
21 beside the River Cree
22 Buittle Castle
23 Alan de Cathcart
24 thirteen castles
25 Lyne, Peeblesshire

BOOK X

1	a great abundance of enemies	18	William de Fiennes
2	Dunstaffnage	19	he soon died and was buried
3	Linlithgow pele [a fortress]	20	Teviotdale
4	great anger and pity	21	romantic
5	the gate	22	breathless and tired
6	was opened	23	the sentries
7	when it was in the middle of	24	Tyre
8	the gateway	25	Alexander the Great
9	protected righteousness	26	berfrois/belfry [a siege tower]
10	Edward II	27	Aristeus
11	Piers Lubaud, a Gascon	28	he who knows all [God]
12	garrison	29	ransacked the buildings
13	Roxburgh and Jedburgh	30	Nithsdale
14	Simon of Ledhouse	31	Rutherglen
15	made ladders of hemp rope	32	Dundee
16	with black cloths	33	Stirling
17	feast days, religious festivals	34	began to run short of supplies

BOOK XI

1	this contract was made	20	pots-defence against cavalry
2	can start an avalanche	21	do their duty as they ought
3	such a long term	22	Falkirk
4	Aquitaine	23	at the church to guard the road
5	paid soldiers	24	Sir Robert Keith
6	never made greater preparation for war	25	embroidered banners
7	earl of Hainault	26	all richly dressed
8	Gascony and Germany	27	Christendom
9	Bayonne	28	chose a brave company
10	pavilions and gear	29	coursers [horses]
11	loaded with hens	30	bannerets [senior knights]
12	helmets and habergeons	31	formation [troops]
13	shields and spears and pennants	32	should we be surrounded
14	Berwick	33	Sir William Dayncourt
15	he deployed in ten formations	34	those that were
16	earls of Gloucester and Hereford	35	unhorsed lost their lives
17	Sir Giles d'Argentan	36	the dust made a murkiness
18	a beardless youth	37	in the air around them
19	earl of Moray		

BOOK XII

1	leather boiled in wax	7	think it wise that we fight
2	Sir Henry de Bohun	8	tomorrow at daybreak
3	easily	9	doughty
4	since he was poorly mounted	10	have heard Mass and prepared
5	they might have lost everything	11	each man in his formation
6	he saw his foes disrupted	12	hindmost

13 no prisoners to be taken
14 until the engagement is decided
15 carse [low ground]
16 thatch
17 doors and windows

18 nor retreat from such rabble
19 set their faces to the enemy
20 lost their lives
21 do their duty well

BOOK XIII

1 rich and royal clothes
2 nothing but groans and blows
3 light [perhaps mettlesome]
4 unarmoured
5 tholing such pains
6 so astonished
7 he fought three times
8 against the Saracens
9 and killed two on each occasion
10 undoing
11 close ordered as you can

12 almost all unarmoured
13 Gilbert de Clare
14 Marmaduke de Tweng
15 joined King Robert's household
16 Laurence de Abernethy
17 a stone's throw
18 Winchburgh
19 Bamburgh
20 wheels
21 fair
22 heir apparent

BOOK XIV

1 Sir John de Soulis
2 Sir John Stewart
3 Ramsay of Aughterhouse
4 Sir Fergus de Ardrossan
5 Larne, Ireland
6 without opposition
7 Carrickfergus
8 Mandeville, Bisset and Logan
9 the Savages [family]
10 hobins [horses]
11 reinforcements
12 Ulster
13 sub-kings/earls
14 where he was obliged to go
15 Kilnasaggart
16 Sir Richard de Clare
17 lieutenant

18 Earl of Desmond
19 Earl of Kildare
20 Birmingham and de Vernon
21 Sir Maurice Fitzthomas
22 the streets
23 plenty
24 he rationed the wine
25 Judas Maccabeus
26 beside a burn [stream]
27 weaken
28 they dammed a loch
29 the Bann
30 Connor
31 Fitzwarin
32 Pascal de Florent
33 Sir Nicolas de Kilkenny

BOOK XV

1 baggage
2 reply
3 so knightly/chivalrous
4 Montpellier
5 he recovered
6 Tuesday in Easter week
7 truce

8 penance
9 Easter
10 Dublin
11 did not omit
12 Sir Neil Fleming
13 Gib [Gilbert] Harper
14 by his [heraldic] arms

15 from Adam's sin
16 Dumbarton
17 Loch Leven
18 Sir Edmund de Caillou
19 the Merse
20 *schiltrom*

21 think of his beloved
22 with a small company
23 fortune deserted them
24 Sir Robert de Neville
25 Hilton, Westmorland
26 scold

BOOK XVI

1 baronage
2 Loch Ryan
3 nephew
4 thus King Robert
5 commanded the rearguard
6 Innermallan
7 burgesses
8 *hobelars* and yeomanry
9 he ignored the rearguard
10 their reinforcements were nearby
11 truncheon [club]
12 persuaded the king to cool off
13 disregarding orders
14 were dashed [dead]
15 nineteen great victories
16 saw him weeping sadly
17 you should be happy
18 that you have avoided death
19 Drogheda
20 Dublin
21 Limerick
22 launderer
23 is giving birth
24 she must be left behind
25 that is why she is distraught

26 that would not take pity
27 he halted the army
28 and had a tent erected
29 Connaught
30 Meath, Uriel
31 Munster and Leinster
32 Lintalee, Berwickshire
33 to clear Jedburgh forest
34 not even a stone's throw wide
35 Douglas leapt upon him
36 turned him over and killed him
37 Elias
38 Eskdale
39 Sir Andrew Harclay
40 around the river Humber
41 Firth of Forth
42 Inverkeithing, Fife
43 Dunfermline, Fife
44 sheriff [of Fife]
45 the Bishop of Dunkeld
46 William de Sinclair
47 prestige
48 fame and leadership
49 on both sides of the River Forth
50 his brother, now made king

BOOK XVII

1 except Berwick alone
2 Simon de Spalding
3 where his sentry duty was
4 Duns, Berwickshire
5 fought fiercely
6 Sir William Keith of Galston
7 beyond the River Tweed
8 John Crabbe, a mercenary
9 Greek fire
10 springald, catapult or ballista
11 Sir Walter Stewart
12 Thomas Earl of Lancaster
13 besieging the town

14 Ripon, Yorkshire
15 Boroughbridge, Yorkshire
16 Myton-le-Swale
17 priests, clerks, monks and friars
18 they were well armed
19 attack the Scots
20 for they were fewer in number
21 deployed in two formations
22 three spear lengths
23   to find safety
24 the chapter of Myton
25 equipment for mining
26 faggots [incendiaries]

27 the eve of the Exaltation of the Cross
28 they quickly surrounded the town
29 scunnered [depressed]
30 sow [a siege implement]
31 operated the engine
32 doubtless
33 the engineer quickly
34 reloaded the weapon
35 landed to the left
36 the strongest part
37 with men in a fighting top
38 well armoured
39 some unconscious
40 those who attacked
41 the Mary gate
42 broke the barricades and
43 burnt the drawbridge
44 women and small children
45 gathered the English missiles
46 and took them up to the parapets
47 and with his following
48 Pontefract
49 hanged and drawn
50 martyr
51 Carlisle
52 masons
53 that knew most about their craft

BOOK XVIII

1 though outnumbered three or four to one
2 I thought never to hear that from you
3 who was without equal
4 among men of his estate
5 John Thommason
6 a causeway
7 done of days [dead]
8 they cut off his head
9 and salted it
10 and sent it to
11 King Edward [II] as a gift
12 they thought it was the head
13 of Edward Bruce
14 overwhelming pride
15 Culross, Fife
16 a lame bull
17 Tranent, East Lothian
18 Melrose, Roxburghshire
19 when the leading ranks
20 had passed out of sight
21 Dryburgh, Roxburghshire
22 Byland, Yorkshire
23 Sir Thomas Ughtred
24 Sir Ralph Cobham
25 Irishry [Highland men]
26 of Argyll and the Isles
27 Sir John de Bretagne
28 two French knights
29 Sir Henry de Sully and
30 the Marshal of Brittany
31 York
32 Rievaulx
33 he was most angry with him
34 your honour
35 would not let you miss a fight
36 free of ransom

BOOK XIX

1 wicked conspiracy
2 to reign in his place
3 Sir William de Soulis
4 Sir Gilbert Malhebe and John Logy
5 Richard Brown, a squire
6 in his livery [uniform]
7 and well-armed knights
8 to prison in Dumbarton Castle
9 where [until?] he died
10 was accused as well
11 he admitted
12 that he knew [of the plot]
13 but was not involved
14 because he hid the plot
15 [Edward II]
16 he treated me with honour
17 and I could not
18 give advice that would harm him
19 each of his [King Robert's] yeomen
20 is as powerful as a knight
21 be dispersed
22 to their normal work
23 their arms will decay
24 or be sold
25 those that are battle-[hardened]
26 will die during a long truce

27 contracted to last thirteen years
28 merchant ships
29 Flanders
30 Bathgate, West Lothian
31 shriven [final confession]
32 Christian
33 Paisley
34 Donald Earl of Mar
35 Weardale
36 dead and buried
37 his young son
38 Windsor
39 Hainault
40 Sir Jean d'Hainault
41 Cockdale [unidentified]
42 River Wear
43 Sir Archibald Douglas
44 Robert Ogle
45 Sir William de Erskine

46 tents and lodges [shelters?]
47 their flight is a ruse
48 but there was a great clearing
49 by a night march
50 strength of position
51 skirmishes
52 he had them cut the rope
53 of tents so that they would
54 collapse on the occupants
55 of great courage
56 it would astonish the rest
57 St Bride
58 a fisherman
59 Thief! You must get out!
60 [the fox] saw a cloak
61 rafts
62 of timber and brushwood
63 the Earls of March and Angus
64 Earl Patrick [of March]

BOOK XX

1 Norham, Northumberland
2 Alnwick, Northumberland
3 Sir Roger Mortimer
4 Queen Isabella
5 the future David II
6 Joanna, sister of Edward III
7 eating, feasting
8 Cardross
9 homage and fealty
10 Robert Stewart (the king's grandson)
11 for the good of his soul
12 to go crusading
13 was the best choice for that task
14 tear out their hair

15 was disembowelled
16 and embalmed
17 Dunfermline, Fife
18 a case of fine silver
19 skilfully enamelled
20 Cornwall and Brittany
21 Spain
22 Seville
23 King Alfonso
24 would have been scarred
25 Morocco
26 had advised his followers
27 Sir William de Sinclair
28 buried with sadness

12

King Robert in romance

*I*t is not the purpose of this volume to embark on a revisionist/debunking exercise, *nor to provide a biography of Robert I, but to make available some of the material that provides the basis for historical analysis None the less, there are a few chestnuts, some venerable, some quite recent, that could do with being laid to rest.*

'King Robert was an Anglo-Norman'… *a description that needs some qual-ification to say the least. The Bruce family arrived in Scotland in the mid-1120s; by the time Robert was born they had been part of the political community for 150 years – they were hardly a new fixture in the national firmament.*

'King Robert spoke French'… *almost certainly true since French was the language of diplomacy and literature, but it is difficult to imagine how anyone could grow up in thirteenth-century Carrick and Annandale without learning to speak both English and Gaelic; how else would they communicate with their tenants and servants? Unless there was a great social upheaval in Scottish society between c.1330 and c.1365 that produced enormous changes in the linguistic constitution of the country and yet made no mark whatsoever in record we must ask how it should be that, if the Scottish nobility spoke French, the greatest – certainly the longest – piece of literature produced by their society was composed in Scots? Without question Barbour's epic was written for the benefit of aristocratic audiences and self-evidently they wanted to be entertained in Scots, not French.*

'The Bruce claim to the throne was superior to that of John Balliol; the Bruces were cheated out of their inheritance by Edward I who had received the homage and fealty of John Balliol'… *Edward had also received the homage and fealty of Robert the Noble, and the balance of expert legal opinion at the time seems to have favoured King John.*

'King Robert was elected king by a group of seven earls in an ancient Scottish tradition of regal inheritance'... *very positive and very patriotic, but not indicated by the evidence. Robert was a usurper. By chance the Balliol line came to an end in John's son, Edward, at which point the Bruce descent became the legitimate line in terms of primogeniture.*

'King Robert was saved at Bannockburn by the intervention of a band of Knights Templar, to whom he offered refuge from their persecution in France and England'... *There is no evidence whatsoever to support this increasingly popular 'tradition', on the other hand there is substantial circumstantial evidence against it. King Robert was an excommunicate and very keen to be re-admitted to the solace of religion. The last thing on his agenda would be to offer any offence to the Pope. Further, the suppression of the Templars had occurred largely at the behest of the king of France, whose support was vital for Robert's diplomatic campaigns; Robert would have been ill-advised to encourage the Templars in any way, let alone give them shelter. Finally, the Templars of the late thirteenth and early fourteenth centuries are probably better thought of as an international property conglomerate rather than an operational military organisation. The senior officers were hardened by conferences and lengthy struggles in courtrooms rather than combat, and the numerical strength of the order as a whole was so slight as to be an insignificant contribution to a major army.*

King Robert was the product of his station and time, the same as anyone else. The activities of his life were perfectly normal for a man of his rank; he endeavoured to protect and extend his family inheritances in both England and Scotland, he performed military and administrative services for his king, he hunted, he ran up debts, he gave to the Church, he hoped to go on crusade and fight in the Holy Land against what Barbour calls 'God's foes'. The regularity with which Robert changes sides in the decade from 1296–1306 is remarkable to our eyes, but not particularly so in the eyes of his contemporaries. Very few Scottish nobles managed to keep their heads above water − or for that matter joined to their bodies − without a few judicious changes of allegiance. King Robert may have been less than constant in his support for Scottish independence before 1306; given his efforts over the remaining twenty-three years perhaps he should be forgiven that inconstancy now.

A Scottish galley, vessels like these were vital to King Robert's littoral warfare in the west of Scotland.

Glossary

Barony:	a landholding with judicial responsibilities
Bondi:	serfs
Carucate:	a measurement of land, nominally 104 acres
Cottars:	smallholders
Desuetude:	to fall into disuse
Gressum:	a payment to the landlord for entry to a leased property
Grieve:	a farm manager
Heriot:	a payment to the landlord on inheritance of a lease
Mainprise:	a guarantee
Merchet:	a payment to the landlord on the marriage of a tenant
Merk:	160 pence, 13s 4d. Two thirds of £1.
Mukkitland:	the regularly manured infield of a farm 'toun'
Nativi:	serfs
Neyfs/Nefs:	serfs
Ploughgang:	one eighth of a ploughgate
Ploughgate:	nominally 104 acres
Runrig:	a form of land division and of ploughing
Rustici:	serfs
Servi:	serfs
Thirled:	to be contracted for life to a particular local service, usually the mill.
Toun:	a farm, usually with a group tenancy
Villeins:	serfs

Notes

7 WHY WAS THERE A BATTLE AT STIRLING IN 1314?

1 G.W.S. Barrow, *Robert the Bruce* (London, 1965) p.281–2.

2 M. McKisack, *England in the Fourteenth Century* (Oxford, 1959) p.30.

3 ibid p.14–22.

4 R. Nicholson, *Scotland in the Later Middle Ages* (Edinburgh, 1974) p.66.

5 Edward's declared intention (November 1313) in reply to a petition from the earl of Dunbar that he would go to Scotland before the feast of St John is not evidence that he was aware of the surrender compact, only that he acknowledged the problem and that he intended to address it during the following summer.

6 Sir Thomas Grey in his *Scalacronica* states that the compact was made by Robert rather than Edward.

7 Edward had campaigned in Scotland with his father in 1301 and 1305, R. Nicholson *Scotland in the Later Middle Ages* p.62, 75.

8 Aymer de Valence and Robert Clifford were both widely experienced commanders.

9 M. McKisack, *England in the Fourteenth Century* p.29–30.

10 Edward's musters at Berwick for 1310/11 did not raise enough troops to allow him to conduct effective operations against the Scots.

11 C. MacNamee, *The Wars of the Bruces* (East Lothian, 1997) p.126.

12 Only Barbour gives a size for King Robert's army – which he puts at the unacceptable figure of 30,000.

13 W.M. MacKenzie, *The Battle of Bannockburn* (Edinburgh, 1912) p.30.

14 G.W.S. Barrow, *Robert the Bruce* p.317.

15 Not only were Edward's subordinates experienced in war generally and against the Scots in particular but it is hard to

believe that none of these men was familiar with the environs of Stirling given its importance as a centre of government.

16 Edward was not expecting the Scots to come to him, but that he would be taking the initiative against them.

17 A.A.M. Duncan (ed.), J. Barbour, *The Bruce* (Edinburgh, 1997) XII, ll.450–70.

18 *Vita Edwardi Secund*, *Scalacronica* and *The Bruce* all describe the Scots as being well protected in light armour.

19 Roxburgh fell to the Scots in February and Edinburgh in March 1314.

20 Robert (King Hobbe) as a bandit in the hills had been an important theme in English propaganda since his seizure of the throne in 1306.

21 The capture and retention of Aberdeen in July 1308 demonstrate the growing strength of Robert's position generally, but also indicate that his 'secured' hinterland was large enough to need an administrative and economic centre.

22 In order to conquer, a 'raiding' strategy must eventually be converted to a 'persisting' strategy to acquire territory and compel the withdrawal of the enemy.

23 Although Scottish attacks across the border are tactically 'raids', because the object of the exercise was to extract so much wealth from the Northern English communities that they could not contribute to Edward's economy these raids were part of a 'persisting' strategy.

24 According to fourteenth-century military thinking, a 'conventional' English army was well balanced in the elements of heavy infantry, cavalry and archers necessary to provide a 'combined arms' force.

25 Almost any stretch along the fifty-foot contour running south east from Stirling could be appropriate.

26 Whatever Edward genuinely believed his 'right' in Scotland to be, he could not give it up without showing weakness and encouraging hostility at home, such as the resistance to the attempted removal of the Stone of Scone from Westminster to return it to Scotland as part of the treaty of 1328; M. McKisack, *England in the Fourteenth Century* p.98/9.

8 THE MORE WE KNOW THE MORE WE KNOW WE DON'T KNOW

1 A. Nusbacher, *The Battle of Bannockburn 1314* (Stroud, 1999) p.85–94.

2 A.A.M. Duncan, *Scotland, The Making of The Kingdom* (Edinburgh, 1975) p.333–38.

3 Wallace's troops were apparently organised in squads of five, the squads in multiples of ten.

4 A. Jones, *War in Western Civilization* (London, 1991).

5 ibid

6 C. MacNamee, *The Wars of the Bruces*, for discussion of the timing of Edward's invasion.

7 J. Barbour, *The Bruce*.

8 There is a military maxim to the effect that 'time spent in reconnaissance is seldom if ever wasted' and it seems clear that Robert chose his theatre of proposed operations with great care, ensuring that the most attractive line of advance for his enemy would afford the best opportunities to his own force.

9   The army mustered at Berwick, but the troops had to march there from all over Edward's dominions before making the journey to Stirling.

10 C.MacNamee, *The Wars of the Bruces* chapter 2, for an outline of the war on land before Bannockburn.

11 C. Macnamee, *The Wars of the Bruces* p.75.

12 The Scots found it necessary to import various commodities, including horses, iron and foodstuffs.

13 R. Nicholson, *Scotland in the Later Middle Ages* p.139. A party of Scots were able to gain entry to Edinburgh Castle by disguising themselves as English merchants.

14 C. MacNamee, *The Wars of the Bruces* p. 4, 207.

15 Oman, Nicholson, Barrow, Prestwich and Nicolle all refer to the shorter bow of the Scots, but none of them offer any support to their statement.

16 See Barrow, Nicholson, Nicholle and Nusbacher.

17 J. Barbour, *The Bruce*.

18 Archers would be most reluctant to loose off their last few arrows for fear of not being resupplied; each may have started the day with perhaps two dozen or thirty arrows, but the rate of shooting required to make an arrow shower was high.

19 David Nicolle, *Medieval Warfare Sourcebook* p.183, 187–88.

20 R.Nicholson, *Scotland in the Later Middle Ages* p.57.

21 A. Jones (ed.), *War in Western Civilization* (2000).

22 Poitiers, Crecy, Halidon Hill.

23 W.W. Scott, *Bannockburn Revealed*.

24 A. Jones, *War in Western Civilization*.

25 A. Jones, *War in Western Civilization*.

26 The 'wardrobe' department of Edward's household was responsible for valuation of horses to be used on campaign and for the replacement of any animals lost in action.

27 A. Nusbacher, *The Battle of Bannockburn 1314* pl.7.

28 C.W.C. Oman, *History of the War in the Peninsula* and J. Naylor, *The Battle of Waterloo* (London, 1960).

29 The compiler of the *Lanercost Chronicle* states that his source was an eyewitness and a trustworthy person; Thomas Grey senior, father of the author of *Scalacronica*, was taken prisoner on the 23 June.

30 Barbour is the sole source for a number of things relating to the battle, including the presence of Scottish cavalry, the selection of men to serve as infantry and the division of the Scottish infantry into four units rather than the three described by all the more contemporary writers.

31 Virtually all modern accounts stress the disadvantage to the English (particularly the cavalry) of fighting on marshy ground, but none of the contemporary writers identify this as a tactical factor.

32 Stirling and Loudon in Scotland, and Courtrai in Flanders.

33 J. Barbour, *The Bruce* 'hard playne field'.

34 R. Nicholson; *Scotland in the Later Middle Ages* p.57/8, for the battle of Falkirk.

35 A. Jones, *War in Western Civilization*.

36 The description of 'standard practice' for English armies offered by A. Nusbacher in *The Battle of Bannockburn 1314* p.76–7 does not seem to be supported by other writers.

37 Barbour, *Lanercost, Scalacronica*.

38 Barbour, *Lanercost, Scalacronica*.

39 C.W.C. Oman, *Art of War In The Middle Ages* (London, 1912).

40 This seems to have been regarded as a real possibility by the English; see N. Denholm-Young (ed.), *Vita Edwardus Secundus*.

41 It was rare for the Scots to fight open field engagements at all and large engagements were very rare indeed. When such actions did occur the Scots had invariably adopted a defensive posture; for the Scots to attack conventionally was unheard of.

42 W.M. MacKenzie, *The Battle of Bannockburn* p.56–62.

43 *Scalacronica* says 300, Barbour says 800.

44 Reference to the demolition of houses to provide bridging material for the English army to cross marshy ground perhaps makes more sense if we think in terms of building ramps to allow wagons to negotiate the narrow, steep gorges – small to a man or horse but a serious obstacle to a wheeled vehicle – formed by the Bannock or Pelstream burns. This would presumably be exactly the sort of 'field engineering' task for which carpenters, labourers and miners were often called up for service in English armies.

45 J. Barbour, *The Bruce* XII, ll.460–63.

46 C. MacNamee, *The Wars of the Bruces* p.63.

47 Sir Thomas Grey, *Scalacronica* p.53 (S.T.S.).

48 ibid.

49 ibid p.54.

50 A. Nusbacher, *Bannockburn 1314*.

51 W.M. MacKenzie, *The Battle of Bannockburn* p.70.

52 ibid.

53 J. Barbour, *The Bruce* XIII, ll.76–7.

54 Barbour is the only contemporary source to mention Scots cavalry, but the value of a reserve that could be deployed in a *coup-de-main* role at a critical juncture would not have been lost on as experienced commander as King Robert.

55 Although no other contemporary writer records this action, Barbour was close enough to the events he describes that too much invention and embroidery in his narrative would undermine his credibility.

56 Archers simply need more space to operate their weapons than spearmen and therefore constitute a less congested target area.

57 A. Nusbacher, *The Battle of Bannockburn 1314*.

10 STORYS... THAT SUTHFAST WER...
HAVE DOUBILL PLEASANCE IN HERYNG

1 The language of medieval Scots nobility has been the subject of some debate, but if his audience had been French, Barbour would have written in French.

2 A.A.M. Duncan (ed.), *The Bruce* p.32.

3 The descendants of these men would want to have their fathers' and grandfathers' exploits recognised.

4 S. Boardman, *The Early Stewart Kings* p.58.

5 ibid p.61.

6 Robert had served Edward 'unobtrusively, but well', R. Nicholson, *Scotland in the Later Middle Ages* p.70.

7 For an examination of pressures on the Scots to accept Edward as king see F. Watson, *Under the Hammer* chapter 5.

8 G.W.S. Barrow, *Robert the Bruce and the Community of the Realm of Scotland* p.278, 280, 414.

9 Randolph had deserted Bruce after the battle of Methven.

10 Edward Balliol resigned his claim to Scotland to Edward III in January 1356.

11 Robert is frequently attacked by three assailants – A.A.M. Duncan (ed.), *The Bruce* footnote p.214. The number three and its multiples sometimes have a literary significance; three equals a few, thirty equals quite a few, 300 equals many, and so on.

12 The ability of the English and the pro-Balliol Scots to win battles was not complemented by a capacity to sustain garrisons and exert lordship.

13 David de Strathbogie was killed at Culblean in 1335, Beaumont was ousted from Dundarg and died in Flanders, the Moubrays changed sides.

14 The political, or perhaps 'personal' or 'familial' prisoners included Bruce's queen and daughter and the countess of Buchan. Bannockburn gave Robert the ransom 'equity' to procure their release.

15 Which says something about the state of Scottish towns perhaps; at least in relation to the towns and cities of France.

16 A.A.M. Duncan (ed.), *The Bruce* p.26.

17 ibid p.25–7.

18 Robert I's legislation refers often to the reign of Alexander III for practical example, and Edward I's peace agreement of 1305 promised the preservation of the laws and customs of the Scots – this was a conservative community with a conservative leadership.

19 Treaty of Edinburgh, Northampton, 1328

20 A.A.M. Duncan (ed.), *The Bruce* footnote p.130; G.W.S. Barrow, *Robert the Bruce* p.227.

Bibliography

PRIMARY SOURCES

Bain, J. et al. (eds), *Calendar of Documents Relating to Scotland* (London, 1881–82)

Denholm-Young, N. (ed.), *Vita Edwardi Secundus* (London, 1957)

Duncan, A.A.M. (ed.), *Regesta Regum Scottorum* (vol.V) (Edinburgh 1988)

—, Barbour, J., *The Bruce* (Edinburgh, 1997)

Laing, D. (ed.), *The Original Chronicle of Andrew of Wyntoun* (Edinburgh, 1872–79)

—, *Scalacronica of Sir Thomas Grey* (Llanerch, 2000)

—, *The Chronicle of John of Fordoun* (Edinburgh, 1872)

MacKenzie, W. (ed.), *The Bruce* (Glasgow, 1912)

MacPherson, D. et al. (eds), *Rotuli Scotiae in Turri Londonensi etc.* (London, 1837)

Maitland, J. (ed.), *Chronicon de Lanercost* (Edinburgh, 1839)

Palgrave, F. (ed.), *Documents and Records Illustrating the History of Scotland* (London, 1837)

Rothwell, H. (ed.) *The Chronicle of Walter of Guisborough* (London, 1939)

Stewart, J. et al. (eds), *Exchequer Rolls of Scotland* (London, 1878–1908)

Stones, E.L.G., *Anglo-Scottish Relations, 1174-1328* (London, 1965)

Watt, H. (ed.), *Scotichronicon of Walter Bower* (Aberdeen, 1991)

SECONDARY SOURCES

Barrell, A.D.M., *Medieval Scotland* (Edinburgh, 2000)

Barron, E.M., *The Scottish Wars of Independence* (Inverness, 1934)

Barrow, G.W.S., *Robert the Bruce and the Community of the Realm of Scotland* (London, 1965)

—, *Scotland and its Neighbours in the Middle Ages* (London, 1992)

—, *The Kingdom of the Scots* (London, 1973)

Dodgson, R.A. (ed.), *Land and Society in Early Scotland* (Glasgow, 1982)

Donaldson, G., *Scottish Historical Documents* (Edinburgh, 1970)

—, *Sourcebook of Scottish History* (Edinburgh, 1952)

Duncan, A.A.M., *Scotland, the Making of the Kingdom* (Edinburgh, 1974)

—, *The Nation of the Scots and the Declaration of Arbroath* (Edinburgh, 1997)

Gemmill, E., and N. Mayhew, *Changing Values in Medieval Scotland* (Cambridge, 1995)

Grant, A., and K. Stringer (eds), *Medieval Scotland, Crown, Lordship and Community* (Edinburgh, 1993)

Grant, A., *Independence and Nationhood* (London, 1984)

Lynch, M. (ed.), *Image and Identity* (Edinburgh, 1998)

Lynch, M., and M. Spearman and G. Stell (eds), *The Scottish Medieval Town* (Edinburgh, 1988)

MacDonald, R.A., *The Kingdom of the Isles* (East Lothian, 1997)

MacDougall, N., *An Antidote to the English* (Edinburgh, 2001)

MacKenzie, W.M., *The Battle of Bannockburn* (Edinburgh, 1913)

—, *The Scottish Burghs* (Edinburgh, 1949)

MacNamee, Colm, *The Wars of the Bruces* (East Lothian, 1997)

McKisack, M., *England in the Fourteenth Century* (Oxford, 1959)

McNeill, P., and H. McQueen (eds), *Atlas of Scottish History to 1707* (St Andrews, 1975)

Nicholson, R., *Scotland in the Later Middle Ages* (Edinburgh, 1974)

Reid, N. (ed.), *Scotland in the Reign of Alexander III* (Edinburgh, 1988)

Watson, F., *Under the Hammer* (East Lothian, 1998)

Young, A., *The Comyns, Robert the Bruce's Rivals* (East Lothian, 1997)

List of Illustrations

Referenced by page number

14 A page from the *Scalachronica of Sir Thomas Grey of Heton*. Courtesy of Jonathan Reeve.

31 Edward I. His aggressive interventions in Scotland destroyed the generally positive relationship between Scotland and England for a century. Despite his posthumous nickname '*Malleus Scottorum*' (Hammer of the Scots) Edward failed miserably in his attempt to annex Scotland. From the author's collection.

52 King Robert Bruce and his second wife from a Scottish Armorial of the reign of Queen Mary, illuminated between 1561 and 1565. Tempus Archive.

82 Brass of Robert Bruce, Dunfermline Abbey. Courtesy of Bob McCutcheon.

89 Seal of Robert Bruce, earl of Carrick. Appended in 1301 to a charter in favour of the Abbey of Melrose. Tempus Archive.

94 The arms of the King of Scotland. The drawing represents a lion within a bordure, pierced by ten fleurs-de-lys. Tempus Archive.

167 The battle of Bannockburn as envisaged by Sir Charles Oman (after S.R. Gardiner). Gardiner and Oman's interpretations were for many years the 'received history' of the battle, although neither bears examination in the light of the documentary evidence. From the author's collection.

168 A sketchmap of the battlefield at Bannockburn on 23/24 June 1314. From the author's collection.

399 A Scottish galley, vessels like these were vital to King Robert's littoral warfare in the West of Scotland. From the author's collection.

Index

Aberconwy 97
Aberdeen 47, 85, 92, 126, 181
Abernethy, Alexander, 54, 119, 120
Abernethy, Laurence, 17
Abingdon, Richard, 122
Achymnasonnee 85
Achynaterman 85
Alexander II 96, 102, 103
Aliores, John, 115
Allerdale 68
Allerton 75
Alnwick 27, 31, 51
Ambassadors 49
Anand, John, 136
Angus, earl of, 65, 66
Annan 19, 111, 123
Annandale, 103, 114, 115, 118, 188
Anointment 81
Appleby, 66, 143
Arbroath 85
Arbylegande, Thomas, 115
Archers 149, 170
Ardena, Ralph, 105
Ardory 86
Ardrossan, Fergus, 130
Argentan, Giles, 25, 119, 196
Argyll 43

Argyll, John of, 129
Arran 76, 193
Artois, Robert of, 20
Arundel, earl of, 25, 134
Askeloc, Ector, 112
Athol, David earl (in English view), 138
Athol, earl of, 18, 55
Auchenbouthy 94
Auchterarder 123, 126
Avers 122
Ayr 19, 116, 126, 131
Ayr Castle 116

Badenoch, John Comyn of, 118
Badewe 122
Baggage 166
Baillies 173
Baker, Geoffrey, 149
Balliol, Edward, 31, 159, 189, 190
Balliol, John (John I, 1292–96), 41, 112
Bamburgh 27
Banaster, Adam, 22
Banff 26, 92
Bannockburn 15, 24, 39, 45, 65, 149, 191
Bardi 147
Barley 143
Basingbourne, Warin, 126

Bastingthwaite 104

Beaumond 76

Beaumont, Henry, 22, 23, 26, 65, 118, 119

Beaumont, Louis, 26

Bedewynde, Walter, 118

Bedford 100, 107, 123

Bell, Thomas, 115

Bentley, John, 130

Berefei 68

Bergen 105

Berwick 16, 25–7, 40, 46–7, 54, 58, 59, 61–2,
    71, 73, 93, 103, 126, 130, 135–7, 153, 156, 177

Betoigne, David, 133

Beverly 78

Bickerton, Walter de, 20, 83, 84

Biknore, Walter, 126

Biland 30, 49, 76

Black Rood 80

Blackhow Moor 30

Blinkers 162

Bohun, Elizabeth, 116, 127

Bohun, Humphrey, 116

Bohun, Humphrey, earl of Hereford, 18, 116,
    123, 127

Bondi 177

Bonkill, Alexander, 104

Bordeaux 100

Borough 74

Boroughbridge 47, 72

Boulton 104

Boyd, Robert, 57, 83, 98, 186

Boyville, Robert, 98

Brechin David, 17, 26, 47

Bremmesgrave, Richard, 113

Brighouse 69

Brittany, John of, 45, 49

Brodie 84

Brough 66

Broune, Richard, 47

Bruce, Alexander, 19, 40, 55

Bruce, Alienora (Eleanor), 122

Bruce, Bernard, 96, 142

Bruce, Bernard, Jnr, 142

Bruce, Cristiana (grandmother of Robert I),
    96, 99, 101, 104–06

Bruce, Cristiana, sister of Robert I, 131

Bruce, Cristina, 50

Bruce, David (David II, 1329–71), 50, 52, 81,
    142, 146

Bruce, Edward, 25, 42, 45–6, 57, 67, 145

Bruce, Elizabeth, queen of Robert I, 127, 128,
    130–32

Bruce, Isabella, queen of Norway (sister of
    Robert I), 105

Bruce, Margery, countess of Carrick (mother
    of Robert I), 189

Bruce, Margery, daughter of Robert I,
    108, 187

Bruce, Mary, sister of Robert I, 130

Bruce, Matilda, wife of Bernard Jnr, 142

Bruce, Nigel, 39, 40, 56

Bruce, Richard, 98

Bruce, Robert, natural son of Robert I, 133

Bruce, Robert, 'the noble', 95, 96, 98, 100–06,
    189

Bruce, Thomas, 18, 40, 55–6

Buchan, countess of, 17

Buchan, earl of, 146

Buchan, earl of, 41

Buchan, earldom of, 42

Buittle 131

Burgh, Richard, earl of Ulster, father of
    Elizabeth (Bruce's queen), 129

Burgh-on the-Sands 41

Burgundy 26

Bute 44, 76

Buttetourt, John, 113

Caerlaverock 131

Caldecote 123

Caldew (Carlisle) 68

Cambuskenneth Abbey 50, 121, 171

Campbell, Donald, 115

Campbell, Nigel, 105

Camphill 182

Cardross 9, 52, 85, 181

Carlisle 19, 36, 40, 54–5, 63–4, 68, 74, 76,
    96–7, 110, 112

Carlisle, bishop of, 136

Carlisle, earl of, 77

Carrick 40, 93, 96–7, 188

Carrick, Matilda of, 112, 113

Cartmel 75
Castle Barnard 79
Castleguard 93, 157
Cattle 174
Chamberlain 91
Chester, bishop of, 123, 125
Chester, earldom of, 96
Cheveroill, Alexander, 119
Chickens, 174
Chivalry, 165, 191–93, 195, 196, 198
Clackmannan 83, 88, 123, 126
Clapham 51
Clement V 71
Cleveland 26, 74
Clifford, Robert, 23, 58, 64, 111, 113, 118
Coket 136
Coldingham 179
Comeston (Comiston), Walter, 115
Commons (of Scotland) 125
Comyn family 154
Comyn, John, 16, 34, 35, 36, 41–2, 53, 56, 116,
    119, 125
Copland 61, 62, 68
Coquina, Gilchrist, 130
Corbridge 59, 60, 67
Cornwall, earl of, 21, 58
Cornwall, Edmund, earl of, 98, 101
Corte Castle 131
Cotingham, Robert, 121, 122
Cottars 177, 179, 180
Courtrai 24
Crail 92–3
Crawford, Reginald, 55
Crokdayk, Adam, 107
Crokedale, Adam, 104
Crombathy (Crambeth) 126
Cromwell, John, 58
Cryn 28
Cullen 92
Cumberland 48, 61–2, 67, 75, 97, 112, 124
Cumin 175
Cupar 20, 85, 92, 137
Curia 72
Currie (Corry), Walter, 104

Dagenham 98
Daliliegh 116, 124, 125
Dalswinton 16, 44
Danande, Walter, 115
David (Biblical king) 194
David I 87
David II 118
Dee, River 42
Denoun, William, 31
Despenser, Hugh, 50
Deyncourt, William, 23
Dickson, Thomas, 196
Dirland, William, 130
Dobery, Robert, 51
Donald (of the Isles) 42
Douglasdale 193
Douglas, James, 22, 26, 44, 49, 51, 57, 69, 74,
    78–80, 186, 191–94,198
Douglas, William, 'le hardi', 98, 108
Downie, Angus, 83
Dryburgh 48
Duddon 75
Dumbarton 26, 93–4, 126
D'Umfraville, Ingram, 65, 165
Dumfries 36, 44, 53, 115, 118–20, 126, 131, 135
Dunbar 21, 25, 59, 65
Dunbar Castle 25
Dundalk 25, 46
Dundee 21, 92, 103
Dunfermline 18, 19, 82, 86
Dunfermline Abbey 87
Dungavel 126
Dunstaffnage 43
Dupplin Moor 160
Durham 26, 44, 48, 60, 66
Durward, Alan, 18
Dyce 85
Dyke 84

Ecle, Matthew, 115
Edinburgh 22, 44, 87, 63, 69, 92, 126, 154
Edward I 16, 19–21, 35–36, 41, 54, 57, 114
Edward II 18, 21, 25, 29, 30, 41, 48–9, 54, 78,
    165, 196
Edward III 31, 44, 50, 78, 142
Elgin 126

Ely, bishop of, 73, 82, 135
Essex 96, 98, 106, 109, 116, 113
Exchequer (of England) 95, 97, 116
Exton 96, 142
Eyemouth 178

Falkirk 48, 151, 166
Fauhope, Adam, 115
Fauside, Roger, 141
Fauside, William, 115
Felton, Robert, 118
Felton, William, 22, 27, 85
Fenygges, William (Fiennes, Gillemin), 22, 63
Fife 20, 93
Fitzcan, Duncan, 115
Fitzkan, Gibbon, 109
Fitzroger, Robert, 54
Fitzwarin, Alan, 111
Flanders 177
Fleckes 115
Flemings 24, 136, 139
Florence 147
Foliot, Edumnd, 126
Fordoun, John, 12
Fordyce 85
Forfar 93, 126
Forres 84,126
Forth 165
Forth, River, 24, 121

Hedgly 121
Hegham, Roger, 123
Heiron, Robert, 133
Herald 39
Hereford 116
Hereford, bishop of, 137
Hereford, earl of, 22, 58, 65–6
Herewynton, Adam, 132
Hert, Durham, 119
Hertford, 106
Hessewell, Peter, 115
Heton, Thomas, 27
Hexham 60, 67
Hilton, Alexander, 111
Holderness 127
Holland, count of, 102

Holm Cultram 75, 100
Holyrood 48
Horncliffe, Robert, 27
Horsley, Richard, 130
Horsley, Roger, 26
Hoystone 59
Huntingdon 102, 111, 114, 123, 142
Husbandmen 179

Improvers 174
Inchaffray 88
Inchaffray, abbot of, 9
Infangtheif 83
Inflation 175
Inglewood 63
Innerpeffray, Malcolm, 123
Inverbervie 103
Inverkeithing 92
Invernairn 126
Inverness 92–3, 126, 181
Irby, William, 106
Ireland 25, 45–6, 67, 70, 95, 145, 154, 159
Irvine 108

Jedburgh 25
Jedburgh, abbot of, 104, 112
Jetour/Jettur 124
Joan of the Tower, queen of David II, 31, 81
John XXII, Pope, 71, 137
Jousts, 31

Keith, Robert, 73, 85, 160, 170, 193
Kelso 181
Kelso Abbey 183
Kemeston 101, 123
Kemston 107
Kendal, Hugh, 98
Kenilworth 96
Kildrummy Castle 18, 40, 116
Killin 88
Kinaldy 85
Kincardine 93
Kinghorn 93
Kingston 121
Kinross 93,
Kintore 116

Kirkconnel, Thomas, 115
Kirkoswald 66
Kirkton of Dyce 85
Knaresborough 72
Kynbauton, Andrew, 128

Lamberton, lands at, 176
Lamberton, William, 52
Lanark 92, 116, 126
Lancaster 75 134, 138
Lancaster, earl of, 29, 70
Lanercost 12
Langeton, John, 106
Latimer, William, 118, 140
Le Bel, Jean, 12
Leases 174–5,
Leicester 16
Leith
Lennox 24
Lennox, earldom of, 120
Lennox, Malcolm, earl of, 40, 83
Letburne, Robert, 138
Level 75
Levington 112
Leware, John, 126
Lincoln 27
Lincoln, bishop of, 81
Lincoln, earl of, 54, 57
Lindsey, Alexander, 57, 108
Linlithgow 92, 126
Lintalee 25
Linton, Bernard, 83
Loch Ryan 40
Lochmaben 16, 77, 111, 118, 123
Logie, John, 26, 47
London 45, 54, 80, 114
Lordship 196
Lothian 25, 58, 115
Loudon 19
Lour 182
Lovel, Richard, 118
Low Countries 154
Lubaud (Libaud) Piers, 22
Lucca 97
Lucy, Antony, 65, 66
Lucy, Elena, 98

Lucy, John, 115
Luxembourg, Henry of, 25

Maccabeus, Judas, 194
MacDoual, Dougal, 55
MacDougall family 154
MacDougall, Duncan, 109
MacGethe, Michael, 115
MacMonhathe, Gilbert, 115
MacRuarie, Christiana, 40
Mainprise 126
Maletotes 146
Malherbe, Gilbert, 26, 47
Manners, Robert, 30, 78
Mar, Donald earl of, 102, 131
Mar, earl of, 79
Mar, earldom of, 102
March, earl of, 26
March, Patrick Snr earl of, 102
March, Patrick, 25
Marechal, Fergus le, 115
Marechal, Richard le, 115
Marechal, Roland le, 115
Marmaduke, Richard, 26
Marmion, William, 27, 28
Mary Rose 160
Maud of Dover 18
Mauley, Edmund, 64
McKisack, May, 152
Meffen/Methven 39, 120, 123, 125
Melrose 48
Meltoun, William, 73
Menteith, earl of, 123, 124
Menteith, John, 36
Menteith, Murdach, 26
Merchants 146
Merlin 127
Meslin 122
M'Gylochery, Morgund, 102
Middlesex 113, 118, 123
Middleton, Adam, 124
Middleton, Gilbert, 26
Middleton, Robert, 45
Midlem 182
Minorites 16–7, 63, 69, 118, 119
Mitford Castle 27, 71

Mohaud, William, 30

Moiller, Jean de la, 26

Monkton 181

Monteault, William, 51

Monthermer, Ralph, 19

Montrose 92

Moray, Andrew of, 50

Moray, earl of, 150, 153, 159

Moray, John, 69

Moray, Thomas Randolph, earl of, 22, 23, 31,
44, 50–1, 67, 74, 78–9, 85, 135, 140, 189, 193

More, Reginald, 94

Moref (Moray), William, 130

Morton 182

Moubray family 17

Moubray, Alexander, 138

Moubray, Geoffrey, 104

Moubray, John, 54

Moubray, Philip, 23, 27, 42, 151

Moubray, Roger, 26, 47

Mouhaut, Bernard, 120

Mountfichet, William, 141

Mountforth, Piers, 23

Mounth (the) 59

Mow 183

Mukkitland 180

Mulcastre, William, 124

Munitions armament 159

Musgrave, Robert, 134

Myton 73

National Trust for Scotland 171

Nativi 177

Nesbit, William, 136

Neville, Robert, 25

Neville's Cross 142

Newcastle 29–30, 70

Neyfs 177

Nith 126

Nithsdale 19, 110

Norham Castle 27, 29, 30–1, 51, 58, 78, 102

Northallerton 72

Northumberland 26, 48, 61–2

Norway, king of, 102

Norwich 81

Oliphaunt, William, 22, 62, 85

Paveley, Sarre de (dame)

Paxton letters 175

Paynel, Thomas, 118

Peebles 48, 181

Peebles, Robert, 92

Penrith, John, 29

Percy, Henry, 31, 108, 118

Perth 17, 22, 39, 44, 54, 58, 61–2, 92, 120, 123,
126, 180, 192

Philip IV 41, 112, 114

Pilmuir, John, 137

Plague 174

Pluscarden 85

Polnacroscel 85

Ponton, William, 124

Pope 47

Porchester 141

Post, John, 113

Poucy, William, 128

Prenderguest 178

Preston 75

Prison 112

Pykard, Adam,

Ragman Roll 80

Rait 182

Randolph, Thomas, see Moray, earl of

Ransom 147

Raploch 94

Rattray (Retreve), Eustace, 47

Recoinage 97

Reddendo 175

Redeman, Matthew, 115

Redesdale 59, 145

Rethy 86

Richard I 102

Richmond, 30, 66, 70, 74

Richmond, earl of, 25, 76, 78

Rievaulx, 76

Ripon, 72, 141

Riveaulx, 30,

Robert, bishop of Glasgow, 131

Roland of Galloway 42

Ross, earl of (William), 39, 83, 102

Roule, Adam, 136
Roxburgh 22, 44, 93, 112, 115, 126, 135, 154
Runrig 180
Rustici 177
Rutland 96
Rye 122

Safe-conduct 88
Sandale, John 116, 121
Scaithmoor 25
Scarborough 21
Scholtrom (Schiltrom) 24
Scone 47, 53, 80, 92, 94
Segrave, John, 65, 66, 133
Selby 133
Selkirk 59, 93, 119–20
Serfs 177
Sergeants 173
Seton, Alexander, 24, 141
Seton, Christopher, 54, 131
Seton, John, 54, 104, 109, 120
Sheriffs 173
Siward, Richard, 109
Skeoch 94, 155
Skinburness 124
Skipton 72
Slane, Philip, 111
Slenach (Slioch) 41
Solway 59
Somerville, John, 121
Soulis, de, conspiracy, 189, 190
Soulis, Nicholas de, 102
Soulis, William de, 26, 47
Siward, Richard, 120
Spalding, Peter, 71
Springwood Park 181
St Andrews, bishop William of, 55, 112, 119,
    141, 181
St, John 113, 118
Stainmoor 66, 74
Stanhope Park 79
Stewart, Andrew, 122
Stewart, James, 108
Stewart, John, 108
Stewart, Robert, 50
Stewart, Walter, 187

Stikelaw, Henry, 105
Stirling 114, 121, 126, 165, 170, 193
Stirling Castle 22, 151, 165
Stobo 181
Stone of Scone 80
Stowe Park 140
Strange, Robert, 126
Strathearn, countess of, 47
Strathearn, earl of, 9, 109, 123
Strathfulane 88
Strivelin, John of Moray, 103
Sully, Henry, 30, 49, 140
Swaledale 66
Swinburne, Adam, 26

Tang, Andrew, 122
Tany, Lucas, 105
Tees 66
Templar, Knights, 9
Teviotdale 31
Thirle(d) 177
Thomas, earl of Lancaster, 18
Tibbers Castle 120
Tiptoft, Pain de, 64, 66
Tony/Tany, Roger, 120
Torthorald, David, 104
Torwood 64
Tottenham 100, 118
Tower (of London) 124
Troupe, Hamelin, 47
Trumpe, Patrick, 112, 113
Tulchys 94
Turmyn, James, 142
Turnberry 109
Twynham, Adam, 106
Twynham, Walter, 115, 141
Tynedale 67
Tyneside 59

Ulster 45, 127
Upsettlington 29
Ur (Urrie/Eure), Hugh, 115

Valence, Aymer de (earl of Pembroke), 17,
    19–21, 26, 39, 54, 113, 118, 135, 196, 198
Vesci, William, 102

Villeins 177
Vipond, Alan, 93

Wake, Thomas, 146
Wales 41
Wallace, William, 36, 55
Ware, Robert, 125
Wark 71
Wark Castle 27
Warrenne, earl of, 58, 59, 109
Weardale 51
Welsh (archers) 126
Westminster 96, 116
Westmorland 48, 61–2, 75
Wetherby 47
Whitehaven 124
Whitwich 16
Wigton 126
Wigton, John, 109
William I (The Lion) 102
Wilmerton, Laurence, 93
Winchester 118
Wincop, John, 121

Windsor 44
Wissard, John, 112
Wold 30, 78
Wolrikesford 129
Worcester, bishop of, 56
Workington 124
Writtle/Writele 96, 98, 110
Wylington, Edmund, 126
Wylringfrith 143
Wymes, David, 119
Wymes, Michael, 119
Wyseman, William, 83

Yair Ford 28
York 30, 49, 73, 109
York, archbishop of, 135–6
Yorkshire 48
Ypres 134

Zouche (Luscpe) Aymer, 118
Zouche, William, 118

If you are interested in purchasing
other books published by Tempus, or in case you have
difficulty finding any Tempus books in your local bookshop,
you can also place orders directly through our website

www.tempus-publishing.com

or from

BOOKPOST
Freepost, PO Box 29,
Douglas, Isle of Man
IM99 1BQ
Tel 01624 836000
email bookshop@enterprise.net